Sport Public Relations

THIRD EDITION

G. Clayton Stoldt, EdD
Wichita State University

Stephen W. Dittmore, PhD
University of Arkansas

Mike Ross, EdD
Wichita State University

Scott E. Branvold, EdD
Robert Morris University

HUMAN KINETICS

Library of Congress Cataloging-in-Publication Data

Names: Stoldt, G. Clayton, 1962- author. | Dittmore, Stephen W., 1968-
author. | Ross, Mike, 1975- author. | Branvold, Scott E., 1949- author.
| Human Kinetics Publishers.

Title: Sport public relations / G. Clayton Stoldt, Stephen W. Dittmore,
Mike Ross, Scott E. Branvold.

Description: Third Edition. | Champaign, Illinois : Human Kinetics, Inc.,
2021. | Previous edition published 2012.

Identifiers: LCCN 2020006738 (print) | LCCN 2020006739 (ebook) | ISBN
9781492589389 (Paperback) | ISBN 9781492589396 (ePub) | ISBN
9781492589419 (PDF)

Subjects: LCSH: Sports--Public relations. | Mass media and sports. |
Communication in organizations.

Classification: LCC GV714 .S77 2021 (print) | LCC GV714 (ebook) | DDC
659.2/9796--dc23

LC record available at https://lccn.loc.gov/2020006738
LC ebook record available at https://lccn.loc.gov/2020006739

ISBN: 978-1-4925-8938-9 (print)

Acquisitions Editor: Andrew L. Tyler; **Developmental Editor:** Judy Park; **Managing Editor:** Melissa J. Zavala; **Permissions Manager:** Dalene Reeder; **Graphic Designer:** Joe Buck; **Cover Designer:** Keri Evans; **Cover Design Specialist:** Susan Rothermel Allen; **Photograph (cover):** Chris Trotman/Getty Images; **Photographs (interior):** © Human Kinetics, unless otherwise noted; **Photo Asset Manager:** Laura Fitch; **Photo Production Manager:** Jason Allen; **Senior Art Manager:** Kelly Hendren; **Illustrations:** © Human Kinetics; **Production:** Westchester Publishing Services; **Printer:** Sheridan Books

Printed in the United States of America

10 9 8 7 6 5 4 3 2 1

The paper in this book is certified under a sustainable forestry program.

Human Kinetics
1607 N. Market Street
Champaign, IL 61820
USA

United States and International
Website: **US.HumanKinetics.com**
Email: info@hkusa.com
Phone: 1-800-747-4457

Canada
Website: **Canada.HumanKinetics.com**
Email: info@hkcanada.com

E7767

Tell us what you think!
Human Kinetics would love to hear what we
can do to improve the customer experience.
Use this QR code to take our brief survey.

contents

Contents

preface

Whether the setting is a college athletics program attempting to increase fan engagement, a professional sport organization advocating the public funding of a new sport facility, a public school system considering a reduction in sport programs, or a coalition of sport organizations promoting better health for the local community, public relations issues are ubiquitous in sport. Public relations practitioners in sport conduct their work in an environment that presents more opportunities and more challenges than ever before. Practitioners can now engage their audiences and tell their organization's stories using a wide range of media types (e.g., social, digital) and specific platforms (e.g., Instagram, YouTube). Public relations professionals must also manage relationships with members of the mass media, the community, organizational employees, and multiple other stakeholders groups, many of whom are highly interested in the organization because of the avidity that often characterizes sports fans.

Given the complexity of the sport communication ecosystem and the high stakes involved in managing relationships with key publics, the study of sport public relations is more important than ever. The purpose of this textbook is to provide such a study.

The authors of the book possess significant professional experience in sport public relations and have maintained that focus in their teaching and research. They recognize that other textbooks have made important contributions in the effort to educate students on the topic. Their aim for this text is to provide a comprehensive treatment of sport public relations. Although the practice of public relations was once thought of simply as publicity in support of the marketing function or media relations leveraging the media's interest in sport organizations, the profession and the communication environment have evolved. The public relations and marketing functions are merging, communication options grow by the day, and the importance of consistent brand communication in a cluttered and challenging marketplace has never

been greater. Sport public relations professionals, now more than ever, must lead their organizations in the strategic management of relationships and communication with key stakeholder groups.

To accomplish their goal of providing a comprehensive treatment of sport public relations, the authors emphasize three themes. First, public relations is a managerial function focused on advancing the organization's brand and successfully engaging key stakeholders. Second, the communication environment has changed significantly in recent years and continues to evolve rapidly. Third, while media relations is a critical form of public relations practice within the sport industry, other areas, such as community relations, employee relations, and donor relations, also warrant significant attention.

This book is written for upper-level undergraduate and graduate students studying sport management, sport communication, or public relations. Practitioners who wish to expand their knowledge of sport public relations may also find the book to be of value. Although the book briefly discusses the foundations of communication, it assumes that readers already have an understanding of effective written and oral communication. The book also assumes that readers understand the scope of the sport industry and have studied fundamental marketing concepts.

How This Book Is Organized

The text begins with a chapter introducing the practice of sport public relations and describing the major changes in the field, including the convergence of the public relations and marketing functions. Chapter 2 examines the linkages between sport public relations and strategic management. Specifically, the chapter discusses the importance of integrating public relations considerations into managerial decision making and the effects that those decisions can have on the brand and reputation of the sport organization. The chapter also addresses the management of public relations and the ways campaigns may be planned to maximize effectiveness.

Chapters 3 through 5 pertain to the different types of media that may be used to engage key publics. Chapter 3 addresses social media, noting these platforms' tremendous potential to both advance and complicate organizational communication efforts. The chapter also covers social media evaluation and engagement metrics. Chapter 4 focuses on digital media, with topics ranging from the still-critical importance of organizational websites to other forms of digital media such as video and podcasts. Chapter 5 covers organizational communication via legacy media with specific topics including media guides, annual reports, and more. A key theme of these chapters, and the book as a whole, is that organizations are most effective when they integrate the various communication platforms to tell stories consistent with the organization's brand.

Chapters 6 and 7 examine media relations. Chapter 6 considers the unique relationship between sport and the mass media and addresses how sport entities can effectively manage their relationships with members of the mass media. Chapter 7 deals with news media tactics such as news releases and news conferences. These chapters also address the significant changes in the media environment and link media relations efforts with the organization's priority of consistently communicating its brand.

Chapter 8 focuses on crisis communication and includes numerous examples of how prominent sport entities have managed recent crises—some effectively, some not. This is yet another area in which social and digital media now have profound impact, so, as in the rest of the book, those topics are integrated into the discussion.

Chapter 9 examines managing relationships with the broader community. The chapter includes topics such as public speeches and open houses, which provide mechanisms for personal engagement. The chapter's primary focus, however, is the broader subject of social responsibility and how the public relations function can play a lead role in managing social responsibility initiatives.

Chapter 10 examines how sport organizations manage relationships with a range of other key stakeholders—employees, investors, customers, donors, and regulators. As the chapter indicates, whether the public is internal or external, the same principles of consistent brand communication and audience engagement are central to successful relationship management.

Within each of these chapters, readers will find a number of elements to assist them in applying the concepts presented. These include a case study in each chapter (in fact, chapter 8 offers four case studies), and a "Be Your Own Media" sidebar, highlighting ways sport organizations are proactively telling their stories across media platforms. Readers will also find examples of public relations materials such as a news release and an employee newsletter. Readers will also find lists of key terms to look for in the chapters and activities for further learning about public relations in sport.

Just as the subject matter of the text is diverse, the purposes of the book are also multiple. More specifically, the text will equip readers to understand the field and apply key skills relating to the following topics:

- The nature of sport public relations, how it is changing in a dynamic communication environment, and how it is critical in advancing an organization's brand

- Reputation management in sport and the ways sport organizations can use public relations programs to foster desirable relationships with key publics and design campaigns to attain specific public relations objectives

- Organizational communication—using social, digital, and legacy media platforms—to tell stories that convey the organization's brand and effectively engage audiences

- The unique relationship between sport and the mass media, and related benefits and consequences

- The foundations for effective media relations in sport, including providing appropriate information services to members of the media, staging media events such as news conferences, and offering necessary services to members of the media at events

- The critical nature of crisis communications plans, including crisis planning and crisis management considerations

- The importance and varied nature of community relations, including direct contact with members of key publics through unmediated communication tactics and the development of social responsibility initiatives to benefit both the sport organization and its community

- The purposes and benefits of public relations programs directed at employees, investors, customers, donors, and regulators

The text is designed to provide both the theoretical basis for sport public relations and also guidance on how to apply those concepts. For example, readers will learn about the importance of integrated communication across varied forms of media. Readers will also learn how to create content that tells brand-centric stories that can be shared across the many available communication platforms in leveraged fashion.

Readers will find general public relations theory frequently woven into the text. It describes the principles of public relations excellence identified by James Grunig, Larissa Grunig, and David Dozier as part of their landmark Excellence Study. It also frequently references the PESO model of media types developed by Gini Dietrich. The text applies these concepts and others in a sport-specific context. The text also incorporates sport-industry specific research and models such as the strategic sport communication model developed by Paul Pedersen, Kimberly Miloch, and Pamela Laucella. The authors are indebted to these scholars and other public relations and sport management academics and practitioners who have made valuable contributions to the field.

Students who want to break into the field can expect to find enough how-to information in this text to help them write their first news release or plan a community outreach event for a sport organization. Future sport managers can expect to encounter ideas that will prompt them to become proactive in their approach to public relations rather than reactive. And ultimately, professionals in the public relations field can expect this book to help them and their organizations become more progressive in their public relations practices, resulting in better relationships between sport organizations and their key publics.

Instructor Resources in HK*Propel*

The following instructor ancillaries are available within the instructor pack in HK*Propel*:

- The **instructor guide** includes a summary of each book chapter, sample lecture outlines, student assignments, and activities with suggestions regarding how instructors may utilize those activities, selected readings that will enable instructors and students to expand their examination of topics addressed in each chapter, and tips for presenting selected key topics for each chapter. The instructor guide also contains a sample syllabus, a semester-long group project, and information about how to assign the chapter quizzes to students within HK*Propel*.

- The **test package** includes more than 200 questions, including multiple-choice and short answer or essay questions. The test package is available in a variety of formats and can be imported into most learning management systems.

- The **presentation package** includes approximately 200 slides of text, artwork, and tables from the book that instructors can use for class discussion and presentation. The slides in the presentation package can be used directly within PowerPoint or printed to make transparencies or handouts for distribution to students. Instructors can easily add, modify, and rearrange the order of the slides.

Instructor ancillaries are free to adopting instructors, including an ebook version of the text that allows instructors to add highlights, annotations, and bookmarks. Please contact your Sales Manager for details about how to access instructor resources in HK*Propel*.

Student Resources in HK*Propel*

HK*Propel* will help you further develop a full understanding of course content, applying chapter knowledge to current issues in sport public relations. You'll find activities with author introductions, discussion questions, and applied learning activities for group or individual completion. You'll be able to tackle tough scenarios, such as escalating workloads faced by many sport public relations professionals and the sign-stealing crisis faced by Major League Baseball. Your instructor may also assign you short quizzes to complete within HK*Propel* to demonstrate your mastery of each chapter's content.

acknowledgments

A number of gracious and skilled people contributed to the development of this text. The authors offer them all a word of sincere appreciation.

Special thanks go to Dr. Lisa Kihl, associate professor of sport management at the University of Minnesota, who wrote chapter 9, Cultivating Positive Relationships in the Community. Her expertise in sport social responsibility and its application in a public relations context represents a valuable contribution to the text.

The authors also offer a word of gratitude to Dr. Anastasios Kaburakis, associate professor of management at St. Louis University, and Dr. Galen Clavio, associate professor of sports media at Indiana University, for their contributions in the area of legal and ethical issues, particularly the sidebar Ethical Issues in Sport Public Relations in chapter 1. The authors also thank Erich Bacher, assistant athletics director for public relations at the University of Virginia, for his contributions to the case study on managing success in chapter 7.

The sample crisis communication exhibits in chapter 8 are adapted from a plan developed by the Wichita State University Intercollegiate Athletics Association. Special thanks to Brad Pittman, senior associate athletic director for facilities and operations, for his assistance in securing them and providing permissions.

Dr. Mike Ross offers a word of thanks to graduate student Courtney Calder for her research in support of the chapters he authored. And each of the authors are grateful to their faculty and staff colleagues for the support they offered throughout the writing process.

Sincere appreciation goes to Drew Tyler, acquisitions editor at Human Kinetics; Judy Park, developmental editor; and the rest of the staff at Human Kinetics for partnering with the authors in the development of this text.

Finally, the authors would like to offer a special word of appreciation to their families for the sacrifices they made while the text was being written. Dr. Steve Dittmore thanks his wife, Andrea, and son, Andrew. Dr. Scott Branvold thanks his wife, Lynda. Dr. Mike Ross thanks his wife, Tonya. And Dr. Clay Stoldt thanks his wife, Sally.

Introducing Sport Public Relations

After reading this chapter, students should be able to

- define public relations in sport,
- understand the evolving nature of the field and its implications for sport public relations students and practitioners,
- recognize the basic skills that sport public relations professionals need to perform their job,
- identify common forms of public relations practice in sport, and
- recognize the benefits that the public relations function brings to sport organizations.

These are the key terms discussed in this chapter:

- brand
- community relations
- media relations
- PESO model

- promotion
- publics
- social media
- sport public relations

ment is critical before the sport organization can develop public relations programs and campaigns.

Finally, if effectively practiced, sport public relations results in desirable relationships. The nature of these relationships varies by public, and many will be addressed in subsequent chapters. One such outcome might be that the organization's fan base is highly engaged with the team. Another might be that members of the community view the organization as socially responsible. Still another might be that the sport organization receives favorable publicity in the mass media. Whoever the public may be, the management team of the organization can define a realistically desirable relationship that might exist between the two parties. The function of public relations is to facilitate achievement of that desired outcome.

Evolution of Sport Public Relations

The global sport industry is ever-changing, and the public relations function has evolved significantly over the past 10 years. These changes merit consideration early on in this text, as they shape much of the discussion that follows. Frankly, a thorough examination of how the field is changing could take up the entire book. For the sake of brevity and as a way of introducing concepts that will be revisited later, this discussion is collapsed into three broad areas: evolution of the sport media, alignment of the public relations and marketing functions, and influence of communications leaders.

Evolution of Sport Media

Change is ever-present in the sport media landscape. Historically, developments such as the establishment of the first newspaper sports section by the *New York Journal* in 1895, the first radio broadcast of a baseball game by Pittsburgh's KDKA in 1921, and the launch of the television network ESPN in 1979 are just a few examples of key evolutionary moments affecting the sport industry and communications professionals. In recent years, the pace of change has accelerated, resulting in new complexities that sport public relations practitioners must address. The following sections describe some of the most important media developments affecting the field.

Growth of Social Media

Social media may be defined as "interactive media technologies that allow consumers to create and disseminate their own content, connect with media outlets and other network users and voice their opinions on any number of topics" (Sheffer & Schultz, 2013, p. 210). Sport is a highly popular topic for social media users, and sports consumers commonly engage in social networking. For example, a 2018 report indicated that 61% of sports viewers followed sports-related accounts on social media (Londergan, 2019).

Table 1.1 highlights some of the key developments in social media's rise to prominence. The table highlights a number of the most prominent applications and does not come close to covering the full range of social platforms, which may number in the

Table 1.1 Key Developments in the Rise of Social Media

Date	New application	Comment
1997	Six Degrees	Launch of first social networking site
2003	MySpace	Launch of popular social network site, with a music and entertainment focus
2003	LinkedIn	Professional networking site for individuals and organizations; purchased by Microsoft
2004	Facebook	Social networking site started at Harvard; quickly grew to become most the popular in the world
2005	YouTube	Video-sharing site now owned by Google
2006	Twitter	Site for sharing messages of 280 characters or less, photos, and videos
2010	Instagram	Facebook-owned site for sharing photos and videos
2010	Pinterest	Digital bulletin board where users can search and share items of interest
2011	Snapchat	Messaging application in which images may be shared for limited time as defined by the source
2012	TikTok	Short form video-sharing application; launched beyond China in 2017

thousands. As of 2019, Facebook had more than two billion users, and YouTube was nearing that mark. Other social media sites may have far fewer users, but they are still enormously popular and highly influential platforms. For example, Twitter had 300 to 350 million users each month through 2018 (Statista, 2019a), but the microblogging site wielded enormous power in sport and many other settings. Globally, the number of people using social media in some form or another is expected to exceed three billion by 2021 (Statista, 2019b).

Clavio (2013) notes that the proliferation and popularity of social media are linked to the introduction of the iPhone in 2007. The iPhone and other mobile devices give users the ability to access and share their own user-generated content almost anytime and anywhere.

While the rise of social media has many implications for sport public relations practitioners, three points seem particularly relevant to this introductory discussion. First, social media have democratized communication so that individuals and organizations can communicate with mass audiences without requiring a mediator such as a newspaper or television network. In sport settings, fans and other stakeholders now have platforms to express themselves, share content they create, and engage with one another. Similarly, sport organizations, athletes, and other sport figures have the same ability to communicate directly with their constituents.

Second, social media have accelerated globalization as social networks span national and cultural boundaries in ways that traditional media platforms cannot. The potential scope of social media engagement presents both tremendous opportunities and challenges for sport organizations and individual sport figures. The National Basketball Association (NBA) dealt with this reality on at least a couple of occasions in 2019. First, controversy resulted from the way the NBA Turkey Twitter account reported playoff results involving Enes Kanter of the Portland Trail Blazers. Kanter, a Turkish citizen, was the subject of an arrest warrant in Turkey based on his criticism of the Turkish president and support for a Muslim cleric deemed a terrorist by the Turkish government (Young, 2019). The NBA Turkey Twitter account, managed by a Turkish vendor, omitted Kanter's strong performance from its report on a playoff win by the Trail Blazers. Kanter called out the snub using his own Twitter account, and the league promptly fired the vendor. An even more consequential issue arose when Daryl Morey, general manager of the Houston Rockets, posted a tweet in support of protestors in Hong Kong who opposed Chinese actions to exert greater influence in the ter-

ritory. China, however, is a key market for the NBA, with more than 600 million people who watch the league (Perper, 2019). Severe backlash from China, Chinese organizations, and social media users ensued; among other things, the Chinese Basketball Association discontinued its work with the Rockets, and Chinese broadcasting properties dropped their coverage of the team. The league initially deemed the tweet "regrettable," in turn prompting criticism from American politicians. The NBA modified its public stance to emphasize its support of free speech, but the league continued to lose partners in China. And LeBron James, the league's most popular player, criticized the tweet as "uneducated."

Third, social media have hastened the speed at which information, and often disinformation, is shared. Sport organizations now have the ability to share content consumed by social audiences in real time. Organizations must also diligently monitor the social environment. In a non-sport-specific report, *The Evolution of Public Relations* (ANA/USC Annenberg Center for Public Relations, 2017), the

Enes Kanter of the Portland Trail Blazers became the center of controversy when the NBA's Twitter account for Turkey ignored his strong performance in the 2019 playoffs.

Jonathan Ferrey/Getty Images

top trend practitioners identified was "social listening." Gibbs and Haynes (2013), who interviewed 18 Canadian and U.S. sport media relations and media professionals for their research, reported that this change in the environment means media relations professionals must be prepared to respond more quickly than ever when news breaks. In assessing Twitter as an influential platform in the sport industry, the authors concluded that "to manage Twitter effectively, teams need to understand the nuances of the system that make it controllable and uncontrollable" (p. 404). Chapter 3 of this text examines how to engage publics via social media. The chapter discusses key social media platforms and how to strategically use social media and assess results.

Fragmentation of Media Environment

In addition to the powerful social platforms affecting the environment, other forms of digital communication are contributing to an increasingly fragmented media environment. For example, digital streaming enables multimedia content distribution via the Internet. In sport settings, streaming gives consumers the ability to watch or listen to live games or view highlights online. ESPN+, YouTube TV, and Hulu are three prominent examples of streaming services popular among sports fans. Twitch.tv established itself as a leading source of esports gaming distribution but has diversified into other types of content. Many sport organizations have embraced streaming to distribute live and recorded content to their audiences. In some instances, the content may be available free of charge; in others, it may be subscription-based.

Downloads differ from streaming in that the digital content may be saved to the user's computer or mobile device. While a range of sport-specific content is available to sports consumers, podcasts merit special mention because they represent a significant growth area. A Nielsen research report indicated that nearly 50 million U.S. households had a resident who was a fan of podcasts in the sports category ("Top Podcast Genres in U.S. Households," 2018). That number represented significant growth from the previous year, and such growth was expected to continue in the years ahead.

One of the primary drivers behind the growth in digital streaming and downloads is mobile device usage. Statista (2019c) projected the number of smartphone users worldwide to reach 2.7 billion in 2019. That growth, combined with increased availability of wireless Internet access and advancement of cellular networks, is spurring increased usage of a range of content delivery options. And that, in turn, is resulting in an increasingly cluttered media landscape. Nielsen Sports *Top 5 Global Industry Sports Trends* report (2018) characterized this environment as "a maelstrom of change" and concluded "as the quality, volume and variety of content increase, it will be harder and harder to cut through" (p. 9). The increasingly cluttered communication environment is also having profound impact on legacy media such as newspapers, magazines, terrestrial radio, and broadcast and cable television networks. Chapter 4 of this text focuses on digital media, including the use of blogs, vlogs, and podcasts. The chapter also devotes considerable attention to websites, key communication platforms for almost all sport organizations.

Changes in Legacy Media

Cord cutting has resulted in a diminishing number of people who receive content via cable television. The percentage of U.S. households subscribing to a pay television service (e.g., cable) dropped from 77% in 2016 to 67% in 2018 (PwC, 2019). The number of people subscribing to cable and satellite services still represents a massive audience, and the ability to conveniently receive live sport programming continues to be a key asset for pay television. In fact, pay television's capability to serve as a hub for live sports programming may be its most important advantage in the competitive marketplace.

Nonetheless, the cord-cutting trend has had profound effects on the sport media industry. For example, ESPN laid off hundreds of people, including a number of popular on-air personalities, in the mid-2010s. Cord cutting, and the lofty rights fees the network committed to paying its partners, were the driving factors behind those layoffs.

Traditional print media have also been hit hard by changing consumer habits. Over the past 15 years, nearly 1,800 newspapers in the United States (Abernathy, 2018) and 250 in Canada (Public Policy Forum, 2017) closed or merged with other properties. U.S. newsroom employment dropped by 23% (Grieco, 2018). Other forms of print media, even dedicated sport publications such as the iconic magazine *Sports Illustrated*, are also feeling the pinch. In recent years, *Sports Illustrated* has seen multiple rounds of layoffs; the magazine was sold once (in 2018) and then nearly immediately afterward seemed poised for another ownership change (MacCambridge, 2018). Legacy media continue to hold relevance for sports consumers, even though these media are not as predominant as in the past. Chapter 5 describes the use of legacy

Case Study

DIVERGENT PATHS OF THE NBA AND NFL

Recent changes in popularity in two major spectator sport properties offer evidence of just how important public relations is to organizational success. The National Football League (NFL) dropped in popularity among sports fans in the United States, falling from being cited as their favorite by 43% of U.S. adults in 2007 to being cited by 36% in 2018, according to a Gallup poll (Norman, 2018). A separate Gallup poll in 2017 indicated that the percentage of Americans saying they were pro football fans had dropped 10 percentage points over a five-year period (Jones, 2017). The National Basketball Association (NBA), on the other hand, has been fairly stable in terms of the share of U.S. adults citing it as their favorite (10% to 12% over the past decade). The number of Americans saying they were fans of professional basketball, a category that includes the NBA and more, was up three percentage points over the same five-year period.

While it is important to recognize that the NFL is still clearly U.S. fans' favorite spectator sport, numerous factors may be causing the league's drop in popularity, including a number of damaging public relations issues. Among these issues are incidents of domestic violence by high-profile players, studies citing negative health effects suffered by players, and political controversy surrounding player protests during the national anthem (Norman, 2018). The NBA, on the other hand, has largely avoided such public relations problems and has soared to new levels of fan engagement as a result of its social media strategy. The league has been particularly successful on Twitter. As one writer described it, "there's nothing like NBA Twitter. It's a sports bar that doesn't close, a barbershop with unlimited seating, a family cookout where the NBA stars show up to hang" (Maese, 2018). The league's star-oriented, personality-driven approach, coupled with a fan-friendly stance on sharing video, has served it well. Little wonder that in a 2018 ranking of fan social media activity across the five major U.S. sport leagues, NBA teams held four of the top five spots: Golden State at number 1, Cleveland at number 2, Los Angeles Lakers at number 3, and Boston at number 5 (MVPindex, 2018).

Discussion Questions

1. What traits have accounted for the NBA's relative stability in popularity?
2. Among the issues described here, or others of which you may be aware, what would you argue has most contributed to the NFL's change in popularity?
3. What are the key takeaways from this brief case study in terms of how sport organizations should be managing relationships with their fans?

---

media in sport public relations. Discussion covers newsletters, annual reports, media guides, and more.

Alignment of Sport Public Relations and Marketing

Sport public relations and sport marketing have always been linked, and that alignment has only increased in the current communications environment. To understand the current trend, however, some background on the two functions is necessary.

Traditional View

Sport marketing is an organizational function that focuses on consumers, identifies how the sport organization can fulfill consumers' needs or wants, and structures marketing programs accordingly.

The sport organization provides its consumers with something of value—entertainment, recreation, fitness, or some other commodity. In exchange, consumers provide the sport organization with something of value—commonly money, but sometimes things such as the consumers' time, energy, or attention.

Sport marketers seek to develop a marketing mix that will attract and retain customers. The traditional marketing mix is made up of the "four Ps"—product, price, place, and promotion (McCarthy, 1960). The product component focuses on developing goods or services customized to consumers' needs. The price component specifies the costs that consumers will incur in exchange for the product. The place component relates to distribution decisions, physically linking the consumer and the product. And **promotion** relates to communicating messages to the consumer regarding the product and attempting to motivate the consumer to make the exchange.

Sport marketers have traditionally viewed public relations as a promotional tactic. Four elements make up the promotional mix: advertising, personal selling, sales promotions, and publicity. Advertising may be described as paid commercial messages about the product carried by mass media. In personal sales, a representative of the sport organization interacts with consumers in an effort to motivate them to buy. Sales promotions vary, but they frequently include additional incentives to the consumer such as premium giveaways, discounts, or other attempts to add value to the core product. Finally, publicity refers to information regarding the product or sport organization conveyed through the mass media for free.

Figure 1.2 portrays the marketing and promotional mixes as they are traditionally described. Some sport marketing experts, recognizing the increased importance of public relations to effective marketing, have added public relations as a fifth *P* to the marketing mix (Mullin, Hardy, & Sutton, 2014). Their rationale is that some sport businesses

(e.g., professional sports, collegiate sports) experience such high levels of media visibility that public relations warrants consideration as a distinct aspect of the marketing mix.

Key Distinctions

Sport public relations has traditionally varied from sport marketing in at least two fundamental ways. First, marketing focuses on consumers, but public relations focuses on more diverse groups of publics. Consumers are a stakeholder group critical to both functions, but the scope of public relations activity extends well beyond customers.

Another difference between the two functions is that the goal of marketing differs somewhat from the goal of public relations. As noted, exchanges are at the heart of marketing activities. Public relations, however, focuses on the broader concept of relationships. The two concepts are related but not synonymous. Scholars differentiate between exchange relationships and communal relationships (Clark & Mills, 1979). Exchange relationships are based on the sharing of benefits between the

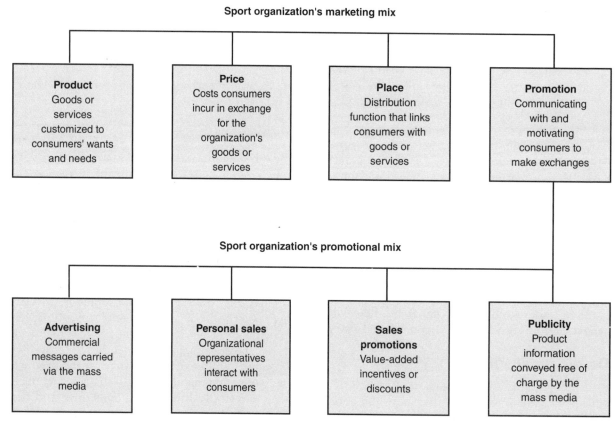

Figure 1.2 The sport marketing and promotional mixes.

parties involved. One provides benefits and expects to receive benefits in return. Communal relationships, however, are predicated on concern for the other party. One provides benefits to the other but expects nothing in return except to see the other party benefit. Athletes and other sport figures who dedicate themselves to serving people in need may exemplify communal relationships. For instance, Norwegian speed skater Johann Olav Koss, four-time Olympic gold medalist, has committed himself to using sport, the arts, and play as a mechanism to educate and empower children in disadvantaged settings around the world (Right to Play, n.d.). Koss founded Right to Play in 2000, and the organization has grown to serve millions of children since.

New Reality

In light of the changing media environment and an advanced understanding of branding and organizational communication, the public relations and marketing functions have become more closely aligned. Mitch Germann, a communications executive with Nike, astutely described this new reality:

> Gone are the days of the PR director serving as a cog in the marketing mix, charged only with obtaining media impressions and mitigating issues.

Today's CCO [chief communications officer] is a credible member of the C-suite, directing content and channel strategy to engage internal and external stakeholders in a way that achieves business results. Building the brand and protecting its reputation still serve as the core focus of the CCO, but given today's convergence of paid, earned, shared and owned media in an always-on digital environment, achieving those goals requires a broader and more progressive approach than in the past. (Germann, 2015, para. 3)

Branding is at the heart of this evolving approach to communications. The alignment of public relations and marketing fully activates the brand by incorporating it into communications with all stakeholders. Figure 1.3 depicts this approach. As indicated, the sport organization's communication efforts, led by both public relations and marketing, consist of brand-driven communications with important stakeholders and the distinct publics that often exist within them. The arrows depicting such communication are two-way in recognition that stakeholder engagement also entails receiving feedback. Much more will be said of two-way communication through the course of this text.

Right to Play is a not-for-profit organization serving children who live in hardship.

Steve Russell/Toronto Star via Getty Images

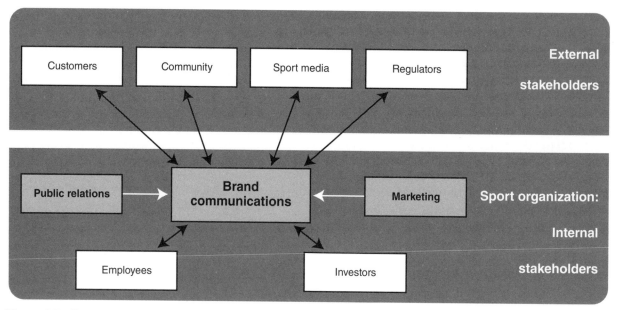

Figure 1.3 Sport organization stakeholder communication.

Glenn Gray, senior executive for a communications agency that specializes in working with the sport industry, has described how the alignment of public relations and marketing has driven the evolution of his firm. Gray (2017) indicated that the Buffalo Agency started as a public relations firm exclusively serving clients in the golf industry. In the ensuing 15 to 20 years, the agency expanded its services to include strategy development, social media, content and creative services, and more. As the agency grew, it diversified its employee base to include team members with skills in campaign development, tickets sales, and online advertising. The business growth that resulted drove the firm's expansion into other sectors of the sport industry, including soccer, fitness, and outdoor.

One of the models that has best captured this integrated approach to organizational communications is the **PESO model** (Dietrich, 2014) (*PESO* stands for paid, earned, shared, and owned media). The sidebar PESO Model of Communication introduces this model, which will be revisited multiple times in this text. Notice that, in the quotation included earlier, Mitch Germann referenced "the convergence of paid, earned, shared and owned media," the very framework of the PESO model.

Influence of Communication Leaders

Recent examples from the College Football Playoff and Nike illustrate how public relations and com-

munications professionals are increasing their influence at the highest levels of their organizations. Gina Lehe is the senior director of external relations and branding for the College Football Playoff. Lehe indicated that the role of the organization's top communicator has evolved, as evidenced by the scope of responsibilities—which encompasses "anything that speaks to who and what the College Football Playoff is" ("Sports Biz Mom," 2019). She views the changes in the field as providing significant opportunities: "We've had to evolve what we do, and those of us that have, have reaped some benefits of not getting left behind with social and digital media" (quoted in "Sports Biz Mom," 2019).

Similarly, Nigel Powell serves as chief communications officer at Nike and relishes this role: "I love working in communications as we can have impact in every area of the brand and business" (quoted in "The Influence 100," 2015). In his senior communicator role at Nike, Powell leads a communications team of 250 people, and his responsibilities include brand and reputation management, as well as corporate, consumer, and employee communications. Though Powell works with one of the largest and most prestigious brands in the world, his role as a thought leader and influencer within the senior management team is one that skilled public relations professionals in varied sport organizations, large and small, are assuming with greater frequency.

Citing coverage in the sport business media and observations of public relations work in British football, L'Etang (2013) observed a trend toward communicators more frequently serving as thought

PESO Model of Communication

Gini Dietrich's book *Spin Sucks: Communication and Reputation Management* (2014) is one of the more important public relations and marketing books of the past decade. In it, Dietrich defined a new model for communications that combines publicity, a traditional aspect of public relations work, and advertising, traditionally part of marketing, with "two new kids in town" (p. 38)—shared and owned media. The four elements make up the PESO model and may be summarized as follows:

- Paid media: The advertising element. In addition to more traditional advertising outlets, the PESO model recognizes social and digital options as well.
- Earned media: The publicity element. The model again goes beyond more traditional placements such as print or broadcast to recognize opportunities with bloggers and influencers.
- Shared media: Social media, essentially. The word *shared* emphasizes the importance of engagement beyond mere audience consumption.
- Owned media: Organizational or individual methods of distributing self-generated content (e.g., blogs, videos, podcasts) directly to audiences.

Spin Sucks is not sport-specific, but it does feature numerous examples of application of the PESO model in sport settings. One such example was Adidas' adjustment of its communication strategy around a new shoe launch when its athlete namesake, basketball star Derrick Rose, suffered a major injury shortly after signing a six-figure endorsement contract. Adidas opted to utilize owned media, specifically a documentary series titled *The Return* that the company created and released online, to tell Rose's story of coming back from a bout with adversity. Adidas leveraged the content via shared (i.e., social) media to build online buzz, gain followers, and generate searches for the product.

The full PESO model details the various tactics that fall under each of the four major categories and identifies zones where the four types of media may overlap. Please see spinsucks.com to access the detailed model.

leaders within their organizations. As they did so, the scope of the stakeholders with whom they engaged expanded beyond fans and media to sponsors, shareholders, and others. Such significant changes were an "acknowledgement of strategic aspects and their importance to sports business" (L'Etang, 2013, p. 160).

Differences exist about the functional label—public relations, communications, external relations—that should be associated with this work. The term *PR*, rightfully or not, is often linked with a more narrow view of the role (i.e., media relations only). As Germann (2015) writes, "Today the role of the chief communications officer is increasing in both importance and remit—guiding a brand's storytelling efforts to all relevant stakeholders in order to achieve business objectives."

Sport Public Relations in Practice

Although the practice of sport public relations is diverse, practitioners must possess certain basic skill sets. The sidebar Essential Skills Underlying the Practice of Public Relations in Sport lists these skills and offers some ideas regarding potential resources for developing them.

Some forms of public relations practice are more common within the sport industry than others. Media relations and community relations have traditionally been at the top of the list. Subsequent sections address those two forms of public relations as well as other types, such as employee relations, investor relations, customer relations, donor relations, and government relations. The discussion begins with an examination of social and digital communication, which has emerged as a common category for job opportunities in sport and is also usually a competency required to be effective in other sport public relations specializations.

Sport Social Media and Digital Communications

Social and digital communications is the professional specialization experiencing the greatest

Essential Skills Underlying the Practice of Public Relations in Sport

Sport public relations is predicated on basic yet essential skills that serve as the foundation for multiple competencies applied in the industry. Readers likely already possess some competency in these basic skill areas. A summary of these underlying skill sets and recommendations for ways students may further develop their capabilities in these areas follows.

Writing Skills

Although the channels through which information is carried vary from news releases to publications to blogs, the core competency remains constant: being able to write effectively. Writing skills cannot be developed simply by accessing educational resources. They must be honed through practice. Students interested in sport public relations or even those who anticipate using writing skills in non-PR jobs should look for any opportunity to develop these skills. Writing for campus media can provide invaluable experience, as can volunteer work alongside sport public relations professionals. Newspapers often hire "stringers," who write small stories (e.g., high school sports reports) on a part-time basis. Students should also consider taking writing-intensive college courses, such as those offered in many mass communication programs. The key element in each of these settings is that professionals or educators critique the students' writing and offer suggestions for improvement. Students looking to develop their writing skills can also access a variety of resources that provide insights on writing effectiveness. One commonly recommended resource is *The Elements of Style* (Strunk & White, 2008), a handbook that addresses basic grammatical and syntax issues writers commonly encounter.

Public Presentation Skills

Although sport public relations professionals may not be called on to give speeches as often as high-profile coaches and organizational executives are, these professionals frequently moderate news conferences and other special events and serve as organizational spokespersons. Furthermore, they may be called on to coach other members of the organization, such as senior managers, coaches, and athletes, as they seek to develop their own public presentation abilities. Like writing, this skill requires practice. Communication courses that focus on public speaking can offer invaluable experience, and the professional literature includes many books on the topic. In addition, professional organizations such as the National Speakers Association and Toastmasters International offer a range of services to support their members in advancing their public speaking skills.

Interpersonal Skills

Sport public relations professionals who enjoy interacting with others and can quickly form social connections typically find that skill to be a professional asset. Some people's personalities naturally lend themselves to success in this area; others may need to cultivate these qualities. Courses in leadership or team building are often beneficial in building interpersonal skills. Many colleges have counseling centers that offer interpersonal skill assessments and services that may assist in the development of these critical qualities. Students and practitioners who continue to develop their interpersonal skills are also likely to gain improved public relations acumen, since many of the relational dynamics affecting interpersonal relationships also apply to organizational relationships (Turney, 2011).

Technological Skills

All prospective sport managers, whether public relations is part of their position or not, need to possess basic technological competencies in a range of areas including the use of e-mail and common software applications (e.g., word processing, spreadsheets). Public relations professionals commonly need even more advanced technological skills. Social media skills top this list; the abilities to develop and share content and successfully engage others are relevant to nearly every facet of public relations practice. It may not be possible to be adept in the full range of existing social media networks. Skill in using the most common platforms such as Instagram, Twitter, and Facebook, however, is critical. In addition, other technological competencies, such as basic coding, graphic design, and other digital skills (e.g., Adobe Suite), also serve as good supports for public relations skills. While the scope of relevant technological skills may seem overwhelming, the good news is that resources are abundant. College courses pertaining to technological skills are common, but software providers such as Google and Microsoft also offer a range of training resources online, and many are free. In addition, books such as *The Dragonfly Effect: Quick, Powerful and Effective Ways to Use Social Media to Drive Social Change* (Aaker & Smith, 2010) and *Developing Successful Social Media Plans in Sport Organizations* (Sanderson & Yandle, 2015) are also excellent resources.

Research Skills

Public relations professionals must be able to search out, understand, and synthesize existing research within their own organization or developed by people outside the organization. Such work requires data literacy—the ability to make sense of data and develop accurate and appropriate conclusions based on data. Common sources of useful information may include not only organizational records but also other information such as directory sources (e.g., a Google search on the Internet) or subscription-based data from data providers (e.g., Sports Market Analytics). Some public relations professionals not only employ secondary research skills (i.e., using research conducted by others) but also engage in primary research activities. These may range from conducting polls or surveys to staging focus group discussions to interviewing. As with the other skills discussed earlier, students and practitioners benefit from a range of resources to assist them in advancing their research skills. Data analytics and research methods courses are common at both undergraduate and graduate levels. Online resources such as Hootsuite Academy provide training programs and related research tools. In addition, a wide array of research-related books and texts may serve as valuable resources. One such example specific to the field of sport management is *Research Methods and Design in Sport Management, Second Edition* (Andrew, Pedersen, & McEvoy, 2020).

growth within the sport communication field. This is a direct result of the manner in which the field has evolved over the last decade, as previously discussed. And while digital and social communications responsibilities may be integrated into the job descriptions of other forms of sport public relations work (e.g., media relations), the industry now supports a large number of jobs fully dedicated to this specialization.

Integral to the effective use of digital and social media is the concept of storytelling. Stories often elicit emotional responses from consumers, and as a result, they are particularly powerful forms of communication. Jennifer Aaker (n.d.), professor and coauthor of the influential social media book *The Dragonfly Effect*, indicates stories can be more than 20 times more memorable than facts. As such, stories have the ability to persuade people and fundamentally shape how they perceive the storyteller.

Rush (2014) encouraged communicators, marketers in particular, to employ storytelling for more impact, noting that both psychology and consumer behavior research support such an approach. "Stories stimulate the mind; it is now in our job descriptions to send consumers on journeys that lead them to solve their problems and, hopefully, boost our bottom lines" (Rush, 2014). The same principle applies to communicators in varied public relations settings working to achieve diverse objectives. Chapter 2 offers additional principles of good storytelling, and the subject of storytelling will be revisited multiple times throughout the text.

Goals of Digital and Social Communications

The NFL's Dallas Cowboys are one of many sport organizations that have adapted their communications management strategy and structure to the new realities of the market. Recognizing that the organization produces content through its television broadcasts, website, social media accounts, and in-game productions, the team aligned its efforts with the goal of maximizing its viewership and audience engagement (Abeza, 2018). The team now uses analytics to inform content development and then matches content to the best channels to reach its audiences. Shannon Grosse, the organization's

Two models commonly describe the practice of sport media relations. The first is a press agentry and publicity model (Grunig & Hunt, 1984). Practitioners employing this model seek to cultivate as much publicity as possible for their organizations. Some even violate the boundaries of what many people consider acceptable behavior to receive that publicity. "There's no such thing as bad publicity," these practitioners rationalize, and their tactics are often successful in gaining media coverage. LaVar Ball, father of a trio of basketball star sons, embodied this model in creating a personal brand that served as a platform for promoting his sons and launching a new business—the Big Baller. As his son Lonzo Ball, then at the University of California, Los Angeles (UCLA), emerged into national stardom, LaVar Ball relentlessly sought media attention, making one outrageous claim after another. Among them, LaVar claimed Lonzo was better than then-two time NBA most valuable player (MVP) Steph Curry and that LaVar himself would easily defeat Michael Jordan in one-on-one. One industry writer, in an article titled "LaVar Ball: Marketing Genius, Out of Control Dad, or Both?," described him as "a 100 percent marketing genius—even in his insanity" (Mazique, 2017, para. 3).

The press agentry and publicity model may also be used in an ethical fashion. For example, many professional and college teams hold media days at some point during their preseasons. One of the primary purposes of media days is to generate favorable publicity in advance of the new season. Perhaps the largest (and, in some instances, the zaniest) media day is the one staged by the NFL each year before the Super Bowl. Now known as "Opening Night," the event has evolved from the traditional media-centric event in which players and coaches were available to credentialed media members only for interviews. While members of the sport media are still on hand to ask questions, they are now joined by other celebrities while a venue full of ticket-purchasing spectators watch and the league network carries the event live. Longtime print and broadcast journalist Peter King observed, "Media Night used to be, 'Let's spread the gospel of this Super Bowl and how wonderful the NFL is.' Now it's, 'Let us spread our wings into alternative media.' It doesn't matter how circus-y it is, it's show business" (quoted in Wilder, 2019). Information pertaining to more conventional media days is presented in chapter 7.

The second model is a public information model that focuses on providing effective service to members of the mass media who are already inclined to cover the sport organization (Grunig & Hunt, 1984). Professionals using this model do not want to risk embarrassing their organization by using questionable methods to seek attention. They may not even actively solicit media coverage, but they do nurture the coverage that they receive by effectively meeting the informational needs of the media. For instance, these professionals may accommodate a television reporter who contacts them in the hope of arranging an interview with a player or coach, or they may produce a media guide that members of the media can use as a reference tool throughout a particular sport's season.

The NFL's "Opening Night" may have evolved over the years, but its purpose is still to generate buzz and anticipation of the Super Bowl.

Nick Wosika/Icon Sportswire via Getty Images

Grunig and Hunt (1984) argued that sport was one of the most common settings in which the press agentry model is employed. Sport media relations professionals with minor league sport teams, athletics programs that are not National Collegiate Athletic Association (NCAA) Division I, sport service providers, and sporting goods manufacturers are among those who operate as press agents, proactively seeking publicity for their organizations. Those working at the highest levels of professional and college sport are much more likely to be able to operate from a public information model and still secure substantial media presence for their organizations. Sometimes media relations professionals within a single organization use both proactive and reactive models depending on the season or time of year. For example, public relations staff members at the Maryland Jockey Club function as press agents for most of the year, proactively seeking attention in the mass media. But they shift to a public information model each spring as their marquee event, the Preakness (the second leg of horse racing's Triple Crown), approaches (Henniger, 2003). Similarly, the communications staff with the Premier League's Arsenal Football Club shift from reactive to proactive media relations practices when scheduling variances, such as the lack of a major international tournament, may contribute to diminished media coverage (Black, 2007).

Favorable publicity is an asset that sport organizations covet, but unfavorable publicity is usually viewed as a liability that they cannot afford. Results of an experiment regarding how audiences responded to positive and negative news relating to a Major League Baseball (MLB) team indicated that the publicity affected readers' feelings and beliefs about the organization, and these effects were particularly pronounced among some segments of the audience (Funk & Pritchard, 2006). Specifically, audience members who were not predisposed to a high level of commitment to the team were particularly affected by the publicity. The researchers observed that "negative publicity can pose a very real threat to a sport organization's market base and affect revenue beyond the turnstile" (Funk & Pritchard, 2006, p. 619). Arguably, the potential for damage resulting from negative publicity is even greater in today's communications environment of social media platforms featuring real-time communication, much of which comes from individuals who are not necessarily concerned with traditional journalistic values such as accuracy and fairness. A study on how sports fans perceived information about a controversial referee's decision during a men's soccer semifinal in the 2012 Summer Olympic Games indicated that fans found Twitter messages from nonprofessional writers to be just as reliable as those from professional journalists (Lee, Ryu, Clavio, Lovell, Lim, & Pedersen, 2014). Popular, and sometimes uninformed, sentiment expressed via social media can have serious consequences for sport organizations. For instance, when news leaked in 2017 that the University of Tennessee was negotiating with then–Ohio State defensive coordinator Greg Schiano to become the Volunteers' football coach, fans responded with a social media backlash that resulted in the scuttling of the candidacy. Furthermore, the school's athletic director, John Currie, was fired the following week. The Twitter mob phenomenon sometimes makes the platform resemble a modern-day Roman Colosseum where the masses render their verdicts (Fontaine, 2018).

Media relations professionals can sometimes negate unfavorable publicity and social media backlash by advising members of their organizations how to avoid public relations mistakes. These professionals can choose to withhold embarrassing or damaging facts from members of the media and can even lead their organization in successfully weathering a crisis when embarrassing or damaging facts about the organization have been publicized. But it is inappropriate for media relations professionals or other sport organization employees to ask members of the mass media not to report such information after it has been discovered. The sidebar Ethical Issues in Sport Public Relations, by Dr. Anastasios Kaburakis and Dr. Galen Clavio, addresses other topics sport public relations professionals often face.

Ethical considerations are usually relevant to crisis situations that sport public relations professionals may face. Chapter 8 addresses crisis communications, including how to develop a crisis plan and select appropriate strategies when faced with a crisis.

Jobs in Sport Media Relations

Sport media relations professionals work in a variety of settings, including professional sport teams and leagues, college athletics programs and their conference offices, and national governing bodies. Media relations responsibilities may be among those assumed by marketing and promotions directors at fitness centers or by the corporate communications staff at sporting goods companies. When it comes to full-time jobs in media relations, however, the two most common job settings are professional sport, where job titles usually include the term *media relations*,

Ethical Issues in Sport Public Relations

The ethical dimension of sport public relations does not receive a great deal of attention, but it can be extremely important for both the individual public relations practitioner and the organization as a whole. The way that a public relations department treats ethical considerations sets the tone for external perception of the organization as a whole.

Many sport media organizations have their own codes of ethics, which act as guidelines for professional behavior among workers in the field. For sport media relations professionals on the collegiate level, a professional organization—the College Sports Information Directors of America (CoSIDA)—publishes a code of ethics, which contains behavioral guidelines and parameters.

Whether or not their organizations have formal codes of ethics, sport public relations officials are expected to conduct themselves professionally while simultaneously acting in the best interests of their organizations. This responsibility includes producing positive content relating to athletes, coaches, and team officials. Two other ethical issues commonly warrant careful consideration among sport public relations practitioners.

Questions of Fairness in Coverage

Media relations professionals are often concerned with equity in coverage of their sports by the media. The process of dealing with inequities in coverage through external media is a long-standing ethical concern, but the growth of organizational social and digital communications has led to ethical issues of fairness in coverage within these organizations. Collegiate and scholastic athletic departments are faced with a difficult question: Does the school provide equal promotion to stories about all varsity sports on its website, or does it focus its coverage on sports such as football and men's basketball, which are liable to attract greater web traffic and therefore generate more revenue?

Moral Differences in Domestic and International Sport

The sport experience in the United States features several intense rivalries, on both the professional level (e.g., New York Yankees and Boston Red Sox, Chicago Cubs and St. Louis Cardinals, Green Bay Packers and Minnesota Vikings) and the collegiate level (e.g., Michigan and Ohio State, North Carolina and Duke, Texas and Oklahoma). But the way that people treat sport in other parts of the world is vastly different, and it begins with team affiliation by youth essentially "out of the womb." Socioeconomic, religious, cultural, and demographic differences render certain teams' competitions as classic rivalries, essentially becoming battles in a long-standing war against supporters of the opposite camp or team, often with religious, political, and socioeconomic overtones. Thus, sport communications professionals need to be aware of the sensitivities of each region. Before a Celtic–Rangers, Barcelona–Real Madrid, Partizan–Red Star Belgrade, or Panathinaikos–Olympiakos game, public relations workers need to attempt a balanced report and try to ease the inherent pressure. Furthermore, public relations professionals need to do the same on the national team stage before classic rivalries with historical underpinnings (i.e., Argentina vs. Brazil, Serbia vs. Croatia, Russia vs. United States).

Dr. Anastasios Kaburakis and Dr. Galen Clavio

and intercollegiate sport, where job titles often include the terms *athletic communications* or *sports information*.

Professional teams and leagues at the highest levels may employ multiple employees in their media relations departments. On the other end of the continuum are minor league teams, which are more likely to have just one full- or part-time media relations employee. The Toronto Maple Leafs of the National Hockey League have a communications staff of nine, four of whom are fully dedicated to media relations work. The Wichita Thunder of the East Coast Hockey League (ECHL) have a single communications staff member, who also has other responsibilities with the team, including serving as the team's play-by-play broadcaster.

The college media relations setting is similar to professional sport in that the size of the staff varies according to the size of the organization. Within the National Collegiate Athletic Association (NCAA), some of the larger programs have more than 20 people working in their media relations departments. Athletics programs at the NCAA Division II or III level, the National Association of Intercollegiate Athletics (NAIA), the National Junior College Athletic Association (NJCAA), and the Canadian Collegiate Athletic Association (CCAA) usually have a full-time or part-time media relations employee, or they may assign media relations to a coach or university public relations employee. Ohio State University, an NCAA Football Bowl Subdivision program, employs 12 full-time media relations staff members along with an intern and 10 students who work on a part-time basis. Langston University, a NAIA Division I program in Oklahoma, has one staff member working in media relations.

Media relations professionals in professional and collegiate sport assume a similar set of primary responsibilities. These responsibilities focus on

- publicity,
- social and digital media,
- statistical services,
- media services, and
- other forms of organizational media.

Publicity

As noted, publicity is a powerful tool for sport organizations, and soliciting and nurturing it is a critical part of the media relations professional's job. Practitioners use a variety of techniques to generate publicity. They issue general news and event information releases, stage news conferences so that members of the mass media may personally interact with important newsmakers, host media days and other special events tailored to the mass media, and may even develop publicity campaigns for players and coaches in contention for various honors. These topics are all addressed in subsequent chapters.

Social and Digital Media

Given that the media relations office is usually the information hub for professional sport franchises and college athletics programs, it is not surprising that many media relations professionals are responsible for content on their organization's website. In addition, media relations professionals may interact with audiences through social media platforms such as Facebook, Instagram, and Twitter, although primary responsibility for social and digital communications may be assigned to other units in some sport organizations.

Statistical Services

Tracking, analyzing, and storing statistical information is a major responsibility for many sport media relations professionals. They track statistics on a game-by-game or event-by-event basis and produce in-depth statistical reports, many of which are detailed enough to offer play-by-play information regarding how the contest unfolded. They also calculate season totals that can be disaggregated for analysis by category (home versus away games, nonconference versus conference contests). Sport media relations professionals are also archivists in that they maintain past records and update them as subsequent seasons unfold.

Media Services

Sport media relations professionals are responsible for much more than tracking statistics at games and events. Managing the media at those events is a critical aspect of their jobs. They are responsible for cultivating media attendance at the competitions, administering credential requests, providing media work space and other relevant services, and generating information on-site for members of the media.

Organizational Media

Media guides, game programs, posters, and schedule cards are just a few examples of the publications that sport media relations professionals create in the course of their jobs. *Media guide* is the term traditionally used to describe the information-rich publications that these professionals create on an annual basis, but those publications can serve multiple promotional purposes. Many media relations professionals are also responsible for producing game programs and other print pieces. Further, some of these publications are moving online as sport organizations look to save money on printing costs and to connect with web savvy audiences.

Sport Community Relations

Community relations may be defined as organizational activity designed to foster desirable relationships between the sport organization and the communities in which it either is located or has strategic interests. Accordingly, community relations is connected with corporate social responsibility, which is considered to be an organization's discretionary practices that positively affect its community (Freitag, 2008). Community relations programs can be complex given that they encompass a range of activities ranging from managing a speakers' bureau to initiating a charitable program to touting environmental initiatives. Further, sport organizations often wish to cultivate multiple communities. Some sport organizations have offices and manufacturing facilities, or sell their products, in a multitude of communities. For instance, shoe and apparel manufacturer New Balance has five footwear factories in the United States and another in England (New Balance, 2012). Other sport organizations may be located in a single place, but their "community" may extend well beyond the physical boundary of the host municipality. For example, the University of Nebraska's football program draws fans from towns and rural areas across the state, not to mention other states and countries. It hardly makes sense for the university to limit its community relations programs to its home community of Lincoln. Location is not the only relevant factor for sport organizations with constituents dispersed over broad areas (Irwin, Sutton, & McCarthy, 2008).

Chapter 9 focuses on how sport organizations may cultivate positive relationships with their communities. Much of the discussion in that chapter centers on social responsibility and how it may be strategically designed and communicated to key audiences.

Goals of Sport Community Relations

Community relations has traditionally been described as a long-term investment in community goodwill (Mullin et al., 2014). For that reason, among others, sport organizations have traditionally devoted more resources to media relations, which is perceived to provide a quicker return on investment through the publicity that it generates. Nonetheless, the value of community relations should not be underestimated. Favorable attitudes among community members may be fostered by positive interactions between representatives of the sport organization and the public and by the charitable contributions, financial and otherwise, that a sport organization makes to its community.

Because of their community relations programs, sport organizations may realize such outcomes as demonstrating social responsibility, building public awareness, generating favor with customers, increasing employee morale, contributing to their community's well-being, and gaining tax advantages. Organizations may also be able to reach publics who are not targeted by the organizations' other marketing and public relations activities (Berkhouse & Gabert, 1999).

Community relations may be particularly important for sport organizations that have difficulty attracting positive media attention for being successful in other areas (Irwin et al., 2008). One such example may be a professional franchise or collegiate program that has a losing reputation and limited prospects for improvement in the near future. Such a franchise could receive favorable media coverage if its players and coaches were to serve meals to the homeless. Another example may be a sporting goods manufacturer or an event management group that endures frequent public criticism. By making

Community relations programs that demonstrate a sport organization's social commitment are a key facet of public relations practice.

Michael Reaves/Getty Images

financial donations to worthy causes like educational programs, these organizations may be portrayed in a positive light by members of the media. In such cases, community relations activities may be particularly critical in cultivating more favorable attitudes among key constituents.

Jobs in Sport Community Relations

Fewer full-time positions exist in sport community relations than in sport media relations, although opportunities are plentiful as organizations embrace the value of strong community relations programs. Community relations responsibilities are sometimes included in the job responsibilities of sport managers with other titles. For example, the director of media relations for a minor league baseball team may also be responsible for coordinating public appearances by players and coaches. College athletic administrators coordinating student–athlete support services may be called on to involve their student–athletes in community relations initiatives. And marketing personnel in the fitness sector of the industry may collaborate with nonprofit health advocacy groups to promote wellness in their communities.

Most teams and governing bodies at the highest levels of professional sport employ full-time employees in community relations. For example, MLB's St. Louis Cardinals have seven employees in their Cardinals Care and Community Relations department. Sport organizations in other industry settings may also employ community relations personnel, although their job titles may not necessarily include the term *community relations*. Maple Leaf Sports and Entertainment (MLSE)—a corporation that owns four major-level professional teams, three minor-level teams, and six sport and entertainment facilities—lists nearly 20 people on the staff of its MLSE Foundation, an organization for community outreach (MLSE, 2009).

Whether the community relations function is executed by someone with full-time responsibilities in the function or not, it generally involves two sets of tasks—coordinating direct contact initiatives and executing charitable programs.

Personal Contact Programs

Face-to-face contact between representatives of a sport organization and members of the general public can be a powerful public relations tool, especially for professional and collegiate organizations whose coaches and athletes are likely to be both recognizable and respected because of the media attention afforded them. Making players and coaches accessible to members of the public is conducive to desirable outcomes such as building fan identification (Milne & McDonald, 1999).

Representatives from sport organizations make speeches and other public appearances. Elite professional teams and college athletics programs stage caravan tours promoting their upcoming seasons, and a variety of professional and college teams host fan days. Unmediated communication initiatives are also employed by health clubs, golf courses, and tennis centers as they seek opportunities to attract prospective customers by hosting open houses.

Social Responsibility Programs

Social responsibility is one of the dimensions that affects an organization's reputation. Specific considerations include supporting good causes, being environmentally responsible, and treating people well (Value Based Management.net, n.d.). Community relations activates many socially responsible programs and supports others. For instance, professional sport teams, sporting goods manufacturers, and fitness and recreation service providers frequently make cash and in-kind contributions to charitable causes. Some stage events for the express purpose of making money for charity (see the examples earlier of Cardinals Care and the MLSE Foundation). Community relations units may also highlight sport organizations' environmental initiatives.

Other Public Relations Program Areas

Sport organizations may also plan public relations activities to cultivate desirable relationships with other key publics such as employees, investors, customers, donors, and governmental parties and other regulators. These topics are examined in greater depth in chapter 10.

Customer Relations

As noted, the sport organization's marketing staff designs programs to facilitate transactions with customers, and public relations plays a key role in the promotional mix. But public relations can make other contributions toward fostering desirable customer relations. Some public relations professionals frequently communicate with their organization's customers. For example, they may include customers on their distribution list for news releases, publications, and other forms of communication.

The public relations office is sometimes a point of contact for customers who have questions or complaints. Public relations professionals may also communicate with customers through social and digital media.

Sponsor Relations

In a sense, sponsors are also customers of sport organizations. Given their importance as a separate source of revenue and their distinct reasons for engaging in partnerships with sport entities, sponsors warrant separate discussion in this text. Sponsor motives range from increased sales to philanthropic outcomes, but they all relate to tapping into the sport property to reach a target market. Public relations plays a key role in activating sponsorships as sport organizations integrate their partners into their communication activities. Sport organizations may also bolster their partners' content creation when the organization's content can be integrated into the stories sponsors share with their own audiences.

Donor Relations

Given the vast number of sport organizations that operate in nonprofit settings, donor relations are an important sport public relations consideration. Fitness and recreation providers such as the YMCA need donors to support sport programs, particularly those designed for children from economically disadvantaged backgrounds. College and high school athletics programs establish booster clubs, some of which require substantial membership fees, to enhance their programs. Individuals and organizations who donate to such programs must be recognized for their generosity, presented with benefits of value, and groomed for future donations. Frequent communication between the sport organization and its donors is at the center of such processes.

Government and Regulator Relations

Sport organizations frequently function in relationship to numerous government agencies and other regulatory organizations. Most sport businesses are highly regulated by federal, state, and local laws. Sometimes, sport organizations advocate certain policies that are beneficial to their sustained existence, such as the Sports Broadcasting Act, which allows professional sport leagues to gain antitrust protection in packaging their games for sale to broadcast partners. Sport organizations may also seek public support in the form of tax dollars for facility initiatives. In such situations, sport managers must devote considerable effort to developing relationships with key governmental agencies as well as public constituencies.

Other sport organizations face additional regulation through voluntary affiliation with organizations such as college athletics associations (e.g., NCAA, CCAA), state interscholastic athletics organizations, athletics conferences, national governing bodies, and even professional leagues. These organizations commonly lobby their regulators for the implementation and maintenance of particular policies deemed desirable by the organization.

Employee Relations

Although often taken for granted, employees and volunteers are critical stakeholder groups that deserve specific public relations consideration. Fostering frequent communication between senior management and employees and between employees in various functional units is an important part of the equation, but employee relations extends beyond these efforts. Some sport organizations design employee relations programs to enhance employee motivation, performance, and job satisfaction.

Employee relations also relates to organizational culture (Pettinger, 1999; Sriramesh, Grunig, & Buffington, 1992). The communication environment fostered within the organization, not to mention the way that the organization addresses diversity within its staff, has important ramifications. Such considerations are particularly important given that each member of the organization is in essence a public relations representative. By cultivating a public relations orientation among employees, an organization is more likely to enjoy positive relationships with other publics such as customers, neighbors, and the community in general.

Investor Relations

Some sport organizations are publicly owned. This form of ownership is most common in the sporting goods industry. Manufacturers such as Adidas and Callaway Golf and retailers such as Foot Locker and Dick's Sporting Goods have stockholders who have invested in the company. Some sport facilities, such as Churchill Downs and Charlotte Motor Speedway (owned by Speedway Motorsports), are also publicly held. Publicly owned sport organizations must pay special attention to their investors and related publics such as financial analysts to keep investors informed about the company's financial performance and to convince them that investment in the organization continues to be a sound financial strategy. Given the importance of investors to the continuing existence of publicly held sport organizations, this aspect of public relations is critical. This area is also highly regulated, meaning that public relations professionals must know which information is mandated for disclosure and how to present information in ways that do not violate the law (Broom, 2013).

Public Relations Value

Public relations offers two broad benefits to sport organizations. First, it advances the organization, primarily by establishing and building the brand. Public relations can also generate revenue by producing content that may be monetized. The second benefit, broadly speaking, is protecting the organization by avoiding mistakes that would damage the brand, alienating customers and other important publics.

Advance the Organization

Public relations advances sport organizations in several ways, but brand building tops the list. Ries and Ries (2002) contend that brand building is the fundamental role of public relations; without a great brand, they argue, other public relations functions will have little effect on organizational success. Certainly, sport organizations have an interest in developing an identity that is viewed positively and serves the operation well. Effectively built, a brand is associated with positive characteristics and benefits in consumers' minds. For example, the Olympic brand is commonly associated with elite sport competition and community building on a global scale. People seeking the thrill of watching elite performers compete and the inspiration that comes from seeing diverse people join in a common cause are likely to attend Olympic events or at least watch television broadcasts of the Games because they know the brand represents those qualities. Brands possessing value in consumers' minds enjoy significant advantages in a cluttered, competitive marketplace.

Public relations is an effective brand-building tool because of its ability to tell compelling stories. When organizations are able to align messaging through paid, earned, shared, and owned platforms, they are well positioned to advance their brand. Consumers may be particularly receptive to communication from earned media or publicity. Because most consumers perceive publicity information as coming from a nonbiased third-party member of the mass media, publicity is a highly credible form of communication. In *The Fall of Advertising and the Rise of PR*, Ries and Ries argue this point persuasively: "To get something going from nothing, you need the validity that only third-party endorsements can bring. The first stage of any new campaign ought to be public relations" (2002, p. xx). Gatorade, the authors note, is an excellent example. The Gatorade brand is built largely on the publicity that the product received in the mid-1960s when the University of Florida football team used the product during a highly successful season. Since that time, Gatorade's advertising and endorsement programs have served simply to remind consumers of what the brand offers. The product was initially positioned in consumers' minds through public relations. The power of public relations to build brands will be addressed in much more detail in chapter 2.

A second way that public relations can generate revenue for the sport organization is by producing content that can be directly monetized. Many sport properties, particularly higher-profile professional and college organizations, offer premium levels of team and athlete content on a subscription basis. Fans may gain access to a range of content, often including digital video game coverage, via their subscriptions. In addition, many public relations professionals in professional and collegiate sport produce publications such as game programs and media guides. Game programs generate revenue through advertising sales, and both forms of publications are commonly sold to members of the public.

Protect the Organization

Although public relations has plenty to offer in terms of advancing the sport organization, its other major contribution is helping the sport organization avoid costly mistakes. Reputation is a topic that will receive considerable attention in chapter 2. The point, for now, however, is that mistakes can be enormously damaging to brands and have severe reputational consequences.

The value of public relations in avoiding costly mistakes is illustrated in the following three vignettes:

• The Mount Vernon (Texas) school district waded into controversy in 2019 with the hire of disgraced former college coach Art Briles as its new high school football coach. Briles had been fired as head coach at Baylor University in 2016 as a result of a sexual assault scandal involving a number of football players. Many, from local residents to national media outlets, criticized the Mount Vernon hire as highly inappropriate (Hoyt, 2019).

• Soccer coach Phil Neville is one of many athletes and coaches who have had old, insensitive Twitter posts come back around in embarrassing fashion. In Neville's case, six-year-old sexist tweets, including one joking about domestic violence, were particularly damaging after he was named head coach of England's women's national soccer team in 2018 (Edwards, 2018).

• The Bradley University athletics program made a public relations miscue in 2019 as its men's basketball team was making its first appearance in the NCAA national tournament in 13 years. The program denied media day access to a longtime, respected sportswriter, reportedly after indicat-

ing he had failed to promote the Bradley brand (Lawhon, 2019). The subsequent national media backlash resulted in the program reinstating the writer's access with apologies from both the university and the basketball coach.

All organizations, sport and otherwise, make public relations errors. The key point, however, is that by attuning themselves to public relations considerations, sport organizations may minimize the frequency and severity of those errors.

The precise financial impact of this benefit is impossible to determine. What was the financial value of the media airtime and space devoted to controversy in each of these situations? As difficult as it may be even to estimate the cost of the errors, it is even more difficult to determine the financial value of avoiding a mistake thanks to public relations counsel.

SUMMARY

Sport public relations is a brand-centric communication function designed to manage and advance relationships between a sport organization and its key publics. The field is rapidly evolving as a result of changes in the media environment, including the rise in prominence of social and digital media. The new media landscape enables organizations to adopt better integrated communication strategies, resulting in much closer alignment of the public relations and marketing functions. Telling stories via the various platforms linked by the PESO model (Dietrich, 2014) enables sport organizations to meaningfully engage their key publics.

The practice of public relations within sport is diverse, but three common forms are digital and social communications, media relations, and community relations. Digital and social communications work involves social media management, digital content creation, and website management. Media relations programs focus on building relationships with members of the mass media to maximize positive publicity and minimize negative publicity. Community relations programs are structured to allow members of the sport organization to come in direct contact with their constituents and to allow the sport organization to gain public favor by contributing to charitable initiatives. Other forms of public relations in sport include employee relations, investor relations, customer relations, donor relations, and government relations. Regardless of the nature of the specific public relations activity, effective practice is based on several fundamental skills, including the ability to write well, make public presentations, interact effectively with others, research audiences and issues, and utilize relevant technologies.

Effective public relations offers two broad benefits to the sport organization. First, public relations advances the organization through contributions to brand development and management. The content public relations professionals develop may also be directly monetized via subscriptions and sales. Second, public relations counsel can help sport organizations save money by preventing the occurrence of damaging mistakes in relation to key publics.

LEARNING ACTIVITIES

1. Conduct a brief in-person, telephone, or e-mail interview with a sport public relations professional. Media relations professionals who work with professional teams or collegiate programs may be the easiest to identify. Your community may also include professionals in sport community relations, employee relations, or even investor relations. How does that person describe the public relations function within the organization? How does he or she describe the relationship between public relations and marketing?

2. Find examples of organizational communication relating to each of the following forms of sport products and services, providing source information:
   - An upcoming professional or college game
   - A service being offered by a local fitness center
   - A new sporting goods product being introduced to the marketplace

3. For the examples you provided in question 2, list where each fits within the PESO model.

4. Visit the website of the professional sport team of your choice. Based on the staff directory and any staff profiles that it may provide, describe the way that its public relations responsibilities are assigned. Does it have a public relations or communications staff? If so, how is that staff organized? If not, is there any indication of who is responsible for executing the public relations function?

5. Access a website such as Teamwork Online or the NCAA's The Market, where sport industry jobs are posted. Search for jobs such as those described in this chapter (e.g., media relations, digital communications). What types of responsibilities are included in the position descriptions? What required and preferred qualifications must successful applicants possess?

6. Assess your own competencies in terms of the five basic skills that underlie public relations practice. If you are considering a career in sport public relations, you may benefit by having a trusted faculty member assist you in this evaluation. What skills should you seek to develop further while pursuing your education?

Integrating Public Relations With Strategic Management

After reading this chapter, students should be able to

- articulate how public relations can drive strategic management,
- describe the nature of integrated communication and the importance of storytelling,
- identify key organizational stakeholders and publics and the various factors that have an impact on organizational relationships,
- specify the process associated with public relations communication, including programs and campaigns,
- detail the connection between issues management and relationship management,
- describe the importance of and approaches to public relations assessment, and
- outline the components and value of reputation.

These are the key terms discussed in this chapter:

- active public
- aware public
- brand
- brand equity
- campaigns
- Grunig's four models of public relations
- integrated communication
- issues management
- latent public
- nonpublic
- proactive public relations
- programs
- reactive public relations
- reputation
- strategic management

Sponsor logo placement on professional sport uniforms has been common in many settings for some time, but major-level U.S. sport leagues have been slow to adopt the practice. In 2017, the National Basketball Association (NBA) became the first within that group, which also comprises Major League Baseball, the National Football League (NFL), and the National Hockey League, to place sponsor logos on jerseys. As that season opened, 19 of the league's 30 teams had agreements for sponsor uniform patches (Kutz, 2017). The logos were limited to a single 2.5- by 2.5-inch patch on the jersey, but despite the league's relatively modest approach, many fans, at least initially, panned the development as compromising the league's integrity and sacrificing team identity in favor of more revenue (Block, 2016).

In such a climate, the Utah Jazz and its jersey sponsor Qualtrics, a research software company, took a unique approach in launching their partnership, displaying a high level of public relations savvy in the process (Frederick, 2017). Rather than simply place the Qualtrics name on the jersey patch, the partners launched a charitable initiative to promote donations to cancer research. The patch read "5 for the Fight," and the campaign's call to action was to encourage people to contribute $5 to cancer research while asking five friends to do the same.

Working in concert with two communications firms, the partners structured a promotional campaign that included traditional media relations tactics, the production of a campaign video, and social media outreach. The video featured stars from both sports (e.g., Jerry Rice) and entertainment (e.g., Michael Peña). The same day the campaign was announced, the patch and video were introduced at a Jazz game. The crowd's response was a standing ovation (Frederick, 2017). The campaign exceeded its goals in areas such as media placement, audience impressions, social media metrics, and views on YouTube.

The "5 for the Fight" campaign is an example of how public relations can drive organizational decision making in a complex and challenging environment. Performance on the campaign's goals indicated that the Jazz had successfully engaged the team's key stakeholders while also advancing corporate objectives specific to sponsor revenue.

In chapter 1, public relations and marketing are described as distinct organizational functions that increasingly work hand in hand to attain key communication outcomes. Marketing tends to focus on consumers and an exchange of value, whereas public relations is likely to focus on a wider range of targets as well as the building and nurturing of relationships with a wide variety of publics. Connors (2014, p. 314) defined PR for the purposes of sport marketing as "an interactive marketing communication strategy" consisting primarily of a combination of media relations and community relations. However, Connors also acknowledged that public relations is a management function that reflects policies set at the top levels of management.

Similarly, Hopwood's (2007) sport marketing public relations model depicts the aspects of public relations that contribute to the marketing function. The model notes distinctions between sport public relations and sport marketing, however, and characterizes both functions as existing within broader internal and external environments. Recognizing

The Utah Jazz and jersey sponsor Qualtrics partnered to promote the highly successful "5 for the Fight" campaign.

Gene Sweeney Jr./Getty Images

this context and citing the work of Ledingham and Bruning (2010) and Shilbury and Rowe (2010), Hopwood (2010a, p. 23) stated, "Sport public relations is all about relationships—relationship management and relationship building." Given such versatility, public relations is uniquely positioned as an organizational function to lead organizational decision making. Such decision making spans the range from smaller day-to-day decisions that over time influence the organization's key relationships to major planning initiatives at the strategic level.

Public Relations as a Strategic Management Driver

Strategic management "involves the analysis of an organization's position in the competitive environment, the determination of its direction and goals, the selection of appropriate strategy, and the leveraging of distinctive assets" (Hoye, Smith, Nicholson, & Stewart, 2018, p. 9). As indicated, strategic management begins with some effort to identify what an organization is and wants to be. This effort typically involves developing vision and mission statements and performing a SWOT (strengths, weaknesses, opportunities, threats) analysis. The sidebar Conducting a SWOT Analysis describes this process. These steps establish a foundation for organizational direction and for developing goals and objectives and crafting broad organizational strategies. These steps are important because they lay the groundwork for the desired image of the organization and begin the process of positioning the organization in the stakeholder environment.

Many sport organizations have embraced the use of some combination of mission statements, vision statements, and values statements to provide

Conducting a SWOT Analysis

SWOT (strengths, weaknesses, opportunities, threats) analysis is an important assessment and planning tool that involves evaluating both the internal attributes of an organization (strengths and weaknesses) and the external environment in which it operates (opportunities and threats). Although SWOT analysis can be used in a variety of ways, when used as a strategic management tool the focus is on assessing the primary functions of the organization.

The internal assessment attempts to identify what competencies and capabilities exist within the organization and how effectively they are being employed to achieve organizational goals. This analysis is done by addressing questions related to marketing, finance, personnel, structure, leadership, technology, operations, production, adaptability, efficiency, and so on. The analysis should produce insights into organizational capacities and limitations.

The external assessment attempts to gauge what influences the environment of the organization has on its direction and ultimate success. Addressing questions related to short- and long-term economic developments, technological changes, social changes, industry trends, and the actions of competitors will provide information regarding what opportunities and concerns may present themselves in the future.

The two types of assessment interrelate, in that strengths may be the basis for capitalizing on opportunities, and weaknesses must be dealt with to fend off potential threats. The SWOT analysis serves as the basis for refining organizational goals and objectives and for developing a strategic plan.

Effective SWOT analysis usually combines input from throughout the organization. For example, an athletics department SWOT analysis might ask each sport and each functional area (i.e., marketing, ticketing, medical services, development, facilities) to assess strengths, weaknesses, opportunities, and threats from these narrower perspectives. This information is then combined with the insights of upper-level administration to create an overall picture of departmental possibilities and problems. Such an analysis can then be used in planning organizational direction, setting priorities, and supporting priorities with appropriate resource allocation.

Organizations may construct a checklist or create a matrix that is tailored to their specific circumstances as a way of providing focus to the SWOT process. Many templates of varying complexity have been developed that may be useful in getting a SWOT analysis started. One example is a checklist fashioned by Kotler and Keller (2016) that includes both a rating scale and a priority scale in the assessment of various functional dimensions.

fundamental assertions of the organization's purpose, goals, operating philosophy, and priorities. Mission statements should give insight into what the organization does well (distinguishing attributes), who its stakeholders and publics are, and how it views its responsibilities to those publics. Vision statements often furnish a sense of the future direction that an organization sees for itself. Some organizations are now also using values statements to describe organizational beliefs that guide actions and behaviors. Figure 2.1 displays the mission,

vision, and values statements of the Canadian Olympic Committee.

The trends in mission statement development are to make them more concise and explicit and to expend greater effort in identifying the competencies, distinguishing features, and important publics of the organization. Identifying the organization's publics is especially important from a public relations standpoint in that it becomes a focal point for identifying the key relationships that the organization is trying to nurture.

Canadian Olympic Committee (COC) Statements

Vision

Canada is a world leader in sport inspired by the passion and performance of the Canadian Olympic Team.

Mission

To lead the achievement of the Canadian Olympic Team's podium success and to advance Olympic values in Canada.

Core Values

The COC Olympic Values have been established to remind athletes and their supporters that the life skills and experience obtained through athletic preparation, competition and teamwork are far more valuable than any medal ever awarded.

Excellence

We believe in the right of all people to pursue their personal levels of excellence.

Fun

We believe in sport being fun.

Fairness

We believe in fairness on and off the field of play, as characterized by equality, integrity and trust.

Respect

We believe in free and open communication and respect for the views, role and contribution of all.

Human Development

We believe that the short and long term physical, social, mental and spiritual well-being of all should be enhanced through appropriate behavior and practices. We also believe that the visual and performing arts complement sport in the development of that well-being.

Leadership

We believe those who participate in sport have a responsibility to teach and apply the values of the Olympic Movement, involving others in the Olympic experience and inspiring and empowering them to reach their potential.

Peace

We believe in sport as a vehicle to promote understanding and harmony within and among nations.

Figure 2.1 Vision and mission statements from the Canadian Olympic Committee.

Reprinted by permission from the Canadian Olympic Committee.

Relationship Management

Public relations should be integrated into all organizational functions. Integration should begin in the early stages of the strategic planning process and include preparation of organizational mission, establishment of goals and objectives that serve as the basis for evaluating public relations activity, identification of the significant relationships with key publics, proactive strategic consideration of desired reputation and relevant issues, and development of communication systems and processes. Thorough assimilation of public relations into the fabric of an organization requires careful thought in all these areas.

James Grunig, one of the most influential public relations scholars of the last century, contended that organizational success is contingent on the effective management of relationship with key stakeholders:

> Managed interdependence is the major characteristic of successful organizations. . . . Organizations are effective when they meet their goals. However, goals must be appropriate for the organization's environment, or strategic constituencies within that environment will constrain the autonomy of the organization to meet its goals and accomplish its mission. (Grunig, 1993, p. 11)

Strategic emphasis on public relations is designed to create an environment in which the desired relationships with stakeholders are clearly defined, consistently cultivated, and systematically assessed across all areas of organizational operation.

In *Excellent Public Relations and Effective Organizations*, Grunig, Grunig, and Dozier (2002) provided a model regarding the strategic management of public relations. Readers are encouraged to access the source material for a detailed discussion of the topic. To summarize, however, the model's three central elements are (1) management decisions, (2) stakeholders and publics, and (3) relationship outcomes. Management decisions have consequences for the organization's stakeholders. Conversely, the actions and reactions of those stakeholders have consequences for the organization. In some instances stakeholder behavior creates issues that organizations must carefully address, because the degree to which they successfully do so (or not) affects relationships. Those outcomes dictate the organization's reputation and ultimately affect the attainment of organizational goals. Given these high stakes, many organizations establish communication programs to successfully manage stakeholder relationships.

Connors (2014) stated that using varied media to build comprehension, interest, and support within various publics are key PR functions. PR personnel are sometimes left out of the strategic planning loop, however, and have to live with objectives set by others, leading to a reactive approach to public relations.

Although communication must be tailored to the organization's various stakeholders, it must also be consistent with the organization's identity and mission. This undertaking is complex because of (1) the number of people involved in communicating with various publics, (2) the wide range of audiences with which communication occurs, and (3) the vast array of communication tools available.

Grunig's four models of public relations provide an overview of the nature of public relations communications. Two of these—press agentry, which involves seeking attention in almost any form, and public information, which seeks to disseminate accurate and favorable information about the organization—are one-way models, in which communication is directed toward a public. Press agentry and public information have long been common public relations models in sport. These strategies are still employed, although the evolution of public relations has resulted in other practices that are in better keeping with the more current view of relationship-oriented public relations. Grunig's two-way asymmetrical and two-way symmetrical models place much more emphasis on interaction and dialogue. The asymmetrical model incorporates research in an effort to persuade publics to act in desirable ways. The symmetrical model uses both research and dialogue to produce a dynamic relationship between an organization and its publics, resulting in public relations actions that are mutually beneficial (Grunig & Hunt, 1984). The element of dialogue is crucial to modern public relations because it places much more importance on practitioners as receivers of information rather than merely information disseminators. This aspect is particularly true because technology has altered the communications landscape. Social networking technology has given everyone a public forum in which to disseminate information quickly and expansively. Sport organizations can sit by passively and observe dialogue taking place, or they can become an active part of the dialogue that shapes public perception.

Grunig (2006) provided additional clarity to the distinctions among these models by suggesting that the one-way models are largely concerned with using public relations to shape public perception while embracing such concepts as reputation and **brand**. Such an approach reduces public relations to a largely tactical role that emphasizes buffering the organization from its environment. Two-way communication and the symmetrical model in particular take a more strategic view in which public relations serves as a bridging function. This approach places more emphasis on cultivating relationships and collaboration in which publics have a voice that influences organizational behavior and strategic decisions.

Placing public relations at the center of an organization's strategic management means adopting a **proactive public relations** posture, in which the organization concentrates on building and sustaining a desired reputation through successful relationship outcomes. **Reactive public relations,** on the other hand, is limited to responding after damaging issues have arisen. Integral to proactive approach is an understanding of branding, the various facets of organizational communication that contribute to building a brand, and the most effective approaches to brand-related communication.

Branding

L'Etang (2013) listed four ways that public relations contributes to brand management:

- Aligning brand images in light of organizational realities
- Promoting brands via integrated communications
- Building organizational reputation in support of the brand
- Defending the brand, especially in times of crisis

Colleges and universities often attempt to capitalize on the strength of their athletics brand to support the institutional brand. Consider how effectively ESPN

ESPN has been highly effective in its branding efforts that have included everything from its networks to its programs and personalities.

Michael Shroyer/Getty Images

has built its identity over the past 25 years. It has developed a brand name that is virtually synonymous with televised sport and continues to expand its presence with ESPN2, ESPN3, ESPN Classic, ESPN News, and ESPN Deportes, among other offerings.

Forbes assigns a monetary value to the top sport brands globally and ranks the brands across four categories: athlete, business, team, and event (Ozanian, 2017). *Forbes* uses a range of financial indicators to quantify "the amount by which the name contributes to the value of the athlete, business, event or team." The resultant brand values are the basis for a ranking of the top brands. Table 2.1 displays the top 10 in each category.

In looking at this list, readers will note the scope of the sport industry as depicted in the *Forbes* ranking. The inclusion of athletes, teams, events, and leagues likely comes as little surprise. However, the sport industry is broad, also encompassing sport media properties and sporting goods companies. This interpretation aligns with how a number of other scholars (e.g., Humphreys & Ruseski, 2008; Pedersen & Thibault, 2018) define the field. While some sport public relations professionals will spend their entire careers working within a single segment of the field (e.g., college athletics), others will move from one sector to another. While the specific application of public relations knowledge and skills may vary somewhat sector to sector, the foundations and core communication competencies are transferable.

Integrated Communication

The relationship between public relations and marketing was introduced in chapter 1. While tensions may sometimes exist between the two functions because marketing focuses on transactions and public relations on relationship, there is an alternative. **Integrated communication** is "the use of PR along with advertising, direct marketing, promotion, and other tools to shape public opinion and deliver audience actions" (Mogel, 2002, p. 19). It entails a synergistic approach to communications that allows congruent brand-related messages to be delivered through multiple promotional techniques (Irwin, Sutton, & McCarthy, 2008). The formula advocated by Ries and Ries (2002) in their book *The Fall of Advertising and the Rise of PR* assumes such an approach. Public relations may build the brand, and advertising may defend it, but both tools must advocate the same brand identity.

Storytelling

Perhaps the best way to communicate a brand is via storytelling. The concept of storytelling was introduced in chapter 1, along with reasons storytelling

Table 2.1 The *Forbes* Fab 40: The World's Most Valuable Sport Brands

Athlete	Business	Team	Event
1. Roger Federer	1. Nike	1. New York Yankees	1. Super Bowl
2. LeBron James	2. ESPN	2. Manchester United	2. Summer Olympics
3. Usain Bolt	3. Adidas	3 Real Madrid	3. Winter Olympics
4. Cristiano Ronaldo	4. Sky Sports	4. Dallas Cowboys	4. FIFA World Cup
5. Phil Mickelson	5. Under Armour	5. Bayern Munich	5. NCAA Final Four
6. Tiger Woods	6. MLBAM	6. Boston Red Sox	6. Wrestlemania
7. Virat Kohli	7. UFC	7. Barcelona	7. Union of European Football Associations (UEFA) Champions League
8. Rory McIlroy	8. YES Network	8. Arsenal	8. College Football Playoffs
9. Lionel Messi	9. Reebok	9. AC Milan	9. Daytona 500
10. Stephen Curry	10. NESN	10. New England Patriots	10. World Series

Based on Ozanian (2017) and Forbes (2017).

Case Study

BRAND EQUITY AND THE ATHLETE

Suzann Pettersen is a professional golfer who over the span of her 15-plus-year career has been ranked as high as second in the world. Pettersen has played on the Ladies Professional Golf Association (LPGA) tour where she has won two majors, competed in the Solheim Cup on eight occasions, and represented her home nation of Norway in the 2016 Rio Olympics (LPGA, n.d.). As of 2018, her career earnings approached $15 million. Pettersen also has multiple endorsement deals with partners including Nike, Dow, and BMW.

Noting that competitive success as an athlete does not automatically result in a strong brand, Kristiansen and Williams (2015) developed a case study examining the organizational communications strategies Pettersen and her management team used to build her brand. Citing the work of Keller (1993), the focus of their study was **brand equity**, "the assets and liabilities linked to a brand that add or subtract from the brand's value in the mind of consumers" (Kristiansen & Williams, 2015, p. 374).

The authors found that Pettersen successfully built brand awareness in Norway, her primary target market, by making public appearances and conducting interviews whenever she returned to her home country. Her management team also produced sport documentaries to air in Norway. These documentaries focused on Pettersen in anticipation of her competing in the Rio Olympics. Each of these tactics was designed to generate media interest in the golfer. The story Pettersen's team aimed to establish included two brand associations: (1) Pettersen was indeed one of the top golfers in the world, and (2) despite a preexisting perception that she was quite serious-minded, Pettersen was a well-rounded person. The goals of these efforts were to leverage additional endorsements and position Pettersen's management company for sustained success following the conclusion of her playing career.

Discussion Questions

1. What types of brand associations were linked to Pettersen prior to the branding campaign?
2. Beyond those described, can you think of other communication tactics that could have contributed to the campaign's success?
3. How does the concept of authenticity relate to athlete branding?

---

is such a powerful way to communicate. Public relations executive Petra Sammer strongly advocates storytelling and emphasized its centrality:

> PR must learn how to make people laugh and cry, every day. PR must get comfortable with a balance of facts and emotion. PR must focus its stories around heroes and encourage our clients to recognise the need for conflict in our work. We must give equal thought to words and visual communication. (Sammer, 2016)

Storytelling may be uniquely powerful within sport, given the innately emotional aspects of winning and losing. Athletes, coaches, and teams have multiple stories relating to their experiences in training, practicing, cooperating, and competing. Fans also have stories as they relate to their favorite athletes and teams, and those allegiances have meaning for fans' lives (Siang, 2016).

Using Sammer's principles of storytelling and building on them, Stareva (2014) crafted a five-step process relating to breakthrough storytelling. The following sequence summarizes her model:

1. Breakthrough stories need a reason to be told. Begin with the why.
2. Breakthrough stories need heroes. People tend to connect with individuals.
3. Breakthrough stories start with conflict (e.g., head vs. heart, past vs. future).
4. Breakthrough stories evoke emotions (e.g., surprise, love, grief).
5. Breakthrough stories deploy viral power across converged media.

Stareva's fifth step directly intersects with the PESO model introduced in chapter 1. The sidebar focusing on Nike's "She Runs the Night" Campaign provides an excellent example of these elements coming together.

Nike "She Runs the Night" Campaign

The Nike "She Runs the Night" campaign is an exemplar of an effective integrated communications campaign, earning honors from both the Media Federation of Australia Awards and Festival of Media Awards Asia ("She runs the night," 2013). The campaign, designed to enable the brand to better connect with the female running market in Australia, was launched in 2011. Advance research revealed that running was predominantly an individual activity, and one of the barriers female runners faced was concern about safety while running alone at night.

The resultant campaign focused on the development of community among female runners and the staging of a "She Runs the Night" 13-kilometer night race exclusively for women. Nike's communication strategy included a blend of platforms that would traditionally fall under the separate areas of public relations and marketing. Social media—both messaging and listening—were particularly key as brand ambassadors shared their own experiences while encouraging other women to do the same. Nike also produced a film on the topic, sharing it via social media ("She runs the night," 2013). In addition, Nike used paid advertising in the form of billboards and print advertising, and publicity was generated via media coverage of the campaign and race. Nike also partnered with *Cosmopolitan* to more fully leverage the campaign.

Regardless of the channel, storytelling was at the heart of the communication strategy. The stories shared by the brand ambassadors engaged the broader community, and the images conveyed in the visual aspects of the campaign resonated with the experiences of female runners. One of the campaign's central messages was "There's True Power in Numbers," with a key action being the development of running clubs for women to build relationships and train together.

The campaign yielded impressive results. The resultant social community included more than 54,000 female runners ("She runs the night," 2013). The initial 13K even attracted 3,200 runners, a number that grew to 6,000 the following year (Chia, 2018). And in the quarter following the campaign, Nike revenue increased by 9%.

Note: Each of the sources cited in this brief sidebar provides significantly more detail about the campaign. Readers interested in learning more about effective integrated communication are encouraged to access this information.

Organizational Stakeholders and Publics

A fundamental activity that establishes the connection between the strategic management process and public relations is the identification of an organization's publics—those groups of people who have some interest or stake in organizational action. Grunig (2006) described public relations as "a strategic management function that uses communication to cultivate relationships with publics that have a stake in the behavior of the organization—either because they benefit from or are harmed by what Dewey called the consequences of that behavior." Several terms have been used, somewhat inconsistently, to describe the various groups with which an organization has or seeks relationships. Such terms as *stakeholder, constituency, target audience,* and *population* are often used either as synonyms for *public* or as a particular type of public. For the purpose of this text, the term *stakeholder* is used to describe large groups of people who hold similar standing in relation to the organization. The term *publics* refers to specific groups of people within stakeholder groups who hold similar attitudes and dispositions toward the organization.

The uninitiated commonly take a narrow view of a sport organization's stakeholders, often taking in no more than clients, customers, and the media. Yes, these groups are critical, but sport organizations interface with many others. Perhaps the most important skill public relations professionals can possess is the ability to identify organizational publics and the dynamics of those relationships (Dozier, Grunig, & Grunig, 1995).

Stakeholder Identification

Although consumers and the media are publics on which most sport organizations would place a high priority, other groups must not be ignored. The number of publics that have a vested interest in or may be influenced by an organization's operations is often expansive, even for small organizations. Lesly (1998) referred to the scope of public relations as the public relations universe. This universe provides insight into the potential breadth of public relations activity as well as the range of publics with which interaction may exist. Figure 2.2 illustrates this concept.

Developing a thorough inventory of relevant publics serves as the foundation for much of the public relations activity that occurs within any organization. Sport organizations should certainly try to determine what stakeholder relationships exist or are needed and how they might be nurtured. As part of strategic planning, one useful approach would be to begin with broad categories of stakeholders and then narrow the focus to more specific target publics. As an example, many sport organizations place a high priority on the media as a stakeholder group. However, the relational dynamics with the specific media publics differ based on many variables, including the media property's form (e.g., print, broadcast), its geographic setting (e.g., national, local), and whether it is a rights holder (e.g., a holder of broadcast distribution rights). For instance, when a professional

sport organization is making decisions about which media properties will receive credentials to cover a big game, reporters from a major national property such as *The Athletic* will likely receive higher priority than those from a nearby smaller-town publication. Similarly, the broadcast production crew from a rights holder—that is, a media property directly or indirectly paying rights fees to the sport organization for the right to broadcast a game—can expect to be prioritized more highly than non-rights-holding media properties that are covering the same event but not broadcasting it live. Figure 2.3 illustrates this concept of stakeholders and the publics within those stakeholder groups.

After extensive review of stakeholder theory, stakeholder management, and public relations, Rawlins (2006, p. 1) produced a more sophisticated model that prioritizes stakeholders through a four-step process:

1. "Identifying all potential stakeholders according to their relationship with the organization;

2. Prioritizing stakeholders by attributes;

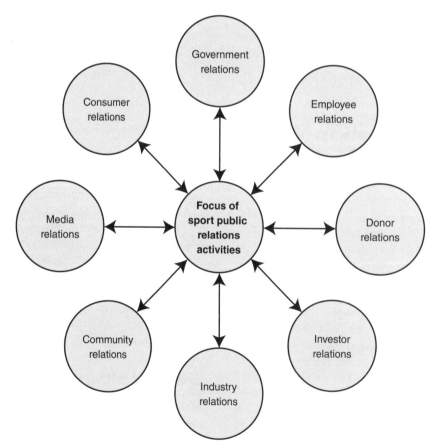

Figure 2.2 Sport public relations universe.

Adapted from Lesly (1998).

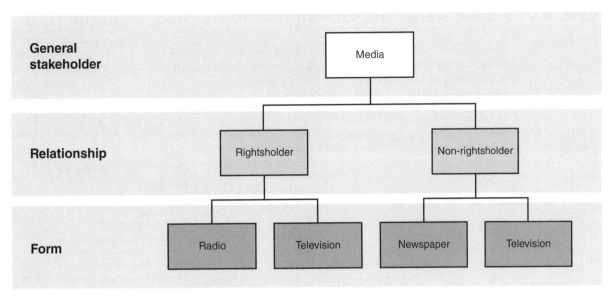

Figure 2.3 From stakeholders to target publics.

3. Prioritizing stakeholders by relationship to the situation;
4. Prioritizing the publics according to the communication strategy."

The first step in the Rawlins process can be accomplished using a linkage model first developed by Grunig and Hunt (1984). The linkages include functional linkages, normative linkages, enabling linkages, and diffused linkages. Table 2.2 provides a brief description of each linkage and some examples of stakeholders that likely fall in each category.

After stakeholders are identified, prioritization can occur. A variety of categorizations may be used to clarify these priorities, including relational attributes, situational factors, and communication strategy. Relational attributes consider such things as the relative power of stakeholders, the legitimacy of the relationship in legal and moral terms, and the urgency of the issues connecting the organization and the stakeholder. As an example, the Major League Baseball Players' Association (MLBPA) is an important stakeholder of Major League Baseball. When looking at relational attributes, the increased power of the MLBPA beginning in the early 1970s has changed the nature of the relationship. A variety of legal constraints shape the behavior of Major League Baseball as it conducts its business with the MLBPA, particularly in the area of labor negotiations. The relationship is also influenced periodically by the urgency of the collective bargaining process. Each of these relational attributes influences the priority of the relationship between the two parties and demonstrates the dynamic nature of the relationship.

Use of situational factors produces a more refined attempt to establish stakeholder precedence. Dozier and Ehling (1992) developed four classifications for describing the situational nature of publics: nonpublic, latent public, aware public, and active public. A **nonpublic** includes people who have no common interest in or connection to an issue confronting an organization. A **latent public** includes people who have some common interest or link to the organization but fail to recognize it. After recognizing that common interest or connection, they become an **aware public**. When an aware public takes coordinated and focused action to affect the relationship with the organization, they become an **active public**. Take, for example, a case in which a city is considering closing a local community recreation center. People in certain parts of the community may have no interest in this issue (nonpublic). Others may be unaware that the center might close (latent public). Another group may have heard or read about the potential closing (aware public), and yet another group may be lobbying city council or initiating a petition drive to prevent the closing (active public). Although the active public will certainly be the focus of public relations efforts, proactive attention to latent and aware publics reflects a more encompassing vision of public relations.

Rawlins (2006) refined the situational nature of publics further by considering whether the stakeholders are supportive or nonsupportive and

Table 2.2 Public Relations Linkages and Related Stakeholders

Linkage type	Description	Example
Functional	Relationships essential to the function of the organization related to input functions that provide the labor and resources to create products or services	Employees Unions Suppliers
	Relationships essential to the function of the organization related to output functions that consume the products or services	Consumers (e.g., fans, members) Retailers Distributors (e.g., media partners)
Normative	Groups that share the organization's interests, values, goals, or problems	Brand ambassadors Peer institutions Professional associations
Enabling	Stakeholders who have some control and authority over the organization, allowing the organization to have resources and autonomy to operate	Board of directors Government regulators Stockholders
Diffused	Stakeholders who may not have frequent interaction with the organization but become involved because of the actions of the organization (publics that often arise in times of crisis)	Special interest groups Community activists Media Social media influencers

Summarized and adapted from Grunig and Hunt (1984).

active or inactive. Strategies for communicating with advocate stakeholders (active and supportive) differ from strategies for reaching dormant stakeholders (inactive and supportive). Adversarial stakeholders (active and nonsupportive) are approached differently than apathetic stakeholders (inactive and nonsupportive). In the community recreation center example, active publics likely exist on both sides of the issue—advocate and adversarial. Such a circumstance is the case with many issues that confront sport organizations.

In addition to relationships with external stakeholders such as the media, consumers, and the community, there is a need to attend to industry-specific relationships as well as relationships with governmental entities, investors, international groups, the financial community, and opinion leaders. Internally, employee relations are important not just from the standpoint of morale and productivity but because of the public relations role that all employees play in projecting the image of the organization. Subsequent chapters will discuss these publics in more detail.

Not all stakeholders are equally vital to organizational success, and resource limitations sometimes necessitate difficult choices that benefit some constituents at the expense of others. A systematic evaluation of the nature and extent of these stakeholder contributions will help managers prioritize

organizational efforts and resources as they oversee these stakeholder relationships.

Relationship Evaluation

Hon (1998) suggested that it is useful to plan public relations systematically so public relations goals are articulated in more specific terms and tied more directly to the organizational mission. Such goals in turn will produce more accountability and clearer assessment and evaluation. Assessment may have both quantitative and qualitative components. As various public relations strategies are developed, effort should be made to attach clear assessment criteria. For some public relations activities, the goals are relatively short-term and quantifiable. For example, a new fitness club that conducts an open house can evaluate the success of the event based on the desired number of attendees or the number of resulting memberships. The club can also collect qualitative information by conducting follow-up surveys to assess visitor attitudes and perceptions.

Grunig (2006) pointed out that many of the metrics used to evaluate public relations tend to focus on tactical activities such as media placements and their effect on sales or consumer preference. Although such tactical measurement is necessary, from a strategic standpoint, public relations strategies and tactics should be evaluated in terms of how effective they are in cultivating quality relationships. Hon and Grunig (1999) identified six components for evaluating the outcomes of long-term relationships, including mutual control, trust, satisfaction, commitment, exchange relationship, and communal relationship. Table 2.3 provides clarifying explanations for each component.

Other public relations activities may have effects that are harder to measure. The college cross-country team that participates in an elementary school program that encourages children to read or the sporting goods store that donates $1,000 of equipment to the local Special Olympics will produce public relations effects that are ambiguous and difficult to evaluate. Poole (2004) acknowledged the often qualitative nature of the contribution that public relations makes to organizational success. This qualitative value involves the vagaries of brand partiality and loyalty that may generate "top-of-mind" brand preferences

when employed effectively. As an example of how public relations can multiply sponsorship value, Poole cited the success of Home Depot's association with the Olympic Job Opportunity Program of the United States Olympic Committee (USOC) before the 2002 Winter Olympics. Interestingly, this program was discontinued in 2009 as Home Depot felt the effects of a drastic economic downturn. Public relations initiatives of more qualitative intent are often at risk when resources are dwindling.

Stakeholder Communication

Hopwood (2010b) introduced a sport marketing public relations (SMPR) model that depicts both the sport marketing and sport public relations functions as existing within the framework of external and

Table 2.3 Relationship Components

Relationship components	Description	Example
Control mutuality	Each party's ability to influence the other to some extent, a basis for strong relationships	Management–union relationship
Trust	Each party's level of confidence in and willingness to be open to the other party (three dimensions to trust: integrity, dependability, competence)	Team–fans relationship
Satisfaction	The extent to which each party feels favorably toward the other because positive expectations about the relationship are reinforced	Team–sponsor relationship
Commitment	The extent to which each party believes that the relationship is worth the expenditure of energy to maintain and promote (two dimensions of commitment: continuance commitment and affective commitment)	Athletics department–donor relationship
Exchange relationship	The sense that one party gives benefits to the other only because the other has provided benefits in the past or is expected to do so in the future	Employee–employer relationship
Communal relationship	The willingness of each party to provide benefits to the other because of concern for the welfare of the other, even when receiving nothing in return	Sport team–charity relationship

Adapted from Hon and Grunig (1999).

internal environments but overlapping in the SMPR zone. This overlap

> represents the potentially powerful collaboration of all sport communication practices and creates the opportunity for true relationship communication in the form of relationship communication and management, promotional communication and transactional communication—a remarkably powerful collaboration which exactly meets the unique needs of the sport organization or entity. (Hopwood, 2010b, p. 58)

Two of the ways that organizations operationalize such communication is through ongoing programs and limited duration campaigns.

Chapter 1 noted that two of the more common forms of public relations within sport are media relations and community relations. These activities are now standardized within many sport organizations, and as such they operate as public relations **programs**. They function continuously in an effort to foster desirable relationships with particular stakeholder groups such as the mass media, community members, investors and employees.

Campaigns differ from programs in several ways (Smith, 2017):

- They have a specific purpose rather than general goals.
- They address a particular issue rather than the overall relationship with a public.
- They are periodic (have distinct time lines) rather than sustained and ongoing.

Table 2.4 highlights the differences between programs and campaigns.

Campaigns often operate within the framework of public relations programs. For example, the media relations program within a college athletics depart-ment may initiate a campaign to gain support for an All-America candidate. The community relations program of a professional sports league may execute a campaign to publicize its charitable donations. Public relations programs may administer several campaigns simultaneously and may even work in consultation with external public relations firms when necessary.

Whether at the program or campaign level, a similar model applies to the public relations process, and it has been described in numerous yet similar ways. For instance, Kendall (1996) used the acronym *RAISE* to describe a five-step model that includes research, adaptation, implementation, strategy, and evaluation. Hendrix (1998) used a similar approach in advocating ROPE, a four-step model whose primary components were research, objectives, programming, and evaluation. Broom (2013) offered a four-step model of defining problems, planning and programming, taking action and communicating, and evaluating.

This chapter uses a four-step model to describe the process. Illustrated in figure 2.4, it is the framework that the Public Relations Society of America uses in evaluating campaigns submitted for the organization's prestigious Silver Anvil Awards, which recognize excellence in public relations. (See the sidebar What Is the PRSA? for information about this organization.) Each step in the model—research, planning, execution, and evaluation—includes multiple considerations.

Research

Research has been described as the compass that guides the campaign planning process (Matera & Artigue, 2000). The authors of the comprehensive Excellence in Communication study argued that research is so critical to success that two of the five competencies that public relations professionals must have to function well as managers involve research skills (Dozier, Grunig, & Grunig, 1995).

Table 2.4 Public Relations Programs Versus Campaigns

	Programs	Campaigns
Purpose	Generally desirable relationships	Specific goals
Focus	Public	Issue
Duration	Ongoing, continuous	Finite
Example 1	Media relations	Heisman Trophy candidate promotion
Example 2	Employee relations	Wellness program promotion

Based on Smith (2017).

Figure 2.4 The public relations process.

What Is the PRSA?

Established in 1947, the Public Relations Society of America (PRSA) boasts more than 30,000 members from a wide variety of industries, including sport. The PRSA serves its members by fulfilling four roles (PRSA, n.d.a):

- Providing lifelong learning opportunities
- Recognizing innovation and excellence within the field
- Advocating for professional ethics
- Giving voice to the profession

The PRSA's highly touted accreditation program offers certification of public relations expertise to professionals in the field. People seeking APR (accredited in public relations) status are required to have five years of professional experience before applying for the examination (PRSA, n.d.b): Those receiving APR status may maintain it by accruing points for professional development and service on an ongoing basis.

Although many who work in sport public relations are PRSA members and possess APR status, others do not. For more information about the PRSA accreditation program, visit www.prsa.org.

The first skill is to use research to identify important publics. The second is to conduct research to evaluate the effectiveness of public relations activities.

Despite the importance of research, some public relations professionals rush headlong into planning campaigns without doing the necessary background work. This approach can be disastrous.

Austin and Pinkleton (2015) indicated that research can assist public relations professionals in a variety of areas:

- Identifying problems that exist, their histories, and their prevalence
- Defining the magnitude of problems and their effects on various publics
- Suggesting strategies for successfully solving problems
- Testing creative strategies to determine whether they possess desired effects
- Tracking implementation plans to ensure that design results in execution
- Evaluating the results of the strategies implemented

Research on the publics involved in a particular problem or issue is typically a good starting place in the planning process. Such research may also provide valuable information regarding what they know, how they feel, and how they are acting regarding the issue. Consider, for instance, a professional sport franchise that seeks public tax support for a new facility. Before launching a public relations campaign advocating such support, the organization's staff and any external agencies it retains should attempt to identify the diverse groups that would be affected by such tax support and how they would be affected. What do they know about the proposal thus far? What are their attitudes regarding the franchise, the prospect of a new facility for the franchise, and the notion of public support for such an initiative? Finally, how might they act when presented with the sport franchise's proposal?

Nike's "She Runs the Night" campaign (see sidebar earlier in the chapter) provides another example of the importance of research. Advance research focusing on female runners determined that running was predominantly an individual activity for women and that safety while running alone at night was a common concern ("She runs the night," 2013). These key findings served as the basis for the highly successful campaign that followed.

Planning

If research is to be considered the compass that orients sport public relations professionals to the most critical considerations about an issue or opportunity, campaign planning may be thought of as the road map that guides them toward a particular destination (Matera & Artigue, 2000). As stated by Jackson (2000), "The biggest mistake practitioners and their clients or employers make is to plunge into tactical activities without a guiding strategy" (p. 104).

The planning process involves multiple decisions, and sport public relations professionals must carefully coordinate each of those decisions. Specific considerations include goals and objectives, publics, strategies and tactics, messages, channels, and budget.

Goals and Objectives

The terms *goals* and *objectives* are often used interchangeably. Practically speaking, the choice of terminology does not usually make a difference in the effectiveness of a public relations campaign. But sport public relations students may find it helpful to consider the terms as two distinct concepts that allow practitioners to think through the planning process systematically.

A public relations goal is simply a desired outcome of a program or campaign. In some cases, public relations goals are stated in a general fashion that do not lend themselves to measurement. In such cases, a series of related and specific objectives may be useful in assessing progress toward the goals. The overall goal of the "She Runs the Night" campaign was to connect Nike with female runners ("She runs the night," 2013). That goal was supported by a number of objectives with key performance indicators pertaining to the number of runners involved in the campaign's community, the number of positive engagements with the brand, and the number of runners indicating they intended to run the race again.

Public relations experts offer four guidelines for writing measurable goals or objectives (Broom, 2013). First, the goal or objective should begin with the word *To* and then be followed by a verb. Second, the goal or objective should define an outcome that is to result from the campaign. Third, the goal or objective must specify the desired magnitude or level of the outcome. Fourth, the goal or objective should define a date by which the outcome is to be attained.

A common mistake that students and even some professionals make is listing strategies and tactics as objectives. "To use Twitter as a communication platform," for example, is a tactic, not a goal or objective. Using Twitter may be a great idea, but it is an action taken in the hope of achieving a desired outcome—it is not an outcome itself. Goals and objectives typically relate to desired knowledge, attitudes, and behaviors among key publics.

Some goals are more difficult to achieve than others. Grunig and Grunig (2001) listed five audience effects that communicators may seek to achieve:

- *Exposure:* Audience members are exposed to the communicator's message.
- *Retention:* Audience members remember the message.
- *Cognition:* Audience members understand the message.
- *Attitude:* Audience members favorably evaluate the message.
- *Behavior:* Audience members act differently in response to the message.

Each of these seemingly simple outcomes relates to multiple complex concepts. For instance, the attitudes that a person holds toward a particular sport organization may have been affected by thousands of expressions throughout the person's life. The fan attitude network (FAN) model developed by Funk and James (2004) recognizes this complexity by noting that an individual's sport identity results from a combination of dispositional needs, such as personality traits and individual attributes, and features found in sport settings, such as performance levels or geographic proximity, that meet those needs. People with different needs may form very different attitudes about the same sport property.

That said, each audience effect following exposure is more difficult to achieve than the previous one. Figure 2.5 illustrates this concept. As indicated, successfully exposing an audience to a message is less difficult than securing retention, which is less difficult than gaining understanding, and so on up the list. Behavioral change is the most difficult outcome to achieve. In fact, some public relations experts argue that even the most skilled campaign planners may have difficulty persuading people to change behaviors (Dozier & Ehling, 1992).

Ahles (2003) recommended that campaign planners work backward from the behaviors they would like their key publics to display in order to identify the attitudes, knowledge base, and awareness levels that must first be cultivated among those publics. The Utah Jazz's "5 for the Fight" campaign described earlier in the chapter illustrates such an approach. In order to achieve the positive public reaction to the Jazz's introduction of a jersey patch partner, campaign planners had to recognize the public's general skepticism about such an arrangement and change attitudes by employing a good cause strategy.

Sport public relations professionals should recognize two other considerations relating to goals

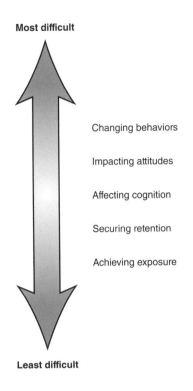

Most difficult

Changing behaviors

Impacting attitudes

Affecting cognition

Securing retention

Achieving exposure

Least difficult

Figure 2.5 Degree of difficulty in attaining communication effects.

Based on Grunig and Grunig (2001).

and objectives. First, goals and objectives should be linked to the organization's strategic direction. The sport organization's mission, its strategic priorities, and the goals of any public relations initiative should be clearly linked. If a program or campaign does not support an organization's general strategy, it is probably not worth the investment of organizational resources. Second, as Grunig's models of public relations would indicate, dialogue with the key publics involved is crucial to determining realistic and attainable outcomes. Persuasion is sometimes achievable, as was the case when community leaders in Wichita, Kansas, used two-way communication to craft a successful communications campaign for a temporary sales tax to fund a new downtown sport and entertainment facility in 2004 (Stoldt, Ratzlaff, & Ramolet, 2009). Poll numbers indicated that 64% of voters opposed the tax in September, but the campaign changed many people's opinions, and the ballot initiative passed with a 54% majority just two months later. Conversely, the NBA's Orlando Magic began campaigning for a new, publicly funded arena in 2001, but after meeting surprisingly strong resistance from the media and members of the public, the Magic

temporarily adjusted their strategy, instead appealing to the public for greater attendance at games to keep the franchise viable (Mitrook, Parish, & Seltzer, 2008). The team continued to explore avenues for a new facility, however, and after years of advocacy and negotiation, the team, city, and county reached agreement for a publicly supported facility that ultimately opened in 2010 (Amway Center, n.d.).

Publics

Public relations campaigns are directed at publics who relate to the sport organization in a particular way. Remember, publics are more specific in nature than stakeholders; a stakeholder group is usually composed of multiple publics. Members of the mass media may be considered a stakeholder group, but a specific group of media members would be considered a public. For example, a number of campaigns touting college football players for the prestigious Heisman Memorial Trophy include outreach specifically to the Heisman voters. Specific tactics have ranged from informational brochures to more unusual items, such as bobbleheads of the player (Allen, 2011). Although some campaigns are designed to reach full stakeholder groups, they are more effectively executed when designed for specific publics. The more specifically that communicators can define their audience, the more likely they will be to reach them.

One common approach is to target influencers within a public. The rationale for such an approach is that if desirable outcomes can be attained with opinion leaders, those influencers may affect other people within the public. For example, college athletic programs promoting Heisman candidates recognize the power of opinion leaders within the mass media, such as the personalities associated with ESPN's popular *College Game Day* show. Public relations scholar Karen Freberg (2016) observed the influencer phenomenon in her analysis of Heisman-related content on Twitter. Tracking Heisman candidate hashtags via analytics software, Freberg identified specific accounts that were particularly strong in connecting with a broader community. Some (e.g., SportsCenter) were common to multiple candidates; others were located within the candidates' unique Twitter communities.

Messages

Having researched the issue or opportunity, specified the desirable outcomes, and defined the publics involved, the public relations planner is now well equipped to define the strategies to attain program or campaign goals. Implicit in this discussion is an underlying mandate that the public relations effort be tailored for the specified audience. Such considerations are especially critical when defining key messages to be conveyed and communication channels to be used. Those choices are inevitably linked to the campaign budget. Figure 2.6 displays the relationships among messages, channels, and budgets.

Message selection is one of the most challenging aspects of strategy planning. Most people are exposed to hundreds of media messages and commercial exposures daily. Given such clutter, what kind of message content will resonate with key publics?

The concepts of selective exposure, selective perception, and selective retention are all relevant to campaign planners (Hyman & Sheatsley, 1947). Selective exposure is the notion that people are most likely to pay attention to messages that relate to subject matter of existing interest. Selective perception means that people interpret the messages that they do attend to through the filters of their life experiences, values, and attitudes. Selective retention relates to people's tendency to remember messages that are consistent with their existing attitudes. A related concept, cognitive dissonance, refers to the inclination to avoid or minimize the credibility of information that conflicts with current values and attitudes (Festinger, 1957).

Sport public relations professionals must strive to connect their message content to topics of interest among key publics. They must be intentional in the ways that they choose either to reinforce current beliefs and behaviors or to argue why publics should reevaluate their beliefs or behaviors. Finally, public relations professionals must craft content that is relevant enough to publics so that they pay attention and ultimately retain information that influences beliefs or behaviors. Storytelling, a concept described earlier in this chapter, is often the best way to attain such relevance, given the emotional power stories possess.

Because persuasion is a common goal of public relations campaigns, practitioners must take care not to violate legal or ethical boundaries with hype. As noted by one set of experts, "Creative presentation is okay. Exaggeration, flattery, and puffery are not" (Schultz, Caskey, & Esherick, 2013, p. 193). In other words, the selective use of statistics in support of an all-star candidate is generally acceptable; the falsification of those statistics is not.

Sport public relations professionals may also be subject to communication regulations imposed by relevant governing bodies. The NCAA, for example, has a number of rules pertaining to social media communication about prospective recruits. As a result, member institutions and their representatives are limited in how specific they can be about their recruiting activities and prospective recruits in particular.

Channels

Just as the key messages must be carefully matched to the intended audience, so too must the communication channels be intelligently chosen. Channels are the delivery systems that carry messages. Public relations practitioners have more choices than ever in making these selections. The primary determinants are the communication goals, the selected public(s), the intended message, and available resources (the budget).

The chapters that follow detail the various platforms available for public relations communication. They include social media, other forms of digital media (e.g., podcasts), and legacy media and direct contact (e.g., public speeches, special events). All of

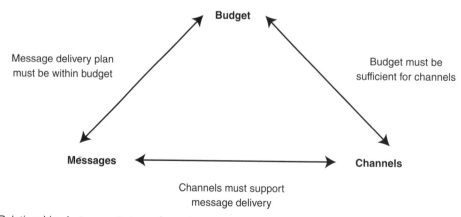

Figure 2.6 Relationships between strategy elements.

these channels relate directly or indirectly to the PESO model (Dietrich, 2014) introduced in chapter 1. While the selection of channels will vary depending on the nature of the public relations effort, the principle of integrated communication applies in all circumstances.

Budget

Because most public relations activities involve some level of cost, budgets are an important consideration in the planning process. The authors of the Excellence in Communication study identified five competencies that public relations professionals must possess to execute a managerial role successfully, one of which is the ability to manage budgets (two others, as mentioned earlier, deal with research skills, and the other two relate to two-way communication practices) (Dozier et al., 1995).

Budgeting for campaigns is usually different from budgeting for public relations programs. Because most programs are continuous, standard budgeting techniques in the field are usually used. For instance, programs may be funded using incremental formulas (e.g., the previous year's budget plus 2.5%) or percentage of sales criteria (e.g., 1% of the previous year's gross sales). Given the short-term nature of public relations campaigns, a historical precedent on which to base a budget is not often available. Campaigns are thus funded in one of two ways: by using whatever money is available in the regular budget or by gaining special allocation of funds based on the specific needs of the campaign. The former approach may seriously compromise the success of the campaign if the amount of funding available does not lend itself to a viable campaign plan. The latter approach is clearly preferable, but the amount of money that senior management is willing to approve for a campaign will likely be linked to the value of the campaign's goals. Campaigns that can demonstrably earn return on investment for the sport organization will gain more funding than those that do not offer such benefits. Nike's integrated communications for the "She Runs the Night" campaign clearly required a healthy budget, given the employment of an external communications firm and paid advertising. The campaign was, however, linked to revenue growth realized in the following quarter.

The good news on the budget front is that the proliferation of communication options, particularly social media, provides public relations professionals with relatively low-cost platforms that enhance effectiveness and protect budgets. In years

Be Your Own Media

Campaigns in support of Heisman Trophy candidates are commonly conducted by college athletics communicators. Conduct some web research on a recent campaign supporting a Heisman trophy winner. In what ways did the winner's program or athletics department serve as its own media? What channels were employed? What key messages were crafted, and what brand image of the candidate did they convey?

past, athletic communicators may have had to incur significant expense to make a splash promoting a Heisman Trophy candidate. Perhaps the best example of this was the University of Oregon spending $250,000 for a giant billboard of Ducks quarterback Joey Harrington in New York's Times Square. In more recent years, digital communications have empowered lower-cost, highly creative campaigns to be equally if not more effective (Gaio, 2013).

Execution

A well-crafted plan is of little value without careful execution. Public relations professionals often use editorial or content calendars to coordinate their actions. While these planning tools may vary in complexity and format, most include dates, content selection, and channels to be employed.

Sport public relations professionals who manage campaigns should monitor the execution of the campaign plan to ensure that the strategies and tactics are being implemented as planned and to assess whether new developments should prompt revisions in the campaign plan. As an admittedly extreme example, Upper Deck, a sport memorabilia company, planned to launch a PenCam product, a video camera within a pen that can document the authenticity of athlete autographs on Upper Deck memorabilia, on September 11, 2001 (Henninger, 2002). The news releases regarding the introduction of the product were distributed just prior to a series of terrorist attacks launched against New York and Washington, D.C. Campaign managers, knowing that their launch would be completely lost amid the day's crisis, decided to act as if the product introduction never happened, and they started over in November of that year.

Evaluation

The final step in the public relations process is to evaluate effectiveness. Just as practitioners have numerous options in the planning process, they also have numerous methods of assessing success. One framework for organizing these options includes assessment of the three phases of communication: public relations activity, intermediary effect, and target audience effect (AMEC, 2011). The three forms of evaluation described in the following sections align with the AMEC typology. Organizational outputs focus on public relations activity. Audience reception may be characterized as an intermediary effect. Impact is the target audience effect.

Organizational Outputs

The most basic level of public relations assessment involves tracking organizational communications. The range of activities that can be tracked is as diverse as the communication options available, but some categories tend to be more common than others. They include content creation (e.g., videos, podcasts), news media communication (e.g., news releases, news conferences), social media messaging, and special events and public speeches (AMEC, 2011).

Analysis of outputs possesses some value as it allows organizations to track whether their public relations programs or campaigns are being executed as planned. Analysis of outputs can also provide an audit of the tactics currently being employed and underemployed tools that may be tapped. Output metrics serve as the foundation for additional levels of evaluation. That said, output alone does not advance understanding of impact.

Audience Reception

A more advanced level of evaluation is assessment of what AMEC terms intermediary effects. These metrics address how organizational communications are received. Outputs such as social media postings or news releases are of little value if they are not received, understood, and possibly embraced and shared. The AMEC model includes more than 20 indicators of intermediary effects that may be applicable, depending on the nature of the public relations activity and intended audience. For instance, the number of impressions within the target audience or the number of placements within the media may serve as indicators of establishing awareness. Social media metrics such as number of retweets or shares indicate interest. Endorsements by influencers and likes on social media are evidence of support.

Both the "She Runs the Night" and "5 for the Fight" campaigns described earlier in the chapter attained noteworthy intermediary effects. Nike's "She Runs" Facebook page received 16,000 likes in a single month and, overall, positive engagements exceeded campaign goals by 40% ("She runs the night," 2013). The Utah Jazz campaign resulted in the #5ForTheFight hashtag trending on Twitter and more than 1,000 mentions (Frederick, 2017). The campaign also generated 266 articles in the mass media with a total audience of 1.2 billion.

A metric that has sometimes been employed to provide evidence of public relations effectiveness is advertising value equivalent (AVE). AVE is typically calculated by measuring the space or time earned by a media placement resulting from public relations communication and then determining the dollar amount that would be associated with an advertising purchase of the same amount of time or space. While AVE can demonstrate public relations clout, it is sometimes discouraged within the industry. Placement data and AVE may document the effectiveness of a program or campaign in gaining media coverage, but placement is rarely the goal in and of itself. More than 40 years ago, Marker (1977) offered a story still relevant to public relations evaluation today. He shared how he had been asked to make a presentation to his boss regarding the value of his company's public relations efforts. Marker carefully documented the vast amount of publicity that had resulted from the company's public relations programs and felt quite comfortable in his defense of the expenditures. "And then it came," he recounted, "the question no one had asked before: 'But what's all this worth to us?'" (p. 52). The answer to that question requires a measurement of impact.

Impact

The highest order of evaluation is impact. This form of measurement attempts to assess the effect of an organization's communication outputs and the audience's reception to messages. Impact on a public may occur at any one or more levels—awareness, retention, understanding, attitude, behavior. The variables are, of course, sequential, so behavioral change within the audience is the ultimate effect.

The best way to assess impact is to close the loop to the goals and objectives specified in the program's or campaign's plans and evaluate the degree to which they were met. Keep in mind that the best goals and objectives are specific and measurable, so they may often be assessed by employing the same research techniques used when planning for the campaign.

Nike's "She Runs the Night" campaign resulted in more than 3,000 female runners competing in its 13K event.

Christopher Lee/Getty Images for Nike

Both of the campaigns referenced throughout the chapter were designed to attain higher orders of public impact. The Jazz's "5 for the Fight" campaign was crafted to achieve public support for the jersey patch sponsorship evidenced by behavioral indicators. The standing ovation for the campaign's announcement was one such behavior. Other behavioral indicators included the hundreds of e-mail and Twitter direct messages (DMs) sent to the CEO of the sponsor, Qualtrics, expressing appreciation for the campaign's focus on such an important cause (Frederick, 2017). Nike's "She Runs the Night" campaign was designed to connect the brand with female runners and generate buzz within that audience. Multiple behavioral indicators documented the campaign's success, including the size of the social community, the number of runners participating in the 13K and indicating they intended to do so again, and Nike's revenue growth (Chia, 2018).

Issues Management

Although identifying relevant publics is a fundamental public relations activity, equally important is recognizing the concerns that are likely to create the connection between the sport organization and those publics. **Issues management** is defined by the Public Affairs Council, a nonpartisan association for public affairs professionals, as "the process of prioritizing and proactively addressing public policy and reputation issues that can affect an organization's success" (Pinkham, 2004). Lesly (1998) noted that an issue is a matter of mutual concern about which there are differing points of view regarding the appropriate action to take. Dale (2002) described issues as the product of problems, opportunities, uncertainties, and controversies, and suggested that issues warrant strategic consideration by key organizational decision makers.

Organizational action that has a substantive effect on one or more of its publics may qualify as an issue. Anticipating a public's reaction and developing an organizational response are key public relations responsibilities. For instance, the use of Native American nicknames and mascots for sport teams has been prevalent in the United States for many years. Protests have periodically raised awareness of the issue and, in educational settings in particular, many organizations have changed their nicknames. Organizations still using such names can reasonably expect that the name will become an issue at some point and should plan accordingly. What is the organization's position on the issue, and what publics are likely to have an interest? What public relations activities will be required to produce acceptance of the organizational position? Will the organizational position need to be modified to align more closely with a public's position? On this issue, several organizations have in recent years moved away from the existing organizational stance.

Some issues can pose public relations problems when an organizational action contradicts the organization's stated mission or position. As an example, the NCAA and its members continually stress the student in the term *student–athlete* but, according to some, often make decisions that don't appear to be in the best interests of the students.

Schedules become longer, and the financial stakes associated with football and men's basketball success continue to grow. The conflict between the NCAA's stated priorities and some of its actions has stirred debate and lawsuits surrounding issues related to commercialization and professionalization and is consistently a public relations challenge for the NCAA as it deals with critics of college athletics.

From a strategic perspective, issues management provides a foundation for a great deal of public relations activity because issues serve as the connection between organizations and their publics. Grunig et al. (2002) observed that the degree to which an organization resolves issues has an impact on relationships, and important issues that are not successfully resolved possess the potential to evolve into crises. A study of sport communication professionals in Northern Ireland indicated that practitioners are well aware of this reality and watch carefully for the "tipping point" in the evolution of an issue to a crisis (Kitchin & Purcell, 2017).

An example of a sustained issue with such potential is the concussion problem confronting the NFL. The league began studying the issue 25 years ago, and since that time, it has faced lawsuits from thousands of former players, a hearing before a U.S. House of Representatives committee, and media criticism regarding its positions on the issue and related actions or lack thereof. Concern around the issue extends beyond the health of former players to the long-term viability of the NFL if the concussion linkage leads to substantially reduced fan interest and sponsor support, as well as a reduction in the number of players in the developmental pipeline.

The concussion issue flared again in 2017 when a medical journal article reported that a study of deceased football players found chronic traumatic encephalopathy (CTE) in 110 of the 111 former NFL players examined (Mez et al., 2017). Coombs (2017) evaluated the league's response to the article and its evolving position on the issue. Noting that the league had denied a linkage between football and CTE until 2016, Coombs (2017) observed the NFL's position had changed to one of acknowledgment and that its "strategy seems to be to accept CTE as part of the game." Aside from offering an observation of the study's limitation (i.e., use of a convenience sample), the league's response to the 2017 journal article was subdued, an attempt to avoid drawing even more media and fan attention to the story.

The issues management process has been described in a variety of ways. Dougall (2008) crafted a three-step process integrating the commonalities in the other models. The first step is issue identification, which involves monitoring the organization's environment for emerging issues and scanning for newly developing ones. In one respect, the proliferation of communication technologies makes such monitoring highly challenging. However, public relations professionals have available more tools than ever to monitor both the traditional news media and social media.

The second step is strategic decision making—prioritizing which issues, among the myriad that may exist within the public relations universe, warrant organizational action. Assessing an issue's likelihood to adversely affect an organization and the potential impact are key considerations in this decision. Once an issue has been prioritized for organizational attention, actions may be defined either to persuade the public to accept the organization's position (i.e., Grunig's two-way asymmetrical model) or to modify that position and communicate a new organizational stance that will result in a more accepting stance by the organization's public (Grunig's two-way symmetrical model). The evolution in the NFL's position on the relationship between football and CTE is an example of an organization moving from an asymmetrical to a symmetrical strategy. Once the organization selects its strategy, aligned messaging and engagement actions are necessary to fully implement and communicate it.

The third step is evaluation, a process that may be applied to issues management in much the same way as it is to a campaign or program. Assessment is best driven by intended outcomes, with the most challenging result to achieve being behavioral change within a key public. Issues are often so complex that it is unrealistic of organizations to expect that all negative consequences will be ameliorated, as evidenced by the NFL's tolerance for costs associated with the CTE issue. Citing the league's $13 billion in revenue in 2016, Coombs (2017) contended:

> "For the NFL, the CTE issue is more about legal liability and what the NFL will pay for it. . . . The NFL can afford to pay for its CTE liabilities. What the NFL cannot afford is a crisis that drives fans from the game."

The importance of issues management should not be underestimated. It can serve to clarify, maintain, and even enhance relationships with key publics. How issues are handled is likely to be a primary influence on stakeholder perceptions of reputation. When organizations proactively consider issues and give stakeholders the sense that their views are considered and that dialogue is possible, they may be able to defuse potentially serious public relations problems.

Reputation Management

Descriptions of public relations often include the management of image or **reputation**. Such a reference may cause some confusion. Reputation management is often narrowly perceived as the protection or repair of reputation during a crisis. This important aspect of public relations is considered in some depth in chapter 8, but it is shortsighted to think that an organization should attend to reputation management only during a crisis. Many decisions made during the strategic management process have great influence on organizational reputation, which brings us to the source of confusion on a conceptual level: What is reputation? How is it different from brand? Are the distinctions important, and if so, what are the implications for public relations practice?

Contributing to the uncertainty about the concept of reputation is the interchangeable and inconsistent use of other terms such as *brand*, *identity*, and *image* and the combination of such terms (e.g., *brand identity*, *brand equity*). Many attempts have been made to define reputation and to distinguish reputation from brand. One distinction between reputation and brand is the idea that brand is a "consumer-centric" term more associated with marketing and marketing communications. Reputation is a "company-centric" term that focuses on credibility and respect among a broader set of constituencies and is more likely to rely on public relations techniques (Ettenson & Knowles, 2008; Macnamara, 2006). Drew (2016) distinguishes the two by stating that brand is what the organization says and how it behaves, while reputation is what others say about the organization based on shared perceptions.

Either way, reputation and brand are clearly connected. Damage to one can create problems for the other, and there is surely interest at the strategic level for development of strategies to establish a brand identity and to sustain reputation.

Some sport organizations have improved their strategic focus on reputation in recent years by devoting more attention to mission development and identification of publics. Prominent individual athletes such as LeBron James and Serena Williams have some of the same public relations concerns as organizations do and take a strategic look at reputation as they position themselves in the marketplace. Unfortunately, many sport figures still tend to ignore strategic reputation management and settle for crisis management.

Scandals and misbehavior seem to be a routine part of the sport landscape. The Tour de France and Major League Baseball are among the prominent victims of image problems created by use of performance-enhancing drugs. Some local YMCAs have been challenged for appearing to operate much like commercial health clubs while enjoying tax-exempt status. Various professional teams have been characterized as extortionists for using money from local taxpayers to build new stadiums and arenas. The list of athletes and coaches who have tarnished their own reputations as well as those of their employers seems to grow almost daily. Few examples of the effect of behavior on reputation have been as spectacular as the Tiger Woods scandal that began in 2009. Tiger's carefully crafted public image quickly crumbled under the scrutiny of all forms of media, which not only left Tiger's reputation in tatters but also put the PGA and Woods' endorsement partners in difficult positions.

Elements of Reputation

As sport organizations examine the benefits of reputation management, they must first determine the attributes that their publics are likely to find important. This process is more complex than might first be imagined. The first complication is that most organizations have multiple publics and accordingly multiple reputations. Different publics are likely to have differing opinions about what makes an organization reputable. Duke University receives accolades for its rigorous academic standards and high graduation rates. Would as many dedicated fans camp out for basketball tickets if the team didn't also win plenty of games? Would the faculty be willing to accept lower academic standards if that were necessary to continue to win basketball games? In this case two publics with somewhat different priorities are appeased, and each has its expectations met. In many cases reconciling competing expectations may not be so easy.

Beyond the complication of multiple publics is the variation among publics even within a single stakeholder group. Among long-suffering fans of MLB's Pittsburgh Pirates (26 seasons without a division title as of the writing of this manuscript) are those who are outraged with the team's continual trading away of some of the fans' favorite players.

Others contend that the most popular players have not been able to prevent losing seasons and that building the system through trades is the way to move the organization forward. A third group of fans want to see a winner but are perfectly willing to follow the team and attend a few games a year in a great ballpark as long as prices remain reasonable. Three sets of fans have three different sets of expectations of the organization. Each of the three publics has the potential to feel betrayed if the strategic choices made by Pirates' management fall short of their expectations. Some of each group will likely feel let down when stories come out about the Pirates' ownership making a profit while the team continues to lose. Reputation is built largely on confidence and trust. When organizations or individuals undermine the faith that their publics hold in them, they jeopardize the relationships that public relations is trying to build.

Non-Sport-Specific Reputation Frameworks

Fombrun (1996) described reputation as a reconciliation of all the images people have of an organization that convey the relative prestige and status of a company compared with its competitors. Reputation is an intangible corporate asset that can enhance success and temper the damage of crises. Reputation reflects the ability of an organization to meet the expectations of its publics and the strength of the relationship that various stakeholders have with the organization. As organizations seek to develop, enhance, and preserve their reputations, they must have clearly identified publics and know what those publics value in their relationships.

Corporate Reputation Quotient

Fombrun, Gardberg, and Sever (1999) developed an instrument that attempts to measure reputation. The corporate reputation quotient of Harris-Fombrun (*Corporate Reputation Quotient*, n.d.) is a multidimensional assessment of reputation that recognizes that various stakeholders have different perspectives and expectations. The model is designed to measure corporate reputation by assessing stakeholder perceptions and also clarifies what attributes tend to be the most influential determinants of reputation.

The model identifies six reputation drivers and 20 attributes. The reputation drivers include emotional appeal, products and services, vision and leadership, workplace environment, financial per-formance, and social responsibility. Each of these drivers has an associated set of attributes, most of which can be applied to any organization. Both the reputation drivers and many of their associated attributes are summarized in table 2.5. Note that this model was designed to include the perceptions of multiple stakeholders, not just consumers or members of the media. This feature enhances its usefulness because the model becomes more of a strategic management tool rather than simply another consumer behavior model. It can also serve as a tactical assessment and development tool as organizations attempt to discover how they are perceived by various publics.

Although not constructed specifically for sport organizations, the corporate reputation quotient has been applied to sport settings. Tomiyama (2012) administered the measurement scale in five Japanese venues, including professional basketball teams, an independent baseball league, and a sport university. The resultant analysis of data found that each of the model's six elements "were a viable measure to a certain degree" (p. 309).

Emotional appeal includes attributes associated with admiration, respect, trust, and positive regard. Many companies would love to see the same type of emotional attachment that some fans exhibit for their alma mater or hometown team. National Association for Stock Car Auto Racing (NASCAR) fans are particularly well known for their loyalty, not only to the race car drivers but also to the sponsors who fund them. Sport organizations must identify what produces such loyalty and take steps to foster it.

Products and services incorporate reputation-related attributes such as product quality, innovation, and value. For example, a sporting goods manufacturer such as a producer of golf clubs must weigh a variety of options as it positions itself in the marketplace: quality versus value, high-end versus mainstream, broad distribution versus narrow distribution, skim pricing versus penetration pricing, and cutting-edge innovation versus established technology. Sport organizations must be aware of the significance of this facet of reputation in establishing and maintaining relationships with customers, sponsors, and investors.

Vision and leadership deal with perceptions of who is directing the organization as well as the direction that the organization is taking. Vision and leadership are of particular importance to employee relations. Relationships with the financial community and political community are also influenced by the quality of leadership in an organization. Leaders in high-profile sport settings such as commissioners

Table 2.5 Corporate Reputation Quotient

Reputation drivers	Driver attributes
Emotional appeal	Good feeling Respect Trust
Products and services	Stands behind products Innovative High quality and good value
Vision and leadership	Excellent leadership Clear vision Opportunistic
Workplace environment	Well managed Appealing place to work Good employees
Financial performance	Profitable Good investment with bright future Outperforms competition
Social responsibility	Supports good causes Environmentally responsible Treats people well

Adapted from Fombrun, Gardberg, and Sever (1999).

and owners are highly visible and, when controversial, may create public relations problems at times.

Workplace environment focuses on attributes of reputation concerned with employees and the conditions under which they work. Although the focus of this reputation attribute is directed toward an internal public, it has important external implications. Because all employees are reflections of the organization, they will have an effect on the perception held by the publics with whom they interact. Organizations that ignore how their employees feel are failing to pay attention to an important public relations asset.

Financial performance includes profitability, investment potential, and competitiveness. Sound financials have great appeal for investors and donors and give the impression that the organization is well run. The trappings of financial success are also important to the perception of an organization. For example, sport organizations try to reflect financial success and stability through facilities. College athletics programs are caught up in an arms race of facility development that involves building bigger and better stadiums, practice areas, weight rooms, and support facilities to lure recruits.

Social responsibility consists of supporting causes and community—in essence, corporate citizenship—and sport is replete with examples of such endeavors. For instance, the Women's National Basketball Association (WNBA) has a sustained commitment to inclusion and equality as part of its Pride initiative. And the LeBron James Family Foundation supports a public school in Akron serving educationally challenged students (Zillgitt, 2018). Another avenue of social responsibility that has been embraced in recent years is the growing emphasis on "green" operations and sustainability. Sustainability in its broadest interpretation looks to provide integration and balance of environmental, social, and economic concerns and the tradeoffs that exist among them (Adams, 2006; Gibson, Fairley, & Kennelly, 2019). Social responsibility and its various facets are explored in greater depth in chapter 9.

FleishmanHillard Model

Public relations and marketing firm Fleishman-Hillard employs a reputation model that, similar to the Reputation Quotient, is not sport-specific but has been successfully applied in sport settings (Drew, 2016). The model is composed of three key pillars, each with three related drivers:

- Management behavior, including doing right, consistent performance, and credible communications
- Customer benefits, including better value, customer care and innovation

- Society outcomes, including employee care, community impact, and care for the environment

As evident, multiple alignments (e.g., innovation, care for the environment) exist between the FleishmanHillard and corporate reputation quotient frameworks. FleishmanHillard reports this framework may be applied across business categories as "regardless of industry, reputation is made up of the same nine ingredients" (Drew, 2016).

Sports Team Reputation Model

Noting the lack of a scale to measure reputation specifically to sports teams, three sport management scholars developed and validated a scale to serve such a purpose (Jang, Ko, & Chan-Olmsted, 2015). The result was the spectator-based sports team reputation (SSTR) model, which consists of six dimensions:

- Team performance as it leads to team success
- Team tradition as it relates to overall achievement and business success
- Team social responsibility as indicated by the team's relationship with the community
- Spectator orientation or the degree to which the team's central focus is its spectators
- Management quality and strategic vision of the team as compared with similar organizations
- Financial soundness and profitability

The strength of the SSTR is that it is a team-specific reputational model and incorporates some domain-specific dimensions such as team tradition. Other elements of the model, such as social responsibility, management quality, and financial soundness align with one or both of the more general reputation models previously discussed. The SSTR, as its name clearly indicates, focuses on a single yet critical stakeholder group, team spectators. Further, the sport industry is broad and diverse, consisting of teams, of course, but also athletes, coaches, governing bodies, and more. Other approaches to analyzing reputation are necessary for those other groups.

Reputation Assessment and Valuation

Each of the reputation frameworks just described can be employed to assess sport organizations.

The reputation drivers incorporated in each model may be incorporated into surveys administered to appropriate stakeholders. The resultant reputation ratings may then shed light on a variety of questions, including how the organization's reputation may change over time, how it may vary among different stakeholder groups, and how it may compare with similar evaluations of competitors.

Using the distinction between brand as what the organization says about itself and reputation as what others say about it, FleishmanHillard uses the term *authenticity gap* to describe instances when the firm's research identifies important differences between an organization's brand and its reputation (Drew, 2016). In applying the model to sports leagues as a category, the company assessed eight major leagues relevant in Canada and found that consistent performance was the most important driver of reputation. All eight leagues were perceived as delivering in that respect. However, some differences existed between the leagues, such as the NHL outpacing the NFL and MLB on consistent performance, value, and innovation. The research also indicated authenticity gaps in at least two areas: credible communications from the leagues and delivering value to fans.

The value of reputation, an intangible asset, is difficult to establish in precise and objective terms. What value can be attached to names like the FIFA Women's World Cup, New Balance, or the Toronto Maple Leafs? In a *Street & Smith's SportsBusiness Journal* column titled "In Pure Dollars, What's Your Reputation Worth?," Jackowski (1999) referenced a significant difference between Nike's market capitalization (i.e., the market value of the company's outstanding shares) and its book value (i.e., the evaluation of the company's current assets). That difference, Jackowski contended, was a financial indicator of Nike's reputation. Although not sport-specific in its focus, the *2018 UK Reputation Dividend Report* found that, on average, 38% of a company's market capitalization was driven by reputation (Sims, 2018). Of course, market capitalization as a reputational measure can be applied only to publicly traded companies. Other types of organizations must rely on different indicators. As stated by Jackowski (1999, para. 15), however, "the knowledge of whether your company has an excellent reputation or a poor one goes a long way toward determining the long-term success of your enterprise. If you have not already paid attention to the value of your organizational reputation, consumers and investors will not pay attention either."

SUMMARY

As sport organizations vie for attention and support in a competitive marketplace, they must strive to accommodate the expectations of their publics. The demand for immediacy can produce impatience on the part of both organizations and publics. This compressed window of opportunity may entice some to disregard the ideals of their vision for more immediate rewards, resulting in an environment in which relationships are viewed as short-term commodities rather than long-term assets. The temptation to take shortcuts often results in action that is inconsistent with the mission statement and creates public relations problems. If public relations is to take a leadership role in attaining organizational success, it must be integrated into the strategic planning process. Sport managers must have a clear understanding of what their organization's mission is, who its key publics are, and what issues connect the organization to its publics. With this knowledge, public relations can proactively serve as a key driver in managing the reputation of an organization and developing and prioritizing the relationships crucial to the success of virtually all sport organizations.

The real measure of an organization's values is how its managers direct their resources. Many organizations profess a commitment to public relations without allocating the necessary resources to integrate public relations into the fabric of the operation. Without dedicating both human and financial resources to public relations, this commitment lacks substance.

This chapter has provided an overview of the key dimensions and concepts related to public relations as a driver of strategic management. Beyond emphasizing a proactive approach to public relations, the chapter has addressed how public relations may be integrated into the marketing function to build a brand and attain brand equity. The chapter has also discussed how organizations may identify and prioritize their key publics and then build programs and campaigns to manage relationships with those publics. In addition, the chapter has covered the nature of issues management and how it pertains to key organizational relationships and reputation. Organizations that effectively apply these concepts and related processes will be well positioned to meet organizational goals and realize their vision.

LEARNING ACTIVITIES

1. Select a sport organization and identify the publics with which it likely has relationships. How might the organization prioritize those relationships? Do the organization's actions appear to be consistent with those priorities?

2. Choose from among the publics mentioned in the previous activity and identify two or three issues that will likely connect the organization and each specific public. What are the benefits of handling the issues well? What are the consequences of handling the issues poorly?

3. Access the PRSA's Silver Anvil Award website (https://apps.prsa.org/awards/silveranvil /Search). Conduct a search after selecting Sports from the Industry menu and then review the summaries of five winning campaigns. *Note: Only PRSA members can access the PDF files with more detailed campaign information.* What type of sport organizations do you see represented? What were the overall purposes of their award-winning campaigns?

4. Evaluate a selected sport organization's reputation using the six drivers of reputation in the corporate reputation quotient. Which of the six drivers are most and least critical to the organization's reputation?

5. List three sport-related entities with a strong brands that are not included in table 2.1. Discuss what attributes contribute to their brand equity and what potential threats exist to their reputations.

Engaging Key Publics via Social Media

After reading this chapter, students should be able to

- articulate the uses of social media as a means of engaging key publics in sport public relations practice;
- describe general approaches to the development of social media content;
- identify strategic considerations for social media management;
- understand broad categories of social media metrics;
- illustrate how social networking sites can be used in public relations efforts; and
- describe skills of social media practitioners and qualifications to manage social media in sport.

These are the key terms discussed in this chapter:

- acquisition metrics
- average engagement rate
- conversion metrics
- demographics
- hashtags
- psychographics
- reach
- retention metrics
- shared media

- social listening
- social media activity
- social media content
- social media voice
- social networking sites
- social networks
- strategic social media management
- virtual communication communities

The rapid evolution of Internet-based technologies continues to have an extraordinary influence on our global society and organizations of all types around the world. Sport public relations practitioners, in particular, continue to adjust to these relentless changes in technology, which create a variety of unique opportunities and daunting challenges. The chance to communicate to mass audiences and a variety of publics appears to be a significant benefit of technology. But these platforms also come with a variety of strategic considerations for sport public relations professionals and need to be appropriately managed as part of an organization's overall communication efforts.

The worldwide digital revolution has significantly changed the way people communicate, collaborate, and consume information. Social media has provided a new tool that gives fans preferred mechanisms to receive information from and interact with trusted organizations, friends, and social influencers. These tools offer a significant degree of freedom for various publics to interact with organizations they choose to follow, doing so whenever—and often wherever—they want to communicate. This shift in communication and information consumption requires a strategic response from all ranges of businesses, but especially in the sport industry, where fan identification and commitment are notably strong.

Social media, as a tool for sport public relations professionals, fits under the **shared media** element of the PESO model discussed in chapter 1. The model defines social media as an element of a broader public relations strategy, but for smaller sport entities (especially youth teams and organizations), social media may be the primary tool of communication and interaction with critical publics. The shared media element of social media interacts at times with both earned and owned media elements of a public relations brand. While social media makes up the vast majority of shared media tactics used by public relations professionals, there are interactions with other elements of the PESO model. Interactions with earned media elements of the model include enhancing partnerships with external publics (such as community partners and charities) and increasing influencer engagement (often these interactions will occur with members of traditional and digital media on the same platform). Additionally, the content that an organization owns (stories about the organization's athletes, coaches, front office, and so on) can be effectively disseminated using social media. Interaction with the paid media element of the PESO model comes with sponsored content, as well as the authority the organization gains with highly engaging content, which can become viral and spread quickly among large groups of people.

In previous chapters, the focus has been on public relation's role in communicating to a wide variety of diverse publics. This and the following chapter address how technology can assist in efforts by sport public relations professionals to communicate to those publics. This chapter focuses on social media's role in engaging key publics, and the next chapter will address the role of other digital media in strategic public relations management.

Social Media Use in Public Relations

The accelerated growth of communication platforms such as Facebook, Twitter, and Instagram have forced sport public relations professionals and their organizations to take notice. Researchers have worked for years to define social media, and the results of that work have produced conclusions as various as the people using social media. Freberg (2016) stated that social media can "provide a personalized, online network hub of information, dialogue, and relationship management. These new communication tools allow individual users and organizations to engage with, reach, persuade, and target key audiences more effectively across multiple platforms" (p. 773). Social media is also often defined by the Internet-based tools used to conduct dialogue and relationships online. Carr and Hayes (2015) defined social media as "Internet-based channels that allow users to interact opportunistically and selectively self-present, either in real-time or asynchronously, with both broad and narrow audiences who derive value from user-generated content and the perception of interaction with others" (p. 8).

Social media, for the purpose of this textbook, was defined in chapter 1 as "interactive media technologies that allow consumers to create and disseminate content, connect with media outlets and other network users and voice their opinions on any number of topics" (Sheffer & Schultz, 2013, p. 210). These technologies produce platforms that provide opportunity for connection, communication, and collaboration manifested in two forms: first, in the use of social networking sites (e.g., Facebook and Twitter, sometimes also referred to as social networking services) and, second, in **virtual communication communities** (instant messaging, blogs, and online fan communities) as well (Chugh & Ruhi, 2018).

Social Networking Sites

Boyd and Ellison (2007) defined **social networking sites** as "web-based services that allow individuals to 1) construct a profile within a bounded system, 2) articulate a list of other users with whom they share a connection, and 3) view and traverse their list of connections and those made by others within the system." (p. 211). These connections and interactions vary in their names across various platforms, but the definition provides a foundation for more productively examining this realm of social media. The most popular and most used social networking sites can be divided into two categories: social networks and media-sharing networks.

Social Networks

Curtis Foreman, a content editor for the popular social media management tool Hootsuite, described **social networks** as broad methods to connect to people and brands for the purpose of sharing information and ideas (2017). Social networks include the popular platforms Facebook, Twitter, and LinkedIn. These social networks can help organizations build relationships with a variety of publics but also serve as sources of news and information in socialized experience within the bounds of the social media tool.

Sport organizations not using these platforms are missing out on the opportunity to connect, communicate, and collaborate with a core group of global users. Facebook has been reported to have 2.41 billion monthly active users (Statista, 2019a), and each one of those users has the opportunity to choose to interact with a sport organization's brand. Twitter has sustained similar success, with 330 million active users (Statista, 2019b).

The Los Angeles Lakers, with more than 21 million followers, were the most popular U.S. sport team on Facebook in 2018. In comparison, popular soccer player Cristiano Ronaldo boasted 122 million fans on his Facebook page in 2019, leading all athletes on the platform. According to MVPIndex (2019), the Golden State Warriors were reported to have the most valuable social footprint, valued at an estimated $512 million. The MVPindex compiles rankings using an algorithm of social activity, including fan reach, engagement, and conversation.

Premier League soccer fans follow their teams passionately through social media, as Newsweek reported in 2018 that 50% of the top 50 sport teams on Twitter in terms of followers came from the most-watched soccer league in the world. In comparison, only three National Basketball Association (NBA) teams made it to the top 20 of that list, and only one Major League Baseball team managed to make the top 50, while four cricket teams from the Indian Premier League were ranked among the top 50 worldwide. While social media growth in the United States has continued for sport teams, there is obviously room for growth internationally for all the major U.S. sport leagues.

Facebook

With nearly 1.6 billion daily active users, Facebook (www.facebook.com) is by far the most popular social network in the world. The platform's company employs nearly 40,000 people and has offices in over 50 cities worldwide. These numbers translate into a broad reach for sport public relations professionals, providing access to millions of people who may have a specified interest in a professional's organization, especially in a digital format native to their everyday interactions with other people.

Personal connections on Facebook are called "friends," but sport public relations professionals are likely managing a Facebook page or group on behalf of their organization. Pages are the main way that brands can interact within the Facebook community and can be created for free on the platform. A Facebook page allows sport public relations professionals to post on behalf of the brand, run advertisements, and build a following with the posting of **social media content**, which is original text, photos, video, and links produced by the organization or shared on the platform from another entity—such as a highlight video from a traditional media outlet such as local news or ESPN or from a governing body such as a college athletics conference or FIFA (Fédération Internationale de Football Association).

What people see after they log in to Facebook is called a news feed. Understanding when, why, and how fans are interacting with content on Facebook is key for sport public relations professionals. The Facebook news feed is governed by an intricate algorithm that takes into consideration a variety of user interactions and develops a formula to determine what is seen at the top of the news feed when a user logs in. Users have some control over their news feeds through the settings of their own profile, but sport public relations professionals should always be monitoring changes in the platform's algorithm that can impact the reach of content posted.

Potential user interactions with content on Facebook can be classified into three categories. The first category includes the emoji reaction. This reaction can

Case Study

CRISTIANO RONALDO ON FACEBOOK

Arguably one of the world's most popular athletes, Cristiano Ronaldo's brand is an excellent example of how social media can be incorporated into and interact with other media in the PESO model. All of the content produced by the athlete's public relations team fits within the shared element of the model, but other interactions also exist. For instance, Ronaldo's Facebook account boasted a variety of paid partnerships, highlighted mainly by his cologne brand, CR7.

Some of the owned content shared on Ronaldo's account includes behind-the-scenes photos of practices and preparation for the Union of European Football Associations (UEFA) Champions League season. Ronaldo also shares content that only he owns and chooses to post, namely, personal images of his family and travel. An element of media relations (part of the earned circle of the PESO model) is evident as well, with photo galleries and scores of Juventus matches as well as documentation of Ronaldo's presence as captain of Portugal's national team.

A combination of all the elements of the PESO model is enhanced by engaging, high-quality photography and video production, which adds to the authority of Ronaldo's presence on social media. More than 122 million people follow Ronaldo's Facebook page (www.facebook.com/Cristiano), adding legitimacy to the influence of his social media presence, which enhances all content associated with the various elements of the PESO model. Paid partnerships with his cologne, Nike Football, and Visit Madeira, among others, give Ronaldo an opportunity to bring one of the largest audiences of any person (or organization) on the Facebook platform to the pursuit of connection, communication, and collaboration with those partnerships.

Ronaldo's team produces a variety of content targeted at both very broad and very narrow publics. That content resides in a variety of categories of the PESO model, giving one of the world's most famous athletes a social media presence that is as well balanced and successful as the forward is on the pitch.

Cristiano Ronaldo's cologne brand CR7 is featured prominently throughout his Facebook time line. Notice at the top that Facebook explains that this is a paid partnership and how the social network describes the details of how partnerships work.

Discussion Questions

1. What are two key takeaways from this brief case study for how sport organizations should be managing their social media presence in relation to the PESO model?

2. How much does an organization's or athlete's authority factor into your decision to pay attention to paid partnerships the organization or athlete promotes?

---

be what is universally known as a "like" (connected to a thumbs-up emoji) but also can be another emoji attached to emotion (including a sad or angry face). The second category of interactions includes users' comments on posted content. Organizations have some control over which comments appear and can even designate certain user voices as top fans, giving the user a small tag under the user's name in comments that signifies significant interaction with the organization's content. Comments can commonly include text, photos, video, and GIFs (animated images, in graphical interchange format, that repeats in a loop). The third category of interactions includes the user's choice to share content from other users and organizations to the user's time line (a historical representation of the user's brand on the platform).

Organizations have unique opportunities related to content on Facebook. A Facebook page can interact with other pages (by liking, commenting on, and sharing content) as a user and follow other Facebook pages. Organizations can also produce live video, create events, offer special promotions, and even post job announcements, all of which can foster interaction with fans of the organization's page. Each page also comes with an instant messaging element that Facebook calls Messenger, which allows for private group and one-to-one interactions in a text-like format. Organizations can also create polls for their fans to vote on, host watch parties, and check in to places with the account.

The organization's page can be run by multiple employees, all of whom may have varying roles in content production. Employees who manage social media for organizations can become admins, editors, moderators, advertisers, and analysts, and custom roles can even be created for users, a feature that can be helpful during a social media takeover by a member of the organization or selected individuals outside of it. Each of these roles has different permissions within the structure of the Facebook page the organization manages.

Twitter

While Facebook provides a significant audience and a variety of interactions, Twitter is another popular social networking platform on which fans can interact with sport organizations. Twitter, which began its rise as a social networking platform in 2006, now ranks as one of the most popular social networking sites today, with approximately 500 million tweets sent by 100 million daily active users each day (Forsey, n.d.).

The ability to follow another user defines connections on Twitter. Those who connect to a user's particular account are called followers, and when users decide to connect to another account, they do so by following another account. Called a post on Facebook, shared content on Twitter is defined as a tweet. A user's tweets are historically collected and organized on a profile, which gives necessary information about the user and the user's twitter handle, which always begins with the symbol @.

While Facebook casts a wide net with billions of users, Twitter provides a sport organization with the ability to get information and news out quickly. Originally limited to 140 characters of text, users today enjoy the ability to post up to 280 characters while also posting images, videos, and GIFs. As on Facebook, users and organizations can also create polls and express emotion with the use of emojis. Emojis used on Twitter have become an increasingly more popular method of communication on the platform as a result of Twitter's character limits and the ease of using emojis on the platform. Users and organizations can interact with one another via tweets, retweets, replies, and likes (which on Twitter, in contrast to Facebook, are designated by just one symbol, a heart).

Unlike Facebook, Twitter requires signing in to a particular account to manage content. Still, users do have the ability to connect to multiple accounts on the same device, primarily through the use of third-party services like Hootsuite, HubSpot, and TweetDeck. Twitter also has an instant messaging element, called a direct message (DM), which allows users to send information privately between accounts. Direct messages can be sent with any account that follows the user, although many organizations will choose a setting that allows them to receive direct messages from any Twitter account, even if the user does not follow the organization on the platform.

Twitter's unique interaction tools include the tag and the use of hashtags. Twitter allows users to tag other profiles by using the @ symbol followed by the username of the profile. For example, if one were commenting on the play of the University of Connecticut women's basketball team in the Final Four and wanted to tag the team's official account, a tweet might read, "It would appear @UConnWBB is poised to return to the national championship game." Tagging the organization in the tweet allows for the brand to be not only mentioned but also notified of the interaction. Tweets that begin with by tagging another user fall under the reply category and are not automatically shown on the user's profile as a tweet. **Hashtags** always start with the # symbol and are an excellent way of strategically connecting content to topics (#fantasytips), brands (#NHL), or events (#WorldSeries).

Twitter can also be integrated with other social media platforms (such as Instagram) and does provide some data via Twitter Analytics (analytics.twitter.com). Users logged into their Twitter accounts who go to the site are given information about trends with the account over adjustable periods of time, making Twitter an excellent platform to use for public relations campaigns.

Media-Sharing Networks

Media-sharing networks differ only slightly in purpose from social networking sites. Foreman (2017) defines media-sharing networks as places for users and brands to find and share media content online. This shared media content includes photos, produced video, and live video. The framework of media-sharing networks is very similar to that of social networking sites, and the ultimate purpose is also to share media content with various publics.

Media-sharing networks are still crucial in communicating with and establishing relationships with different publics. While the original content may be images or videos, the platforms do still allow text in posts for some context and, more importantly, allow text in response to posted material.

Cristiano Ronaldo also has a successful presence on other platforms in addition to Facebook. Ronaldo (@Cristiano) has 184 million followers on Instagram (making his the second-most followed account on the platform) and gained more than 35 million followers in 2018 after his transfer from Real Madrid to Juventus Turin. LeBron James (@kingjames) is the most popular U.S. athlete on Instagram, with 47.9 million followers (Jahns, 2019). In comparison, Nike (@Nike) has nearly 93 million followers. Video-sharing platform YouTube has a widely diverse audience that includes an extensive presence in the esports environment. Popular professional esports player Tyler Blevin (also known as Ninja) boasts more than 22 million subscribers to his YouTube account (youtube.com/NinjasHyper), which features Blevin playing Fortnite and Player Unknown's Battle-grounds (PUBG), among other games.

Instagram

Instagram has over a billion people using the platform each month and more than 500 million people sharing images and videos via the platform each day (Newberry, 2019). Instagram's function is primarily to share photos; however, with the addition of IGTV, which features longer videos (between 1 and 60 minutes) in a vertical format, longer-running video is quickly becoming more popular.

Each Instagram user has a profile, which serves as the historical repository of the user's content. Profiles show previous content chronologically in rows of three that flow vertically down the profile page. Profile names are similar to Twitter and start with the @ symbol. User profiles also allow users to upload to IGTV and to access a private selection of posts that the user has saved or bookmarked as well as a section where users can see other content in which the user or brand has been tagged. Instagram also has a stories feature that allows users to highlight and group particular elements of content based on a specific topic or event, using media to tell the story of anything from the user's day to breaking news.

Instagram's interaction features include a "like" option (designated by a heart), the ability to post text replies, and the opportunity for users to bookmark content by saving a post. Users can also share content to other platforms (like Facebook and Twitter) directly from a post. A significant amount of content on Instagram is shared and consumed on mobile devices. The platform does include specific size and dimension requirements for posting (posted photos are usually in the shape and size of a square, and video content is vertical, similar to the way a smartphone would produce this content). The platform allows users to tag other users in their posts, and hashtag use is as prevalent on Instagram as it is on Twitter. Photos and videos can be created within the Instagram app itself or can be uploaded and customized after being created by the user on another device. One of Instagram's most popular features is the ability to use filters, which users can choose from and then apply to enhance the colors and look of the content.

Instagram's content can be integrated easily with other platforms, including websites, thanks to a feature that generates code to embed content on another site. Users can also share content can to Facebook, Facebook Messenger, and Twitter with the touch of a button in the Instagram app.

One sport account that occupies significant influential space on Instagram is ESPN's SportsCenter (@sportscenter) account. The account, which has more than 14.5 million followers, uses a variety of publishing methods to reach SportsCenter's following. The SportsCenter account posts multiple IGTV videos per day, allowing followers to stay up to date with the latest and most celebrated plays of the day and information from the world of sport; the SportsCenter name has become synonymous with quick highlight hits.

SportsCenter also uses stories to its advantage with other branded ESPN content such as its "SC Featured" stories of triumph through adversity in sport, as well as other events such as the U.S. Women's National Team participation in the 2019 World Cup. Also included are photos, many of which are similar to graphical pieces that would be seen on a broadcast; graphical representations of prominent athletes' social media posts; and short videos that may go viral in the world of sport. The content creators produce diverse content that is informative, relevant, and timely.

YouTube

The other of the top two media-sharing networks, YouTube, has seen significant growth in the social space. In 2005, a trio of PayPal employees began the social video sharing site for users to upload, share, and view video content (Chi, 2019). Use of the site snowballed, and within months users were posting more than 60,000 and watching more than 100 million videos per day. That type of web traffic quickly got the attention of Google, which purchased YouTube in 2006 and has turned it into the second most-visited website and the second-largest search engine in the world. By 2017, more than 400 hours of video content were being uploaded to YouTube every minute, a number that continues to increase.

The site now averages 2 billion active monthly users and has created a cord-cutting venture called YouTube TV that for approximately $50 per month offers access to 70+ channels (including ESPN, NBCSN, FOX Sports, and the Big Ten Network, among others). Additional networks are available for purchase that include FOX's popular soccer add-on, FOX Soccer Plus. YouTube has also ventured into the world of music, capitalizing on a constant stream of video content coming from the music production industry. YouTube continues to be a pioneer on the revenue generation front as it relates to social media, with a premium capability that includes the elimination of ads (which content producers often allow to monetize YouTube accounts) and the ability to download videos for offline use.

User pages on YouTube are called channels, which are historical representations of previous content produced and organized into various playlists. Connections on YouTube are called subscribers, and the site allows those who produce content also to have those subscriptions listed with content provided on their channel.

With video content come some unique strategic considerations, including the amount of video watched on mobile devices. Google reports that 75% of adults watch video on mobile devices, and 7 in 10 users default to watching video horizontally, in contrast to Instagram's vertical video styles. With YouTube's presence as a powerful search engine, Google also reported that 68% of YouTube users watched a video to assist in making a purchase decision.

Video on YouTube can be preproduced in formats up to 4K resolution, and creators can show live video as well. YouTube video can also be produced inside the YouTube Studio, which is a section of a user's account that provides significant analytics and performance metrics, as well as an area to edit footage the user wishes to produce. With such a broad audience worldwide, consideration should also be given to language translation if analytics prove it to be necessary and to accessibility standards for those who might not be able to see or hear content.

YouTube has its own sport channel, which has more than 75 million subscribers, with content generated automatically by the site's video discovery algorithms. Playlists included on the channel include top stories, highlights, popular videos, live sport, upcoming livestreams, and channels dedicated to a wide variety of content specific to sport, such as Ultimate Fighting Championship (UFC), tennis, and horse racing.

The platform continues to be very shareable, primarily because of YouTube's relationship with Google, which allows anything put into the world's largest search engine to return information on videos that exist on YouTube. Within the video player on YouTube, users have the opportunity to choose playback speeds and video quality based on capacity for data or the strength of an Internet connection. Also embedded in the player are options for closed-captioning and for changing the size of the video player from full screen to other modes that allow smaller versions of the video. Users can also like videos or show disagreement with some part of the video using a thumbs-up or thumbs-down button, can share video via a link, and can embed code that allows the video player to appear in a website. Below the player, as a video is playing in regular mode, appears a list of related videos that YouTube produces through its video algorithms.

Users who produce content on YouTube must be wary; use of copyrighted material can result in the removal of the video and the user ultimately being banned from posting future content. Producers may also choose three different settings for displaying the video. The first and most popular setting is public, which allows the video to be viewed by anyone on the user's page and also to appear in search results on YouTube. The second setting is unlisted, which allows only those with a dedicated link to the video to be able to view it, with the video not appearing in YouTube's search results. The third setting is private, which allows only the producer to view the video in the player on the site. Producers should take into consideration which setting might work best for content being produced for the platform and which public or publics should ultimately see the content.

Strategic Considerations for Social Media Use

The use of social media by sport organizations has long moved past the stage of being a fad. In chapter 2, a discussion of Grunig's two-way symmetrical

Dude Perfect's YouTube Trick Shot to Subscription Success

In 2009, a group of college friends who all played high school basketball and went to college at Texas A&M University decided to upload a video on YouTube full of basketball trick shots. Included in the original video were shots that ranged from bouncing the ball off the roof of a house to placing a goal in the back of a truck—shots that most people could only imagine sinking. Since that video, Dude Perfect has earned one of YouTube's most significant presences, with more than 46 million subscribers and nearly 9 billion video views in 10 years on the platform (Larson, 2019).

Attracting 46 million subscribers put Dude Perfect into the top 10 of all YouTube accounts and very near the top sport-specific account, belonging to WWE (World Wrestling Entertainment), which boasts 49 million followers and

Dude Perfect's self-grown, family-friendly brand has used YouTube to help produce the visibility necessary to secure lucrative sponsorship deals and a variety of traveling shows and worldwide tours.

Logan Bowles/PGA TOUR

ranks as the seventh-most viewed channel on the platform. While Dude Perfect produces a variety of video content that includes anything from comedy routines on stereotypes to videos featuring one member of the group dressed as a panda, the most popular content on the channel continues to be videos of battles between group members and trick shots. A video titled "Ping Pong Trick Shots 3," published in 2017, has been viewed more than 230 million times, and videos featuring the group members battling each other in shark fishing and with bubble wrap have each achieved more than 60 million views.

Those numbers have helped the group attract sponsorships. Secondary ticketing market merchant StubHub has sponsored trick shot videos and provided a partnership for users to sign up to win a trip to watch a National Football League (NFL) football game with the group. The association works well for StubHub, too, as Dude Perfect members have also taken their trick shot wizardry on the road to large indoor and outdoor venues.

Both Bass Pro Shops and Cabela's sponsored a video on camping stereotypes produced by Dude Perfect that was already viewed more than 13 million times within the same week it was posted in September 2019. Hasbro Gaming signed on to sponsor a helicopter battleship battle that in the comments included links to Hasbro games that could be purchased at Target. The audience Dude Perfect brings in can undoubtedly attract the attention of plenty of advertisers, but the group continues to stay on-brand with their public relations goals as well. The group also did a stunt-driving video that partnered with auto brand Fiat that produced more than 23 million views on YouTube.

In a 2015 appearance on ABC's late-night series *Nightline*, the group described the importance of maintaining a family atmosphere in their videos and in their shows when on tour. Dude Perfect had been approached by alcohol brands about partnerships but has maintained that a family-friendly audience is their aim (Chang, Kapetaneas, & Valiente, 2015). The group has also been able to create a presence on other social media platforms and even sell merchandise through the group's website and has evolved into one of the most popular YouTube accounts on the planet. And it all started with a group of friends having fun making a trick shot video in someone's backyard.

communication model provided the groundwork for how social media can provide a strategic communication benefit to sport organizations. Grunig's representation of the symmetrical benefits of dialogue between the organization and its publics makes social media an imperative element of overall strategic public relations management.

Keeping Grunig's symmetrical model in mind is critical for those coordinating social media efforts for a sport organization. Grunig stated in 2013 that organizations "should think of digital media as a way of identifying problems, publics, and issues that require the attention of strategic managers and as a way of engaging in dialogue with publics" (para. 4). Kapoor and colleagues (2018) agreed, in a summary of social media research that suggested organizations should not ignore the opportunity for social media engagement because of a potentially negative impact on a company's image. Plainly stated, a sport organization not using social media as a public relations tactic to inform and engage key publics fails to reach its full potential to accomplish organizational communication objectives and build relationships with a variety of key stakeholders.

Cawley (2018) defined **strategic social media management** as "the process of creating, scheduling, analyzing, and engaging with content posted on social media platforms" (para. 1). Of primary concern to sport public relations professionals is **social media content**, or the information the organization wishes to use to accomplish public relations objectives via social media. This content can come in a variety of formats, including text, photos, videos, and motion graphics.

Content shared on social media should be related to engaging the audience by one or more of three action steps:

1. Giving audience members something to think
2. Giving them something to feel
3. Giving them something to do

Focusing on those three broad goals—to cause the audience that the organization wishes to communicate with to think, feel, or do something, or any combination of the three—and understanding that audience, can provide a simple overview of the complex strategy behind the use of social media. The following is a list of critical strategic considerations for sport public relations professionals to consider as they develop content:

- Planning
- Alignment
- Voice or tone
- Social listening
- Social media tools
- Evaluation metrics

Planning

As discussed in chapter 2, planning is a key element of strategic public relations management and the management of campaigns. The planning stage should take into consideration a variety of factors, including short- and long-term communication goals, opportunities to engage key publics in the conversation using elements of the PESO model, and the calendar.

Social media can accomplish a variety of public relations goals. That knowledge should be built into planning how social media should be used. Social media is an excellent place for organizations to conduct short-term campaigns. Using hashtags and time-specific specialized content are good examples of engaging in short-term conversations to satisfy public relations objectives. Short-term goals may be to create awareness about specific initiatives (e.g., color-based games like "Think Pink!" for breast cancer awareness or "whiteout" or "blackout") or to exploit an upcoming rivalry game.

As the Houston Astros began their World Series run in 2017, the organization used the hashtag #EarnHistory to connect and engage fans on social media with the emotional punch of potentially bringing the franchise's first world championship home. This particular short-term goal of engaging the fan base was part of a larger social media push by the organization, which hosts a Social Media Night each season for fans connected to the organization on social media platforms like Facebook, Twitter, and Instagram. The building of this connection to fans via social media is important to note, as the Astros were later found to have cheated during that World Series championship season, and were forced to use social media as a form of crisis communication (see chapter 8). The connections made through social media efforts during times of success are crucial to how easily an organization can manage communication tactics on social media over the course of a crisis when it hits.

The organization's calendar plays a key role in planning. The calendar includes not only events but also promotional efforts, television schedules and information, and stories to share throughout the season (and in the off-season) as they develop. A social media calendar is a helpful way to keep content on task and organized for peak impact in obtaining public relations objectives. A simple Google search can yield a variety of templates that can be used to develop a social media calendar, but most include the platforms the organization owns, the type of content to be posted (video, text, photo, etc.), the subject of the content (player introduction, Q&A, photos and information used to promote an upcoming game, sharing of influential media posts, etc.), and a time period when content will be posted (morning, lunch, etc.). Included in some models are connections between content and public relations objectives, as well as owners of specific content pieces (specific employees noted using their initials, or particular departments within the organization) for accountability. Table 3.1 provides an example of what the calendar could look like.

Issues such as injuries, suspension, personnel changes, and so on create the need to be able to adjust to specific situations. Still, planning content ahead of time offers the opportunity for the organization to engage with key publics strategically.

Alignment

In the previous discussion on planning, the idea of tying content to specific public relations goals and objectives was presented. It is also key to align the organization's social media goals with the overall goals of the organization as a whole.

If the organization is focused on revenue generation, then social media goals should be centered around assisting with increasing revenue for the organization. Perhaps content can support marketing efforts to generate new leads through sign-ups or click-through links back to the organization's website.

A smaller sport organization with a desire to build its brand at a broader level can be supported on social media with goals that increase awareness. With content that can easily be shared, and with the fan base spreading the word via retweets or shares, social media can assist in the accomplishment of the organizational goal. Social media is a tactic that can be used as part of the overall communication message. Utilizing the shared element of the PESO model helps organizations accomplish broader goals by communicating messages that shape attitudes

and ultimately change behaviors to move the brand forward.

Voice and Tone

Each brand has a persona. Each individual within the public relations staff has a particular persona as well. When strategically planning the use of social media, the **social media voice** of the brand should be unified, and the tone should be aligned across all of the social media platforms. Communication should be consistent with the personality of the brand and the culture. Under Armour's use of the hashtag #IWILL is a good example of staying consistent with the organization's branding and reflecting the organization's culture, as the company produced numerous commercials of athletes claiming, "I will protect this house."

Also included in voice and tone is a consideration of the organization's audience on social media. **Demographics** include information on audience age, gender, and location. **Psychographics** include information on the behaviors of fans or followers. An analysis of both gives organizations a better sense of their audience on particular social networking sites.

Demographics

Facebook's insights provide this information for the platform in a graphical format. Included in insights (which are accessible by someone with administrative access to the Facebook page while that person is on the organization's page) is information about the age, gender, country, city, and languages of those who are following the page. Twitter's analytics provide statistics on the gender and location of followers but do not include age. Additional demographic categories that Twitter's analytics does provide information on include estimated home value (using data from partnerships) as well as household income. YouTube analytics (provided in YouTube Studio) give information on gender, age, and country of origin as well. Business profiles on Instagram also have access to some demographic data via the platform's insights (individual users do not have access to insights for their own pages). Gender, age, and location are the primary demographic data available to organizations on Instagram.

Psychographics

Psychographic data on social media followers includes a wide variety of categories based on the behavior of individuals who are connected to the organization's platforms. Facebook's insights provide information on when content was viewed

Table 3.1 Social Media Calendar Example

	Subject/topic	Content	Timing	Owner	Objectives
Facebook	• Rivalry Week amp up • #BeatState hashtag engagement	• Photo of 1986 game • Throwing back to the Miracle in '86 #BeatState	• Tuesday morning 10 a.m. post (leading up to media availability) • Engage conversation through noon	• Strat comm (JRD) • Follow-up comments from multiple staff with #BeatState	• To increase use of #BeatState hashtag • To create excitement and engagement surrounding Rivalry Week
	• Remaining tickets for Saturday	• GIF of rowdy fans • Limited tickets remain for Saturday night! #BeatState • Emojis with ticketing phone and web link to single-game tickets	• Two posts each day (scheduled 11 a.m. and 5:30 p.m., until tickets are gone)	• Strategic communications and ticket office (AGR will work with tickets on updates)	• To create awareness of remaining tickets and purchase urgency • To increase use of #BeatState hashtag
Twitter	• Top 25 tweet	• Retweet of coach's Top 25 tweet • Movin' on up to No. 8 #BeatState	• Monday approximately 1 p.m. (likely will be No. 8 but adjust accordingly)	• Strat comm (AGR)	• To increase awareness of national ranking • To increase use of #BeatState hashtag
	• Rivalry week amp up	• Amp up video • We're ready for #BeatState week!	• 4:30 p.m., Thursday (before coach's radio show)	• Strat comm (LCL) & digital (BDC)	• To create excitement and engagement surrounding Rivalry Week • To increase use of #BeatState hashtag

or engaged with by fans (including the time of day and the day of the week). Also included are how long videos are viewed and where the organization's fans are coming from (website link, search engine, a follower's news feed, etc.). Twitter's analytics provides a variety of psychographic data, including interests of followers, which wireless carriers followers use, and even consumer goods purchases through a data partner (these are estimates that come from the partnership and should not be taken as 100% valid information). YouTube provides information on where subscriber traffic is coming from (internal or external to YouTube) and the average duration of views of videos on the page.

Instagram analytics for business profiles provide information on when followers are viewing the page and posts and which times and days of the week followers are most active.

Once organizations have better information on their social networking sites' audiences, the accounts have a better opportunity to align the voice and tone of the platform to the overall voice and tone of the organization's public relations efforts. Consistency between social networking sites and knowing the audience on those sites can successfully keep brands on target with their global public relations efforts.

Authenticity is another characteristic of social media voice and tone that is important to engage an audience on social networking sites successfully. Content should be genuine and not just a cookie-cutter copy of the latest fad and craze on another social networking platform. Sport public relations professionals should remember that those following the account already have some level of identification and commitment to the organization (and that connection is not always positive). Knowing who your audience is allows you to build authentic relationships with followers right where they are in terms of interaction, and to accomplish a wide variety of outcomes, from building awareness to changing behaviors. These outcomes are not achieved if fans feel the relationship is not authentic or the presence of the account is not genuine. If a high-profile coach has a Twitter account but has members of the public relations team posting information throughout a game, the authors of the content can attach their initials to the end of the tweet. Doing so signals to the audience that someone besides the coach is tweeting, and the words are not coming directly from the coach on a sideline during a game. Another step toward authenticity includes social networking site verification, which usually involves adding a direct phone number and an e-mail address and verifying the identity of the organization with social networking site representatives through one of those methods. This verification represents itself differently by platform, but a checkmark has become a somewhat universal representation of a verified account.

Social Listening

Part of creating a two-way dialogue with key publics includes listening to fans and followers of the organization's social networking sites. Paying attention to engagement by fans of an organization's social networking site can accomplish a variety of public relations goals. Amaresan (2018) defined **social listening** as "the monitoring of the brand's social media channels for any customer feedback and direct mentions of your brand" (para. 4). Social listening is more than just collecting analytics on posts. It also includes dialogue with key publics that ultimately meets their needs. Listening to how fans are commenting about entry policies, game-day experiences, and even promotional efforts are key takeaways a public relations staff can deliver to important internal stakeholders.

Reactions to entry policies might include how the public is adjusting to a new "clear bag" policy for personal items brought into the stadium. If fans are responding on social networking sites with confusion, a stronger public relations effort might need to be made to assist in dispelling misinformation or rumors that can quickly spread in new and confusing periods for fans. The ability of a sport public relations professional to engage in this dialogue promptly could allow the information to flow forward to key internal stakeholders for clarification and potentially an adjustment to the policy if needed. Fans are also an organization's first line of defense in the stands; fans can spot potential trouble areas and may offer comments about things impacting their game-day experiences inside the stadium as well. The amount of traffic a post gets about a bobblehead night might provide valuable insight into whether a marketing team needs to adjust expectations for how quickly they will run out of product on a promotional evening. Social media has allowed sport public relations professionals to become the central hub of information, interaction, and engagement with key external stakeholders. That information should be passed on to crucial internal personnel with the ability to clarify issues and decision-making authority to make adjustments if needed.

A majority of social listening can be accomplished on each particular social networking site by engaging in conversation and reading comments that receive a lot of interaction from other fans. However, a variety of tools are available to assist in social listening, primarily if the organization uses third-party social media management software like HubSpot, Hootsuite, or Sprout Social.

Social Media Tools

A variety of tools exist to assist in the creation of engaging social media content. From graphic design to motion graphic creation, these tools can help a sport public relations professional or staff member become more proficient with branding content, save time, and produce a consistent look and feel for interactions on varying social networking sites.

A simple and affordable tool for sport public relations professionals to use in the creation of social media content is Adobe Spark. The web-based platform provides a wide variety of storytelling templates that can produce web pages, social media graphics, and even short videos. Organizations that choose premium subscriptions can also create their brand inside the platform, including colors, fonts, and logos that can be used by anyone with access to the account. The platform is a web-based "light" version of the popular Adobe products Photoshop and InDesign, and require very little knowledge of either to produce engaging content that is consistently on-brand for the organization. For organizations that do not have the budget to access premium Spark services, a free version of the platform is still available and accessible with the creation of an Adobe account. The free version does not include branding tools but does include a wide variety of templates that can save public relations professionals extensive amounts of time in the production of social media content.

The web page creation tool's highly graphical interface can be used to create one-off sites for particular events, to display photo galleries in a vibrant format, or to produce other public relations outcomes like campaigns or year-in-review documents. The social media templates are designed explicitly for social networking sites' dimensions for graphics (including an Instagram post, YouTube video thumbnail, Facebook cover photo, etc.). There are also templates for flyers, newsletters, advertisements, and infographics. The short video templates include interchangeable graphics based on the type of video the professional chooses to create (game teaser video, campaign highlight video, recap video, etc.).

Canva is another free content design tool available online. Canva comes with a variety of templates used for posts on social networking sites, infographics, and an online library of stock photo images that can be used in a variety of ways. Sport public relations professionals should always be aware of copyright regulations when using free stock photos, as many images are free for download and use but cannot be redistributed or sold in any form or fashion. Many sites have varying licensing levels for downloading stock images and videos, so social media curators should use due diligence to protect the organization from copyright infringement liability. Canva also includes the ability to edit pictures, and professional paid versions, similar to Spark, give the user the ability to create and maintain brand logos, colors, and text.

TweetDeck is an application featured by Twitter that allows users to create tweets, view multiple time lines, and even conduct social listening through searches using key terms or hashtags. The ability to manage multiple Twitter accounts on one app makes TweetDeck an excellent tool for sport public relations professionals who may be charged with managing multiple accounts at one time. The tweet creation tool allows the user to attach images and GIFs to text and to schedule tweets in advance. The ability to add multiple columns, including activity (which is a report of what the accounts you follow are doing in terms of likes, follows, etc.), hashtag searches, and multiple users, make TweetDeck an excellent application for managing an organization's Twitter presence.

Tagboard is a powerful social listening tool that allows users to search for a particular topic, term, and hashtag to see online conversations involving a diverse array of topics. Tagboard will incorporate posts from a variety of social networking sites and has features that allow integration of in-venue video boards as well as websites. Google Trends is another social listening tool that enables users to search for trending topics online. The site allows users to monitor specific keywords and even provides a "Year in Search" feature that gives information about trending topics, news, athletes, and more for a particular year. Google Trends provides users the opportunity to search by country or globally.

Link-shortening tools like Bitly, TinyURL, and Hootsuite's Ow.ly are useful for managing social media accounts as well. These tools allow users to take very long links to websites and boil them down to just a few characters, which take up far less space in a social networking site environment. While Facebook does not have character restrictions on posts, Twitter does, and a link that can be shortened from 50 or 60 characters to 10 to 14 characters can make a vast difference in posting content.

Sport public relations professionals can access an array of free and paid tools that can assist in a variety of ways. The key is to learn what the tool can do and how it can best be incorporated into an overall social media management strategy. A simple web engine search may provide a list of new tools available to users to enhance their social media content creation, social listening, or analysis of social media effectiveness.

Social Media Metrics

Like all public relations tactics, the use of social media by sport organizations should be monitored and evaluated for effectiveness and impact. While the complete return on investment (ROI) in a tweet may not be able to be formulated, a variety of evaluative measurements exist to determine overall social media effectiveness. No one metric should be deemed a global evaluative measurement, because what sport public relations professionals are measuring should be guided by what they wish to know, and how that information aligns with the goals and objectives of the organization and its public relations efforts. Ultimately, social media and overall organizational goals will determine the type of metrics that are important to measure.

Each of the four social networking sites (Facebook, Twitter, Instagram, and YouTube) previously discussed have varying internal analytics tools embedded within the platform. Seiter (2018) described social media analytics as fitting into six different categories:

1. Activity
2. Reach
3. Engagement
4. Acquisition
5. Conversion
6. Retention and advocacy

Depending on the organization's goals, a varying combination of these categories should be used to provide information on the effectiveness of social media content and strategy.

Seiter defines **social media activity** as output or the amount of content produced by the public relations professional. That could include the number of statistical infographics created to showcase a particular team or the number of Instagram posts per month during the season. Tracking the numbers of varying content by type (post, photo, video, etc.) may be helpful as well in ensuring dynamic engagement with the audience. Seiter comments that the amount of money spent producing content should be factored into the tracking of activity.

The second category of metrics includes measurement of the audience and the potential audience, which Seiter defines as **reach**. Included in these metrics are post reach and impression, which are the estimated numbers of people who do see and could see content, respectively. If a new youth sport facility wishes to use social media to grow awareness of the brand, the total number of fans or followers within the specified time would be monitored for growth. The organization may also wish to track fan sentiment, or the percentage of fans or followers who react negatively, positively, or neutrally to mentions of the brand.

Shleyner (2019) defined engagement metrics as the measurement of how people interact with content produced. These metrics are action-based, functional measures of content seeking to give an audience something to do. The average engagement rate is one metric to track in this category specifi-

cally. **Average engagement rate** is the number of engagement actions (such as a retweet or like) on a social network post, divided by the number of total followers of the page or organization on a particular social network. As an example, envision world soccer giant FC Barcelona posting on Twitter a photo of one of Lionel Messi's most memorable goals in the matchup in advance of the team's upcoming El Clásico match against bitter rivals Real Madrid. This photo is intended to stir a memory and give the audience something to feel. The average engagement rate would be calculated by the number of followers who reacted to the post (on Twitter that would be the number of likes plus replies plus retweets) divided by the number of followers the team has on Twitter.

Acquisition metrics are focused on the building of relationships and are especially crucial for sport public relations professionals in proving the value of social media efforts. The amount of traffic that a social networking site can drive back to a website is one example of an acquisition metric. Seiter (2018) describes that many of these metrics can come from Google Analytics and may also involve other elements such as the number of new subscribers to a blog after it is linked to on a social networking site, the number of people who signed up for e-mail based on a specific post, and so on. Acquisition metrics are a good measurement of posts that give an audience something to do.

Conversion metrics are most closely related to marketing metrics, such as sales and revenue generated by social media efforts. These metrics are essential for public relations professionals who may be managing social media efforts as proof that those efforts do play a part in converting a fan into an active consumer, which ties directly to marketing and revenue generation efforts.

The final category of metrics is **retention metrics**. These measure things such as satisfaction rates (which can be collected through a poll). Also in this category would be the number of and quality of reviews left by fans or followers (these metrics are especially useful with Facebook). Another metric is the number of positive testimonials collected through social media (these may come in comments, mentions, or even via direct message).

New metrics for social media effectiveness seem to appear each day. The ultimate guides to what should be measured are the organization's goals, the alignment of public relations goals and social media goals, and any other variables that provide information about the effectiveness of a particular social media strategy or tactic.

Careers in Social Media Management

One area of growing popularity for careers in public relations or marketing is the strategic management of aspects of the overall social media efforts for a sport organization. A wide variety of roles exist that require a wide range of skill sets. Still, ultimately, the number of opportunities to work directly in social media content creation continues to rise.

TeamWork Online is an excellent source of job information related to social media positions. At one point in 2019, there were 34 posted openings at a variety of sport organizational levels, including jobs at Major League Baseball, the National Football League, the New Hampshire Motor Speedway, Minor League Baseball, professional minor league hockey, sport venues, and governing sport bodies like USA Baseball and the United States Specialty Sports Association. Positions included internships and full-time roles as a social media producer, social media content specialist, and social media editor.

A content analysis of job openings produced a list of various skill sets necessary to work in social media production, either as an intern or as a full-time member of a public relations or marketing staff. While some differences in specific requirements and responsibilities existed, many job descriptions looked similar at a full-time and internship level. The review of full-time postings made it clear that to work in social media, applicants would need some experience managing organizational social media accounts and the ability to stay current on digital trends (or, as one position description described it, "whatever the next big thing the kids will be into by the time this position is filled").

Be Your Own Media

Conduct some research on the top five players on the LPGA (Ladies Professional Golf Association) Tour Official Money list for the last year. Then, find as many of them on social media as possible (including multiple social networking or media-sharing sites such as Facebook and Twitter). Are the social media efforts of these athletes consistent across platforms? Is there room for improvement? If so, what suggestions would you make? How does the presence of these players differ from that of other athletes on social media you may follow? Pay special attention to the content the athletes produce on Twitter. How much of the content is video? Photos? Branded content associated with sponsors that the athlete retweets? Do you find this particular mix to be effective for the athlete's overall brand?

An analysis of internship positions resulted in much more vague information, with several job descriptions requiring strong writing and interviewing skills. It appeared that social media interns would be active participants in the development of social media content under the guidance of full-time personnel responsible for the scheduling and analytics of that content.

Table 3.2 summarizes responsibilities and required skills to maintain an internship or full-time job in the sport public relations field of social media. It can be expected that these requirements and responsibilities will continue to develop and adapt with new trends and platforms.

Table 3.2 Social Media Job and Internship Responsibilities and Qualifications

Full-time position responsibilities	Internship responsibilities
Coordinate planning and development of social media content on a variety of platforms	Provide coverage of games, practices, and events
Work with multiple stakeholder groups (staff, vendors, media)	Conduct interviews to develop written and video content for social media distribution
Ensure content across platforms is on brand	Monitor and engage in social conversations regarding the brand
Stay current on developing social media trends and best practices	Assist in the development of social media content
Assist in collecting social media analytics across platforms	Assist in tracking social media analytics
Full-time position qualifications	**Internship qualifications**
Bachelor's degree in related field, and one to five years of experience in social media	Current student pursuing degree or receiving academic credit for experience
Excellent organizational skills	Experience with social media platforms and tools
Experience with design and graphical software (Adobe Photoshop, Adobe Illustrator)	Experience with software such as Microsoft Office
Experience with video and motion graphics editing software (Final Cut, Adobe Premiere, After Effects)	Some experience with image and video editing software preferred
Strong writing skills	Strong written and verbal communication skills
Ability to work independently and in teams	Ability to maintain a flexible schedule and handle multiple projects at the same time
Knowledge of the sport (organization, statistics, etc.)	Basic knowledge of the sport

SUMMARY

The advancement of social media as a communication tool has arguably impacted the sport public relations professional more than anything else over the past 10 to 15 years. The ability to instantly connect, engage, and inform broad publics with a simple post on a social network brings immense opportunity and a set of challenges that force professionals to adapt tactics constantly. Social media fits into the shared element of the PESO model described in earlier chapters. What makes social media so powerful, however, is the connection it can make to the other aspects of the model, with the central authority that builds relationships between brands and the fans who love them. Social networking sites allow users to create a profile, develop a connection with other users they share a connection with, and then connect with the interactions that those connections and other users make within the system. Facebook, Twitter, Instagram, and YouTube continue to be the dominant players among social networks and media-sharing networks. Still, they are not alone, and sport public relations professionals must continue to have an ear to the ground to be aware of the next significant development.

The development of media content continues to be at the forefront of developing relationships with fans and followers online, with consistent engagement a key concern. The two-way communication method of social media should be used to enhance online relationships with fans strategically, but comes with a variety of critical considerations. Content should include one or more action steps of giving fans something to think, feel, or do, with planning, alignment, voice and tone, social listening, tools to create social media, and evaluation metrics all factoring into strategic social media management. Sport public relations professionals must continue to stay current on social media metrics and ensure the organization is measuring the right things to determine successful outcomes, which are tied directly to the public relations goals of the organization. Finally, this chapter described a new line of careers that combine sport public relations and social media, as organizations continue to move toward positioning themselves in the new digital environment.

LEARNING ACTIVITIES

1. Compare the content of a variety of sport organization social media accounts (e.g., NFL franchise, Major League Baseball [MLB] franchise, National Collegiate Athletic Association [NCAA] Division I institution, National Association of Intercollegiate Athletics [NAIA] institution, fitness center, sporting goods manufacturer). Based on the content, what appear to be potential public relations goals of the content posted?

2. Compare the design of social media posts for a variety of sport organizations (e.g., NFL franchise, MLB franchise, NCAA Division I institution, NAIA institution, fitness center, sporting goods manufacturer). What themes do you see that are similar among the posts, and what differences are immediately recognizable? Discuss whether or not these posts appear to be on-brand for the organization.

3. Conduct a sentiment analysis of your favorite sport team's Facebook page. Is sentiment in the comments by fans generally positive? Neutral? Negative? Determine one step the organization could take to move the conversation forward in a more positive way.

4. Determine the average engagement rate for five tweets on your institution's athletics department Twitter account. Are the numbers consistent? Discuss potential reasons why the numbers are or are not consistent based on recent tweets by the organization.

Engaging Key Publics via Other Forms of Digital Media

After reading this chapter, students should be able to

- articulate the purposes and capabilities of websites in the context of public relations;
- describe general approaches to website design, development, and management;
- identify ways in which websites can advance relationships with various stakeholders;
- illustrate how blogs, podcasts, virtual fan communities, and video can assist in accomplishing key public relations objectives; and
- characterize Internet-related challenges for sport public relations professionals.

These are the key terms discussed in this chapter:

- blogging
- bounce rate
- conversion rate
- domain name
- e-commerce
- intranet
- key performance indicators (KPIs)
- mobile application
- podcasting

- score bug
- search engine optimization (SEO)
- site structure
- spam
- viral marketing
- virtual communication community
- website accessibility
- website service provider

Computer technology has had an extraordinary influence on society in numerous ways. One particular advancement that has had a profound effect on organizations of all types is the Internet. While the previous chapter discussed the impact of social media, technological advancements in digital communication do not stop there. The Internet, manifested through websites, podcasts, and video, provides apparent advantages for many organizational functions, including public relations, and the benefits grow as access becomes more prevalent and technologies progress. You may even be reading this chapter in an e-format while connected to the Internet. Much of daily life is now related to our growing connections online.

World Internet Users Statistics (internetworldstats .com) reported that 94.6% of the population of North America uses the Internet and that over 4.5 billion people worldwide use the Internet, which is nearly 60% of the world's population in 2020. Internet access has become a routine part of our existence, and wireless technology and mobile technology now allow for virtually constant Internet access anytime, anywhere. Technology has also created the capacity for us to experience a nearly continuous state of connection to one another. The relentless and rapid changes in technology have created unique opportunities and daunting challenges for public relations.

It would be difficult to imagine an organization not having a web-based presence, as websites in particular allow sport public relations practitioners to accomplish a variety of critical strategic purposes. Organizational websites are important channels for the distribution of messages to many of an organization's key publics. These websites not only carry the organization's message to a variety of interested parties, but also allow the organization to have a significant amount of control over the message. Many news outlets now will quote an organization's website as the "source" of the news they are reporting, better allowing the organization to have ownership of that news (and the narrative) instead of a news outlet being "the first to report." This shift in sourcing has allowed public relations practitioners to use organizational websites to better shape both the information being presented to a variety of publics and the identity of the organization as the accurate, reliable authority of that information. Given the potential of a website to quickly deliver messages to a mass audience and provide public relations professionals with a high degree of control over that message, organizations must spend the time and resources to strategically develop and enhance their online presence.

In previous chapters, the focus has been on public relation's role in building relationships with the different publics of sport organizations. Chapter 3 addressed how technology can be used to enhance these relationships in the form of social media. The emphasis of this chapter will be on the website as a tool for advancing public relations efforts; the rise of blogs, podcasts, and virtual communication communities; and the importance of video for building connections with key publics online. Public relations professionals must always be alert to technological advancements that alter the tools and subsequently the practice of public relations. Websites are used for a variety of purposes and can play different marketing and public relations roles for sport organizations. Websites have become organizational assets, and care must be taken to construct them well and utilize them to their fullest potential.

The opening section of this chapter discusses the capabilities of the Internet for public relations and outlines the purposes of organizational websites. The second section considers general approaches to website development. The third section addresses the ways that sport organizations can use digital media to communicate effectively with various stakeholder groups, including members of the media, sponsors, employees, investors, customers, and donors. The next section describes the development of web-based tools such as blogging and podcasts, and the chapter concludes with strategic considerations for sport public relations professionals as they consider the use of new media.

Digital Media Use in Sport Public Relations

The use of the Internet, especially in the form of organizational websites, provides a continuous link with organizational stakeholders that never sleeps and that offers an opportunity for a variety of interactive exchanges. For public relations, websites provide a platform for building and sustaining relationships and present an opportunity for a public relations professional to accomplish a wide variety of overall public relations goals.

Websites have evolved from being primarily information repositories to being interactive centers of information and commerce. They serve a variety of audiences and perform a variety of functions, including education, entertainment, and engagement. As a communication tool, websites (and the more recent addition of social media) have completely changed not only what sport public relations professionals do, but also how they go about trying to communicate with key publics.

Many sport organizational websites incorporate several purposes into their function. As an example, many professional sport team sites primarily serve purposes of e-commerce (purchase of tickets and merchandise), information (statistics, rosters, directions to the stadium), and entertainment (video and audio clips, pictures, livestreaming of game audio and video). Although these purposes have the highest priority, the site content is likely to reflect other purposes as well. Websites can often include explanation of the rules of the game (education); links to other sites or features such as a staff blog, podcast, coach's show, or sign-up forms (web portals); and community service events and activities (community building and engagement). Websites for other types of sport organizations contain content that reflects different priorities. A local golf or tennis club may use its website primarily as an electronic newsletter to inform its members, tell viewers about upcoming events, take online reservations, describe the facility's amenities, and provide directions to the club as well as contact information for staff.

From a public relations perspective, most of the publics of any organization can be served by websites in some way, and the benefits of a well-maintained website can serve to enhance the organization's relationships with those publics. There are seven key public relations benefits to an organization continuing to enhance its digital presence with thoughtful production of a website:

- Global reach
- Speed and user choice
- Support of multiple content types
- Support of transactions
- Computational functions
- Interactive capability
- Adaptability and customizability

The extraordinary scope of the web may expand the size of various publics or provide constituents much easier access to information about the organization. The scope of content included on a typical professional team's website will accommodate even the most demanding site visitor. A sporting goods firm may experience quantum leaps in its customer base and revenue with a well-developed and interactive Internet presence. In 2017, the total sporting goods industry revenue was $45.1 billion in the United States, with an incredible $16.9 billion of that coming from electronic and mail-order shopping (O'Connell, 2020). The speed with which information can be disseminated and accessed is another attractive aspect of the Internet. In the context of public relations, this speed is particularly appealing because stakeholder satisfaction is often related to timeliness and convenience.

The ability to support different types of content allows organizations to build sites with information that goes beyond text to include audio and video along with graphics and animation. Virtual views allow ticket buyers to select a seat based on desired sight lines, and often the website will now allow buyers to download tickets to their mobile devices and use those for entry into the facility. Webcams can be used to generate excitement about progress on construction of new facilities. Streaming audio and video turn computers and various mobile communication devices into radios or televisions and provide access to games that are simply not available through traditional media in real time. For example, a grandmother can now hear her grandson's high school basketball game on the Internet even though she lives in a small town 1,200 miles (2,000 kilometers) away. College athletics programs may be able to persuade recruits to move farther from home because all their games are streamed on the school website, or through an athletics conference streaming rights agreement, for athletes' families to follow.

Websites also provide a platform for transactional activity. The extraordinary growth of e-commerce demonstrates the capability of the Internet in this regard. **E-commerce**, also called electronic commerce, is "the buying and selling of goods and services, or the transmitting of funds or data, over an electronic network, primarily the Internet" (Rouse, n.d., para 1). In 2017, e-commerce produced approximately $2.3 trillion in sales, and that amount is likely to double by 2021. The transactional capability of the Internet encompasses everything from purchasing an authentic jersey to ordering a new set of golf clubs to submitting a bid for an appealing piece of memorabilia. This capacity extends to recording and processing information. One example is the fantasy leagues popular in many sports. Online fantasy sites provide computational services to manipulate salary data, statistical information, and player transactions in determining fantasy winners and losers. Two other emerging areas of e-commerce related to sport are online sports betting and esports. The U.S. Supreme Court voted to lift the federal ban on sports betting in 2018, and numerous states have since passed legislation to legalize sports wagering. One thing standing in the way of widespread online betting is the Wire Act of 1961. U.S. President Obama's administration felt that the act did not apply to gambling, but President Trump's administration had a differing opinion, setting the stage for a future political battle about the legality of sports betting online (Licata, 2019). Russ (2019) produced a Reuters report on esports and projected that advertising, sponsorship, and media rights for multiplayer competitive video gaming could bring in more than $1 billion in revenue over the course of a year. At the organizational level, online fan stores have allowed sport teams to capitalize on the e-commerce frenzy. Many professional and college teams have partnered with online retail giant Fanatics, which expected to generate more than $2.5 billion in revenue in 2019 (Murphy, 2019).

But perhaps the most significant influence of websites and digital organizational media from a public relations perspective is the prolific growth in interactive capability that not only connects organizations with their constituents in many ways but also connects constituents with one another. As discussed in chapter 3, social networking sites (e.g., Facebook and Twitter) and media-sharing networks (e.g., YouTube and Instagram) have created extraordinary opportunities for connecting with various publics and sharing information with them on a scale that was unimaginable only a few years ago. The connections established through these sites have the potential to create bonds and engage the most actively involved constituents. The development of Internet-related communication tools like social media and organizational websites has become an essential activity in brand management and control in an ever-growing environment of discourse. Lowes and Robillard (2018) found that social media has had an immense impact on the profession of journalism. Media professionals are no longer the gatekeepers of information as a result of the rise of social media and the ability for anyone to report breaking news, rather than access being limited to particular media outlets. This discovery and the continued rapidly development of technology should give sport public relations professionals pause. As discussed in chapter 3, social listening and monitoring the communication that is taking place may lead to quicker and more effective public relations responses. The PESO model discussed throughout this textbook shows the power of Internet-related communication tools as part of an overall public relations communication strategy. Most websites now include not only links to organizational social media accounts but also interactive windows where

the latest tweets and Facebook and Instagram posts can be seen in a designated area of the website, often in what was formerly used as advertising space on the right-hand side and bottom of related pages on the organization's official website. As was previously stated, but is worth repeating, an organization's website is no longer simply a repository for information; it is a highly interactive hub for a variety of communication-based activities.

As social media has developed, mobile technologies have also rapidly advanced. Our phones have now become devices we can use for a variety of interactions with other people and sport organizations. For example, the Los Angeles Football Club (LAFC) built stronger connections with fans by establishing mobile ordering through Apple's iMessage service in 2019. The program allows fans to scan a QR (quick response) code that opens menu options on their mobile devices from their seats in the stadium. Luong (2019) described the program, which positively increased social media buzz about the organization. Gone are the days of long lines at concession stands, as a **mobile application** can now give reports on the length of lines, where specialty items can be found, delivery or express pickup options, and in-venue promotions that can be sponsored (e.g., a click-through advertisement in the app for water from the designated bottled water provider in the venue). Game patrons can download these applications, an app that coordinates an audience color and light show, and a variety of other interactive experiences through an organization's website—all in the service of the public relations game of assessing and enhancing relationships with key stakeholders.

Finally, websites can be tailored to the needs of specific users. Websites can be programmed to greet users by name, direct them to parts of the site that users' history suggests they might be most interested in, and personalize the presentation of information that they have requested. For example, many sites now allow users to customize scoreboard tracking information to include only those games or players specified by the user, all while integrating fantasy sports, betting trends and lines, and click-through links to live broadcasts as well.

As website purposes and content continue to evolve and shape public relations efforts, new and expanded services for site visitors could enhance the speed and convenience with which interaction occurs on or off site. These user benefits can create opportunities for developing and enhancing relationships with an organization's publics and also connect those key publics to important information from a variety of internal groups and stakeholders (game-day policies, facility rental information, ticket information, etc.).

Website Development

The development of a website involves a range of considerations that determine its functional effectiveness and usefulness. Such considerations include goals and objectives, site provider and management, content, site design, site promotion, and site evaluation. These site planning and maintenance issues are addressed in the sections that follow. While the advancement of social media has been rapid in improving public relations efforts, Ryan (2016) explains that an organization's website is "the most valuable piece of digital real estate you will ever own" (p. 40). The importance of building and maintaining a high-functioning, highly interactive website cannot be overstated.

Goals and Objectives

As with any planning, website development involves establishing goals and objectives. This step is an essential part of producing a website that engenders loyalty and serves organizational needs. Ryan (2016) adds that a website should be the meeting of organizational business goals and the needs of the organization's key publics. The goals of a website are related to its purposes and to the audiences being targeted, and alignment in purpose is a key consideration for the sport public relations professional. If the primary purpose of the site is e-commerce, identifying the targeted consumers and developing goals relevant to that primary purpose will be necessary. Such goals would likely include desired revenue production, profitability, sales volume, market share, customer retention, and customer satisfaction. If the primary purpose is to provide entertainment, the target audience of that entertainment must be determined, and goals will be related to the frequency of use, length of use, and user satisfaction with the entertainment. Investing effort at this stage of website development will prove beneficial when it comes to evaluation because the foundation for assessment will already be in place.

Hosting and Management

The selection of a **website service provider** is an initial decision critical to the hosting and manage-ment of the organization's online presence. Service providers vary in how much they charge and what they offer to get a website created and running. Several issues should be discussed before deciding on a website service provider, or alternatively deciding to build the website in-house using the talent and resources already available. First and foremost, sport public relations managers should consider the amount of technical assistance they will need from the service provider. These providers will range in the expertise they offer, from simple outsourced management of a website already in place to the building of a website from scratch and management of the site after launch. Website service providers can offer anything from cookie-cutter style templates to unique designs and functions created specifically for an organization. The primary advantage to sport public relations professionals in the use of external website service providers is their technical expertise, which may not be readily available internally. Price is always a concern when dealing with big-ticket purchases from a public relations perspective, and the building and maintenance of a website using an external service provider firm may be one of the largest line-item expenses in the public relations budget. Some providers can charge an annual fee of $10,000 to $40,000 for website hosting and support, which does not include the day-to-day management of website content (Smith, 2016).

Some sport organizations outsource the entire design of their web pages to professional developers who may have more insight into the complexities of a multipurpose site. Many college athletics programs contract with website developers such as SIDEARM Sports or PrestoSports to construct their sites. Among the major collegiate conferences, SIDEARM Sports is one of the prominent service providers. Many sites also partner with other companies to provide live video and statistics services. The major professional sport leagues in North America maintain their own in-house website development. As an example, Major League Baseball (MLB) controls league and franchise websites through MLB Advanced Media, LP, and the National Basketball Association (NBA) does the same through NBA Media Ventures, LLC. The National Football League (NFL) and the National Hockey League (NHL) also have moved to more centralized and interactive versions of league and team websites. The NFL has an array of websites that include the NFL Network site, sites for special events (such as the Super Bowl and Pro Bowl games), sites directly related to fantasy football games, and geographically targeted sites such as NFL en Español.

As previously mentioned, cost is a major consideration that must be weighed in development and, later, management decisions. A study of college athletic administrators indicated that those who managed their websites in-house reported enjoying greater control over what information is posted on their sites, at what speed (Stoldt et al., 2001). Those who outsourced the management of their sites reported that the primary advantages of such an arrangement were the technical expertise offered by the service providers and the freeing up of department personnel because of the service. When selecting a service provider, sport managers should consider how effective the service's current sites are in terms of loading time and visual appeal as well as the currency of the information on those sites. A portfolio of strong sites currently in operation may be predictive of satisfactory service. Sport managers are encouraged to seek multiple bids from service providers, and check with already established partners as a reference regarding prices, technical support, and services that those site providers offer.

One additional development decision that rewards careful attention is the **domain name** or website address. Generally, the simpler the name is, the easier it will be to find the site; many sport organization domain names include more recognizable elements rather than just using "TeamName .com" (mgoblue.com—the official website of the University of Michigan—is a prime example of this tactic). The site name should reflect the team name or a universally common reference or connection to the organization to be most effective. Domain names are usually constructed with three elements: top-level domains, second-level domains, and machine names, read from left to right and often separated by periods, which are also referred to in domain reference as dots (domain.com). Top-level domains appear on the right side of the domain name, and premium names will end in *.com*; *.org*; *.net*; *.biz*; or, in the case of interscholastic or intercollegiate organizational site names, *.edu*. Second-level domain names appear in the middle and are what most consider to be the domain name itself. This is where common reference or connection comes into play to make the domain name more recognizable, and individual athletes will use these recognizable domain names (e.g., lebronjames.com) to enhance identity and personal brand construction (Barnett, 2017). Finally, on the far left, a machine name is used, which typically is associated with *www* or *en*. All domain names must be registered with the Internet Corporation for Assigned Names and Numbers (ICANN), a nonprofit organization that procures several databases related to Internet name space. Assuming that a desired domain name has not already been purchased, the cost of securing the address can vary based on the registrar selected (e.g., GoDaddy, Wix.com). Often website service providers include registration in the overall cost, which averages $10 to $15 per year. New domain names are usually registered for 1 to 10 years, with discounts often applied for longer registration periods (ICANN.org). Strategic maintenance of this registry (e.g., awareness of renewal deadlines) is critical to keep the domain from falling into the hands of those interested in just profiting off a quick "swoop and sell" to the organization if the registration expires.

A final development consideration is **website accessibility**, which Ryan (2016) described as "the process of designing your website to be equally accessible to everyone" (p. 44). The mission of the World Wide Web Consortium (W3C) is to provide protocols and guidelines for all websites to create an environment that is accessible by all, including those with visual and hearing impairments. These standards address not only accessibility but also usability. The ability for elements of an organization's website to address a variety of browser setting preferences allows everyone to have a similar experience on the website. As an effort to ensure that a website meets the minimum standards, W3C provides accessibility but also sets up an organization to easily integrate new technologies such as newly developed web browsers that may quickly become popular to use when navigating web content.

Content

Website content is a function of the site's purpose and audience. It is a reasonable assumption that a website visitor is likely to have a specific purpose in mind. Without substantive and useful content, other aspects of website construction and design will have little meaning. Sport managers planning or managing websites have an array of content options from which to choose. Website provider SIDEARM (sidearmsports .com) provides a list of key content features including rosters, schedules, photo galleries, video distribution, and fan engagement. This list can be refined when the material is organized and site constraints are considered. The process can be combined with envisioning how the content might best be presented using several categories of content type, including text, graphics, video, audio, animation, multimedia, and interactive tools (e.g., information requests, purchase tools). Some examples of the type of content that might be included on the websites of various sport organizations are summarized in table 4.1.

Table 4.1 Potential Website Content

College athletics sites	Pro team sites	Fitness club sites	Retail sites
Team rosters	Team rosters	Membership information	Merchandise
Schedules and results	Schedules and results	Programs	Prices
Statistics	Statistics	Facility location	Store locations
Historical records	Historical records	Directions	Special sales
Ticket information	Ticket information	Hours of operation	Gift cards
Facility information	Facility information	Newsletter	Loyalty programs
Booster club	Fan clubs	Services and amenities	Prominent brands
Directory	Charity partners	Staff directory	Return policies
Links to other sites	Merchandise	Special events	Employment
Camps	Fantasy camps and games	Community programs	Community programs, rebates, and recalls
Photos and video	Photos and video	Facility photos	Investor information
Links to social media accounts	Links to social media accounts	Links to social media accounts	Contact information for customer service including live chat when available

Content should be offered that can quickly meet the minimum expectations of potential visitors. Internet software developer HubSpot describes the vision of "understanding the world through the eyes of your user" (Summerfield, n.d., para. 1) as a critical element in website building. As technological capability and Internet speeds have progressed, the limitations to what can efficiently be included in website content have been reduced. Material that once required too much computer power to make it viable (e.g., video clips) now is routinely available, allowing for much more extensive and creative website content. Video is now even used as motion-generated background instead of the previously preferred static images or contextually color-coordinated graphic design.

Although many websites contain primarily marketing- and commerce-related information, much of the content can and should have a public relations orientation as well. A well-constructed website provides constituents with a broad range of information that creates opportunities to connect with the organization in a variety of ways—not just as a consumer. Ryan (2016) cautioned that in an era of multimedia advancements on the web, text still resonates as the most viable content in establishing connection to key publics. The words on each page still provide meaning and require careful consideration to ensure that the tone and

voice meet the standards of the organization's established brand.

A key advantage of the web over other information sources is the capability of modifying and updating in near real time. Providing site users with current and regularly updated content serves as incentive for more frequent visits to the site and enhances user loyalty. The credibility of a website often hinges on the accuracy and currency of the information presented.

Design

Identifying the content to be included on a website is one step, and determining how it should be organized and presented is another. Website design is part art and part science, and several general guidelines should be considered in the site construction process. Victor Thomas (2020), owner of the San Francisco–based web design company Thomas Digital, suggested elements of site design that most successful designs have in common:

- Minimal design
- Well-organized design
- Design that is ready for conversion
- Design that keeps mobile in mind
- Fast loading times

Professional sport organizations may have a combined public relations and marketing group who work together to coordinate media materials and promote events.

©Tom Merton/Caiaimage/Getty Images

Developing a sound **site structure** is an important first step and allows a logical arrangement of content that makes it easy for users to search, browse, and navigate. While the tendency might be to just "throw the kitchen sink" on the site, Thomas (2020) suggested that the best sites actually have less going on. He described this concept as minimal design, which includes font styles and sizes, colors, and alignment. Websites should not use a myriad of fonts, and the website should be kept to two or three total visible font styles. Fonts used should be recognizable and adhere to any organizational visual identity standards related to the type of fonts used. Since many typefaces come organized as a family now (e.g., Arial, Arial Condensed, Arial Black, etc.), typeface visual identity standards are usually established by marketing or public relations professionals well in advance of a website build or redesign. The sizes of these fonts play a role in minimal design as well, and minimal design includes limiting font sizes differences as

much as possible. Obviously page headlines will be a larger font size, but much of the rest of the text content should be kept to a similar size. Colors are an important selection in design as well, as public relations professionals will again want to reference their own visual identity standards for guidance on selecting the proper color in the RGB system. The RGB system is defined as the combination of red, green, and blue to produce a variety of different colors visible on screens, with more than 16 million possible combinations (RGB Colors, n.d.).

How information is organized to be navigated on a website can have a variety of potential impacts. For example, a site may be composed of a series of layers that provide related information for users who want it. A headline and paragraph about game results may lead someone to a second layer with a more extensive game description. From there another layer may include the box score and statistics for the game, and a further layer could contain video highlights or postgame interviews. When building a new website, or redesigning an existing one, public relations professionals should consider previous users' keyword searches to strategically determine what content is the most searched for and to coordinate that information into themes to use in future site navigation structures. Three common structures are linear, hierarchical, and hypertextual, and some sites blend characteristics of multiple forms depending on the complexity of the site (Baehr, 2007). The importance of the home page cannot be overemphasized because it is usually the first contact that the user has with the site. The home page must have a positive impact and provide the platform for efficient navigation. The home page is also where the aesthetic quality of the site is likely to have an important influence on user behavior; this is likely to be where first impressions are formed, especially as they relate to the initial navigation system of the website. Site navigation involves helping users know where they are and find what they want. Well-designed website navigation reveals content (Krug, 2006). A variety of tools can help users steer their way through the site, including toolbar menus and buttons, hyperlinks, search utilities, and site maps. The complexity of the site determines the extent to which these tools are employed (Baehr, 2007). Tracking user navigation patterns is an important assessment tool in evaluating site content and design. Continual site evaluation will keep the information current and the structure consistent with user needs.

Websites should also take into consideration the needs of the user and the organization. While information organization needs to be tailored to the user, it should also be optimized to maximize the relationship with that user, including monetization. Thomas (2020) states that websites designed with conversion in mind "take visitors down a clear path to success. [The website] then identifies the needs of the visitor and gives them a clear next step to take." For a sport organization, this kind of design could include consistent and well-placed links to a ticket marketplace or a fan-related online store, or give users the ability to renew donations with the click of a mouse.

As mobile technology continues to dominate how we access sport, the mobile functionality of websites should be taken into consideration. Design should take account of how the user's needs may shift from website to mobile device, and the impact that shift might have on the optimal design and layout of information. Website service provider SIDEARM Sports boasts a responsive site design that promises to deliver a user experience whether "fans are on their smartphone, a tablet, or the computer at their desk" (SIDEARM Sports, 2019).

Finally, websites should be optimized for fast loading times. Thomas (2020) describes successful website design as "invisible" when it comes to loading. Loading time is so critical that Google takes website loading times into consideration as part of its search rankings. Keeping loading times as short as possible is a critical element of minimal design. Daniel An, from Google, reported in 2018 that page loading time is significantly related to an increase in the visitor **bounce rate**, which Ryan (2016) defined as "the number of people who arrive on your site, scan the landing page and then leave immediately" (p. 121). An found that as loading times increased from 1 to 10 seconds, bounce rates increased more than 120%. In the modern era of Internet technology, it is obvious that speed matters.

Design has important implications for both initial visitor impression and ease of use. If users can find the information and services that they are looking for quickly and easily, they are more likely to return to the site in the future. Keeping the user in mind during the design process will enhance the chances of effectively meeting user expectations for the site.

Promotion

Getting users to the website is certainly an important consideration, because a great website with no visitors is of little use. The purposes and goals of the site have a significant bearing on how much effort is put into promoting the website as well as how it will be promoted. Some sport organizations provide websites primarily as a service or a convenience to their stakeholders. The incentive is largely to serve existing stakeholders rather than to attract new visitors. Most organizations, however, are much more interested in expanding their reach. Some sites generate significant revenue by selling advertising space, hosting online stores, offering pay-per-view opportunities, and providing insider access (through paid subscriptions to videos, blogs, and other updates). Media giant ESPN years ago produced a print magazine with a variety of features and photos. Now, ESPN+ provides content and articles from personalities like Mel Kiper Jr. and his mock draft pages leading up to the NFL college draft, in addition to a wide variety of live and on-demand video. For organizations that have e-commerce as a primary purpose, promoting the site becomes a key element in its success.

Given the importance of the sport organization's website to its public relations and marketing efforts, it only makes sense for sport managers to seek effective avenues to promote the site. Posters, business cards, and even sales receipts can be promotional devices. Website addresses can be listed not only on these organizational print media pieces (see chapter 5), but also on the organization's social media profiles, providing an instant link back to the site. Much like other service industries such as restaurants and hotels, sport organizations may use ticket receipts to solicit online feedback by offering an incentive for completing a satisfaction survey. On-site signage should also be allocated for promoting the website; in addition, often, the website address will be visible on the playing surface of the organization's facility.

Another essential strategy in website design is **search engine optimization (SEO)**. This tool is still crucial as the most common route to a website is likely still to be one of the major search engines (e.g., Google, Yahoo!). Those whose sport sites rely on viewers to come to the site via a search engine should understand how search engines evaluate websites. Search engines operate in a highly complex environment of search algorithms that scan billions of web pages to provide the best and most relevant search results for their users. With more than six billion indexed websites as of 2019 (worldwidewebsize.com), and the Google Search Index more than 100 million gigabytes in size, maintaining a website that is primed for search engines is a key strategic approach.

In Google's explanation, "How Search Works" (google.com/search/howsearchworks), the organization provides details about ranking systems that sort through those billions of websites in an effort to find relevant results that are useful to the end user. Words that users input in a query, the relevance and usability of pages, the expertise of potential sources, and the end user's geographical location all play a role in the results produced to a user entering a search into Google. Google uses not only search algorithms that index results, but also "search quality raters" who are stationed around the world.

Ryan (2016) suggests a variety of strategies for optimizing search engine attractiveness. Content is more important than aesthetics in website rankings, and content is evaluated based on keywords, phrases, and page titles. Knowing the target audiences and the types of search phrases that they are likely to use is fundamental to improving the ranking of a site. Using the websites of successful competitors as a benchmark for keywords may also be useful. Interior links that connect pages within the site and the quality of other sites that link to a site are all important in moving up the ratings scale. Text is again emphasized, as the algorithms used by search engines are most interested in and guided by text. While graphics are aesthetically pleasing to users, they are ignored by search engines trying to index sites. Heavy use of graphical elements involving Adobe Flash Player, JavaScript, and frames are detrimental to search engine optimization because they are more difficult for search providers to read electronically.

With YouTube's ascendance to the rank of the second most-used search engine in the world, one can argue that SEO is not as important as it used to be. The development of social networking sites and the more widespread use of high-speed Internet access via mobile devices have made the days of sitting in front of a computer to search for something on Google or Yahoo! seem to be coming to an end. However, building a usable site that can easily be navigated by search engine algorithms and search quality raters continues to be an important strategic consideration in maintaining an organization's website presence.

Evaluation

Because the website is an important interface between the organization and constituents, evaluating and subsequently improving the user experience are important. As with any evaluation, website assessment should be tied to identified purposes, goals, and objectives. If the site is primarily oriented toward commerce, business-focused metrics are likely to be central to evaluation. From a public relations perspective, however, user-focused measures are essential to determining the effectiveness of a website.

When measuring website effectiveness, the previously mentioned goals of the site will drive the questions that need to be answered by analytics through the development of **key performance indicators (KPIs)**. For example, if a youth sport facility is interested in generating revenue through e-commerce, the most useful indicator may be a **conversion rate**, a metric which takes the number of conversions (website visitors that eventually produce a defined action such as a purchase or sign-up) and divides it by the total number of website visitors. For other public relations outcomes such as information dissemination and building brand awareness, the number of website visitors over a defined time span may be helpful to determine effectiveness. Another key metric may be the site's bounce rate, which was discussed previously in the section on website design.

Many of the needed metrics for evaluation are accessible from the website management provider or from Google Analytics for a specific site. How that data is used, however, is driven by the organization's goals for the website and the KPIs that are chosen to determine the effectiveness of the site in meeting those goals. These will differ for nearly every organization, but the blueprint to website evaluation is often the same: Determine what you want to know, and find the relevant performance indicators that give the needed information on the utilization of the website to meet public relations goals.

Websites for Specific Stakeholders

Throughout this book, several stakeholder groups are identified as primary targets for sport organizations in their public relations efforts. These publics are also important audiences for organizational websites. Constructing a website that accommodates the needs of constituents such as the media, community, consumers and fans, members, donors, and business partners and sponsors will help enhance these relationships.

Media Relations

One of the most important relationships that many sport organizations have is with the media, particularly in high-profile spectator sports at the professional and college levels. Websites can help accommodate the needs of the media, especially through the provision of news and information. Members of the media rely on information in many forms, and spectator sport counts on the media for the exposure to new potential fans. Teams, leagues, conferences, and governing bodies all maintain websites that are at least partly devoted to the kinds of information that the media require. In some cases, team and league websites provide distinct sections accessible only to credentialed media. Major League Baseball serves the media with access to a centralized bank of reference information through MLB Pressbox (mlb-pressbox.com). Although much of the information could be accessed from a variety of sources, this centralized repository includes nearly everything that the league can provide for the media, including links to a "press box" for each team. This material includes game schedules, game notes, lineups and injury reports, statistics, press releases, media advisories, special events, rules, record books, and league executive information, as well as downloadable audio, video, and photos of players. The site offers one-stop shopping for information that media professionals need to do their jobs.

News releases that were once faxed or mailed in hard copy are now routinely transmitted and stored electronically. The same is true of media guides. The advantages of this technology are obvious and go well beyond the financial savings associated with reduced printing and mailing costs. Speed of communication, convenience of access, timeliness of information, and ease of updating all provide added value. Even when information is not actually sent directly to the media, it can be stored on the website where media members can access the information when they need it. The best way to serve the media relationship is to find out what information media members want and in what form they want it. The more convenient and usable the information is, the more likely it is that media members will view the organization as a reliable partner.

A broad range of information is desired by the media, and the type of information varies by medium. As an example, visual media outlets will have more need of photos and video clips, whereas print and online media outlets may need more statistical information, historical background, and feature material. Local media may want information that ties an organization to the media's market area, such as the success of local athletes. Websites can provide a wide range of material, and electronic transmission of this material to the media can be done efficiently when necessary. Modern sport is oriented toward statistics, and the current and historic statistical detail available is often extraordinary. Technology and the Internet have greatly simplified the media's ability to access and manipulate statistical data and incorporate it into their work.

Most team sites have a wide range of information, including team rosters and individual player biographies, game schedules and results, coaching staff information, game and cumulative individual and team statistics, archived historical records, personnel updates (recruiting, trades, injuries, roster moves), facility information, staff directories, and visitor information. Other content that may be beneficial to the media as well as other constituents involves links to other information sources such as league, conference, and opponent websites. Virtually all college and professional league websites contain links to the sites of each league member as well as links to a variety of other sources. Individual team websites often reciprocate, with links to the websites of various leagues of which they are members and of other relevant governing bodies. Some organizations have sites capable of providing live updates of games or events through the use of live statistical updates (often referred to as live stats). The National Collegiate Athletic Association (NCAA) typically has ongoing updates of championship events on its website. In many cases the sites also include access to live broadcasts (both audio and video) of games, and the distributing media become website partners in some respects. Information may also be available on the process used for distributing press credentials and the protocol for visiting teams who desire to broadcast events. Organizations such as the PGA provide the same types of content but also serve as the conduit to the individual tournaments that serve as the components for the PGA Tour.

Community Relations

Sport organizations commonly use their websites for community relations in several ways. The first and probably most common way is as a platform to promote the organization's good works in the community. In some cases, especially in the off-season for professional sport teams, this information can become a prominent element of the site. Each of the teams in the four major professional sport leagues in the United States has a "community" section on its website, and other major professional sport operations around the world often have some form of community connection such as a foundation. Photos and video clips are frequently used to display these community efforts. Organizations are likely to use their websites to promote and solicit support for their own (or their foundation's) charitable initiatives or the good works of their affiliated coaches and athletes. The Houston Texans post an annual impact report on the community relations area of the organization's website. The report includes information on the number of personal appearances, donations awarded to organizations from the foundation, the foundation's mission and vision statements, relationships with community partners, and specific theme-oriented initiatives such as NFL PLAY 60 and Salute to Service games and partnerships.

Some sport organizations, particularly those in the high-profile entertainment segment, use their sites as tools for managing charitable requests. The site provides information regarding the organization's policies for donation requests and, sometimes, interactive tools that enable web users to submit their requests online.

The second way that sport organizations use their websites as community relations tools is by promoting direct-contact initiatives. Organizational websites may promote speaking and other public appearances by the organization's personnel, mascots, and cheerleaders, and special events such as caravans, open houses, exhibitions, and conferences. Organizations with personnel in high demand for public appearances may also use their sites to disseminate information regarding appearance policies and to provide mechanisms for submitting requests for personal appearances.

The third way that websites may be used to improve community relations is by offering services specifically designed to maintain or enhance a sense of community among stakeholders. For example, organizations that may not be prominent enough to secure broadcast distribution outlets may choose to webcast audio or video coverage of their events. This tool enables fans, alumni, and family and friends of competitors to enjoy events even if they are not able to attend.

Other organizations have taken community-building efforts to recognize the diversity of the organization's fans. For example, the NFL's New York Giants have established a Giants Women's Club (GWC). Users enter their names and contact information and get access to special Giants Women's Club member–only events throughout the year and exclusive promotions and giveaways specifically targeted at female fans. There are also user blogs on fashion, fitness, and wellness and information on insider tours of the organization's various facilities, which provide a direct connection to members. Membership also includes an invitation to the GWC Big Blue Challenge flag football event, a training camp event, and other exclusive interactive organizational activities. Social networking sites are particularly valuable tools for community relations efforts as well. Many community relations efforts conducted by sport organizations have their own dedicated social media accounts for foundations, organization and player charitable initiatives, and large fundraising efforts that benefit charitable partners. Dellarocas (2010) suggested that successfully harnessing these social communities depends on establishing a reputation built on attracting the right people and content that fits the organization's vision for the site. Sport organizations are only beginning to tap into the potential these tools have to nurture the relationships fundamental to the practice of public relations.

Employee Relations

As will be discussed throughout the text, employees make up an important internal public that is at times overlooked in public relations efforts. One method for communicating with and fostering interaction among employees is through the use of protected internal servers where a variety of information may be stored, shared, and accessed by those who need it the most. Many segments of the organization have specific uses for those servers, particularly for sharing information and data across departments. An athletics department might need to share facility scheduling information among various units within the program. Sales and marketing can access market research information, customer service can gain entry into a client information database, and accounting and finance can quickly access payroll information.

Another use of websites for employee relations comes in the form of outsourced **intranet** connections. An intranet is a privately accessed and restricted website structure for communication, collaboration, and sharing of important information among employee units. Although one driving force for intranet use is logistical efficiency, public relations applications are present as well. Human resources can use the intranet in a variety of ways to enhance and expedite important internal communications. Possible examples include individualized employee interfaces, personalized content feeds, analytics to track employee engagement, social interactions such as likes, comments, etc., and integrated internal communication tools (Weaver, 2019). Effective intranet use may help the organization become less compartmentalized and promote a more open operational environment that can enhance communication and create a more collaborative atmosphere. The key to a successful intranet is its content. It must be relevant, accessible, available in a timely manner, and updated regularly.

Donor Relations

The importance of fundraising for many sport organizations is addressed in later chapters of this text. For now, suffice it to say that technological advances have provided valuable tools to assist in development efforts. Nonprofit organizations have benefited greatly from the communication and interactivity of the Internet. Waters (2007) reported that the most common methods organizations used to keep in contact with key donor stakeholders included the collection of e-mail addresses, and stakeholder feedback forms. Online stores and auctions have proven to be popular methods of fundraising via the Internet. The sidebar 10 Rules of ePhilanthropy Every Nonprofit Must Know sum-marizes some basic considerations for using the Internet in fund-raising.

Although a website may serve as a center for information and the host for online donations, donor relationships can be nurtured through a variety of electronic communications options. E-mail can be used in direct solicitation, but the real public relations value of e-mail is its contribution to maintaining a communication link with donors. E-mail allows efficient and inexpensive communication with large groups of constituents. It provides an opportunity for dialogue rather than one-way communication and can direct a tailored and targeted message to supporters (Olsen, Keevers, Paul, & Covington, 2001). These contacts should be made only with permission to avoid communication being perceived as **spam**, which will impair effectiveness. E-mail can also be passed from initial recipients to many others. This practice, known as **viral marketing**, can be effective in expanding the donor base because it uses existing donors as promoters of the cause (Hart, 2002). Connection to social networking sites and external virtual communication communities are also excellent ways to increase the probability that shared content will go viral. Although the term *viral* may have a negative connotation, it is simply the electronic version of word-of-mouth marketing. Wilson (2000) defined viral marketing as "any strategy that encourages individuals to pass on a marketing message to others, creating the potential for exponential growth in the message's exposure and influence." In the context of fund-raising, viral marketing attempts to capitalize on existing networks of donors to grow the donor base. Having a good cause, presenting it in the right way, and providing attractive incentives will encourage existing donors to pass along the fundraising appeal to potential donors. Having donors forward the fundraising appeal personalizes the message for recipients and makes it appear less like spam, which allows organizations to reach prospects to whom they have little direct access in a way that has considerable influence.

The Network for Good (networkforgood.com) has compiled an extensive list of resources that discuss various aspects of fundraising, including how to develop websites and integrate social networking as part of an integrated communication and fund-raising strategy. A website can serve as an information hub and be a communication link for a much wider audience. A website can also keep donors and prospective donors informed about an organization's mission and needs, the status of fundraising efforts, and the way the money raised is being used.

The 10 Rules of ePhilanthropy Every Nonprofit Must Know

Rule 1: Don't be invisible.

If you build it, they won't just come. Building an online brand is just as important and difficult as building an offline brand.

Rule 2: It takes know-how and vision.

Your organization's website is a marketing and fundraising tool, not a technology tool. Fund-raisers and marketers need to drive the content, not the site developer.

Rule 3: It's all about the donor.

Put the donor first! Know your contributors and let them get to know you.

Rule 4: Keep savvy donors; stay fresh and current.

Make online giving enjoyable and easy. Give the donor options. Use the latest technology. Show your donors how their funds are being used.

Rule 5: Integrate your site into everything you do.

Your website alone will do nothing. Every activity that you have should drive traffic to your site.

Rule 6: Don't trade your mission for a shopping mall.

Many nonprofit websites fail to emphasize mission, instead turning themselves into online shopping malls.

Rule 7: Ethics, privacy, and security are not buzzwords.

Many donors will be making their first online contribution. They will expect your organization to maintain the highest standards of ethics, privacy, and security.

Rule 8: It takes the Internet to build a community.

Many nonprofits, particularly smaller groups, lack the resources to communicate effectively. The Internet offers the opportunity to build a community of supporters.

Rule 9: Success online requires targeting.

The website alone is not enough. You must target your audience and drive their attention to the wealth of information and services that your website offers. Permission must be sought before you begin direct communication through the Internet.

Rule 10: ePhilanthropy is more than just e-money.

ePhilanthropy is a tool to be used in your fund-raising strategy. It should not be viewed as quick money. There are no shortcuts to building effective relationships, but the Internet will enhance your efforts.

ePhilanthropy.org © 2005

Most college athletics websites contain a link to their booster or support organizations. The content includes justifications for considering making a contribution, an outline of rewards associated with certain donation levels, and an opportunity to join the booster group. In some cases the website allows direct online donations or provides links to the institutional fundraising arm. Often the site provides information about support group events and media content of past booster group occasions.

Blogs

Another Internet-based tool at the disposal of sport public relations professionals is **blogging**. Blogs, which are websites containing a writer's or writers' experiences, opinions, and observations, have become a useful tool for the fulfillment of public relations goals. While blogs may have begun as static musings and information, they have become more interactive, frequently including the opportunity for comment and discussion and embedding links to related sites and information. As print media organizations continue to downsize, former beat reporters and columnists are now being hired by organizations to internally produce content that may include blogs.

The structure of blogs presents opportunities and concerns for sport organizations. One type of blogging involves pieces written by members of the organization or its constituents that provide behind-the-scenes or personal insights about various aspects of the operation. This internal form of blogging housed on organizational websites gives the organization tight editorial control over content. As an example, the NBA's website features nearly 20 blogs from players, league insiders, and coaches. In fact, athletes' voices in blogging have become so popular that Derek Jeter founded a new media outlet, *The Players' Tribune*, to further promote the voices of athletes on topics they deem important, such as mental health and labor relations. This format gives athletes definitive control of their messages, which come directly from their own thoughts and beliefs.

Another form of blogging involves blog sites developed by people outside the organization that may be a part of a **virtual communication community**. Sport fuels passion that fans like to share. Blogs, vlogs (video commentary), and other media content have become frequently used outlets for these exchanges. In some respects these outlets have become the Internet version of sports talk radio, except that every fan who signs up for the community

now has a voice. One obvious concern about these sites is that they are largely outside the control of the sport organizations. While content on the website that hosts the community may be developed by professional journalists who are credentialed for similar access to traditional media outlets, responses to that content are normally written from the viewpoint of the fan, which brings with it bias that may raise issues of accuracy and credibility in an environment that provides little to no accountability. Some communities require registration and even subscription to access content and fan boards where communication is shared among members, but anonymity continues to be an easy choice for those who are part of virtual communication communities to make with secondary e-mail addresses and phone numbers that provide little in terms of identification.

Monitoring the information and discourse on these sites can be useful in gauging consumer attitudes and opinions. Sport organizations may also be able to capitalize on the interactive nature of blogs to enhance relationships. But organizations will also need to confront the problems that sometimes come with rapid and uncontrolled information dissemination. Monitoring these online communities, with the addition of social networking sites, can become a full-time job, but sport public relations practitioners have little choice but to pay attention to communication and even rumors posted anonymously, which can have devastating impacts if ignored.

While virtual communication communities may seem to some public relations professionals like a horrifying nightmare waiting to happen, there are some benefits. Quickly dispelling rumors or misinformation to members of a key public brought together by their vested interest in your organization allows them to become brand ambassadors in defending the organization from misinformed social mobs. These sites also provide the opportunity for grassroots research on fan opinions and issues that might need to be addressed strategically by the organization (e.g., major parking and traffic problems in particular parking lots during postgame egress). These communities are also an excellent way for fans to get involved with their own ideas for assisting an organization and its fans through humorous nicknames or, as the following case study explains, a historic patriotic display.

Be Your Own Media

While blogs have been around for some time, the idea of athletes using their own voices to respond to the media, the public, and sometimes even the organizations they play for is still somewhat new and evolving.

Visit *The Player's Tribune*, and read a post written by an athlete. What differences in tone can you notice from the hard news reporting style of press releases (see chapter 7) normally found on an organization's website? Now that athletes have an opportunity to address issues they deem important, do you feel this improves their image in the eyes of the general public in labor contract negotiations? Should colleges consider creating a similar format for their student-athletes?

Podcasts

Another development of online communication has been the rapid growth of **podcasting**, defined by

PATRIOTISM FROM A POST

In September 2001, the sport universe in the United States was reeling with the emotions from the attacks on the World Trade Center. Hundreds, possibly thousands, of sporting events were canceled and postponed in the wake of the attacks. Many organizations, in the days following September 11, were working to determine when their teams might see competition again, while also juggling a delicate balance. That balance dealt with organizations attempting to plan not just how to pay tribute to the lives lost in the attacks but also how to show unity through patriotic displays when their teams finally returned to the field or court, in an effort to allow sport to serve as a healing mechanism for fans across the country.

In College Station, Texas, that balance was squarely on the minds of Texas A&M University fans and students. As the country began the process of healing, sport was a central element of both moving forward and establishing what a new normal might look like for the nation. While the date of the next home Texas A&M football game was still in limbo, fans were beginning to stir on a growing virtual

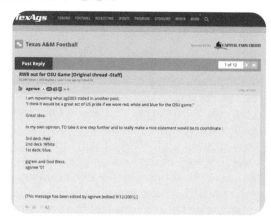

A post from TexAgs.com member agsrwe began an intensive campaign to "Red, White, and Blue Out Kyle Field." This highly successful effort was coordinated by several people but originally started with the post shown here.

Courtesy of Texas A&M.

community home of Texas A&M fans, TexAgs.com. One post by user ag2003 stated a desire to wear red, white, and blue for the upcoming home game against Oklahoma State University. User agsrwe then created a post that started a firestorm of activity and an incredible story of a virtual community quickly coming together and coordinating something truly remarkable.

The massive grassroots effort to coordinate the color of shirts worn by the three expansive decks that held fans at Kyle Field had begun, coordinated by a group of students who quickly sprang into action. Coordinated efforts to "Maroon Out" Kyle Field for big games had been met with outstanding success—but coordinating the production and sale of three different colored T-shirts in 10 days to not only benefit first responders in New York but help ensure a color-coordinated group of 70,000+ fans as a patriotic display? The likelihood of getting that many people coordinated in such a short time frame was daunting at best. That difficulty did not stop a group of five Texas A&M students from trying, however, as they began efforts to coordinate the production of red, white, and blue T-shirts printed with the phrase "Standing for America" on the front. Proceeds from the sale of the $5 T-shirts would go to relief funds for New York City firefighters and police. According to a 12thman.com story recalling the events leading up to the game, the first order of T-shirts was 3,000, but by the day before the game, nearly 40,000 T-shirts had been sold.

The idea was for fans sitting in the stadium's third deck to wear red. White T-shirts were purchased by fans who had tickets to sit in the middle deck, and blue T-shirts were to be worn by fans sitting in the lower first deck of the stadium. In the early morning hours prior to the game, an astonishing 30,000 T-shirts were purchased as word began to quickly spread both on the TexAgs.com forums and also through traditional media outlets.

The students were able to present $180,000 in donations to the first responder relief funds in New York, which benefited the families of fallen first responders in the aftermath of the attacks on the World Trade Center. On the day of the game, the coordination efforts culminated in an inspiring display of patriotism, as the stadium was full of fans in red, white, and blue T-shirts either purchased or brought from home. In one of the greatest stories of a virtual communication community, an idea that came from a single fan's post was put into action.

Discussion Questions

1. What is one lesson that can be learned about the power of a virtual communication community to come together for good without oversight from the organization itself?

2. This event took place in 2001, years before social media's rise to prominence. Does the power of viral information make something like "Red, White, and Blue Out Kyle Field" more likely to occur in the future? Why or why not?

3. What other similar efforts can you find that are fan-generated and that did not initially include organizational oversight?

Brown and Green (2008) as technology that allows the creation and distribution of audio or video files to users who may subscribe to receive the files. Yet another communication tool for the sport public relations professional to use, popular podcasts are often produced by members of the traditional media, traditional media outlets, and social influencers who already have an established following.

Professional sport organizations have made an effort to develop internal podcasts for the use of providing insider access to information, player profiles and interviews, commentary, and even recorded broadcasts of coaches' shows and other audio and video-based content. Podcast content has also become a mainstay of organizational communicators on the college sport level, with coaches' shows, game highlights and analysis, and interviews with student–athletes and department staff. Many times, these podcasts include a radio voice of the organization (play-by-play radio talent) or other members of the public relations staff with the experience and desire to record and produce content on a regular basis.

Podcasts with sport media personalities continue to rise in popularity. The "Skip and Shannon: Undisputed" podcasts, featuring FOX Sports personalities Skip Bayless and Shannon Sharpe and hosted by Joy Taylor, are an example of a podcast that has other integrations including the podcasters' daily national television show. Fantasy sports podcasts are a topical area of interest for many listeners of podcasts. Some independent content providers have been able to carve out a niche market for their content and produce revenue. Podcasting advertising revenue is expected to exceed $514 million dollars in the United States by the end of 2019. The CEO of Barstool Sports, Erika Nardini, commented that half her company's advertising revenue came in the form of podcast advertisements in 2018 (Patel et al., 2019). Winn and colleagues (2019) developed a complete step-by-step guide to creating a podcast (podcastinsights.com) and included information on everything from choosing a topic and show name, to integrating music and cover art, to equipment selection and audio or video recording and editing. Other considerations include uploading to iTunes,

Podcasts are an effective tool for adding personality to public relations efforts with insider access, commentary, interviews, and previously recorded audio and video.

Robert Laberge/Getty Images

Spotify, and other podcast hosting formats, as well as providing a web presence (either embedded in a player on the organizational website or on another medium such as a blog). Transcriptions and show notes are also helpful for some who tune in. Whether one starts a podcast with something as simple as a mobile app or uses a production studio, content will ultimately be what drives the success of the effort. While a variety of formats are used in podcasting, including a single host, a team of hosts, in-studio interviews, remote interviews and more, the content of a podcast should be, like everything else discussed in this chapter, targeted to support the organization's overall goals.

New Media Limitations and Problems

The Internet can be an important asset to sport organizations, but it poses some public relations problems. Coombs (2002) noted that the reach and speed of the Internet are both a blessing and a curse for public relations professionals with respect to crisis management (discussed further in chapter 8). Although the Internet makes connecting with stakeholders much quicker and easier, it also has the potential to give issues such as personnel changes, disciplinary actions, or controversial policy decisions a contagious quality that can rapidly energize publics. Given this potential, sport organizations that operate on a public stage must monitor the Internet closely and evaluate issues for the potency of the threat posed to the organization. As discussed in chapter 3, if the mainstream media are monitoring the Internet for news tips and gauging public sentiment, sport organizations themselves should be involved in social listening as well. This practice requires a multifaceted effort for public relations staff, who must monitor social media, virtual communication communities, and other Internet-related pieces such as blogs, podcasts, and websites.

Often these websites and blogs as part of a virtual communication community are a mix of boosterism and journalism, so questions arise about whether they operate as media or as an arm of the athletics program. In at least one case, the University of Kentucky's athletics program banned a site operator from contact with the program after he reportedly asked subscribers to contact recruits and posted stories about and pictures of recruits online (Harmonson, 2004). Because of the prevalence of small

digital cameras and cell phone cameras, coaches have become wary of conducting open practices and cautious about how they behave in social situations. Although these new media sites enjoy First Amendment freedoms, they can create significant problems for managing organizational image. In some past cases, schools have limited access or refused to provide media credentials to website providers who don't have a newspaper or television affiliation (Matuszewski, 2000). While the practice of keeping Internet-related journalism out of the building by denying credentialed access was common early in the digital media age, the widespread coverage and size of some virtual communities run by fans can no longer be ignored. Rather than seeing blogs, podcasts, and web forums as a threat to an organization, public relations staff members are well advised to build and maintain relationships with those working in digital media in the same way as with those working in traditional media.

Other considerations must also be addressed when employing Internet technology, especially as it relates to live video. Livestreamed content has become popular for not only organizational websites but also the networks created by leagues, conferences, and other governing bodies. Several high school football games are now livestreamed digitally to a worldwide audience either on a network (e.g., ESPN+), or on the high schools' own websites, powered by the same website management providers as some Division I schools. While live video is an excellent vehicle for carrying out a variety of public relations goals, it does not come without strategic considerations. For smaller events, simply livestreaming via one camera may be enough to suffice. For larger organizations, an expectation of quality control becomes a concern, with the need for multiple camera angles, the ability to switch back and forth between those cameras, and a graphical interface that includes a **score bug** that allows the viewer to keep up with the score, time, and which quarter or half is being played. Large events may require the use of instant replay, and the ability to switch back and forth between live action and replay. Previously recorded video known as B-roll (see chapter 7), to be used to fill time at the beginning of a broadcast or when going to and coming back from commercial breaks, may need to be recorded and edited days in advance of an event. With on-site camera operators and production staff, the number of people needed for a live broadcast can approach the double digits for smaller events and exceed the triple digits in the case of major events such as the Super Bowl and the NCAA Final Four.

One final comment regarding technology: Technological capabilities continue to change rapidly. What is commonplace today may be outdated within a short time. This rapidly changing environment has implications for public relations professionals, who must be constantly alert to the technological advances and innovations that alter some of the tools and subsequently the practices of the public relations practitioner.

SUMMARY

The Internet and related new media present a host of public relations opportunities and challenges to sport public relations professionals. New media empower us to communicate directly with and receive feedback from large numbers of people quickly. Sport organization websites are diverse in purpose and complexity. In some instances, sport organizations offer relatively simple sites to provide critical information to fans, customers, and members of the media. In other cases, sites may be highly complex and offer numerous e-commerce options such as ticket and merchandise sales. Given the importance of websites as public relations and marketing platforms, careful planning is imperative. Some sport organizations manage their sites entirely in-house, whereas others outsource at least some site development and management responsibilities. Most sport organizations evaluate the effectiveness of their sites using a variety of metrics that align with the purpose and goals of the website. A sport organization's website may be designed to facilitate communication with diverse stakeholder groups, such as members of the media, the community at large, customers, and donors. Site content varies based on the particular interests of each stakeholder group. The Internet also has resulted in several challenges for sport public relations professionals. Blogging, podcasts, and virtual communication communities have created many new opportunities to connect with various constituencies but can also create public relations concerns. The lack of control over information that exists for many of these new media options poses public relations challenges. Irresponsible content posted on fan-based websites and social networking sites, security concerns, and unfiltered Twitter posts have created a number of Internet-related concerns that require constant monitoring. Finally, this rapidly changing area requires both attention and imagination. Creative use of technological innovation with live video and a variety of other technological advancements can greatly enhance the way that organizations nurture relationships with their stakeholders.

LEARNING ACTIVITIES

1. Compare the content of a variety of sport organization websites (e.g., NFL franchise, MLB franchise, NCAA Division I institution, National Association of Intercollegiate Athletics [NAIA] institution, fitness center, sporting goods manufacturer). Based on the content, what appear to be the goals and priorities of the websites? How do they compare and differ in basic design principles?

2. Select a sport organization and develop a content list of plausible material that might be included in a website. After you establish a content list, identify the elements that require regular updating to increase the potential for repeat site visits.

3. Select a professional sport organization's website and identify the content related to the organization's community relations efforts.

4. Determine whether your institution has a fan-based virtual communication community (such as TexAgs.com or MaizeandBlueNews.com) or visit one of another school. In the

open message board forums, are there any posts that you think an organization might be watching closely?

5. Listen to several sport-related podcasts (both internally hosted by an organization and also externally owned). How do they compare? What are the similarities and differences you can immediately understand? What strategic considerations might be important to consider if you planned to produce a podcast on a sport organization's website?

Engaging Key Publics via Legacy Media

After reading this chapter, students should be able to

- describe the purpose and nature of media guides in professional and collegiate sport,
- specify other types of print media that sport public relations professionals may be required to produce on a regular basis such as game notes,
- address forms of electronic media that sport public relations professionals may be required to produce, and
- discuss the corporate communications function within sport organizations.

These are the key terms discussed in this chapter:

- corporate communications
- game notes
- media guides
- newsletters

- organizational app
- organizational media
- game programs
- schedule card

Most sport organizations employ a variety of tactics to communicate with their publics, many of which do not rely on the involvement of mass media and are published or produced by the organization. Smith (2017) classified these tactics as **organizational media** and emphasized their value as a "middle ground between high-impact, small-audience interpersonal tactics and lower-impact, large-audience news and advertising tactics" (p. 275).

As noted in chapter 1's discussion of the PESO model, organizational media are considered part of the owned category of the model. Smith (2017) stated that organizational media "generally are controlled, internal, nonpublic media" (p. 274). While these tactics may not be targeted to the general public, they are often made available to the public through a variety of digital distribution methods.

The advantage of organizational media is that they can be tailored to specific publics and are often used by information-seeking publics. A notable downside to organizational media is the potential costs associated with their development and distribution (Smith, 2017). These can include production costs, as well as costs associated with the sport public relations professional's time devoted to deploying various organizational media tactics. Accordingly, sport public relations professionals should weigh the use of each form of organizational media carefully and consider how a particular tactic might be used in combination with other communication tools.

The most prominent of these organizational media tactics include the media guide (also known as a fact or record book) and game notes (also known as advances), although the importance and presence of printed media guides continue to decline in the era of social media. The first section of this chapter describes media guides that are commonly produced by professional, collegiate, and elite amateur sport organizations. This section includes an examination of the purposes and components of media guides, other planning considerations, and current media guide challenges.

Sport public relations professionals have many options beyond media guides for organizational media tactics. The second part of the chapter explores additional print tactics including game notes or advances, programs, brochures, newsletters, annual reports, and more. The third part examines electronic tactics such as video and audio recordings. Finally, the chapter concludes with a discussion of the corporate communications function, which often includes production of organizational media.

Media Guides

One of the primary tasks assigned to many sport public relations professionals is the development of **media guides** (Davis, 1998; Hall, Nichols, Moynahan, & Taylor, 2007; Helitzer, 2000). These guides, sometimes also referred to as fact books or record books, are designed primarily for the media but are also used by a variety of other information-seeking constituents such as fans, donors, and prospective partners. Media guides provide detailed information regarding the sport organization and its teams and are generally produced annually. In collegiate settings, a sports information office often produces a separate media guide for each varsity sport and separate publications for men's and women's teams. A single office may produce a dozen or more guides in a single academic year, particularly in higher divisions of competition. In smaller collegiate divisions, multiple sports in a season can be bunched together in one guide.

Media guides vary in size and level of detail. Typically, they are 8.5 by 11 inches (21 × 28 cm) at the college level and 5.5 by 8.5 (14 × 22 cm) or 6 by 9 inches (15 × 23 cm) at the professional level. Most media guides that are printed are bound in some form like a book and have color covers and black-and-white inside pages, but there are exceptions to those standards. Sport public relations professionals at smaller colleges in particular may opt for smaller publications that are less expensive to print. In some instances, even quad- and trifold brochures function as guides. Professional sport teams are much more likely to print media guides at this point for members of the media. With the elimination of media guides in recruiting practices at the college level, guides are much less likely to still be printed at smaller schools and exist in a PDF format on the organization's website instead. In addition to printed versions, many of these media guides are available to anyone via institutional websites. Placing these guides on websites has allowed for greater distribution of information to those seeking it, as well as creating a historical archive to use as a reference from year to year.

While collegiate organizations have a renewed purpose for media guides no longer aimed at recruits (see the sidebar Media Guides and the National Collegiate Athletic Association [NCAA]), professional organizations have continued to print media guides and distribute them digitally as well. The following sections describe the purposes of media guides, content that should be included in the guides, other relevant considerations, and several related challenges that are currently confronting professionals in the field.

Media Guides and the National Collegiate Athletic Association (NCAA)

Years ago professional guides were produced in sizes that would allow them to fit into the pockets of sports journalists, but the size of most guides today precludes that sort of convenience. Before 2005 no regulations governed the size of college media guides. The 2004 University of Missouri football media guide had 614 pages and weighed 2.2 pounds (1 kg). Effective in fall 2005 the NCAA mandated that universities' media guides not exceed 208 pages as a cost-cutting measure and a green initiative supported by several institutions.

Missouri realized a savings of $20,000 in that first year (Cherner et al., 2005). Subsequent revisions to NCAA bylaws (National Collegiate Athletics Association, 2018) have addressed a ban on the use of media guides as recruiting materials for potential student–athletes (Bylaw 13.4.1.1.2 in 2010) and also the required notice of rule violations and penalties issued to the institution by the NCAA. The most recent revisions make it possible for media guides to continue to be sold by third parties designated by the institution or conference, or by those institutions and conferences themselves. Relatedly, a heated national debate continues about the use of the names or likenesses of student–athletes, and the ability for those student-athletes to profit off that use (Bauer-Wolf, 2019).

In addition to their concern with cost, several universities expressed unease about the environmental impact of printed media guides. Guides were often distributed to prospective student–athletes, many of whom were conditioned to consult the Internet for information. Many universities agreed to stop printing media guides after the legislation passed in 2010 preventing guides from being sent to recruits. Since that time, media guides (or whichever of a variety of names they are called, including fact books, record books, and team guides) are being printed more with a renewed purpose of focusing on information useful for media members covering the team as opposed to the large books with flashy pages dedicated to recruiting purposes in the early 2000s.

Purposes

Since the purposes of media guides shifted away from recruiting at the collegiate level, theses guides generally serve the purpose of information distribution. Although members of the media remain the guides' primary audience, they are not the exclusive audience. Guides are useful not only for the media, but also as a potential source of revenue and goodwill for sport organizations.

Media

The information that media guides contain serves as a valuable resource to members of the media who cover the sport organization's teams and events and can generate favorable publicity as a result. Sport organizations typically go to great lengths to make sure that media guides are in the hands of influential media members several weeks in advance of a season, and many journalists rely heavily on those publications throughout the year. Beat reporters may wear out their copies of a media guide, but they are often reluctant to ask for a new copy because they may have made notations and earmarked sections that are especially useful to them throughout the year.

Revenue

Media guides possess the potential to generate significant revenue for sport organizations through sales to advertisers, boosters, and sponsors. Professional and collegiate organizations frequently produce enough copies of these guides to sell them to members of the general public. Priced anywhere up to $30, guides can draw significant fan interest when their sale is promoted to interested parties. For example, officials at the University of Tennessee reported generating $70,000 in media guide sales revenue in 2003 (Brown, 2004), but as the Internet has become a go-to source for information, potential revenue from printed guides sales has decreased dramatically, especially at the collegiate level.

Some sport organizations, particularly professional teams, sell advertising that may be placed within media guides. These advertisements may be particularly marketable when the sport organization uses the guide as both a media tool and a fan publication (e.g., a game program with special inserts). For smaller colleges, the entire media guide printing budget may be funded through advertising sales.

Whereas sales to the public and advertisers can directly contribute to the sport organization's revenue, media guides may also be a source of indirect revenue when used as incentives. Some sport organizations may use media guides as perks to reward season-ticket holders and boosters. Media guides may also be included in proposed sponsorship packages as a way of adding value to the deal. The inclusion of media guides in ticket, booster, and sponsor packages may not cinch the deal, but every element that adds value to sales inventory boosts the potential for closing the sale.

Content

The following sections summarize the major components that should be included in most media guides. This listing is based on media guides that the authors have procured and on judging forms from College Sports Information Directors of America (CoSIDA) media guide contests. (See the sidebar CoSIDA Publications and Digital Design Contests.) Table 5.1 summarizes the content found in four

Table 5.1   Media Guide Content

General category	San Francisco 49ers Media Guide (NFL)	University of Tulsa Men's Basketball Record and Fact Book (NCAA)	Dallas Wings Media Guide (WNBA)	Women's National Team Media Guide (U.S. Soccer and World Cup Team)
General information	Table of contents • 2018 49ers schedule • Levi's Stadium media guide • Social media and organizational contact information • Media guide credits • Corporate partner advertisements and logos • Broadcast information	Table of contents • Media information • City of Tulsa • Facility information • University information • Directions to campus • Athletics department directory • Records against 2018–19 opponents • Quick facts	Table of contents • Staff Directory • Organization ownership and leadership • Media information • Community relations information • Mascot information • Home arena information • Social media and organizational contact information • Broadcast information	Table of contents • U.S. Women's National Team (WNT) programs • Sights set on France 2019 World Cup • Referee program • U.S. Soccer National Training Center • Media guidelines • Important phone numbers • U.S. Soccer communications and content • Programs overview • Girls' Development Academy • TV information
Team and event information	• Club directory • Player and coach bios • Executive leadership bios	• Roster and schedule • Season preview • Player bios • Coaches and staff • Staff directory • TV and radio chart	• Staff Directory • Player and coach bios • Opponent capsules • Promotional schedule	• Player and coach bios (for all women's national teams) • U.S. National Team pool • U.S. WNT headshots
Season review	• Regular-season and playoff statistics • Game-by-game results • Participation chart • Transactions • Starters and inactives • Transactions • Game summaries	• Results • Miscellaneous stats • Game-by-game superlatives • Opponent highs and lows • Game-by-game stats • Box scores • Season notes	• Season Rewind • Regular-season statistics • Scoring breakdown • Team highs and lows	• Final stats • Final results

media guides based on the general categories presented in the following sections. The table shows how content may vary based on the nature of the sport organization.

General Information

The material included in the general information category varies, but some of this information is among the most-used sections of many media guides. General information includes the following:

- A table of contents that assists readers in navigating these large and frequently complex publications
- A staff directory listing phone numbers and e-mail addresses
- Media-specific information such as how to apply for event credentials and make interview requests
- Profiles of the organization and the organization's leadership (e.g., team owner, league

General category	San Francisco 49ers Media Guide (NFL)	University of Tulsa Men's Basketball Record and Fact Book (NCAA)	Dallas Wings Media Guide (WNBA)	Women's National Team Media Guide (U.S. Soccer and World Cup Team)
History	• 49ers Founder • Team awards • NFL awards • 49ers Hall of Fame • Individual and team records • All-time results • Draft history • All-time statistical leaders • Postseason history • Team records • All-Pro selections • Pro Bowl selections • 49ers' all-time roster • Retired 49ers jerseys • All-time 49ers coaches	• Career leaders • Season records • Individual records • Team records • Miscellaneous records • Scoring records and streaks • Honors and awards • Postseason records • Year-by-year results • Year-by-year team statistics • Year-by-year rosters • Letter winners • Poll history • Series records • All-time results • Retired jerseys	• Year-by-Year results • Tulsa Shock year-by-year results* • Record versus opponents	• National Soccer Hall of Fame • All-time players list • Attendance records • U.S. WNT World Cup history • All-time results • All-time lineups • All-time individual and team records • All-time head coaches • Statistics 1994–2016
Governing body information	National Football League • Nationally televised games • Important dates	American Athletic Conference • 2017–18 conference standings and statistics • 2018–19 composite conference schedule	WNBA • 2017 Final standings, leaders, and playoffs • All-Time WNBA award winners • Playoff format • WNBA playoff history • League time line	USWNT • Information on various USWNT competitions • U.S. Soccer Staff Directory • U.S. Soccer Board of Directors and past presidents • FIFA • Confederation of North, Central America and Caribbean Association Football (Concacaf)

*Organization moved from Tulsa to Dallas prior to the 2016 season.

Information compiled from sources: San Francisco 49ers (2018); University of Tulsa (2018); Dallas Wings (2017); U.S. Soccer Communications (2018).

CoSIDA Publications and Digital Design Contests

Competition in collegiate sports extends beyond the realm of athletics. Sports information professionals compete for awards each year in CoSIDA's publications and digital design contests. Media guide contests have eight different media guide categories, and most have several divisions (CoSIDA, 2018). Categories are based on the type of media guide (e.g., lacrosse, women's soccer), and divisions are based on level of competition (e.g., NCAA Division I, NCAA Division II). In addition to media guides, CoSIDA members can submit game notes, game programs, and special event programs, as well as infographic features, motion graphics (GIFs), online magazines, posters, and video features. Members volunteer to serve as judges, and they evaluate submissions for review based on inclusion of required information, thoroughness of presentation, editorial quality, and other design elements.

The purpose of the competition is twofold. First, the competition allows the association to recognize excellence among its members. Second, those who submit their guides for peer review receive feedback from the judges' evaluations that may be helpful as the submitters endeavor to produce higher-quality guides each year.

commissioner, university president, athletic director)

- Information that details how media members can contact representatives of the organization at road contests

Team and Event Information

Information specific to the team or event should include the following:

- Season schedule (placed prominently, often on a cover or in the opening pages)
- Rosters of athletes (preferably with separate alphabetical and numerical rosters)
- Profiles of the coaching staff (if applicable), including relevant coaching records
- Profiles of the athletes, including individual statistical profiles and personal bests
- A thorough preview of the upcoming season or event
- Opponent information (for team guides) that provide overviews of the teams on the upcoming season's schedule
- Facility information that profiles the site at which the sport organization competes

Season Review

Although historical documentation should not be limited to the most recently completed season, the past year is arguably the most relevant historical information in a media guide because current

coaches and athletes are likely to have participated. The season review should include the following:

- Game or event results
- Complete team and individual statistics

History

Information regarding the history of the sport organization should extend well beyond the most recent year. Other historical information should include the following:

- Records, both team and individual, for the organization and its opponents
- Coaching history and records
- Complete list of honors and awards received by members of the sport organization
- Complete list of significant team achievements (e.g., championships)
- All-time results, commonly displayed as year-by-year listings of contests and outcomes

Governing Body Information

Finally, team and event media guides should include information regarding the sport organization's governing bodies. Media guides of professional organizations should include profiles and historical information regarding their leagues and the leaders of those leagues, such as commissioners. College media guides should profile both their conferences and their national organizations, such as the NCAA and National Association of Intercollegiate Athletics (NAIA). Organizations that play internationalally should also include information on governing bodies of contests they may participate in (e.g., FIFA, Formula One, international individual events such as Wimbledon).

Planning

Media guide production is a complex process and one of the more challenging aspects of media relations work. Accordingly, sport public relations professionals must create plans to guide them through the process in a timely manner.

Chris Anderson (1997), former associate athletic director of communications at the University of Nebraska–Lincoln, recommended that media guide planners establish time lines by working backward from the date when the printed guide must be received by the sport organization. Key steps along the way include the following:

- Conducting interviews with coaching staff and other key individuals
- Gathering information to be used in development of player, coach, and staff profiles
- Tracking down information regarding key events and opponents
- Updating historical records
- Securing copyright permissions for the use of photographs and the reproduction of any editorial content originated outside the sport organization

Anderson also recommended that media guide content be reviewed by several individuals to ensure its accuracy before going to press. Capable proofreaders can usually be found among other public relations staff members. In smaller operations, sport public relations professionals may need to work a bit harder at identifying someone with a good eye for editing. Direct supervisors should also be given the opportunity to proof the guide. In addition, head coaches or their designated representatives should review the information for factual accuracy. Anderson also noted that guide covers likely need to be readied for the printer several weeks earlier than the rest of the publication because they are almost always four-color (full-color) and sometimes feature special design elements. Often, covers will feature prominent players and coaches, but the University of Louisville got creative and featured 2018 Triple Crown winner Justify on the front cover of its

football media guide. Along with three Louisville players, the horse was featured with a 100th season anniversary logo and the tag line "Speed City," an approach originally suggested by head coach Bobby Petrino to Louisville communications staff (Lourim, 2018).

Not surprisingly, some media guides evolve into year-round projects—as soon as one year's guide is complete, work on the next year's guide begins. Most of the work on any guide occurs in the off-season, but some public relations professionals recommend that some work on the upcoming season's guide be done during the current season, particularly writing game summaries for that season (Abicht, 2004).

Design Elements and Quality

Design elements are arguably still important for media guides, although less time is spent on cover design at the collegiate level since the guides are no longer used for recruiting purposes. Even so, all sport public relations professionals should strive to make their publications as attractive to readers as possible. Special attention should be paid to cover design, selection of type fonts, graphic elements that may be incorporated throughout the publication, color that may be incorporated into the layout, and the photos that are included in the publication. Care must also be taken to ensure the design can be viewed easily in an online format, as most organizations now produce a digital copy of guides as well.

The list of layout and design principles relevant to these considerations is too lengthy to detail in this text. Table 5.2 offers some guidelines, but it serves only to alert readers to the most critical questions that professionals must consider. Specific training in desktop publishing and layout and design is highly valuable to sport public relations professionals. Even those with some training in publication design may be wise to collaborate with graphic arts specialists throughout the production process.

As with any other type of organizational publication, media guides must be written with the highest level of editorial quality to achieve credibility with their audiences. At a minimum, media guides should be free of grammatical and syntactical errors. Factual errors are also highly problematic, because members of the media are extremely concerned with accuracy. If media members convey inaccurate

Case Study

A MEDIA GUIDE CRISIS RESPONSE APPROACH

In July 2018, Ohio State University football assistant coach Zach Smith was fired from his position following a report from journalist Brett McMurphy on Facebook that provided information on an incident between Smith and his wife several years before. The report included information about a protective order filed against Smith by his wife, and Smith was fired shortly before Ohio State's 2018 football season was set to begin.

While the public relations fallout was extensive enough to touch multiple chapters in this text, the fact that Ohio State's football media guide would have already been completed in advance of Big Ten Media Days deserves a closer look.

Like many schools, Ohio State no longer prints media guides for sale to the public or for recruiting, a practice adopted after NCAA legislation changed their use in recruiting practices (CoSIDA, 2015), the school does still curate its media guides online on the athletics department website (ohiostatebuckeyes .com). A review of the 2018 guide following the season showed that Smith had been removed from the online version of it, a process that would have been much more difficult had Ohio State printed guides as many schools had done in the past (and some larger colleges continue to do in smaller quantities for media purposes). After Smith was fired, Ohio State desired to have his association with the team eliminated; a normal response tactic is to remove the person from organizational media that can quickly be adapted internally, such as websites and online rosters, and information such as media guides (other crisis communications response tactics are described in later chapters).

Discussion Questions

1. Do you think the appearance of the fired coach in the media guide could cause any negative impact with the organization had it been printed instead of online?

2. Do you think the response to remove the coach from the guide would have been the same if McMurphy's report had not gone viral and made national news?

3. How would a similar situation be handled for a coach who retires or desires to pursue other opportunities but leaves on a positive note? Do you think such a person would be eliminated from the guide before the season began?

Table 5.2 Media Guide Design Considerations

Design element	Key questions
Cover	Is it attractive? Does it incorporate key elements (e.g., organization name, logo, year)? Does it possess a recognizable look with the organization's brand?
Type font	Is the body copy easy to read? Is the use of fonts consistent throughout the guide?
Graphics	What visual tools are used to make the presentation attractive? Screens (shaded areas)? Text boxes? Logos and symbols? Is the use of these visual tools consistent?
Photos	Are photos clear (i.e., focus, contrast)? Action photos: Is the ball in the photo? Action photos: Do they capture the moment?

information from a media guide in one of their stories, the sport organization's mistake has cost the media members credibility with their audience. And because media guides are produced primarily for media members, the guides should conform to Associated Press (AP) style guidelines.

Distribution

Multiple methods may be employed to distribute media guides. Public relations personnel often personally deliver guides to members of the media who cover the sport organization on a regular basis. Media guides may also be made available at preseason media days or at the facility on game day in an area specially dedicated to media. Nearly all sport organization media guides also appear on the organization's website in a PDF file or other presentation format.

Guides may be mailed to members of the media who cover the team on occasion but not on a frequent basis (e.g., a writer for a national magazine) as well as to public relations representatives of the opponents that the organization will be facing in the upcoming season. These opponents are likely profiled in the guide, and the publication will serve as an important resource as the opponent's public relations representatives provide relevant information to their own media constituents.

Because significant costs are involved in printing media guides and mailing them, some sport organizations sell the publications to those who are not going to use them for professional purposes.

Postseason Guides

Successful seasons often lead to postseason competition. Although most sport public relations professionals enjoy those winning campaigns, they present an additional challenge in that information in media guides is usually several months old when postseason play arrives. As a result, many sport public relations professionals create special postseason media guides.

Postseason publications are usually less comprehensive than regular media guides and less complex in design and production. They serve as updates because, through the course of a successful season, player and coach statistics have changed, awards have been received, and records have been broken. The postseason media guide documents these changes. A typical postseason guide includes the following:

- Updated rosters and depth charts
- Complete regular-season game results
- Complete team and individual statistical reports for the regular season
- Final regular-season standings
- Updated biographies for players and coaches
- Chronology of how the team was built (at professional levels)
- Team postseason records

Most postseason guides are compiled quickly, so time is not available to dress them up with design elements or color or have them printed on glossy paper. Many are simply copied in-house and bound with staples or spiral binding.

Print Organizational Media

Although the media guide may be a sport organization's largest and most visible organizational media tactic, many other print options exist, each with its own attributes and objectives. These include, but are not limited to, game notes, newsletters, programs, posters, schedule cards, brochures, reprints, and annual reports. Publishing these items is somewhat challenging for the sport public relations practitioner. As Wilcox and colleagues (2016) pointed out, the public relations professional needs to produce media that promotes management's organizational objectives, serves the interests of constituents, and incorporates journalistic standards. These standards are especially important when producing all of the following forms of organizational media, which carry a high degree of credibility because of their design.

Game Notes

Game notes have become an important organizational media tool as a result of the rise in the number of contests now shown on television and in streaming formats. Even smaller organizations may have in-house broadcasts for games, requiring up-to-date information for use by the broadcast production team. The timeliness of these documents (sometimes referred to as game advances and weekly releases) is most critical, placing significant demand on sport public relations professionals, because broadcast teams and other media will be preparing and producing elements of coverage for the event days (and sometimes weeks) before the event.

CoSIDA executive director Doug Vance described game notes as "the [sport public relations professional's] calling card to the media for as long as there has been a sports information profession" (Vance 2018, para. 2). The evolution of game notes has mirrored the evolution of media guides, as sizes, colors, and content have varied over the years.

Sport public relations professionals often attempt to provide more than enough information for a game in their notes, but time and resource demands must be balanced in game notes production.

Game notes can vary in length from as few as 1 or 2 pages to as many as 500, depending on the type of organization and the amount of attention paid to each contest. With some sports playing multiple contests a week, the amount of time and resources spent by sport public relations professionals during the season can be significant enough to require proper planning.

Authors frequently can pull pieces of information from the media guide early in the season. Game notes are often set up to include space for future information as the season progresses, allowing for a quick update of information following each contest. In larger organizations, multiple members of the sport public relations staff may play a role in the development of the entire game notes package, while smaller organizations, especially at the collegiate level, will often have just one person devoted to producing the game notes package prior to each contest. In small college sport public relations offices, these notes may be produced once a week for multiple contests because of the significant amount of time required to update multiple notes packages for multiple sports that may be in season.

Another consideration for sport public relations professionals is the impact that resources used in game notes production can have on internal operations, especially the amount of paper used to print game notes and whether to print any of the notes' pages in color. While color can enhance the appearance of game notes, color printing costs internally can be extensive. Many organizations may choose to print the first page of the notes package in full color for branding purposes and potentially a one-page, printed full-color broadcast chart for detail on player and coach pictures for identification purposes. The majority of the game notes package is likely to be printed in black and white.

With the addition of digital publication of game notes on organizational websites, organizations may choose to print fewer copies of their notes package, reserving printed copies for broadcast personnel (who will also often make their own copies of the notes prior to arriving for the contest).

While media guides may continue to be a publication that prominently represents an organization prior to the start of a particular season, a sport public relations professional's game notes can require just as much planning and attention throughout the course of the season.

While the viewpoint of every organization and every sport public relations professional is different, many elements of game notes, such as the header, media information, team season information, and team notes, can be seen across varying levels of sport organizations.

Header

The header of an organization's game notes is likely to include the team logo and other information important to the recognition of the event, such as the date of the game, game time and place (with stadium capacity information), and the records of both

Game notes have been a long-standing tool for broadcast sports reporters, giving them a bank of facts and statistics to reference during their commentary, reporting, and interviews as part of a broadcast.

teams participating in the contest. Often, broadcast information will appear in the header, and organizations may place social media information as a call to action that allows readers the opportunity to follow teams that are participating in the contest.

Headers usually include some sort of specific branding for the organization, such as word marks, logos, specific fonts, and other recognizable characteristics like team colors. Some design elements might mirror those found on the organization's website, in the official organization letterhead, or even in components of that season's media guide.

Media Information

Often included on the front page, information on game broadcasts (e.g., streaming, television, radio) includes where broadcasts can be found, the talent on the broadcasts, and contact information for sport public relations professionals of the organization. This contact information likely includes sport organization professionals' personal cell phone numbers, e-mail addresses, and even social media information if it is a professionally based account.

The increase in information-seeking publics makes this information important to include, but media will use this information to answer questions from their own information-seeking publics as well. For sports with smaller roster sizes such as basketball and baseball, sport public relations professionals may even include a one-page chart that can be used on site by broadcast professionals and media covering the event, especially at the collegiate level where players are not as recognizable. For example, the Baylor University men's basketball team provides photos of the players for identification purposes, as well as identification information (player numbers, heights, weights, hometowns) and sometimes small bites of information that can be used to describe the player (such as personal superlatives and significant career moments). (Search "Baylor Bears media almanac" online to view the PDF for this publication.)

An easy-to-find series history is also often included, with overall series records for both teams; the number of previous meetings between the teams; and the records of the teams' games against each other at home, away, and at neutral sites. This series history may also include the records of opposing coaches against each other, the overall records of both, and the records of both at their current respective organizations.

Team Season Information

Game notes are often dedicated to an immense amount of information about a team's current season, especially for the opposing team's media, who may not have followed the progress of the organization's season prior to a matchup they will cover.

This category of information includes a schedule that is updated with results up to the present contest. The team's overall and division or conference record is also included. Information on the organization's coach is also present, including the coach's overall and organization or school coaching record. A team's roster is also included, and a pronunciation guide is also an important addition, especially for broadcast personnel.

A large amount of team information in game notes is dedicated to statistics. The types of statistics will vary depending on the sport the team participates in (e.g., basketball, football) but most include updated statistics, statistics on previous games, recaps and box scores, and team and individual superlatives.

Also included in this category are statistical categories often referenced in a broadcast, including team records when playing at home, leading at halftime, and so on. Probable starters are noted, and participation charts from throughout the season are often found in game notes as well.

Team Notes

While team season statistical information produces a large amount of content in game notes, another important category of information is usually delivered in short, easy-to-digest bites of information called notes.

Rece Davis, host of ESPN's popular college football and basketball preview show on Saturday morning, *College GameDay*, described the best written notes as "bite sized and easily understandable, yet not overly simplistic" (Vance 2018, para. 9). Often, these small pieces of information about a team, individual player, season, or organization are one to two sentences, frequently formatted in bulleted lists with categorical headers describing a block of notes devoted to the same topic.

These bites of information are often quickly mentioned in broadcasts but can also promote potential story ideas to members of the media. These notes often include information on previous contests, allowing the sport public relations professional the opportunity to have some notes that do not need updating after every single contest.

Newsletters

Newsletters combine the look and feel of a publication such as a magazine or newspaper with

College game-day hosts often utilize team notes to prepare for interviews and commentary.
© Steve Adelson

organizational publicity information. Newsletters serve a variety of purposes and may be customized for specific publics such as employees, alumni, vendors, donors, and customers. Large organizations may choose to produce more than one newsletter, depending on the public that they are targeting. Smith (2017) estimated that the total number of organizational newsletters in the United States may be as high as one million.

Traditionally, newsletters were distributed in printed form, often on glossy paper with color photographs, through the mail. But technology has changed that model significantly. Now more newsletters are considered e-news, or electronic news, and are frequently delivered directly from the organization to the subscriber in an e-mail or through an organizational app. Smith (2017) warned that while e-mail newsletters create another organizational vehicle to communicate, they should be used strategically with a definitive purpose and targeted to publics that sign up to receive them, in an effort to avoid e-mail inbox congestion. Newsletters may be published on any

schedule from daily to quarterly depending on the targeted audience.

One advantage of a newsletter is that it allows organizations to communicate certain information to a large public all at once. The organization has complete control of the message, and because of its design a newsletter may have more credibility with readers because it is not a traditional form of advertising. Another advantage of newsletters is closely tied to marketing in the ability to get more information from those targeted audiences, such as potential leads that can become beneficial connections. While the paths of public relations and marketing may cross here, Miller (2017) described a need for a 90/10 ratio between educational and promotional content. This ratio makes the communication function, and the information a sport public relations professional can supply, critical to the measurable success of e-newsletters.

Smith (2017) cautioned organizations to follow the principles of newsworthiness (see chapter 7) when writing newsletters. Information in newsletters should be of interest to the readers and not simply

Be Your Own Media

Considering important facts to include in a set of game notes is as easy as thinking of your favorite team or organization. What are the organization's current major story lines? Whatever critical stories need to be told, when developing a game notes package, the sport public relations professional has the responsibility to tell the organization's story in bite-sized pieces of information that resonate with multiple publics.

Go to the website of a sport organization of your choosing that is currently in season, and see whether you are able to download game notes for an upcoming game. Not every organization posts these notes for the general public, so you may have to search multiple sites, but when you do find a set of game notes, read through them and notice elements of proactive and reactive public relations (recall the discussion in chapter 2). Reactive public relations provides a public relations viewpoint on the past, such as a losing or winning streak, and proactive public relations provides information and perspective on upcoming events such as a record about to be set.

From your viewpoint as a fan or casual observer, does the information in the game notes align with the major current story lines of the organization? Is the theme more proactive or reactive? Could your answer have something to do with how the organization's season is currently playing out? If you had to sum up the team's season in one or two sentences (think of Twitter-like character limits here), how easy would that be?

information that the organization wishes to disclose. For example, a sport organization's newsletter targeting alumni may include current information about the performance of the organization's teams as well as updates on the whereabouts of former athletes. Alumni will appreciate learning where former teammates are currently living and what they are doing.

The newsletter's focus will help determine whether it will be an internal or external newsletter. Internal newsletters are primarily for people who are or have been part of the organization, including alumni, employees, and volunteers. A university athletics department may produce an alumni newsletter that focuses exclusively on news and information related to student–athletes. This newsletter would be separate from the university's general alumni newsletter, which focuses on all former students. Alumni newsletters often play on the sentiment of former athletes and their ties to the university. For this reason, messages regarding donations and fundraising are common.

Employee newsletters might focus on human resource information such as benefits and insurance changes. Large organizations with employees in many locations might use a newsletter to update their employees regarding product development as well. For example, a sporting goods company might have its corporate headquarters in a major city, but it might also have distribution centers and manufacturing plants throughout the world. Information that allows employees a measure of pride in the company is common in these newsletters. The sporting goods company may wish to recognize employees for longevity with the company or acknowledge a specific plant that has set a record for consecutive work days without a lost-time injury.

Volunteer newsletters are effective at motivating people who donate their time and energy to the organization. Special Olympics New Jersey offers a monthly newsletter for volunteers. The newsletter presents information on the organization and gives volunteers information about different sports, upcoming events, and future volunteer opportunities designed to increase volunteer retention.

External newsletters generally focus on persuading readers about a particular issue or communicating directly with an influential group of people such as investors, customers, and community leaders.

Newsletters that target customers of the organization are frequently tied into the organization's marketing efforts and can be highly measurable. For example, the Oklahoma City Thunder deliver their *Thunder Insider* newsletter directly to subscribers through e-mail. The newsletter contains exclusive information on ticket deals, merchandise discounts, and calls to action such as All-Star game voting. By supplying the subscriber with a discount code or coupon, organizations can track the success of their newsletters in reaching customers. Many sport organizations connect e-mail newsletters to their affinity marketing programs—programs designed to leverage the strong sense of connectedness that people may feel to a team or organization—and provide these newsletters as a benefit of membership in a fan program (Mullin, Hardy, & Sutton, 2014).

External newsletters may also target specific community leaders, or advocate a specific position on an impending issue. For example, the NCAA

Eligibility Center publishes a monthly newsletter for member institutions that includes reminders, updates, information on resources, and updates to international academic standards for eligibility.

Game Programs

Game programs, sometimes called scorecards, are typically sold on the day of an event and are written, assembled, and distributed by the organization that is hosting the event. Game programs are sold to the general public and provide lineup information for the event along with feature stories and other information about the host organization. Programs can be a revenue source for an organization in two ways. First, the organization can sell the program directly to spectators attending the event, and second, the organization can sell advertising space in the program to local businesses. The marketing department often handles the advertising sales, and many of the ads are provided through trade with sponsors and other businesses.

The public relations staff usually writes, edits, and designs the program. Occasionally the host organization receives publishing support from a league or governing body or from a national sport publisher who will edit and print the cover and several pages of general information along with national advertisements. In such cases, the host organization adds specific stories about the organization and local advertisements.

The typical program is a four-color, high-gloss magazine with color photographs, although some smaller sport organizations might publish a scorecard featuring only the rosters and lineups of the event participants. Memorabilia enthusiasts often collect programs and scorecards, and many spectators view them as keepsakes to remember attending special events. Many programs from previous events can be found and purchased online, potentially with prices in excess of $100 depending on the age of the program and the particular event. Sport public relations practitioners thus have an obligation to develop programs that are professional and memorable.

The more elaborate the program is, the more it will cost to produce it. Organizations may charge between $10 and $20 for programs at premier events such as the Super Bowl or Final Four. For example, Major League Baseball sold copies of the 2017 World Series program featuring the Houston Astros and the Los Angeles Dodgers for $15. Sport organizations typically charge $3 to $10 for programs at regularly scheduled events.

Posters

Like programs, posters often involve both the marketing and public relations departments. Posters are common at the university level and with smaller professional organizations (such as minor league baseball and hockey) and are generally specific to the sport. Posters that are prominently displayed in businesses and storefronts close to the organization provide visibility to the organization (Smith, 2017).

Many posters have a corporate sponsor who helps to underwrite the production costs of the poster—hence the marketing tie-in. Posters usually feature prominent athletes as well as the season's schedule. If the marketing department has developed an advertising theme for the team, the poster often serves as an extension of those efforts. An additional use for posters might be to distribute them to children before a certain game and allow the children to get player autographs after the game, thus combining a direct-contact community relations activity with public relations and marketing objectives.

Schedule Cards

Unique to the sport industry is the **schedule card**, a pocket-sized publication that features the organization's schedule. Schedule cards are intended to be a vehicle for both information and advertising; they are typically considered a marketing tactic and often involve a corporate sponsor or advertiser. Schedule cards may be printed with a prominent athlete on one side and the schedule on the other side. Programs for sports that have lengthy schedules, such as baseball, may opt to create a schedule card with several panels that fold into a pocket-size piece. Cards also may include ticket prices and maps of stadium seating sections that may be priced differently.

Brochures

Sometimes called leaflets or pamphlets, brochures provide basic information about an organization, product, or service. Brochures are distributed through the mail, in information racks, or electronically as PDF files that may be downloaded or sent by e-mail. Sport organizations commonly use brochures in support of marketing initiatives. Prospective season-ticket buyers might receive a brochure that includes specific information regarding schedules, ticket locations, ticket prices, and ordering procedures. The promotion of youth camps sponsored by the organization that include the team's coaches and potentially players is another use for brochures, designed to collect information that again can be used in organizational public relations and marketing efforts.

Brochures are often printed on glossy paper and folded. A standard brochure is often folded into thirds, creating six panels. A ticket brochure might be formatted so that one of the panels is an order form and can be detached and mailed to the organization along with payment for tickets.

Annual Reports

The final organizational media print form discussed in this chapter is the annual report. The annual report as a function of investor relations is discussed later in the text. Increasingly, however, sport organizations issue a season summary as a type of annual report. The season summary is a retrospective of the organization's season, complete with a narrative review of the season as well as final statistics and records. Reprints of news articles may also be included as a way to provide historical context. Season summaries are especially helpful for beat reporters and other media members who cover the organization. The annual report is, in some respects, a media guide for after the season.

Electronic Organizational Media

Smith (2017) noted that electronic forms of organizational media continue to grow in popularity and can enhance the audiovisual aspects of public relations. This is a burgeoning area of public relations, but it comes at a cost for some practitioners. Smaller sport organizations may see these electronic organizational media as a necessity in order to compete with larger counterparts but may not have the resources to invest in the necessary tools and employees needed to compete with larger budgets and staff in bigger organizations. While quality video can now be recorded on a cell phone, in order to add professional graphics, software is needed, and editing takes time, which may be at a premium for a practitioner in a smaller organization who has numerous other duties. While new technologies are developing and making for more meaningful interactions with fans and organizations, it is important

to remember that a balance must be achieved that makes electronic organizational media a positive addition and not something that drains public relations morale.

Video

The decline of print journalism has given birth to a new era of news consumption that includes video as a primary distribution vehicle, increasing the public relations value and versatility of how organizations tell their story.

Michael Sadowski (2018), head of marketing and communications at Intrepid Group, the world's largest adventure travel company, commented that the best video media isn't confined to one digital space but can live in a variety of channels in a variety of formats. Sporting goods manufacturers use videos to demonstrate new products. Teams use highlight videos of a successful season as a revenue stream for the organization. Coaches use instructional videos to reach out to aspiring athletes. Organizations use training videos for new employees or volunteers.

Organizations may consider a variety of distribution methods for video, such as DVDs, podcasts, and streaming video via social media or an organizational website. Regardless of the distribution platform, Helitzer (2000) advised organizations to consider two things when producing a highlight video for public distribution: (1) professional production and editing and (2) sponsor interest. Specifically, videos should have the look and feel of a professional broadcast. Several broadcast-quality cameras, rather than camcorders, should be used to capture the action. Approximately 10 minutes of video should be shot for every minute of highlight video. The sport organization should use an editing studio for postproduction of the highlight video, which may prove to be expensive, depending on the amount of video that needs to be edited. Organizations may want to offer existing sponsors an opportunity to underwrite the production in exchange for advertising or sponsorship presentation associated with the video.

Public relations professionals should view their job in the production of a video as that of project manager. Public relations professionals often conceptualize the video and create a storyboard that includes determining which video to use and writing the script that will be recorded over the video (Wilcox et al., 2016).

Audio

Although less popular than video media, audio represents a publicity opportunity for organizational public relations (Smith, 2017). Common tactics that can be employed in audio media include podcasts, recorded telephone information, and voice mail. A podcast has been defined as "a music or talk program made available in digital format for automatic download over the Internet to a personal mp3 or digital device" (U.S. Environmental Protection Agency, 2009). Podcasts may feature audio only or video as well and may be played on traditional computers or mobile devices such as smartphones or iPods. Users may subscribe to podcasts through RSS feeds or iTunes and receive frequent updates from an organization's key messengers.

The use of automated telephone messages has become commonplace in today's business environment. These recorded messages are an opportunity to promote organizational objectives to audiences who are seeking information. After all, the people who call an organization are doing so because they wish to obtain information about the organization. Sport managers should strive to keep their recorded messages current. Updates regarding ticket availability for an upcoming event or a rebroadcast of positive moments from the previous event are ways that an organization can build on its message distribution.

Electronic Publishing

Smith (2017) stated that nearly every form of print organizational media discussed in this chapter is now potentially distributed in an electronic format as well. Technology continues to impact audio and video media as well, as most recording, editing, and production devices now store everything digitally as opposed to using videocassettes and CDs.

Presentation software, such as PowerPoint, Prezi, and Google Slides, has become universally accepted in today's business environment, and organizations may wish to use this format to deliver information about a product or program that they are promoting. Audience members can download the file from the organization's website or access it from a cloud server, or the organization can e-mail the file directly to audience members. In addition, presentation software allows people to print slides for later reference.

In addition to publishing through social media (discussed in chapters 3 and 4), the use of websites and smartphones has become a staple tactic for advancing public relations and marketing objectives.

Websites have become a tool every organization can use to connect with information-seeking publics. The types and amounts of information may vary, but the website can provide a vast array of information in a way that is easy to find and read. Public relations professionals should be wary of making the organizational website a catchall repository for everything and capitalize on opportunities for interpersonal interactions with publics rather than point them toward a website with little direction. Specific links are helpful to provide a direct pathway to the information needed by the organization's publics.

Information may also be disseminated through an **organizational app**, made available to members of the public via their smartphone's or tablet's operational software. Smith (2017) stated that there are numerous positive implications for public relations professionals in the use of apps by targeted publics including "banking services, voting, ticket purchases, order tracking, maps [and location services], and scanner readers" (p. 284). Other apps, such as Grammarly, can assist public relations professionals in writing, and connecting with other departments in the organization can be made easier using apps like Slack and Trello, which focus on communication and workflow.

Sport public relations professionals are advised to use a cross-section of organizational media tactics in their public relations campaigns (Harris, 1998; Smith, 2017). Table 5.3 summarizes the various organizational media tactics available to sport public relations professionals, the uses of these tactics, and their advantages and disadvantages.

Regardless of the tactic, consistency is vital to integrating organizational messages and achieving organizational objectives. For example, sport managers who want to communicate information about an upcoming season's schedule should not rely on schedule cards alone. Instead, an integrated communication plan might involve a news release, as discussed in chapter 7, supplemented by the production and distribution of schedule cards, posters, newsletters, and direct e-mails.

NEWS. TICKETS. SHOP. GAME COVERAGE.

ALL THE INFO YOU NEED ON YOUR MOBILE DEVICE

Organizational apps can help college sport teams connect with fans.

Corporate Communications

Sport organizations are structured in diverse ways, so considerable variance is present within the field in terms of which unit assumes functional responsibility for organizational media. Media guides are almost always produced by public relations units within collegiate athletics departments. Professional organizations may be structured in such a way that media relations falls to a communications department that also includes community relations and other public relations programs. Other sport organizations, such as the National Association for Stock Car Racing (NASCAR), have **corporate communications** units that oversee public relations activities, including the production of organizational media.

Corporate communications departments vary in size and scope of responsibility. For instance, National Hockey League (NHL) director of corporate communications Michael DiLorenzo stated,

"One of the many goals of the NHL's corporate communications unit is to reinforce key league messages with its corporate partners and other influential stakeholders in the business-to-business marketplace" (DiLorenzo, 2010). The communications division (teamusa.org/media) of the U.S. Olympic & Paralympic Committee (USOPC) assumes responsibility for managing media inquiries for the organization as well as communications efforts at USOPC events. The department also provides media training to representatives of U.S. Olympics and Paralympics. In addition, the department operates the organization's National Anti-doping Education Program. Finally, the unit offers communication services to other USOC departments such as development and entertainment properties.

As with USOC, corporate communications departments often assume both public relations and marketing responsibilities. One of the advantages of this approach is that it may result in more coordinated efforts to integrate organizational media in a consistent manner.

Table 5.3 Organizational Media Uses and Advantages

Organizational media tactic	Target public	Common platforms	Advantages	Disadvantages
Media guide	Primarily members of the media; also may be of interest to fans of the team or event	Print publication, PDF file for download, electronic media guide	Can yield positive publicity from media members who use the guide as a resource; can generate revenue	High production costs; significant time required to plan, develop, and produce
Game notes	Primarily media covering a specific event that includes the organization	Print publication, PDF file for download	Positive publicity yielded on game broadcasts or related programming; can serve as an up-to-date source for information-seeking publics	High production costs; significant time required to produce multiple times throughout a team's season
Newsletter	Customizable to a variety of publics including alumni, employees, customers, and community leaders	Print publication, PDF file for download, e-newsletter	Can communicate similar messages across a variety of publics	Potential costs for production and distribution; timeliness
Program	Customers attending organizational events	Print publication; potential digital distribution via website or organizational app	Potential revenue stream through direct sales and advertising sales	High production costs; changes for every event
Poster	Several but primarily customers (fans) of the organization and community businesses	Print publication	Potential revenue stream through sponsorship; broad publicity	Establishing a consistent distribution network
Schedule card	Existing customers of the organization as well as potential new customers	Print publication	Potential revenue stream through sponsorship	Establishing a distribution network; frequent schedule changes especially for sports played outdoors
Brochure	Several but primarily targeted to customers of the organization and others seeking information	Print publication, PDF file for download or e-mail attachment	Can be used for revenue generation	High production costs; information may become out of date
Annual report	Primarily geared toward shareholders for annual reports but also targeted toward media and general public for season summaries	Print publication, PDF file for download, electronic annual report	Positive publicity; targeted to important publics	High production costs

Organizational media tactic	Target public	Common platforms	Advantages	Disadvantages
Video	Suitable for all publics	DVDs, podcasts, streaming videos	Can be used for a variety of purposes including potential revenue generation	High production costs
Audio	Suitable for all information-seeking publics	Podcasts, streaming audio, telephone messaging	Can be updated frequently to ensure timely content	Limited to information-seeking publics
Electronic publishing	Suitable for all publics but often targeted to media and customers of the organization	Websites, presentation software, e-mail, organizational apps	Can be timely; wide distribution	Message needs to be explicit

SUMMARY

Most sport organizations employ some type of organizational media in support of their public relations objectives. Organizational media tactics available to sport public relations professionals are almost as numerous as the number of stakeholder groups that these practitioners serve. Media guides produced by professional and collegiate sport organizations may represent the most complex form of organizational media in the field. These guides are resources for members of the mass media, promotional materials that may be sent to prospective student–athletes, and products that are sold to the public and included as incentives for donors or sponsors. Media guides contain in-depth information about the sport organization, its representatives, the current season or event, and the history of the organization. Other forms of organizational print media include game notes, newsletters, programs, posters, schedule cards, brochures, reprints, and annual reports. Electronic organizational media include video, audio, and computer-based communication. Each form of media may be customized for specific publics and purposes, but sport public relations professionals should make every effort to achieve some level of consistency in their communication tactics. Responsibility for the planning, design, and production of organizational media is sometimes assigned to a corporate communications department that may assume both public relations and marketing responsibilities.

LEARNING ACTIVITIES

1. Develop a small media guide for a local high school team. Begin by outlining a plan that will guide you through the planning and production phases in a timely manner. Then work through the plan, being careful to involve all the other interested parties (e.g., coaches, administrators) as necessary to ensure the production of a thorough, accurate product.

2. Develop a newsletter for your academic program. Again, start by developing a production plan. As you move to content decisions, be sure to consider the publics who would receive such a document and what their interests may be. Plan to provide information that accommodates those interests while also incorporating elements that will present the program in a favorable light. After developing the newsletter, distribute it to the appropriate publics and solicit informal feedback from them.

3. Secure several types of organizational media produced by a single local sport organization (e.g., team, fitness center). Analyze them to assess their degree of consistency. What elements of consistency can you identify? What recommendations would you make that might enable the organization to achieve greater consistency?

Managing the Sport Organization–Media Relationship

After reading this chapter, students should be able to

- describe the media's structure and influence in society,
- denote the significance of rights fees in the success of sport organizations,
- identify and understand the increasing restrictions sport organizations are placing on media access to their teams, and
- describe basic services expected by members of the media at organizational events.

These are the key terms discussed in this chapter:

- credential
- gatekeeper
- media rooms

- rights fee
- Sports Broadcasting Act
- statistics

Few segments of the business world receive more media attention than sport. Most newspapers devote an entire section to sport. Most local television newscasts allocate an entire segment to sport. All-sports television stations, radio stations, weekly news magazines, and websites exist to satisfy the demands of our sport-crazed society. Complicating the relationship between sport organizations and the media is that the two are often viewed as "partners," with media paying leagues and teams for the rights to broadcast their events, providing sport organizations with an important source of revenue, either directly through rights fees or indirectly through exposure.

Sport organizations produce scarce content that has demonstrated the unique ability to consistently deliver the large audiences and television ratings desired by media organizations. Advertisers use the media's distribution channels to gain access to targeted consumer markets, and consumers buy products sold by those advertisers. Researchers have long noted this symbiotic relationship between media and sport organizations (e.g., Andrews, 2003; Bernstein & Blain, 2003; Evens, Iosifidis, & Smith, 2013; McChesney, 1989; Rader, 1984; Wenner, 1998). Audiences choose particular TV channels to consume sports of interest, and the media outlets harness this opportunity to maximize their revenue through advertising. Andrews (2003) noted that Rupert Murdoch used live sports programming to grow News Corporation into a transnational media corporation, suggesting Murdoch "approached sport as a form of media content whose inherent value lay in its ability to appeal to a mass audience" (p. 238).

Wenner (1989, 1998, 2006) has written extensively about the subject, coining the term *MediaSport* to describe this symbiosis. He differentiated between MediaSport institutions, or how market dynamics shape sport; MediaSport texts, or how the media influences the reality of heroism, nation, race, and gender; and MediaSport audiences, or how most spectators consume sport.

Managing that relationship can be a critical part of any public relations professional's daily responsibilities. Because the focus of most sport organizations is the events in which they participate, it is tempting to think that the relationship between media and organizations is based solely on those events. Increasingly, however, media cover organizations throughout the year, so PR professionals must nurture relationships with the media on a regular basis. Indeed, it is impossible to distinguish the mass media from today's sport consumption experience, but that relationship has not always been this close. Many sport organizations initially viewed the media as a threat to profitability rather than a revenue stream.

This chapter addresses three main topics critical to understanding the sport organization–media relationship. First, this chapter explores the history of that relationship, tracing the evolution from print coverage in the 1800s to the growth of television during the latter half of the 1900s. Emphasis is placed on sport as entertainment by addressing adaptations that sport organizations have made for the benefit of the media as well as sport created solely for television. The second section deals with navigating the structure and landscape of today's increasingly complex media sport environment, with its growing emphasis on direct-to-consumer and mobile applications. Providing facilities and services for members of the media who are covering organizational events enables them to focus on reporting. This subject makes up the third and final section of the chapter.

Definition of Mass Media

Journalists often refer to their role in constructing public ideology as that of **gatekeeper**. They alone decide what to report and when. The *New York Times* states boldly on its masthead that it reports "all the news that is fit to print." Sage (1998) observed that "the media determine what we think, how we feel, and what we do about our social and political environment" (p. 164). Accordingly, the mass media strongly influence the ideologies commonly accepted in most cultures. They accomplish this as gatekeepers, deciding which stories to cover, where to place stories in a newscast or a newspaper, what quotes to use, and which images to accompany the story. If something newsworthy happens, the media's job is to report it. Ultimately, the media decide what is newsworthy through their allocation of resources. The media's choice not to cover a high school volleyball game does not necessarily mean the game is not newsworthy. Rather, it may mean that the media have decided to dedicate resources to other events that they feel are more newsworthy. The core of a PR professional's job is convincing a journalist that news about an organization is worthy and fit to print or broadcast.

Traditionally, scholars have divided mass media forms into print and electronic (Black & Bryant, 1995;

Sage, 1998). Print media include newspapers, magazines, and books, whereas electronic media include radio, television, and film. Some sport governing bodies, such as the International Olympic Committee (IOC), treat each group differently. The IOC refers to non-rights-holding media covering the Olympic Games, such as writers and photographers, as *press*, and it refers to rights-holding media, such as television and radio personnel, as *broadcast* (Samaranch, 1996). Most sport managers refer to print and electronic media simply as *the media*.

That dichotomy fails to consider emerging forms of new media. To that end, Pedersen, Miloch, and Laucella (2007) first conceived a strategic sport communication model in which one of three components focused on sport mass media. In the model, the authors distinguish between three segments of sport mass media: publishing and print communication, electronic and visual communication, and new media. Hutchins (2018) has expanded this line of thinking, calling for a complete mobile media sport research agenda. He argues that mobile media have become the "norm" for how consumers access information: "This focus represents a departure from over a century of institutional and commercial history in which broadcast (radio and television) and print (newspapers and magazines) have been the dominant technologies sustaining the production, representation, and consumption of sport" (p. 2).

As these technologies have improved and become more accessible, any organization can act in a manner consistent with that of a media organization. In fact, many sport organizations have hired former traditional journalists to produce content, both print and video, for official team or university websites. This evolving space has led to challenges to the historical view of the privileges and protections that come with being a member of the media. Discussion of these challenges will be presented later in this chapter.

Mass Media and Sport History

The beginnings of organized sport in North America can be traced back to the early 1800s, but as Rader (1999) observed, the growth of sport was aided by "improvements in communication and transportation, plus the growth of cities" (p. 20). The advent of the telegraph in the mid-1800s began the marriage of mass media and sport. Betts (1953) found that

the new technology, including improvements to the printing press, led to immediate reporting of baseball, boxing, horse racing, and regattas throughout the United States. The symbiotic relationship between the mass media and sport began to play a prominent role in American society in the 1920s, when sport emerged as a social institution (McChesney, 1989), and communication grew to include radio broadcasts and then television broadcasts for which media companies paid leagues and teams a **rights fee**. The role played by broadcast rights fees is central to today's relationship between sport organizations and the media. The following sections discuss how the relationship has evolved.

Print Media

William Trotter Porter started the United States' first weekly sport publication in 1831, the *Spirit of the Times*. At its height in 1856, 40,000 subscribers were reportedly reading it each week (Rader, 1999). Twenty-five years would pass before Joseph Pulitzer established the first sports department in a daily newspaper in his New York Herald in 1883, and another 12 years passed before the first sports section appeared, developed by William Randolph Hearst in the *New York Journal* in 1895 (McChesney, 1989).

The prominence of the sports writer grew immensely in the first quarter of the 20th century. Grantland Rice was the most recognized writer during this period. Known for his poetic prose, Rice inspired a new wave of writers who saw "their task to be the construction of an interesting story of what had happened or what was likely to happen" (Rader, 1984, p. 21). Following a Notre Dame–Army football game in 1924, Rice wrote for the *New York Tribune* what may be the most famous lead sentence of any sports story written in the 20th century: "Outlined against a blue-gray October sky, the Four Horsemen rode again" (Rice, 1954, p. 177). Only after that story did the Notre Dame backfield become known as the Four Horsemen.

Rice and his contemporaries created heroes out of athletes and social drama out of athletic competition. Fans of sport had only two ways to gain a visual image of their athletic heroes at the time—go to a game in person or draw a mental picture in their mind based on the words of sports writers. In effect, the print media legitimized organized sport in the United States and created a rabid spectator following.

Notre Dame famously staged four football players on horseback after Grantland Rice wrote a story drawing parallels between the players and the Four Horsemen of the Apocalypse as described in the New Testament.

©The four horsemen of the football, Notre Dame backfield. Indiana Notre Dame, ca. 1924. Photograph. Retrieved from the Library of Congress, https://www.loc.gov/item/2013646095/.

Radio Broadcasts

If the print media brought the stories of sports heroes into homes, it was radio that brought sounds to those stories, enhancing the spectator experience. Fueled by technology from World War I, radio broadcasts began to transform consumption of sport. Spectators could experience an event as it was happening instead of waiting for the next day's newspaper story (Rader, 1984).

Early technology did not permit radio announcers to broadcast road games live in their local markets. As a result, announcers relied on Western Union tapes for play-by-play action and augmented the broadcast with in-studio sound effects to create the impression of a live broadcast (Hall, Nichols, Moynahan, & Taylor, 2007).

Owners initially feared that free radio broadcasts would cause a decrease in attendance at games, and many were hesitant to embrace the media. This reluctance disappeared as corporate advertisers became willing to pay for sponsorships of marquee events. The Ford Motor Company paid $100,000 to advertise during the 1934 World Series, and Gil-lette Safety Razor Company sponsored the World Series for 32 consecutive years beginning in 1939 (Rader, 1984). Owners' fears eased as they welcomed the additional exposure and revenue that radio delivered. Thus began a relationship between the electronic media and sport that continues today. Media want the opportunity to broadcast sporting events because of the large amount of money that advertisers are willing to pay to reach the audience.

Television Broadcasts

While radio broadcasts of sporting events dominated the period between the 1920s and the late 1950s, televised sporting events did not catch on as quickly. First, the technology at the time allowed the viewer to focus on only one thing at a time. Television was not effective in conveying the experience of a baseball game to viewers. Subtleties such as the positioning of the fielders and the lead of base runners were lost (Roberts & Olson, 1989). As technology improved, innovations such as instant replay and slow motion attracted greater numbers of viewers (McChesney, 1989).

ESTABLISHING A PROPERTY RIGHT

As Wong (2002) noted, while sport organizations have attempted to maximize financial gain from broadcast rights fees to their athletic contests since 1921, the ownership of that right has not always been clear: "The courts and the government initially had difficulty deciding who owned the property right to sports broadcasts: the team, the broadcasting station, the players, or the league" (p. 664). In the 1930s, the Pittsburgh Pirates successfully barred radio station KQV from broadcasting descriptions of games based on information from KQV observers stationed outside Forbes Field. The Pirates had previously entered into an exclusive, paid agreement with KDKA for the rights to its games (*Pittsburgh Athletic Company v. KQV Broad. Co.*, 1938).

Owners did not readily embrace this potentially new and lucrative revenue source, even though they could. For example, during the early days of radio and television in the 1930s and 1940s, Chicago Cubs owner William Wrigley charged nothing for broadcasts. As a result, "as many as seven Chicago radio stations sometimes carried Cubs games" (Rader, 1984, p. 26).

Eventually, owners and leagues realized that the ability of sports programming to draw large audiences meant many broadcast entities were willing to pay large sums for exclusive rights to carry events. The first league to benefit from a surge in rights fees was Major League Baseball, which saw radio and television broadcasting revenues increase from 3% of total revenues in 1946 to 16.8% in 1956. That percentage would increase to 50% of total revenues in 1990. Local team revenues grew as well, and an imbalance quickly developed. Teams in larger media markets, especially successful teams, reaped greater revenues than did teams in smaller markets. During the 1950s, for instance, the Brooklyn Dodgers garnered $580,000 in broadcasting revenues, whereas the St. Louis Cardinals brought in only $9,000 (Zimbalist, 1994).

The court in *Pittsburgh Athletic Company v. KQV* could not have known that the decision it made regarding a radio broadcast of a professional baseball game would forever change the revenue structure in sport. Eighty years later, sport at all levels is funded through rights fees, creating a competition among media organizations to pay more for content that is in higher demand, meaning it has a larger audience.

Discussion Questions

1. What would have been another underlying concern for owners embracing the free dissemination by radio of game play-by-play in the 1930s and 1940s?
2. What are examples of property rights emerging in the digital age?
3. How are sport organizations monetizing these rights?

Second, just as with radio, owners feared that fans would stop paying money to attend games in person if the contests were televised. Indeed, attendance at professional football and professional baseball games declined as television became more prevalent. Out of respect for their concerns, television executives blocked home games from being broadcast in local markets (Fielding & Pitts, 2003). Attendance increased as a result.

A factor that contributed directly to the growth of televised sport was the **Sports Broadcasting Act**, passed by Congress in 1961. Before the act was passed, each team was free to negotiate television contracts with national networks. The Justice Department advised league governing bodies that federal antitrust laws would prohibit them from negotiating national television contracts on behalf of all member teams. As a result, prominent and large-market teams attracted the interest of networks, while clubs in smaller markets suffered from declining attendance and reduction in potential broadcasting revenues (Rader, 1999).

The belief in the 1950s was that "the right to broadcast a game over the air belonged to and thus could be sold by the teams playing in the game" (Weiler & Roberts, 1998, p. 549). The Sports Broadcasting Act took away that right from the individual teams and gave it to governing bodies, such as Major League Baseball (MLB) and the National Football League (NFL). By representing all member clubs, leagues were able to command a greater rights fee in their negotiations with networks than an individual club could. Leagues subsequently developed a system to distribute rights fees equally among member clubs.

The first league to reap the benefits of this antitrust exemption was the NFL, whose commissioner Pete Rozelle ignited the first bidding war among television networks. CBS had signed a two-year deal with the NFL in 1962 at $4.5 million per year. As ratings increased dramatically in the early 1960s, all three national networks—CBS, NBC, and ABC—decided to bid in 1964. CBS ultimately submitted a final bid of $14 million per year for two years, so each NFL franchise received more than $1 million (Rader, 1984).

After CBS signed its 1964 deal with the NFL, NBC quickly signed a deal with the rival American Football League (AFL) for $42 million over five years (Rader, 1984). Networks were in a position to up the ante for professional football rights fees because they had found that companies were willing to pay a premium to advertise during broadcasts. As McChesney (1989) observed, sport "provided access to a very desirable market—not only for 'blue-collar' products like beer and razor blades, but for big-ticket items like automobiles and business equipment" (p. 62).

With his network blocked from the lucrative professional product, ABC Sports president Roone Arledge approached National Collegiate Athletic Association (NCAA) president Walter Byers with a proposal to broadcast college football. The NCAA had shuttled among the three major networks from 1960 to 1965. Arledge promised that ABC would not seek professional football if it was awarded exclusive rights to college games (Rader, 1984).

Despite that pledge, ABC entered an agreement with the pros when it signed a contract for *Monday Night Football* in 1970. Even so, ABC also held its exclusive deal with the NCAA until 1982 (Rader, 1984).

Arledge is acknowledged by most as having done more than any other person to cement the marriage between television and sport. Roberts and Olson (1989, p. 114) called him the "most important single individual in modern sports." He is credited with building ABC from a third-place network in the early 1960s to the top-rated network by the mid-1970s through sport programming such as the Olympics, college football, *Wide World of Sports*, and *Monday Night Football*. The sidebar ABC Television Changes the Olympic Games summarizes how ABC coverage of the Olympic Games in the 1970s made an indelible mark on the sport organization–media relationship.

Although both broadcasters and sport organizations have clear economic motivation to cooper-

The broadcast trio of Howard Cosell, Frank Gifford, and Don Meredith fueled the early popularity of ABC's *Monday Night Football.*

Michael Ochs Archives/Getty Images

ate, Ashwell (1998) observed that both sides need to look beyond the bottom line and consider benefits that are not as easily measured. For example, NBC Sports, which began broadcasting the Olympic Games in 1992, has positioned itself in the marketplace as the Olympic network by locking up television rights for the Games through 2032 for $7.65 billion (Armour, 2014). This agreement gives NBC a clear advantage over rival networks when competing for advertisers wishing to gain access to the huge audiences that the Olympics draw. NBC has used this advantage to promote much of its own programming during Olympic coverage.

As television networks became more aware of how vital rights fees were to the continued success of sport, the networks began to request changes to the sport product. These modifications were embraced by sport governing bodies that saw the changes as a small price to pay for increased television rights fees and larger fan bases.

To a certain degree, each sport that is broadcast on television has permitted the media to alter its core product in some capacity. Video cameras began to be

ABC Television Changes the Olympic Games

No televised sporting events did more to alter the landscape of the sport organization–media relationship than the 1972 Munich and 1976 Montreal Olympic Games broadcast by ABC. The human dramas played out in and around the sporting arenas riveted the American television audience and forever changed the way that Americans approached the Olympic Games. These Games altered not only the financial viability of the Olympics, but also the structure of amateur sport in the United States.

As Rader (1999) observed, ABC's coverage of the Games "contributed immensely to the Games' 'coming of age' as television extravaganzas" (p. 283). Indeed, the percentage increase in American television rights fees from 1972 to 1980 was greater than that in any other period in history. ABC paid $7.5 million for the rights for the 1972 Munich Games and $25 million for the 1976 Montreal Games—a 333% increase. But that dollar amount paled in comparison to the leap that NBC made for the 1980 Moscow Games when it paid $87 million (Senn, 1999). That figure was more than the previous 20 years of U.S. rights fees combined and was a 348% increase over 1976. Through an insurance policy, NBC recovered 90% of the $70 million it had already paid to the Moscow organizers when the United States boycotted the Games (Senn, 1999).

During the 1970s, the IOC was on the verge of financial disaster. The increase in rights fees led to a series of changes in the management of the Olympic Games. Sponsors took a more active role when they realized that the Games could attract large television audiences. The IOC brought rights fees negotiations inside its organization and out of the hands of individual organizing committees, allowing the IOC to control the process. By the 1990s, the IOC was negotiating long-term television deals rather than for one set of Games at a time. The end result was a more financially stable IOC.

Besides paying escalating rights fees, ABC's Olympics coverage created heroes, magnified the struggle between the United States and Communist nations, and legitimized sport on television as both entertainment and news.

Roone Arledge, president of ABC Sports, made a conscious decision in 1972 to focus on a teenage gymnast from the Soviet Union who was a last-minute addition to her nation's roster. For three days Arledge and ABC followed the moves of Olga Korbut as she won three gold medals and, as Arledge (2003) himself wrote, "made a previously obscure sport a television obsession and launched the gymnastics craze among teenage girls in America" (p. 125).

While Americans were becoming fixated on teenage gymnasts like Korbut and, in 1976, Romania's Nadia Comaneci, both from Communist nations, the nationalistic tones of politics took to the Olympic Games as well. American viewers were shocked as television magnified the successes of the Communist bloc nations and the disappointments of American athletes. The United States, tops in the medal count in 1968, finished only four medals ahead of East Germany in 1976 and 31 medals behind the Soviet Union (Rader, 1999).

To address the U.S. decline, President Gerald Ford established a commission to study amateur sport governance (Rader, 1999). This commission eventually passed the Amateur Sports Act in 1978, known now as the Ted Stevens Olympic and Paralympic Amateur Sports Act in honor of the senator from Alaska who chaired the commission. This legislation allowed the U.S. Olympic Committee to govern, manage, and promote all activities of the Olympic and Paralympic teams within and outside the United States (Hums & MacLean, 2004).

Unfortunately, the 1972 Olympic Games were forever scarred by the events of September 5, when members of the Palestinian terrorist group known as Black September stormed into the Olympic Village. The terrorists killed two members of the Israeli delegation in the village and took nine members hostage. All of the hostages were killed in a botched German police ambush attempt at an airport in Munich (Reeve, 2000).

Arledge was producing ABC's coverage of the Games, and as soon as he heard of the takeover in the village, he immediately made plans for ABC to broadcast live, even though it was still the middle of the night in the United States. The network broadcast for 14 hours that day as negotiations between police and the terrorists dragged on for nearly 24 hours.

Americans watched the coverage with an intensity that had not been seen since the 1963 assassination of President John F. Kennedy and the murder of his accused killer, Lee Harvey Oswald (Rader,

1999). ABC's coverage was anchored in its studio by Jim McKay and Chris Schenkel, with reports from Peter Jennings, who had holed up in the village. The network won 29 Emmy awards for its coverage of the tragedy and, by selling commercial spots during the Games, posted the first profit in its history. More than 50% of American households watched some of the 1972 Olympic telecast (Arledge, 2003).

In its coverage of the Olympic Games, ABC, led by Arledge's production, took a sporting event that had previously received little media attention and turned it into a financial success for organizers, advertisers, and the network. By weaving human drama into the competitions, ABC legitimized the Olympic Games as a sporting event. The Games became a television ratings giant—so much so that a little more than 40 years after ABC paid $7.5 million for the rights to broadcast the 1972 Munich Games, NBC paid more than $2.4 billion to be the U.S. rights holder for the 2018 and 2020 Olympic Games (Crupi, 2011).

placed inside automobiles in National Association for Stock Car Auto Racing (NASCAR) races to provide unique viewer angles, shot clocks and three-point lines were introduced in basketball to create more scoring, and ice hockey adopted a brief overtime period to reduce the number of ties in its games. Additionally, baseball and football both have made well-documented adaptations to their products for the sake of television.

Baseball Adaptations for Television

Throughout the 1960s, MLB suffered through a decline in offensive production because of the rise of dominant pitchers. In 1968, Carl Yastrzemski won the American League batting title with an average of .301, Bob Gibson won the 1968 Cy Young Award with a microscopic 1.12 earned run average and 13 shutouts, and Don Drysdale hurled 58 consecutive scoreless innings. To ignite more offense, baseball lowered the height of the pitching mound in 1969, and the American League adopted the designated hitter in 1973 (Rader, 1984).

Bowie Kuhn became commissioner in 1969 and presided over a variety of changes to the league structure, all of which benefited television in some fashion. Baseball expanded from 20 to 26 teams, creating more markets; each league was split into two divisions, creating additional postseason competition; and part of the World Series was scheduled at night, allowing more viewers to watch the games.

Football Adaptations for Television

Rader (1999) observed that "no other team sport was quite as responsive to the needs of television as pro football" (p. 255). Beyond the obvious creation of a special night for its product (Monday night), the NFL embarked on a series of rule changes throughout the 1970s designed to bring more offense and scoring to the game that theoretically would make it more attractive to television viewers. The NFL moved hash marks closer together, moved the goalposts back to the end line, changed the yard line for kickoffs, reduced the penalty for offensive holding from 15 to 10 yards, and permitted offensive linemen to extend their arms and open their hands to protect the quarterback (Rader, 1984).

Even before the boom of television, NFL commissioner Bert Bell allowed "television time-outs" as a means to increase advertising opportunities for the network (McChesney, 1989). Other accommodations by the NFL for the benefit of television included sudden-death overtime, two-minute warnings, and wild-card playoff berths.

Today's MediaSport Environment

The numbers of viewers that television programs draw are central to any study of the success of television programming. Television executives concern themselves with a program's rating and share, both of which measure how many households watch a given program at a given time. The ability of live sports programming to deliver consistently strong audiences, particularly relative to pre-scripted content such as sitcoms and dramas, makes sports programming must-see TV, and, consequently, drives the market price for in-demand rights.

A program's rating is the percentage of the overall population (represented by households with televisions) who watch a particular program. A share represents the percentage of the population watching television who tuned into a particular program. Those figures, however, do not measure actual viewers, just households. Further complicating matters is that the U.S. population has grown, as have the number of television viewing options. Therefore, comparing one event to another is difficult.

For example, Super Bowl XLIX between the New England Patriots and the Seattle Seahawks, played on February 1, 2015, was watched by a record 114.5 million people, making it the most-watched TV program in history. The game drew a 47.5 rating and a 71 share among adults between 18 and 49 years old (Patten, 2015), meaning that 47.5% of overall television households (nearly every other household) watched the Super Bowl and that 71% of households with a television on during that time—more than 7 out of every 10 televisions turned on in the country—were watching the Super Bowl. Still, those numbers do not exceed the 60.3 rating and 77 share that the final episode of *M*A*S*H* received in 1983 (Finale of M*A*S*H, 1983).

Of the 100 most watched U.S. television broadcasts in 2018, 89 were broadcasts of live sport. Super Bowl LII, between Philadelphia and New England, drew a 43.1 rating and 103.4 million viewers. Among non-sport-related broadcasts, only the State of the Union address (second) and the Royal Wedding (ninth), both spread across multiple networks, made it into the top 10 most watched shows. All the remaining top 10 were NFL games, with the 2018 Olympic Winter Games Opening Ceremony coming in 11th (Crupi, 2019). Of the 20 most watched sporting telecasts of all time, 18 were NFL games. Only the 1994 Olympic Winter Games, which featured the Nancy Kerrigan–Tonya Harding controversy, dented the top 20.

Corporate Media Structure and Vertical Integration

The development of large media companies, especially in the newspaper industry, has affected the media on a variety of levels, including consolidation and content, both of which relate to economics. With respect to consolidation, Solomon (1997, p. 75) observed that after a newspaper is bought by a media conglomerate, "its policies and priorities reflect the parent firm's needs, more than the needs of the community in which the newspaper is situated." For the PR professional, the change in ownership might mean that the newspaper devotes less attention to local or community organizations. For example, persuading the newspaper to cover

a local women's volleyball team may be more difficult because the newspaper may be more focused on covering national sports like NASCAR racing that attract more advertisers and readers, creating more revenue.

Consolidation has also reduced the overall number of media outlets, creating a less competitive marketplace. Media organizations do not seek exclusive stories as frequently in markets that lack competition. Consolidation has reduced the number of outlets that a PR professional can use to reach the public at large, although the proliferation of new media outlets available exclusively in digital format, such as *The Athletic*, has begun to reverse this trend slightly.

Vertical integration in the MediaSport complex can be thought of as "the process by which a corporation secures its presence in each aspect of the production of a given product" (Harvey, Law, & Cantelon, 2001, p. 453). Large media corporations have historically filled air time through the acquisition of professional sport franchises (Gerrard, 2000). Ted Turner was one of the first to do so when he purchased the Atlanta Braves in 1976 (Dart, 2014). Other examples of this type of integration include News Corporation's ownership of the Los Angeles Dodgers from 1998 to 2004, the Tribune Company's ownership of the Chicago Cubs from 1981 to 2007, and Cablevision's current ownership of the New York Knicks and New York Rangers.

The majority of these business decisions were based on the idea of synergy, which would make it possible for the media corporation to obtain a greater level of profits once it owned the team (Dart, 2014). The ability to reap increased revenues from a regional sports network (RSN) appealed to professional sport organizations: "Teams quickly realized that they not only stood to benefit by selling their rights, but by also obtaining interests in RSNs" (Peles, 2014, p. 301). Team-owned networks like Yankees Sports and Entertainment Network (partly owned by the New York Yankees) and league-owned networks such as the NFL Network began to proliferate as well (Goldfarb, 2011).

Ownership of sport teams by media companies creates an avenue for vertical integration within the corporation (Gomery, 2000), allowing media conglomerations to promote their sport franchises at little cost to the organization and permitting them to control all advertising revenue during broadcasts by eliminating the need to pay a broadcast rights fee. A downside to this concept, which led several conglomerates to sell their franchises in the early 2000s, is that a franchise that does poorly causes the conglomerate to lose money as well. Because many media conglomerates are publicly traded companies, shareholders may voice dissatisfaction with the investment. As an example of the interconnectedness of sport and media, the Tribune Company owned the Chicago Tribune, Chicago-based WGN television and radio, and the Chicago Cubs from 1981 until the Ricketts family purchased the club in October 2009. Subsequently, the Tribune Company split into Tribune Media (broadcasting) and Tribune Publishing (print). In December 2018, Nextar Media Group announced it would buy Tribune Media for $4.1 billion (Littleton, 2018).

McChesney (2000, 2004, 2008) has studied the problems of media ownership in general from a political economy perspective, and has identified two scholarly dimensions to the issue. The first considers how media and communications reinforce or challenge existing social and class relationships. The second, which has greater application to sport media, examines "how ownership, support mechanisms (e.g., advertising) and government policies influence media behavior and content" (McChesney, 2000, p. 110).

Occasionally, mass media organizations create their own programming, thereby eliminating the need to pay rights fees for a product. The success of ESPN since its inception in 1979 is a good example of how this has been accomplished. The network created a number of brand extensions, including additional cable channels such as ESPN2 and ESPN News, an awards show called the ESPYs, and a failed theme restaurant called the ESPN Zone, as well as other mass media outlets like magazines, radio stations, and websites. ESPN also benefits from a sister relationship with ABC. As will be discussed later in the chapter, ESPN is not the first television network to combine sport, media, and entertainment into a single product for audience consumption.

The ability for media organizations to own or create compelling content that drives audience numbers will remain a hot topic for the foreseeable future. The current media industry model, based on traditional linear channel delivery of programming, is facing threats from multiple fronts. As ESPN president Jimmy Piatro said in late 2018, "Every big tech company is a competitor" (Patel, 2018).

Increased competition comes from technology companies such as Amazon, Facebook, and Twitter, all of which have streamed live sports, but also from over-the-top, direct-to-consumer streaming services such as DAZN, run by former ESPN executive John Skipper, which signed a three-year deal to show nightly Major League Baseball highlights beginning in 2019 (Umstead, 2018). DAZN charges consumers $9.99 per month for its services.

As consumers choose to subscribe to DAZN and other direct-to-consumer services such as Netflix, many are also choosing to "cut the cord" and drop cable or satellite television subscriptions altogether. As the number of pay television subscribers declines, so, too, does the amount of revenue cable and satellite providers bring in, forcing them to raise rates. Rates have been particularly likely to rise for sports packages. In early 2019, both Comcast and DirecTV announced increased fees of anywhere between $1 and $2 per month per subscriber for regional sports networks, to offset losses in total subscribers (Smith, 2019).

Made-for-Television Sport

While many sports were changing rules to make their products more television-friendly, television networks were busy creating their own sport prod-

Be Your Own Media

One of the underserved markets for sport media rights is high school athletics, although the technology exists to easily broadcast high school events online. Further, since most high schools have journalism classes, an eager-to-learn pool of labor exists, enabling a high school to truly become its own media company. Consider how many high school kids participate in athletics and have grandparents or relatives out of state and unable to watch an event in person. Online streaming enables those individuals to watch, creating a market for this service.

Research the court case *Wisconsin Interscholastic Athletic Association v. Gannett Co.*, 658 F.3d 614 (7th Cir. 2011), and evaluate the issues discussed in the case and scholarship related to the case. Who owns the property right in this case? How do the concerns addressed therein impact the ability to broadcast high school athletic events?

Now consider how your high school approached becoming a media company. What strategies did the school employ to create content, and were those strategies successful? Applying the discussion from this chapter, what recommendations would you make to enable high schools to capitalize on their property rights?

ucts suitable for broadcast. ABC and Arledge led the way by packaging 87 different sports into *Wide World of Sports* between 1960 and 1966. Daredevil Evel Knievel appeared 16 times on *Wide World of Sports*, beginning in 1967 when he attempted to jump the fountains in front of Caesar's Palace in Las Vegas (Roberts & Olson, 1989).

Subsequent made-for-television sports included competitions between athletes from various sports and between Hollywood personalities, as well as competition between world-class athletes during the Cold War and the creation of an Olympic-style event for the developing extreme sport market.

The Superstars

In the 1970s ABC developed a program called *The Superstars*, which pitted athletes from all sports in events like obstacle courses, bowling, and rowing (Rader, 1984). The contest sought to identify the world's best overall athlete. The success of *The Superstars* led to a variety of spin-offs on all three networks, including ABC's *Battle of the Network Stars*, which featured the stars of popular prime-time television shows competing against one another in athletic contests.

Lending continuity to these programs during the 1970s was ABC sportscaster Howard Cosell. A lawyer by trade, Cosell was the dominant presence on all of these shows. He served as a color commentator on *Monday Night Football*, as a reporter on *Wide World of Sports*, and as a host on *The Superstars* and *Battle of the Network Stars*. Cosell's presence on a show meant an instant ratings boost. Viewers tuned in just to hear what Cosell would say next. As Jim Spence (1988), former senior vice president of ABC Sports, reflected in his memoir, "We would have been very successful without Howard Cosell; we were a whole lot more successful because of him" (p. 20).

Goodwill Games

Following the boycott of the 1980 Moscow Olympic Games by the United States and the retaliatory boycott of the 1984 Los Angeles Olympic Games by the Soviet Union, Ted Turner created an international competition to air on his cable television networks. Turner's vision was to create an event that would "ease tensions during the Cold War through friendly athletic competition between nations" ("Goodwill Games," n.d.).

The first Goodwill Games took place in Moscow in 1986. The event marked the first time that the United States and the Soviet Union had competed against each other in a multination, multisport format since the 1976 Montreal Olympic Games. Subsequent Goodwill Games would take place in Seattle, Washington; St. Petersburg, Russia; New York; and Brisbane, Australia. After the Cold War ended, the Goodwill Games' focus shifted toward young people.

The Goodwill Games initially succeeded because of the level of competition, not the television coverage. As Taaffe (1986) reported, Turner encountered a conflict of interest between the creation of the Goodwill Games and objective reporting: "Is he selling or reporting? How objective can someone be when he's reporting on his own pet project? Is television in this case serving the sport, or vice versa?" (p. 55).

Many world records were set during the 16-year run of the Goodwill Games, which also included one Winter Goodwill Games. Turner generated worldwide interest from members of the Olympic movement in his event without having to pay the astronomical rights fees that the IOC charges to broadcast the Olympic Games. The Goodwill Games officially ceased operations after 2001.

X Games

ESPN successfully capitalized on the growing segment of the sport industry known as extreme sports when it created the Extreme Games in 1994 as a way to fill programming hours on its new network, ESPN2 (Semiao, 2004). The event, since renamed the X Games, has spawned a winter version, fostered worldwide interest, and developed a loyal following among a segment of the sport industry previously ignored by mainstream media. The rise in popularity of extreme sports has led to sports such as snowboarding being accepted into the Olympic Games.

Similar to Turner's Goodwill Games, the X Games have allowed their creator and owner, ESPN, to control the details of the games and provide ideal programming for the network while pocketing all of the advertising revenue without having to pay rights fees to broadcast the event (Pitts & Stotlar, 2007).

Serving the Media at Organizational Events

Chapter 1 defined media relations programs as programs designed to generate favorable publicity and minimize unfavorable publicity by fostering desirable relationships with members of the mass media. Many members of the media attend organizational events to report firsthand on what transpired. Although sporting goods manufacturers, fitness centers, and health clubs do not have games or events, they may hold open houses or other functions that may attract media attention.

Working with media at these organizational events is a key part of any PR person's job. Sport PR professionals must understand the needs of media members who cover organizational events and provide services for them. This aspect of the organization–media relationship is unique to the sport industry. At any given sporting event, media members covering the event need a place to observe the event, a place to work on their stories, access to statistics and other related information, and access to the participants after the event for news and opinions. In addition, representatives of the different types of mass media have different needs, many media members are in competition with one another, and some of the media in attendance have likely never been to the facility in which the event is taking place.

Credential Policies

At most sporting events, people can enter the facility in two ways, with a ticket or with a credential. A **credential** is a pass that allows the bearer access to the facility without paying for a ticket. Credential holders have the additional expectation of having access to areas of the facility that the ticket-buying public does not.

Because media members need access to athletes and coaches for interviews, providing media representatives with credentials is appropriate. But the organization should exercise some caution when distributing credentials. Accordingly, many organizations develop credential policies that address eligibility requirements and set limits for media outlets. Other concerns relating to credentials include distribution, application forms, and supplementals. Figure 6.1 outlines typical credential policies adopted by professional sport organizations.

Application Forms

Sport PR professionals should require all media outlets, even beat reporters with whom they are familiar, to submit some form of credential application. Typically these forms are filled out by a sports or photo editor at a print media outlet and by a sports director at an electronic outlet. These forms are relatively standard and should ask for basic information such as the name of the media outlet, contact information, the individual's name, and the

type of media (print, photo, or broadcast). The latter information will be helpful in budgeting for supplementals, which are explained in the next section.

As a part of the organization's media credential policy, PR professionals need to determine whether they will accept credential requests through e-mail, via fax, in person, or over the phone. Although media members expect to fill out a credential application form for most events, many believe that sending an e-mail or picking up the phone to request a credential is more efficient. In addition, the organization's policy commonly indicates a specific time after which the organization will not accept applications for a given event.

Eligibility and Limits

Because a credential permits access to an event for free, the first thing that the organization should address when forming a credential policy is deciding who is eligible to receive one. Typically, organizations focus on local media because they are likely the ones who cover the organization closely. Being familiar with the reach and circulation of local media is a critical first step to determining eligibility. Is a local weekly community paper that focuses primarily on high school sport eligible for a credential to cover a professional football team? What about the writers for an Internet-only fan site?

Those questions can be difficult to answer. On the one hand, the organization is seeking to maximize exposure for its programs and should welcome all forms of media. On the other hand, the space available in the facility for media seating is finite. What will happen if a national news outlet requests a credential just before the event? Surely the sport PR person would welcome the national exposure for the organization, but accommodating the national outlet might be a challenge if space is limited because several smaller media outlets have credentials.

When determining eligibility requirements, organizations should consider what benefits they might derive from the media's presence. Hall and colleagues (2007) observed that a university may wish to exclude representatives from gambling-related publications and media outlets that do not regularly offer sports coverage. In the case of gaming publications, including fantasy sports publications, league or governing body policy may already address their exclusion.

Consider hypothetical media outlet eligibility for an Iowa State University basketball game. The university is located in Ames, Iowa, just north of

Media Credential Policy

Welcome to our online media credentialing system. Please fill in all prompts in the sections that follow. At the end you will be asked to submit a passport-sized photo, which is necessary to complete the process for full-season requests. Single-game credentials should be submitted via e-mail to our Media Relations Coordinator, no later than one week before the event.

Please note credentials will not be issued without the following information:

- Media organization for which the individual will be working (note that freelance requests will be considered on a space-available basis only)
- Name, e-mail, and mobile phone number of individual to whom the credential will be issued
- Contract information from editor authorizing the request

Parking

Media parking is limited. Please request through the full-season credentials online system, and passes will be distributed as available. Television stations seeking satellite truck parking should contact our Director of Operations.

Credential Pick Up

Credentials will be at the PRESS WILL CALL window, and available three hours before the event start. Press entry is on the north side of the stadium. Credentials should be worn at all times.

Press box

Our press box is located on the northwest side of the stadium, gate A20. Please use the elevator bank between gates A19 and A20 to access the press box.

Media work room

Media work space is located immediately behind the press seating area in the press box.

Wi-Fi passcode

Please see a media relations staff member to obtain that day's Wi-Fi passcode. We change the passcode for each event.

Interviews

Ten minutes following the conclusion of the game, the head coach and two or three players will be brought to the interview room, located next to the locker room on the ground level. Media requesting specific players for interviews should make those requests to a media relations staff person with no less than five minutes remaining on the game clock.

Photographers

Sideline credentials are limited to photographers employed by (or with a specific freelance assignment from) a recognized sport or news agency. Single-game credentials should be submitted via e-mail to our Media Relations Coordinator, no later than one week before the event.

Figure 6.1 Sample organizational policy for media covering an organization's sporting event.

Des Moines. Both Ames and Des Moines have daily newspapers, and the market has three television stations and several radio stations. In addition, the sports information office at Iowa State will likely get requests from the university's student paper and television or radio station. Because the university is a large state institution, it may also receive requests from television stations in the Cedar Rapids, Sioux City, and Mason City markets, as well as requests from daily newspapers in Cedar Rapids, Waterloo, Iowa City, and many other towns. Iowa State will want to consider how frequently those organizations cover Iowa State athletics and whether their audiences and circulations reach important publics such as alumni. From that information, the university can develop some sort of internal pecking order for determining eligibility. For example, if the only time that the Iowa City Press-Citizen covers Iowa State is when it is playing the University of Iowa, which is located in Iowa City, then the Press-Citizen might be lower in the pecking order for a contest not involving both Iowa State and Iowa than the Mason City Globe Gazette, which is closer to Ames.

Like eligibility, limits are somewhat subjective and vary among organizations. One factor may be physical space. If an organization's press row for a basketball game has 15 seats and one newspaper is requesting 5 of them, the PR staff needs to decide whether providing one-third of available media seating to one news outlet is appropriate. If the organization issues more credentials than it can accommodate, it may need to find alternative seating for the media or perhaps squeeze them into existing space. One option would be to assign the media specific seats in the seating bowl, which may not have a view as good as that on press row. This option should be the last one, however, because it eliminates potential revenue (i.e., forgone ticket sales) for the organization.

Developing a pecking order for media outlets with respect to eligibility and limits of credentials carries some risk. Media outlets may feel slighted if they are considered a low-priority outlet, and regular media may resent being forced to compete with low-priority media for space and access. Hall and colleagues (2007) advised sport organizations to stick to a policy rather than try to accommodate everyone. Trying to squeeze in extra reporters "may cause greater relationship problems with those media organizations that regularly cover the team. Better to deny access to low-priority journalists at the outset than to provide substandard work space and assistance to all" (p. 157).

Many writers and photographers work as freelancers, meaning that they contract their services to various media outlets. Freelance photographers may ask for credentials to shoot a sporting event without an affiliation. Their hope is that they can sell their photos to media outlets after the event is over or on an as-requested basis. Sport organizations need to address freelance requests in their credential policy. Ultimately, each organization needs to evaluate credentials for freelancers as appropriate. One common tactic is to grant a credential to a freelance journalists only if she or he can produce a letter from a legitimate media outlet indicating that a contract exists between the individual and the media outlet. This letter should be forwarded to the PR person on the media's letterhead to ensure authenticity.

Restrictions

As mentioned earlier, sport organizations are increasingly behaving like media companies, producing unique content that looks like what would be considered traditional media content. In many ways, these in-house media operations are better positioned to provide unique and compelling content because of the access they can provide themselves. Chris Freet, formerly the senior associate athletic director at the University of Arkansas, suggested that his department's digital strategy was one of supplementing traditional media. He stated that the department identified "where we can be unique and where we can fill a void left by the traditional media. . . . We can offer expert opinions and more behind-the-scenes access while providing a greater level of consistent engagement. Most coaches don't want outside media covering their practices and potentially giving away game plans, but they don't mind if we are there" (Read, 2015, p. 32).

Sport organizations increasingly place restrictions on how and when media can share information they observe at practices. In 2017, the University of Notre Dame released guidelines for how media could cover football practice, including no references to plays, no reporting of players practicing with specific units, and no video of trick plays and other strategic elements (Notre Dame football, 2017).

Research into the legality of such restrictions is inconclusive. Although facts from sporting events are available in the public domain and are not protected under the Copyright Act of 1976, sports broadcasts are protected because each game is a unique script, the result is unknown, and the camera angles represent original interpretations of the game (Garmire, 2000).

Creation and Distribution

Sport organizations distribute credentials to their regular media and beat reporters in advance, often creating a pass that is good for the whole season. The PR professional should also create a number of event-specific credentials that can be distributed to opposing media and any nonregular media. Credentials are best displayed on a lanyard and worn around the neck. The credential should be laminated to prevent falsification. Credentials of different colors are often given to different groups of people. For example, media representatives may wear red credentials, whereas coaches may wear blue credentials. This system helps event security personnel identify who has access to specific areas.

Another method involves printing a new pass for each game, perhaps in a different color from the previous games. This method helps event personnel recognize proper credentials for any given game, although the method may be problematic for sports like baseball and basketball that have many games and therefore require many colors.

Regardless of which method is employed, the credential must be both person-specific—that is, it must have the individual's name and organization on it—and event-specific. Some high-profile events such as the Olympic Games require the person's photo as well as name. This system prevents the transfer of the credential to an unapproved individual. Sport organizations may wish to print the person's name on the credential with a computer program or simply write the name in permanent marker. A credential should also include the date and time of the event for which it is valid.

Distributing credentials before the season to beat reporters is often accomplished in person, perhaps at the organization's offices or at a media day. For opposing media and game-specific media, the organization should create a media will-call window near the media entrance to the facility. Credentials should be available for pickup by the media no later than three hours before the event begins. The will-call window should remain open throughout the event because some media representatives may not arrive until after the event begins. Media members should be required to show some form of photo identification when picking up their credentials. Condron (2001) cautioned against underestimating this aspect of the process, stating that "a good media will call system is the key to an overall media operation."

For high-profile events, such as the National Collegiate Athletic Association (NCAA) men's and women's basketball championships, advance planning time may be limited. Organizations hosting an event similar to these championships may choose to create a credential pickup area at the official media hotel for the event, although the organization should still arrange for a will-call pickup site at the facility on the day of the event.

Supplementals

Most sport event managers place restrictions on who can access areas close to the field of play such as the sidelines at football games and the baselines at basketball games. These locations are desirable for photographers and television broadcasters, who need to be as close to the action as possible to capture the best images. Many organizations require some form of additional credential, called a supplemental, to access these areas.

Common supplementals include wristbands, stickers, or sleeves that members of the media are required to wear at all times to gain access to those areas. Supplementals along with a valid media credential should provide access to field-of-play areas. Sport PR professionals should closely regulate who receives supplementals and should develop event-specific supplementals similar to event-specific credentials. This system prevents people from attempting to use one supplemental for several events.

Press Box

The late Leonard Koppett, a legendary sports writer for the *New York Times*, titled his memoir *The Rise*

Media members who need special access to restricted areas are often designated with supplementals.
© David H. Lewis/Getty Images

and Fall of the Press Box (2003). The book is a collection of stories from his career combined with lamentations regarding the current state of the sport organization–media relationship. Koppett began by stating that, once upon a time, the press box was a "special place where millions of Americans of all ages and all segments of society yearned to be" (p. 3). It was, he said, restricted to working press. Koppett was referring to a period from the 1930s to the 1970s when the importance of newspaper coverage of sporting events was at its height. The press box in baseball was controlled not by the organization, but by the local chapter of the Baseball Writers Association of America.

The press box in today's sport environment is still used by working media, but access is no longer exclusive to that constituency, and management of the press box rests squarely with the sport organization. The press box has become a gathering place for sponsors, scouts, agents, team officials and their guests, and many other groups invited into the space by the organization governing the press box. Koppett (2003) blamed this change on television broadcasters, who closely protect access to their broadcast booths, and on sport organizations, which concentrate their efforts on servicing the broadcasters who reach the public more quickly than newspapers and pay the organization for that privilege.

Given the premier location of the press box in most stadiums and arenas, it is not surprising that groups other than the media want access. Sight lines from the press box are among the best in the building, and sport organizations give those seats to members of the media for free. Imagine how much revenue the organization could generate by selling the 50-yard-line seats given to the media at football games. The idea is that the publicity generated by media coverage of its events is worth more than the revenue that would be produced by selling those seats to the public. Sport organizations provide a variety of services to members of the media in the press box as a way of promoting positive publicity. Many of these services have become so commonplace that media members frequently take them for granted. These services include workspace, technology, hospitality, and statistics.

Workspace

The primary purpose of a press box is to provide accredited, working members of the media with a place to sit and record the actions of the event. The location of this space varies from sport to sport. In baseball, the press box is typically located halfway up the stands behind home plate, whereas in basketball the press box may consist of a row of tables and chairs along the side of the court. Regardless of the location, certain fundamental and often unstated rules govern the workspace.

First, the press box is intended for the media who are covering the event. Public relations professionals should make every attempt to remove people who do not meet this criterion. Second, the workspace should be free of cheering on the part of the occupants. Most members of the media understand the need to remain objective and adhere to this code. PR professionals and other organizational employees must subscribe to this policy as well.

A third assumed policy of the press box is that some level of hierarchy will be evident through the assignment of seat locations. Separate booths or rooms are generally provided for broadcast media, including television, the home organization's radio broadcasters, and the visiting organization's radio team. Within the main press box workspace, PR professionals should assign space to specific media organizations. There is no set formula or protocol for this. Helitzer (1996) suggested using a seniority hierarchy for assigning seats. Hall and colleagues (2007) advised providing beat reporters and other regulars the same seat locations each week. Public relations professionals may wish to group visiting media together in one section.

Regardless of how the space is assigned, PR professionals should place name tags on each seat to eliminate confusion. They may also wish to post a seating diagram on the wall throughout the press box to help members of the media identify their assigned seats.

Another service provided by sport organizations to accredited, working members of the sport media is technology to assist with their work. Technology includes a variety of services such as telecommunication and televisions.

Telecommunication

Most writers and photographers desire to submit stories and pictures over a wireless or broadband connection. Sport organizations are expected to provide access to telephones throughout the workspace; however, most media members will bring a mobile phone for personal calls.

Wireless broadband connections have become commonplace in press areas. Often these wireless networks are password protected, and members of the media need to obtain a password from a PR staff member. Media outlets may wish to install their own broadband connections or phone lines in the press box at their expense, a practice common at mega sport events like the Olympic Games. Sport PR professionals should assist the media in setting up this service and should monitor use of that connection to ensure that only the correct media organization is using the service. Sport organizations should also provide a fax machine for media use and apply similar restrictions on long-distance dialing as for telephones.

Televisions

If a sport organization's event is being televised, members of the media working in the press box expect a feed of the telecast to be available on television monitors in the press box or on tables along a basketball press row. Media members use this service to view replays of controversial or important plays as a way of formulating story ideas and angles. If millions of people are watching an event in their living rooms on television, journalists covering the

event in person must be able to see what the television audience is watching as well.

Hospitality

Condron (2001) stated that a hospitality area for the media "doesn't help the writers write a better story or the radio play-by-play men do a better broadcast, but it is usually appreciated by the various media." Because event times often overlap with normal mealtimes, having some type of food service will assist the media covering the event. Food may also encourage media members to arrive earlier or stay later, affording the sport organization a greater opportunity to discuss story ideas in person.

The downside to providing food and beverage is the cost incurred. Because of the cost, hospitality varies from soft drinks and cookies to a full buffet. By working with the organization's marketing department, the PR department may be able to secure donated sandwiches or pizza from one of the organization's sponsors, reducing out-of-pocket hospitality expenses.

The best sight lines in the stadium are usually found in the press box.

Jim McIsaac/Getty Images

Media Rooms

In contrast to press boxes, which are places to work, **media rooms** are "fundamentally a hospitality suite to serve management's varied interests" (Koppett, 2003, p. 16). That differentiation is fairly accurate, although media rooms serve a work function as well, especially at events such as basketball games that do not have a large press box. Media rooms may offer many of the same amenities and services as a press box does, including technology, hospitality, workspace, and statistics. In addition, the sport organization should provide a photocopier for media use and to photocopy statistics and other publicity materials.

Media rooms also function as a base from which PR staff may distribute publicity materials to the media such as game notes, media guides, and schedules. Each of these items is discussed in more detail in chapter 5. Media representatives expect visiting organizations to have similar materials available in the media room. An organization that has a separate media room should plan to have a staff member present in the room before, during, and after an event. Journalists frequently use media rooms to store belongings.

Parking

In addition to the press box and media room, journalists expect the organization to provide free onsite parking in proximity to the media entrance. The organization's marketing department may protest, arguing that those close-in parking spots could be sold to groups who actually pay the organization money, such as season-ticket holders or sponsors. Sport managers may choose to combine the media parking lot with other VIP or reserved parking at the facility.

The media's expectation of parking is based on a couple of factors. First, media members generally bring bags of heavy equipment with them to cover an event, whether they are writers, photographers, or broadcasters. A close-in parking space minimizes the distance that they have to walk from their vehicles to the facility. Second, media members often stay at the facility to file stories long after the ticket-buying public has left. The proximity of media parking may alleviate any concerns about leaving a facility late at night.

A final concern for sport PR professionals at an event is a formal interview area. Chapter 7 presents more information on formal interview rooms, and the sidebar titled Media Operations Checklist provides an inventory of items and issues that sport PR professionals should consider before hosting an event.

Reporting Statistics

Statistics have evolved in sport as a way of comparing performances over history. Barry Bonds's pursuit of the all-time baseball home-run record was important because it compared his ability with that of Babe Ruth and Hank Aaron. If no one had kept statistics when Ruth played in the 1920s there would have been no way to compare Bonds's ability with his predecessors'. The Base Ball Reporters Association of America invented a standard method for keeping score and statistics in baseball in 1887 (Seymour, 1960/1989). This standardization led to the regular inclusion of box scores with game stories.

Keeping and tracking statistics has evolved into a large part of the sport PR professional's job. Archival statistics and historical records can be found in every organization's media guide. Story ideas emerge from players' or teams' pursuit of statistical records, many of which are documented in the PR office. Recording and distributing these statistics in a timely fashion is a critical component of a sport organization's public relations.

Professional sport leagues typically use standard statistical programs to record an event's action, but the NCAA does not mandate use of specific statistical programs by member institutions. Certain programs, however, are widely used and are available from several vendors.

Among the vendors offering statistical programs for various sports are StatCrew, Daktronics, and HY-TEK. Among the mostly widely used programs are those offered by StatCrew, which claims to have hundreds of colleges as well as conferences, high schools, and minor league teams as customers (What is StatCrew?, n.d.). StatCrew produces statistical software programs for basketball, baseball, softball, football, volleyball, ice hockey, soccer, field hockey, lacrosse, and tennis. These providers now boast compatibility with mobile apps, HTML or XML options, integration with governing body offices, and "live" web stats.

Statistical software programs can be used to track cumulative season statistics as well as individual events and offer a variety of output options. During an event, frequently generated reports include play-by-play reports, scoring summary reports, team and individual statistics, drive charts, and quickie stats, which are brief statistical synopses that may be generated during time-outs.

Media Operations Checklist

Sport PR professionals may find it helpful to develop a generic checklist for each event that their organization is running. This checklist can be used to track milestone completion dates as well as delegation of responsibilities. The following items are essential for a successful media operation.

Credentials:

- Application form
- Will-call distribution
- Design of pass
- Supplemental for on-field access

Press box:

- Seating chart
- Name tags for assigned seats
- Telephones
- Internet access
- Power
- Television monitors
- Fax machine
- Photocopier
- Statistics crew with computer and software
- Hospitality

Media room:

- Publicity materials
- Telephones
- Internet access
- Television monitors
- Power
- Fax machine
- Photocopier
- Hospitality
- Coat racks
- Designated storage areas

Parking:

- Location
- Design of pass

Organizations purchase statistical software programs directly from vendors. After the program is installed, the organization must train people on data-entry operations for the software. Procedures, equipment, and individuals needed to operate statistic programs will vary based on the budgets and practices of the organization. No set policies exist for the number of staff required to work an event.

For basketball, most statistical programs require six or seven people. One person is needed to enter data into the program, and one or two people function as spotters, dictating the event action to the data-entry person. One or two people are needed to map the shot chart manually, and at least three people should be conducting simultaneous manual statistical calculations in the event that the data on the computer is lost.

Statistics should be available at regular intervals, such as between quarters or halves, to the media in attendance at events. The PR professional should oversee staff whose job is to secure a printout of the statistical summary from those running the statistical program. That summary should be photocopied and literally run to the media in attendance. Priority should be given to members of the electronic media who are covering the event live. Writers and other media members not on urgent deadlines should be next. In some cases, the PR staff may also be responsible for delivering statistics to the coaching staffs of both teams. At the end of a contest, copies of the summaries should be taken to the interview room where reporters will gather to ask questions of coaches and players.

Reporting Play-by-Play Information

The courts have held that statistics and information produced during an event are facts and therefore are not copyrightable. Still, sport organizations have sought to control the distribution of such information if it mimics play-by-play "descriptions or accounts" of games. This is especially the case when sport organizations are attempting to maximize their own business interests. For example, the PGA Tour threatened to pull credentials from journalists who tweeted during the Farmers Insurance tournament in early 2013, citing the tour's credential regulations, which "prohibit the use of real-time, play-by-play transmission in digital outlets" (McIntire, 2013). The PGA Tour preferred that fans interested in the event either attend the event in person, watch it on television with the official rightsholder, or visit the official websites of the association or the tournament.

The court in *National Basketball Association v. Motorola* (1997) relied heavily on *International News Service v. Associated Press* (1918), and lack of case law following the 1976 Copyright Act, when determining whether the defendant, Motorola, was infringing the copyright of the National Basketball Association (NBA) when Motorola transmitted score updates and statistics from NBA games via subscription pagers. Because Motorola transmitted only facts, and not descriptions or expressions of games, the court affirmed the dismissal of the misappropriation claim. Judge Ralph K. Winter wrote, "We believe that the lack of caselaw is attributable to a general understanding that athletic events were, and are, uncopyrightable" (p. 847).

A similar case had arisen two years earlier when the NFL challenged Stats, Inc.'s creation of a text play-by-play description of NFL games distributed over the Internet. That case was settled prior to the NBA's case. The impact of *NBA v. Motorola* is, as Wong (2002, p. 700) noted, that "Internet sport sites are able to provide real-time sports scores for their visitors without fear of infringing upon copyrights."

Because owners of a property right generate revenues by licensing that right to broadcast entities, misappropriation of that right is a major concern for the licensee and the licensor. As technology has advanced, college athletics organizations have become increasingly concerned about protecting game content beyond facts and statistics.

Like the court in *Pittsburgh Athletic Co. v. KQV Broadcasting* (1938), the court in *National Exhibition Co. v. Fass* (1955) had to consider the difference between facts and descriptions. The defendant, Martin Fass, would listen to radio broadcasts of baseball games and teletype details to other radio stations. The court found for the owner of the property right, suggesting the defendant had deprived the plaintiff "in respect of the creation and production of baseball games and public dissemination of descriptions and accounts thereof" (*National Exhibition Co. v. Fass*, p. 777).

The idea of play-by-play representation, and how it differs from statistics, was at issue when Brian

Bennett was "ejected" from the press box of an NCAA Baseball Tournament game in 2007. Bennett was a *Louisville Courier-Journal* sports reporter covering the NCAA Baseball Tournament when he was removed for simulating a play-by-play of the event in violation of NCAA media guidelines. The Bennett case raised questions about credential policies and play-by-play representation. In particular, an NCAA memo issued to media organizations stated implicitly "blogs are considered a live representation of the game" (Keeney, 2008, p. 88). After the NCAA tried unsuccessfully to have Bennett stop blogging, the organization removed his credential and ejected him from the press box, claiming that his ejection was necessary to preserve the valuable revenue the NCAA received as a result of broadcast rights it had licensed to ESPN. The negative publicity surrounding the event led the NCAA to amend its policy for the following year, permitting blog updates limited to score and time remaining.

Two years later, the Southeastern Conference (SEC) enacted a short-lived policy that initially would have prohibited spectators from producing or disseminating material about an SEC event, including descriptions, pictures, videos, and other information. The policy also contained restrictions on the amount of content traditional media organizations covering SEC events could use, prompting criticisms from major news organizations including Gannett and the Associated Press Sports Editors (Sheppard, 2010). The policy was amended within 24 hours to include less restrictive language (Ostrow, 2009).

Technology has evolved greatly since the Bennett incident and the SEC controversy. No longer are media restricted in the amount or timing of blog posts. In fact, many athletics departments maintain play-by-play-style updates on departmental websites and social media. From roughly 2009 to 2011, college sports information directors regularly engaged in live in-game blogging using a third-party software known as CoverItLive. These blogs included a textual play-by-play and permitted users to simultaneously comment on the action. Fans were also encouraged to share their social media posts during the game.

Concerns sport organizations have expressed regarding play-by-play representation of live events differ slightly from the previously discussed issue of sharing highlights on social media. The value in sports rights lies in the unscripted live broadcast. Property rights owners believe unauthorized representation of the live event is a threat to the owners' financial stability. Sheppard detailed both logistical and legal problems with policy enforcement in this area, concluding sport leagues "must adopt a policy based on norms that see fans as partners in protecting the league's interests, rather than adversaries" (2010, p. 446).

Finally, sport organizations are increasingly controlling access to nongame information by restricting access to team practices, limiting student–athlete and coach availability and regulating the amount of content news organizations can distribute to their audiences. Indeed, as Austin (2015) stated, "information management is the name of the game these days in college football." Recognizing that rabid fan bases are aggressively seeking information about their teams (Clavio, 2011), college athletics departments are able to drive traffic to their media platforms by limiting traditional media access to players and coaches and, simultaneously, distributing unique content on those platforms, creating a scarcity effect of sorts.

Other factors influencing colleges to impose limitations on access include gambling and match-fixing activities and infringement on broadcast contracts (Hutchins, 2011), as well as the idea that college athletics departments do not need to abide by collective bargaining agreements with their athletes, as most professional leagues do.

While there is a rationale for the aforementioned access restrictions, as the quote from Freet earlier in the chapter suggests, the overwhelming reason for decreasing access appears to be that coaches do not want media present. After being denied "media access to football players or assistant coaches for the third consecutive week" in October 2015, the *Clarion-Ledger* newspaper in Jackson, Mississippi, ceased covering Jackson State University (JSU) sports. JSU acknowledged not making assistant coaches or players available for interviews following the midseason dismissal of its head coach. Only the interim head coach was available for interviews, prompting concerns about objectivity and points of view (Morales, 2015).

Increased traffic on athletics department media platforms could lead to increased advertising and sponsorship revenue for the athletics department. Newcastle United approached generating revenue and restricting access simultaneously in 2013 when it sent letters to national newspaper editors in the United Kingdom indicating the club's plan to make papers pay for access to players (Douglas, 2013). Additional interests may also be present, including maintaining secrecy around game plans and injuries that, if made public by the media or other source, could negate a competitive advantage.

These examples of nongame information restrictions prompted a critique from former *Chicago Sun-Times* sportswriter Ed Sherman on the Poynter Institute website. Sherman pointed to specific examples of media experiencing reduced access to college athletes, noting that "access, or a lack thereof, continues to be a major problem for college football reporters." While Sherman identifies specific anecdotes to support the notion that access is dwindling, he stops short of characterizing the perspective of journalists and how access impacts their job, something Suggs (2016) endeavored to argue in his research: journalist access equates to legitimacy.

> Should reporters get subsidies such as open access to events and individuals, and should they be allowed to record and publish whenever they choose? Or should teams limit access to press-box seating and news conferences with coaches? The extent to which journalists can gain access, work independently, and publish in the context of an organizational field can be conceptualized as legitimacy. . . . However, if new platforms and broadcast partners are providing teams with alternative channels to reach fans and constituents, then independent journalists may be losing that legitimacy. (Suggs, 2016, p. 267)

SUMMARY

The media are a significant enterprise in society, often influencing what the public sees and hears. Today's mass media include traditional forms such as print and electronic but have also grown to include the Internet. The current relationship between sport and the media is symbiotic: Each needs the other to survive. This circumstance represents a shift from the days when many sport organizations resisted television and radio for fear that they would decrease revenue. As sport on television flourished, many sport organizations made concessions to their rules to maximize publicity. The media have developed the relationship further by creating sport as entertainment and programming. As sport has grown more comfortable in its relationship with the mass media, the need for PR personnel has emerged.

Defining media accreditation policies, providing adequate workspace, and offering critical services such as technology support and statistical reports are important aspects of service planning. Because media interest in many sport organizations extends beyond game days, other organizational media policies may be necessary, ranging from defining appropriate organizational spokespersons to specifying interview policies.

LEARNING ACTIVITIES

1. Research the role of the mass media in a sport not discussed in this chapter, such as golf, tennis, or auto racing. What sort of financial benefits does the sport receive from television exposure? Has the sport altered its core product to accommodate the media?

2. Watch a sport segment of a local television station's evening newscast with a stopwatch. How much time was devoted to the entire segment? To each story in the segment? How many stories were reported?

3. Visit the websites of two newspapers in the same city, such as Chicago or Salt Lake City. Compare the coverage emphasis of each paper in terms of national versus local sport and professional versus amateur sport. What, if any, recommendations would you make to sport PR professionals in those markets to increase the amount of coverage that they receive for their organizations?

4. Interview a sport PR professional in your community regarding her or his organization's accreditation procedures. Who is eligible for media credentials from their organization? What sort of application process is required? Does media demand for game credentials and media services ever exceed supply? If so, how does the organization address that concern?

Employing News Media Tactics

After reading this chapter, students should be able to

- understand the role of the sport PR professional in distributing content to publics;
- appreciate the value of news and its effect on media coverage;
- describe how to use an interview to communicate organizational messages;
- illustrate the steps necessary to prepare someone for a media interview; and
- identify the key elements of a news conference.

These are the key terms discussed in this chapter:

- B-roll
- inverted pyramid
- lead
- message development
- news conference
- news value
- self-presentation
- teleconference

It has been said that information is the currency of a public relations person. The communication of that information, often to the media, ideally results in favorable publicity for the professional's organization. In turn, the favorable publicity might lead to increased awareness about the organization and ultimately increased revenue. Recently, the role of a PR person has moved beyond generating favorable publicity into developing a variety of positive content about the organization.

As discussed in chapter 1, two models are commonly used to turn information currency into organizational revenue. The model most commonly employed by sport public relations professionals is the press agentry and publicity model, in which practitioners seek to cultivate as much publicity as possible for their organizations (Grunig & Hunt, 1984). This goal is frequently achieved by disseminating newsworthy information to the media.

A variety of communication tactics are available for distributing information, each with its own relative strengths and weaknesses. Traditionally, these tactics can be divided into four categories: advertising and promotional media, news media, organizational media, and interpersonal communication (Smith, 2017). Table 7.1 illustrates some advantages and disadvantages of the various communication tactics.

Advertising and promotional media are generally reserved for the marketing department and will not be addressed here. *Organizational media* is synonymous with *legacy media*, a topic that is addressed in chapter 5; legacy media tactics include specific tactics such as media guides and programs. Interpersonal communication, or face-to-face personal involvement, is addressed in chapter 10. This chapter focuses on news media tactics, which Smith (2017) defined as "opportunities for the credible presentation of organizational messages to large audiences via journalistic organizations" (p. 260).

The rest of this chapter focuses on the responsibilities of PR professionals in managing an organization's message through interviews and news conferences. The chapter examines how to prepare individuals to be interviewed by encouraging responses that are consistent with organizational goals and objectives. This chapter also provides a basic checklist for staging a successful news conference as well as a formula for identifying the best timing and location for a news conference. Finally, the chapter explores how sport organizations can

Table 7.1 Communication Tactics: Advantages and Disadvantages

Tactic	Public reach	Public impact	Sport examples	Advantages and disadvantages
Advertising and promotional media	High	Low	Newspaper advertisements that promote an upcoming event	Reach large numbers for low cost; dismissed by the public as a paid message
News media	Medium to high	Medium to low	Press conferences; news releases	Reach large numbers for free and are highly credible; rely on a third party (media) to deliver the message
Organizational and social media	Medium to low	Medium to high	Programs; media guides; digital or social media	Reach publics interested in the organization; often require an additional purchase by the consumer
Interpersonal communication	Low	High	Community open houses; facility tours	Use highly persuasive face-to-face involvement; reach only those in attendance

Based on Smith (2017).

benefit from hosting a day for the media to interact with players and coaches.

Media Policy Development

Sport organizations command a high level of media attention, so sport managers should consider developing a media policy. Mathews (2004) defined a media policy as "a set of guiding principles and behaviors to help ensure consistent, fair and ethical communication with all of your constituents" (p.46). Those principles and behaviors should include identifying who within the organization speaks to the media, what employees should do if they are contacted by the media, and when coaches and players are available to the media. These policies should apply when individuals are being interviewed for a media story and are not just playing an information services role.

Identifying the Organizational Spokesperson

The organizational spokesperson is the voice of the organization and answers the media's questions. The spokesperson may be a senior member of the organization, such as a president or general manager, or may be one of the organization's PR professionals, such as a sports information director.

Some sport organizations develop a hierarchical approach to the spokesperson role based on the information that the media are seeking. Senior management may speak on topics of importance, and the PR professional may address routine operations. For example, in the case of an announcement about a coach's dismissal, the organization's general manager or athletic director would be the best person to act as spokesperson because he or she is likely the person who decided to dismiss the coach. But if a media member is looking to confirm when tickets will go on sale for an organization's postseason game, the PR professional would usually handle the request.

A final rule of thumb for identifying an organizational spokesperson is to allow the person who has the greatest knowledge about a given subject, and thus the highest degree of credibility, to speak on behalf of the organization. As an example, let's say that a university is building a new on-campus natatorium. A reporter may be interested in knowing precisely how much dirt needs to be moved to grade the land or how much concrete needs to be poured. In this case, the project manager is likely to have the most intimate knowledge of such details and would be the most credible spokesperson.

Developing an Employee Media Policy

Journalists are taught to be creative and enterprising when it comes to gathering information for a story. Occasionally, a reporter will bypass organizational protocol and contact an employee directly. Organizations should therefore have an employee media policy stating that only the organization's PR office will speak to the media.

If employees in another department such as accounting receive a call from a reporter, they should refer the reporter to the PR office. In certain situations, the PR person, after learning the nature of the reporter's inquiry, may have the accounting employee talk to the reporter because that employee may be the best person to answer the question.

Determining Coach and Athlete Availability

Unique to sport organizations is coach and athlete availability. Coaches and athletes devote a great deal of time to competition and training and may view media interviews as a disruption to their preparation for an upcoming event. To minimize these intrusions, many sport organizations adopt media policies that set aside specific times when coaches and athletes will be available to speak with the media. Media members understand that requests that fall outside those times may not be honored. Limitations might be considered for practice days as well as competition days.

Most policies on coach and athlete availability are communicated to the media either in the organization's media guide or a news release. Media members are usually required to contact the organization's sports information or PR office to arrange the interview ahead of time. For example, Clemson University employs a strategy typical of many college athletics departments. Prior to its game against North Carolina on September 28, 2019, Clemson restricted football player interview availability to the Monday prior to the game, with the possibility that a "few players may also be available" after Coach Dabo Swinney's Tuesday press conference. Coach Swinney's only media availabilities that week were on Sunday evening during a teleconference and at his Tuesday press conference. All other times had to be coordinated in advance (Clemson Football, 2019).

Adopting a policy such as the one used at Clemson allows better planning on the part of the media, coaches, and athletes. Members of the media know that if they wish to speak with someone, they should plan on being at a certain location at a certain time. Coaches and athletes know that they will not be continually distracted by interviews as they prepare for an upcoming competition.

Following an event, an organization may choose to open its locker room to the media following a cooling-off period of around 10 minutes. Most professional sport leagues mandate that coaches and athletes be available for interviews following a game. For example, the National Basketball Association (NBA) mandates that each team have an open locker room before and after a competition. Media representatives are allowed in the locker room for a minimum of 30 minutes before a game, ending 45 minutes before tip-off. They are allowed back

into the locker room within 15 minutes of the conclusion of the game. All players must be available to the media for a minimum of 5 minutes during this period. On nongame days, players must be available for 15 to 30 minutes.

Failure to adhere to guidelines such as these may result in sanctions against the team or individual. Former National Football League (NFL) running back Marshawn Lynch showed up at the 2015 Super Bowl Media Day and announced, "I'm here so I won't get fined" (Newport, 2015). Lynch had been previously fined more than $100,000 by the NFL for failing to make himself available to the media.

News Releases

Despite the presence of alternative forms of communication, the news release, still one of the most common news media tactics, is commonplace in the sport industry (Davis, 1998; Hall, Nichols, Moynahan, & Taylor, 2007; Helitzer, 1996). Although

Athletes may be required by their organizing body to be available for media access after events and face fines if they do not comply.

it is sometimes called a press release, *news release* better describes the intent of the communication tactic. The goal is, in effect, to release newsworthy information to the public in as positive a light as possible. Although organizations historically relied on media organizations to report on a news release in order to disseminate the information, that is no longer the case. This shift opens up the possibility for organizations to function as their own media organizations by distributing news and information directly to consumers without relying on the media.

Sports news releases are written about anything relative to the organization. They may include a preview of a competition or the result of a competition, even if the organization's team lost. They also include announcements regarding personnel, schedules, product launches, event sponsorships, event time changes, and more. Note that not all news releases communicate positive messages. Although distributing a news release that announces the hiring of a new women's volleyball coach is appropriate, it is equally appropriate to distribute one announcing the firing of the previous coach. Often the PR person will be placed in the unenviable position of writing a news release following an event in which the organization's team has performed poorly.

The focus on positive messaging may not entice a member of the media to pick up on the news value of the information. However, sport PR persons should remember that their audience also includes ticketholders, alumni, boosters, and general fans. In other words, the release should emphasize information that may be of interest to both the media and the broader public.

News Value

Although a given sport organization may think that a piece of information is newsworthy, the news media may not. This does not mean the broader public won't find the information relevant. For example, a sporting goods manufacturer may think that the launch of a new line of tennis rackets is newsworthy. The news media may not see the launch the same way, because the production of tennis rackets is the core business of the manufacturer; rackets are what the company is supposed to make. But if the production of this new line of rackets will take place entirely in Fargo, North Dakota, and will create 50 new jobs in the community, the news media in that area will be interested. The information has the news values of proximity and impact.

The determination of **news value** is somewhat subjective, based on the audience, location, and focus of the recipient. In the aforementioned example, it is easy to see that media that cover tennis, North Dakota and surrounding states, or the sporting goods industry would be interested in the story. It probably does not have nationwide appeal, however, because it lacks value for most recipients.

William Thompson (1996, p. 133) developed an easy-to-remember term for information analysis focused on six basic news values: *TIPCUP*, which stands for timeliness, impact, prominence, conflict, unusualness, and proximity. The TIPCUP analysis can help the sport PR professional determine whether or not to write a news release.

Timeliness

Information that is new, and therefore "news," is always timely. A good PR person, however, can devise ways to make old information timely, depending on what is happening in the world or within the organization (Treadwell & Treadwell, 2000). A 25-year reunion of a championship basketball team is timely and newsworthy, although the reason for the reunion occurred 25 years ago.

Another consideration regarding timeliness concerns news from other industries that may compete for the public's attention. The first week of April is a good time for organizations involved in baseball-related news to seek publicity, because the Major League Baseball season is beginning and the sport media is focused on baseball and the optimism surrounding a new season. That period would probably not be timely for a university to announce the hiring of a new basketball coach, because the story might not receive much attention.

Impact

When a PR person is evaluating the impact of a particular piece of information, the focus should not be on the impact the information will have on members of the news media, but rather the impact on their readers and viewers. If members of the news media can see potential relevance to their audiences, they will likely cover the story (Treadwell & Treadwell, 2000).

Prominence

Using prominent organizational spokespersons or VIPs to attract the attention of news media is a common PR strategy (Treadwell & Treadwell, 2000). Senior managers in an organization are generally more credible than midlevel managers and therefore generally garner greater media attention.

Conflict

The nature of sport is rooted in conflict and battles. Successful organizations win more battles, or competitions, than they lose. Conflict, however, goes beyond the physical confrontation (Thompson, 1996). Each year the National Collegiate Athletic Association (NCAA) issues a news release placing individuals who may be selling unlicensed Final Four merchandise on alert that it will prosecute them for trademark infringement. This battle to protect unauthorized use of a protected mark represents a conflict for the NCAA. Information regarding this conflict would likely be considered newsworthy.

Unusualness

Certainly the announcement of the 68 teams that qualify for the NCAA Men's Basketball Tournament is timely and has considerable local news value for the institutions chosen. But consider the 2019 tournament, for which Gardner-Webb University, in Boiling Springs, North Carolina, qualified. The news value was easy for the local media to recognize, but adding the fact that no Gardner-Webb team had reached the NCAA tournament since the university entered Division I in 2000 created a story that had nationwide appeal because the news was unusual.

Proximity

Although sport organizations love the glamour of being featured on national media outlets such as Bleacher Report and *USA Today*, the reality is that news must be extremely relevant to warrant national attention. Most PR persons do well to focus on local connections, even for national news. When the Premier Lacrosse League announced High Point University player Tim Troutner Jr. as its 2019 Rookie of the Year, the High Point athletics department picked up on the award and publicized it through a news release (Troutner wins PLL Rookie of the Year, September 20, 2019).

News Release Elements

After a sport organization has decided to release newsworthy information, attention turns to writing the news release. By adhering to a universally accepted format, a PR person can increase the likelihood that the media will use the information (Treadwell & Treadwell, 2000). Central elements of this format make the release easy to identify, easy to read, and easy to edit (Lorenz & Vivian, 1996).

Be Your Own Media

As the public relations person for a professional baseball team, you have been approached by a veteran starting pitcher who is planning to announce his retirement. While not All-Star caliber, this pitcher was a part of your organization for 12 years and contributed to a number of playoff teams. He was a fan favorite who always volunteered to speak at schools, sign autographs, and regularly granted interviews to the media. He needs your assistance in coordinating this announcement.

Given the plethora of platforms available for this type of announcement, how would you advise him to proceed? Should he announce his retirement in an Instagram or Twitter post? Should he author a piece for organizational website? Should the team stage a press conference at the stadium? Consider the pros and cons of each available option.

Those elements include a header with key contact information, a lead paragraph that summarizes the newsworthy elements of the release, text that provides additional details of the newsworthy elements presented in an inverted pyramid style, a tag that identifies the organization, and a symbol to let the reader know that the release has ended. All of this should be written in accordance with the journalistic standards identified in *The Associated Press Stylebook and Briefing on Media Law*.

Header

The most important element of a news release is a header placed at the top of the page that should contain, at minimum, the organization's name, address, and telephone number; the name of a media contact with phone number; the release date and time; and a headline (Simon & Zappala, 1996).

The name of the media contact should include a phone number that will be answered, whether it is a work, home, or mobile number, along with an e-mail address. Because the news media do not work a conventional eight-hour work day, the PR person must be accessible should a question arise about the information (Helitzer, 1996; Lorenz & Vivian, 1996; Treadwell & Treadwell, 2000).

All news releases should carry the date and time to indicate to the media when the information can be used and where it originated (Treadwell &

Treadwell, 2000). Most releases will be available "for immediate release" (Helitzer, 1996; Lorenz & Vivian, 1996; Simon & Zappala, 1996). Occasionally, an organization updates a developing news story by issuing a second news release on the same day. In those cases, including the actual time of day when the news release was written is essential so that journalists can identify the most recent information.

Because sport-related news is frequently reported as it happens, an organization may need to disclose sensitive information, such as player injuries or coaching changes, before the organization wishes the information to be in the public domain. In that case, the news release should be "embargoed" for a later time (Lorenz & Vivian, 1996).

Disclosing information under an embargo is risky business for the organization. What guarantees does it have that the media will not violate the embargo? Generally, the organization is engaging in a good-faith gesture with the media when it embargoes information. Treadwell and Treadwell (2000, p. 231) identified two reasons why news media will honor embargoes. First, no professional wants to disclose information in advance that may be subject to change. Second, news media that leak embargoed material may find it difficult to gather information from the organization in the future. Given the challenges, the best advice for sport PR professionals is to avoid embargoing information unless absolutely necessary.

The release location, called a dateline, identifies the city in which the release originates and is usually typed in all capital letters, followed by a hyphen, just before the beginning of the first sentence of the release. Newspaper stories almost always include the location if the news originates outside the local newspaper market (Hall, Nichols, Moynahan, & Taylor, 2007).

The final element of the header is some sort of headline as a means to catch the attention of the release's recipient (Helitzer, 1996; Simon & Zappala, 1996; Treadwell & Treadwell, 2000). Journalists are in no way obligated to use this headline, and most will not. But there is always a chance that the headline will be used verbatim, so it should put the organization in the best possible light. Notice the differences between the following possible headlines for the Seattle Storm of the WNBA:

> Dream flattens Storm, 75-62, to win
>   WNBA title
> Storm falls to Dream in WNBA
>   championship game

The first headline places the emphasis on the Atlanta Dream and connotes dominance through use of the verb *flatten* and the statement of the score. The second headline, likely from the Seattle Storm, provides a more positive image of the game through use of the verb *fall* and mention of the championship.

News Release Content

The flow of a news release should follow the journalistic standard of the **inverted pyramid**, so named because this standard form places the most important information first in the release and the least important information last, creating what resembles an inverted pyramid of importance. This style works well for straight news releases and competition stories because the information being disseminated is likely new information that the readers do not already know.

The opening one or two paragraphs of a news release is called the **lead** and should contain a summary of the most newsworthy elements to the release. A widely accepted practice is to include the who, what, where, when, why, and how (five Ws and one H) within the lead paragraphs (Hall, Nichols, Moynahan, & Taylor, 2007; Helitzer, 1996; Lorenz & Vivian, 1996, 2000; Treadwell & Treadwell, 2000). But in sport it is frequently difficult to summarize the why or how elements of an event in a concise manner.

Following the lead of a news release written in the inverted pyramid style, subsequent sections also have specific functions. Thompson (1996) suggested that the second section should explain the lead, often completing omitted information, and that the third section should present information in support of the lead by offering evidence to back up the lead.

A fourth section provides background to place the news in perspective, and a fifth section includes any specific call to action that readers might want to take (Thompson, 1996). For example, a news release announcing the beginning of season-ticket sales for a minor league baseball team might close with information about the price per ticket and a phone number that will accept orders. Unlike some other forms of writing, news release writing should involve short, succinct paragraphs, many of which do not exceed one sentence or one new idea (Thompson, 1996).

Ending

The ending of a news release is just as important as its header, or beginning. Certain stylistic elements are accepted and expected, including a boilerplate paragraph and a notation indicating that the release is complete.

Many organizations develop a standard boilerplate paragraph that provides basic information about the organization (Treadwell & Treadwell, 2000). Organizations may wish to use the boilerplate to position themselves within the sport industry in their own terms by identifying key elements of their business strategy and by including information about the organization that a reporter might want to incorporate into an article. For example, Gatorade ends its corporate news releases as follows:

> About Gatorade: The Gatorade Company, a division of PepsiCo, provides sports performance innovations designed to meet the needs of athletes at all competitive levels and across a broad range of sports. Backed by more than a 50 year history of studying the best athletes in the world and grounded in years of hydration and sports nutrition research at the Gatorade Sports Science Institute, Gatorade provides scientifically formulated products to meet the sports fueling needs of athletes in all phases of athletic activity. For more information and a full list of products, please visit www.gatorade.com. (Gatorade® launches, 2019)

The inclusion of Gatorade's various products positions the company as being a diverse worldwide sporting goods manufacturer, despite the focus of the news release, which was about tennis. In addition, the boilerplate paragraph provides context about the longevity of Gatorade by including information about the company's history.

The journalistic standard for ending a news story is to center the number *30* at the end of the story.

The same applies to news releases, although three consecutive pound signs or an organizational hashtag have become acceptable variations for ending a release.

Without some sort of ending to a news release, the reader will be inclined to think that more information is contained on a separate page. Given that, if a news release exceeds one page, it is common to center the word *MORE* at the bottom of the page, indicating that more is to come (Lorenz & Vivian, 1996). If a second page is used, it should be identified with a header in the upper right-hand corner indicating the subject of the release and the page number. Table 7.2 provides a summary of the basic news release elements and their purposes.

Visuals

In addition to the written portion of a news release, media outlets and social media increasingly rely on visuals to help with storytelling. As such, sport PR professionals should be prepared to incorporate B-roll, video news releases, and photos into their releases.

B-roll

Organizations frequently provide video B-roll to television media as means to deliver quoted statements or other visual information. A video **B-roll** is a taped series of unedited video shots and sound bites related to a news story (Smith, 2017). B-roll is also sometimes referred to as cover video (Cremer, Keirstead, & Yoakam, 1996). Typical video shots may include behind-the-scenes video that a sport organization would like to release to the media. But the organization may not want to allow the media unfettered access to shoot. For safety reasons, a university that is building a new arena may shoot B-roll of the progress inside the construction zone rather than have media representatives shoot it themselves.

Table 7.2 Basic News Release Elements and Their Purposes

Element	Purpose
Header	Contains contact information for the organization's public relations person as well as the date and time when the media can use the information
Lead	Summary of the most newsworthy elements of the release
Body	Follows the lead with supporting information in the inverted pyramid style
Boilerplate	Standard information that communicates an organizational position
Ending (30, ###)	Indicates to the reader that no more information is available

An obvious consideration for the sport organization is performing a cost–benefit analysis of shooting B-roll. An organization will incur a significant expense to hire a freelance videographer to shoot B-roll. Additional cost is associated with editing the B-roll into logical sequences and producing individual tapes to present to television stations. All this expense will be wasted if the stations do not air the video—and they are not obligated to do so.

Video News Releases

Although similar to B-roll, a video news release (VNR) has a slightly different objective. B-roll contains unedited video that the sport organization provides to the television station in hopes that the station will edit it into a story. A VNR is a ready-for-broadcast package that the organization offers to the television station in hopes that the station will "plug and play" (Treadwell & Treadwell, 2000, p. 263). Lorenz and Vivian (1996) advised keeping a VNR to between 60 and 90 seconds and preparing it to have the feel of a news story.

Organizations often have similar reservations about the costs and benefit of a VNR as they do about B-roll. VNRs carry increased expenses because of the time necessary to edit B-roll into video that matches the audio script. In addition, the organization may need to hire someone to record the voice-over for the VNR if no one within the organization is available to record it. VNRs frequently have a lower usage rate by television stations than does B-roll (Treadwell & Treadwell, 2000).

The popularity of social media and video-sharing sites has created an additional avenue for organizations to post versions of their own video news releases. By creating official YouTube, Instagram, and Snapchat accounts, organizations can easily share their video content with fans of the organization. These distribution channels can create significant brand engagement.

Photos

A sport PR professional must have access to a reliable photographer who can capture the organization's successes to be forever reproduced. The old saying that a picture is worth a thousand words is definitely true in sport. Lechner (1996, p. 157) called photography the "best medium to convey positive information in a story-telling manner with memorable impact."

Sport PR professionals use photography on a daily basis as a means to promote the organization. Two types of photos frequently used by PR profession-als are head shots and action shots. Head shots, or mug shots, are basic portrait photos of an individual commonly used in organizational media. The sport PR person should organize a day before the beginning of the season to shoot photos of team members and coaches. Individuals should dress similarly to one another, perhaps in dress clothes or the team uniform (Lechner, 1996).

Action shots, as the name implies, are photos made during an event of some kind, such as an athletic competition or a press conference, that the organization intends to use for publicity purposes in the future. A good rule of thumb for the organization is to have a photographer present at all official functions to capture the spirit of the event.

Because photos shot by photojournalists are copyrighted by the photojournalist's news organization or the individual photographer, an organization typically may not use such photos for publicity purposes without consent. Therefore, a sport organization should either hire a permanent in-house photographer to serve on its staff or contract with local freelance photographers. An organization that chooses the freelance route must consider several points when contracting with a photographer.

First, the parties must be certain to agree in advance on the pay rate. Some photographers charge by the hour, whereas others charge per day or half day. The organization must clarify whether the rate includes expenses such as travel and special equipment (Lechner, 1996). Often, those expenses are in addition to the hourly or day rate.

Second, the organization must pay attention to the terms of the contract with the photographer. Of particular importance to the organization are the usage rights and ownership of the photos. The organization should strive for usage rights as broad as possible that permit the organization to use pictures made by the photographer in media guides, programs, websites, posters, and other organizational media without paying a royalty to the photographer. This stipulation may increase the hourly or daily rate charged by the photographer, but it will save the organization headaches and money in the future.

Usage rights should also clarify whether the organization can provide the photos to news organizations for publicity purposes. Finally, the contract should specify the byline to be used in conjunction with the published photos. Organizations typically provide credit to the photographer in the front of media guides or program, but doing so is less common in other forms of organizational media such as posters. Frequently, a byline will include both the organization's name and the name of the photographer.

Third, an organization should get subject permission when using photos for commercial purposes. This point is generally not a problem for people associated with the organization such as coaches and team members, but it might be an issue for a prominent guest speaker or alumni who may want compensation for the use of his or her likeness. Photos made exclusively for editorial usage in programs, websites, and media guides are protected under the First Amendment's freedom of speech clause (Lechner, 1996). For example, if a college athletic foundation hires a speaker for a luncheon, the speaker's image can likely be used in association with noncommercial content.

Media Pitches

The nature of big-time sport guarantees media coverage. Daily newspapers cover a Major League Baseball team whether the team is in first place or last place. Therefore, some sport PR professionals do not need to pitch story ideas to reporters, but practitioners with less prominent sport organizations do have to pitch stories on a regular basis.

The actual sales process for the PR professional is a pitch to the media that something is newsworthy enough for them to cover. The pitch is often, but not always, accompanied by some sort of tactic like a news release. Public relations professionals should never just send a news release without

following up with a journalist, and that follow-up is the pitch.

Pitching to the media is common practice in the sport organization–media relationship, and journalists expect stories to be pitched to them. While the initial idea pitch may come via text or e-mail, PR professionals should explain more detail about the content of the idea through a personal phone call. This pitch is also an opportunity to divulge new or updated information to the reporter. For example, if a sporting goods manufacturer is unveiling a new line of shoes at its manufacturing plant, PR staff may offer claims that the new shoes are lighter than the competition's sneakers. After the PR staff has distributed a news release or media advisory announcing the unveiling, a PR professional might want to call reporters, remind them of the unveiling, and ask for their shoe size. When the reporters show up to cover the event, they can try on a shoe that fits properly and judge firsthand how light the shoe really is. See the sidebar Pitching a Story Effectively for additional insights.

Interviews

One of the most basic ways in which a journalist gathers information for a story is through interviews, defined as a session in which journalists ask questions and someone from the organization responds.

Although that process sounds simple, sport interviews are much more complicated. Many interviews are conducted following an event in which the team lost on a last-second play, an occurrence that could

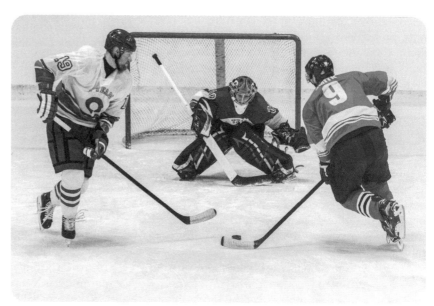

Action shots taken at events are used by sport PR professionals on a daily basis to promote their organizations.

© simonkr/Getty Images

Pitching a Story Effectively

Public relations professionals working for less well-known sports or minor league organizations cannot automatically assume that the media will report on the professionals' organizations. The practitioner must have some tactics in mind when pitching a story to the media. Several strategies can be effective:

- Know your sport inside and out. Be in a position to explain to a reporter the intricacies of the sport, including the scoring system, the rules, and judging, and seek to identify unique aspects of your sport that the reporter might find interesting.
- Know your athletes and coaches. Understanding the off-field interests of athletes and coaches can lead to additional publicity opportunities.
- Develop your own sources. Suggesting to reporters where they may turn for another perspective may lead to favorable mentions in the media or additional stories. Be certain, however, that the source will speak favorably about your organization before directing a reporter there.

adversely affect an interviewee's mindset before he or she addresses the media. In one memorable moment after the Seattle Seahawks defeated the San Francisco 49ers in the 2014 NFC Championship, Seahawk defensive back Richard Sherman told FOX Sports' Erin Andrews on live television, "I'm the best corner in the game. When you try me with a sorry receiver like [Michael] Crabtree that's the result you're going to get. Don't you ever talk about me" (Brinson, 2014). Many pundits criticized Sherman for saying what he did, but the situation is illustrative of what can occur following an emotionally charged athletic event, particularly one in which the winner qualifies for the Super Bowl.

Hall, Nichols, Moynahan, and Taylor (2007) identified specific characteristics of a sport interview: It is an interchange of information between two or more parties who ask and answer questions, and it has a specific purpose. Examining those characteristics provides insight into how a sport organization can use an interview situation to its advantage. Rather than simply respond to a reporter's questions, interviewees should think of the interview as a two-way street that the organization can use to reach a wide audience through the media (Hall, Nichols, Moynahan, & Taylor, 2007; Hessert, 2002).

In all likelihood, the reporter's purpose is to report a story that will inform readers, viewers, or listeners. The organization's purpose may be to explain a critical moment of the game or reinforce positive images of the organization (Hall, Nichols, Moynahan, & Taylor, 2007). A sport interview is thus an opportunity for organizational representatives to respond to media questions with organizational messages. Media interviews can be used to the

organization's benefit. PR professionals can assist the process by fielding interview requests professionally, selecting an appropriate interviewee, and preparing the interviewee.

Fielding Media Requests

Often a sport organization reacts to inquiries from the media for interviews as opposed to proactively seeking interview opportunities. The PR person is usually the first contact between the media and the organization. As such, when fielding media requests, the PR person should seek to gain information that will help prepare the best response possible.

Specifically, PR professionals should attempt to determine the reporter's deadline and the story angles that the reporter is working on, including any specific technical information that the reporter might be seeking. Many reporters will comply with these questions because they recognize that they will likely receive better responses from prepared interviewees. Some may be reluctant, however, for fear that the information might hold up the interview process or eliminate the element of surprise (Lorenz & Vivian, 1996).

Early identification of the reporter's time line allows the organization to gauge how long it has to develop a response before the reporter's story will hit the newspaper or airwaves. Understanding what story angles the reporter is working on will help PR involve the best spokesperson. For example, if the reporter wants to know why the team is not interested in offering a contract to its free-agent pitcher, the organization may want the owner or general manager to respond because the decision may involve complicated financial issues.

Preparing the Interviewee

In a memorable moment from the movie *Bull Durham*, the character of Crash Davis, a veteran catcher, advises hotshot rookie pitcher Nuke LaLoosh to commit a series of clichés to memory for use whenever he's interviewed. LaLoosh responds that the clichés are boring, but that is Davis's point. Sport media have an insatiable appetite for quotes, regardless of how substantive the quote may be. Sayings such as these dominate today's sports pages: "They need to step up and make plays"; "She plays within herself"; "He's coming into his own." Representatives of sport organizations must recognize that interview opportunities are just that—opportunities for the organization to communicate messages to its targeted publics, not to spout tired clichés. This example represents the challenge of media members' seeking quotes of substance while athletes do not want to elaborate on certain topics. PR professionals should help educate interviewees to view an exchange with the media as an opportunity to build an image and articulate desirable messages.

Gauging a PR professional's direct value to a sport organization is often difficult, but astute PR practitioners recognize their contribution in preparing interviewees. Harvey Greene, vice president of media relations for the Miami Dolphins, views his role in the interview process as one of helping the team focus by limiting off-field distractions (Greene, 2003). He never wants coaches or athletes to be surprised by what they are asked.

Hessert (2000) advised PR professionals to have a strategy in place that anticipates questions from the media and determines specific goals and messages to be communicated. In many instances, professionals can coach interview subjects regarding those central messages. The sidebar Tools for Controlling the Interview describes three techniques for getting to central messages.

PR professionals can contribute positively to the interview process in several ways. First, as stated, PR professionals are usually the first line of communication between the media and the organization. They can exploit this power by gaining as much knowledge as possible of the reporter's topic, story angles, and sources, which will aid in developing and shaping a response (Rowe, Alexander, Earl, & Esser, 2001).

Second, a fundamental responsibility is to understand the media and the external environment of the organization. By trying to think like a reporter,

Tools for Controlling the Interview

Although the interviewer is the one asking the questions, the interviewee may exert considerable influence on the direction of the conversation. The following list offers three tools for exerting some level of control.

- *Bridging*: Deal with the question honestly and briefly and then move logically to your message. Before you bridge, you must answer the question. Examples include the following:

  - Yes, and in addition . . .
  - No. Let me explain . . .
  - I don't know. I do know that . . .
  - That's the way it used to be. Now . . .

- *Flagging*: Emphasize to reporters what you want them to highlight—what one piece of information you want them to print or broadcast. Examples include the following:

  - The most important thing is . . .
  - This is the bottom line . . .
  - If you remember one thing about our organization . . .

- *Hooking*: You can prompt the next question you want asked by ending your response with a hook. If the interviewer doesn't respond to hooks, then bridge. Examples include the following:

  - And that's just one possibility . . .
  - We've done something no other organization has done . . .

the PR professional is better able to anticipate what questions might be asked before the interview begins and develop a possible response.

If a member of the university football team is placed on academic suspension, the PR professional should outline information that will be helpful to the head coach when being interviewed. A reporter is likely to want to know whether the player is the only one suspended or whether other suspensions might follow. The reporter may also ask how the player's absence will affect the lineup and game preparations. Arming the coach with specifics such as team grade point average can help emphasize a positive rather than dwell on the negative.

Additionally, PR professionals may assist organization representatives in preparing interviewees by offering coaching in the areas of **message development**, presentation skills, and the notion of information that is "off the record" or "not for attribution."

Message Development

The media use various tactics to elicit responses from an interviewee. The mere phrasing of a question can affect how a person responds to a given question. Reporters often use open-ended questions, which don't limit answers (Wilstein, 2002). Consider the following questions from a reporter to a coach:

1. Have you ever been more frustrated by your team's play?

2. You must be frustrated. Describe your thoughts on your team's play.

In the first question, the reporter is asking a simple yes-or-no question in a negative tone. If the coach were to answer no to that question, it is easy to imagine a headline the next morning that reads, "Coach Frustrated by Team's Play." In the second question, however, the reporter is leaving the door open for the coach to influence the interview by falling back on one or two organizational messages.

As Hessert (2000) pointed out, the average audience member recalls one major point from any given speaker. If the PR professional and interviewee decide on several key messages in advance and stick to them, they can influence the direction of the interview.

One method of identifying messages and repeating them throughout an interview involves keeping in mind the rule of threes (Rowe, Alexander, Earl, & Esser, 2001). Write down the three message points that the organization deems the most important. State each of the three messages three different times during the interview, bearing in mind that

you may be able to convey the same message in different ways (Rowe, Alexander, Earl, & Esser, 2001). Although the organization may not have three different message points that it wants to convey in the interview, the concept of repeating key points multiple times throughout the interview is fundamental to the organization's ability to communicate.

Presentation Skills

Interviewees should consider the form of mass media in choosing their approach to each interview because each form is seeking something different. In the event that representatives of more than one form of media are present, interviewees should generally use the approach with the widest appeal.

An old saying in business is, "Image is everything." Image plays a vital role in sport as well, especially in interviews. Athletes and coaches can use media exposure to alter or reinforce their public image. In addition, interviewees who put extra effort into their dress, composure, and mannerisms present a better image of themselves than those who don't. Appearance is important not only for television but for all media. Each of the three major media types has unique qualities that, if the interviewee recognizes them, can facilitate positive impressions of the organization. Further, athletes and administrators are advised to consider their social media status updates as a form of interview.

Television and Video

Most television news stories run approximately 60 seconds, and most clips during those stories are 10 to 20 seconds in length—hence the term *sound bite*, which effectively describes what television provides: a bite of sound.

How can interviewees get their message across in 10 to 20 seconds? Several pointers can help them improve their organization's image and deliver their key message on television.

First, interviewees should keep answers concise and try to avoid rambling. Hessert (2002) equated good interviewing to good driving: "It's awfully hard to crash and burn at 30 mph" (p. 24). She advised interviewees to pause a few seconds to collect their thoughts before answering, even in broadcast interviews. Unless the interview is live, the broadcaster will likely edit out the silence.

Second, interviewees should repeat messages. Because television journalists are likely to use only 20 seconds of an interview, interviewees increase the odds that key messages will make it into those 20 seconds by going back to the message frequently.

Third, interviewees should look at the reporter, not the camera. Typically, a television reporter stands to one side of the camera or the other, and because the reporter, not the camera, is asking the question, the interviewee should focus on the reporter.

Finally, interviewees should practice posture, appearance, and nonverbal gestures. Most newspaper writers do not incorporate gestures like slouching or lip licking into their stories, and they generally eliminate "ums" and "uhs" from quotes. Broadcast, however, amplifies those images and sounds (Weisman, 2002).

Radio and Podcasts

Radio is similar to television in that interviewees should seek to limit the length of their answers and not provide rambling responses. But unlike exchanges on television, radio interviews do not need to be face to face. Through the use of telephones, sound can be recorded anywhere, allowing a radio reporter to conduct an interview from halfway around the world. That flexibility means that radio is an informal medium. Interviews tend to be more conversational than in other media. Because of that informality, interviewees should be wary of becoming too relaxed and deviating from the pre-determined messages.

Print Reporting

Although both television and radio interviews can be conducted live, print interviews are typed, edited, and published online or through traditional print media. This process can be both an advantage and a disadvantage for the interviewee.

Because print reporters are not limited by time constraints, interviewees can provide more in-depth answers to questions, improving the odds that the organizational message will be conveyed in the story. However, many journalists will live-tweet postevent interviews, sharing content immediately. Interviewees should be cognizant that anything they say to a reporter can be distributed and published immediately. In a rush to "break news," reporters may fail to provide proper context for a quote. Many reporters tape-record interviews, but others do not. As Wilstein (2002) stated, using tape recorders has several drawbacks, including time and inconvenience. Transcribing an interview generally takes up to four times longer than conducting the interview.

Even the best reporters find it difficult to listen to an audiotape of an interview and type at the same time. Most play a portion of the tape, stop the tape, and type what they just heard. They repeat the process until they have typed the entire quote. This process is more common in long-form feature writing, which is not as time sensitive. Reporters working on these types of stories may pose follow-up questions to interviewees.

Social Media Status Updates as On-the-Record Content

People are continually cautioned about how they represent themselves when updating popular social networking sites such as Facebook, Twitter, and Instagram. Journalists consider those comments and updates as being on the record, and they frequently report those details. Increasingly, athletes are being reprimanded by team, league, and other organizational authorities about inappropriate status updates.

At the same time, proper usage of social media, particularly by athletes, can present an image different from their identity as an athlete. Olympic athletes in particular have capitalized on the popularity of the Games and its global media presence to promote themselves and develop their personal brand through appropriate **self-presentation** (Geurin-Eagleman & Burch, 2016).

Lebel and Danylchuk (2012, 2014) classified athletes' social media messages in the service of self-presentation into two main categories: front stage and back stage. Front-stage messages include interactions with fans and messages initiated by the athlete. Self-promotion and back-stage messages include messages sharing information from other platforms, disclosing behind-the-scenes stories, expressing support to other athletes and teams, and analyzing the games.

Off the Record and Not for Attribution

The notion of presenting information in an interview off the record poses a problem for journalists. Reporters add credibility to their stories when they identify sources (Lorenz & Vivian, 1996). When interviewees say that something is off the record, journalists are placed in a difficult position: Should they report the information, which is likely newsworthy, or not?

Lorenz and Vivian (1996) defined off-the-record information as information given "so that a reporter will better understand a confusing or potentially harmful situation. . . . The information is not to be disseminated, even in conversation" (pp. 374–375). Hall and colleagues (2007) similarly defined off-the-record information as subject to "an agreement prohibiting the reporter from using the information in any way in pursuit of the story. . . . He or she also pledges not to repeat it to other sources" (p. 216). Note the emphasis in both of those definitions is on not repeating the information.

Understanding the definition of *off the record* and deciding whether to make a statement that is off the record are two different things. After an organization has disclosed sensitive information, it can no longer control it (Hall, Nichols, Moynahan, & Taylor, 2007). The organization should probably not disclose information that it does not wish to see publicized in the media, even if the disclosure is off the record.

Information that is off the record differs somewhat from information that is not for attribution, a tactic commonly employed in politics to release information to the media on the record but without identifying the speaker. "A White House spokesperson confirmed" is a frequently heard statement around Washington, D.C. The practice is becoming more commonplace in sport. Organizations often disclose information, such as a pending news conference, to stimulate interest from the media.

Controlling Postevent Interviews

Immediately following any sporting event, participants and coaches face a number of demands. Depending on the type of competition, these demands can include live television interviews, radio shows, team meetings, award ceremonies, drug testing, and media interviews.

Every organization should develop a media policy that clearly communicates postevent interview procedures to the media. PR professionals also have several responsibilities as the event draws to a conclusion, including polling the media to find out who they wish to interview and arranging for live television and radio interviews.

The advantage of an open locker room, which is mandated by most professional leagues, is that media members can interview anyone they wish. For organizations with a closed locker room, the PR professional is responsible for asking media representatives whom they wish to interview (Davis, 1998). This task should be done toward the end of the contest, although the PR person should understand that the media will want to talk to anyone who scores a game-winning goal or makes a last-second basket.

Media members often request the same interviewees, making the PR person's job easier. Requested interviewees should be brought to the news conference room for the benefit of all media in attendance. Occasionally, a reporter may ask to interview someone to whom no one else wishes to talk. In that case, the PR professional should arrange for the reporter and the individual to meet, perhaps in the hallway outside the interview area.

Perhaps no situation is more chaotic postgame than after a PR person's organization wins or loses a championship. The following case study illustrates how Erich Bacher, assistant athletics director for public relations at the University of Virginia, helped manage the Cavaliers' 2019 NCAA championship after the Virginia men's basketball team became the first number 1 seed to lose to a number 16 seed in the 2018 NCAA Tournament.

Postevent Interview Priorities

Organizations love the publicity generated by live television broadcasts of their athletic events. For PR professionals, live events mean increased responsibilities. Television production groups usually meet with the organization at least a day in advance. Any in-game or postgame interview possibilities should be discussed at this meeting. Assuming that both sides agree to in-game or postgame interviews, the PR person will need to escort the coach or athlete to the area where the interview will take place (Davis, 1998). Taking the organizational representative to the television camera is much easier than the reverse. Rights-holding media such as television and radio networks are frequently given preferential treatment regarding live postevent interviews because they have paid for the right to cover the event while other media outlets, such as newspapers, have not.

Many organizations have a postgame radio show during which the coach and a player of the game are interviewed. The challenge for the PR person is to balance the needs of the radio affiliate doing a live broadcast and the other media representatives seeking to interview the same coach and athlete in the interview room.

One strategy is to have the coach conduct a news conference first and then do the radio show. This approach allows the coach to limit time in the news conference and conduct a more relaxed interview with the affiliated radio announcers, who are likely to be less confrontational than the media representatives in a news conference in which multiple people ask questions.

MANAGING SUCCESS

Whether preparing for a regular season game or the Final Four championship, public and media relations professionals need to be ready for a potential win or loss. For a win, being ready means serving the rights-holding TV and radio broadcasters with head coach and student–athlete interviews on the court or podium following the game. Afterward, the public and media relations staff lead the way through the awards and net-cutting ceremonies, before the team returns to the locker room where any additional postgame press conferences interviews may take place. Erich Bacher describes the scene:

A loss is more challenging. We are preparing possible talking points and potential questions that could be asked for our head coach and student–athletes, and identifying which student–athletes will represent us at the podium following the loss. Dealing with the aftermath of the historic UMBC [University of Maryland, Baltimore County] loss in 2018 was certainly challenging, but I don't think our head coach or student–athletes could've handled it any better than they did. I was really proud of Tony [Bennett] and our student–athletes.

Erich Bacher, assistant athletics director for public relations, University of Virginia.

Photo courtesy of University of Virginia Athletics

In explaining the role of communications staff, Bacher notes that in addition to serving the media at the conclusion of the game, staff members also secure postgame statistics for the coaches and prepare the student–athletes with talking points and questions that may be asked for the postgame interviews. While the NCAA media relations staff and Final Four press volunteers were also helping to ensure successful coverage, three Virginia staff members were tasked to handle postgame responsibilities during the Final Four. Their roles were as follows:

1. Manage the postgame for Coach Bennett
2. Manage the two to three student–athletes who went to the press conference
3. Manage the open locker room

After the 2019 championship win, Bacher describes the media requests and events:

We received about 200 media requests in the first 24-48 hours following the national championship win. We couldn't fulfill them all, but we knocked out many one-on-one interview requests from the local, regional and national media, including TV, radio, newspapers, magazines and on-line sites. We also held a media availability with Coach Bennett and our players following an incredible celebration at Scott Stadium that week that attracted over 21,000 fans.

Discussion Questions

1. How would you prioritize the 200 media requests Virginia received? Which ones would respond to first? Why?
2. Analyze Virginia's use of three staff members to manage media immediately following the basketball game.
3. How do you believe Virginia handled its own social media accounts during this chaotic ending?

Media Tours

Traveling from one media outlet to another may be necessary, in a sort of media tour. Harris (1998) defined media tours as "tours of major markets for the purpose of obtaining publicity in local media" (p. 257). Media tours are popular in mainstream business, and although this tactic sounds simple, it may be difficult and time-consuming to execute. The goal of a media tour is to maximize media publicity for the organization while minimizing cost and demands on representatives. For example, a U.S. figure skating athlete who wins an Olympic gold medal overseas will be in media demand when he returns to the United States. To minimize the effects on his schedule, the national governing body may organize a media tour in an area with a significant media presence, such as New York City. This tour may include stops on morning talk shows as well as a publicity stop at an ice rink. The organization may invite sponsors and vendors to attend, further strengthening organizational relationships with those partners.

An alternative form of media tour is a satellite media tour (SMT). An SMT is similar to a teleconference, but it is done with satellite video technology and is used almost exclusively by television reporters. SMTs allow journalists anywhere in the world the opportunity for a live one-on-one individual interview, usually of five minutes or less (Smith, 2017). SMTs allow local television stations to ask specific questions of an interviewee that may be of interest to a local media audience. Think back to the figure skating athlete just described. Instead of a tour of media outlets in New York, U.S. Figure Skating may choose to position its athlete in one television studio and schedule a series of interviews with media outlets across the country using satellite links originating from the studio.

News Conferences

As is true of news releases and other forms of information services discussed in this chapter, the goal of a **news conference** is to disseminate noteworthy information from an organization to its targeted publics. Smith (2017) stated simply that "a news conference is a contrived media happening in which an organizational spokesperson makes a newsworthy statement. Generally this is followed by a question-and-answer session with reporters" (p. 316). After the spokesperson finishes the state-

ment, reporters usually have the opportunity to ask questions.

This definition addresses two key aspects to consider when calling a news conference—namely a newsworthy statement and an organizational spokesperson. In other words, what is the organization saying, and who is saying it?

A wise first step for an organization is to address why it is considering holding the news conference before going to the trouble of actually doing so (Condron, 2001). An organization should always consider whether holding a news conference will achieve its intended goals. Many organizations wrongly believe that staging an elaborate news conference to impress the team owner automatically results in positive news stories.

As discussed earlier, members of the media generally use six criteria to determine the news value of a story: timeliness, impact, prominence, conflict, unusualness, and proximity (Thompson, 1996). The same criteria should be used to determine whether a sport organization should hold a news conference (Hall, Nichols, Moynahan, & Taylor, 2007).

Although the announcement of a new head coach or a trade involving a star player almost always warrants a news conference, the announcement of a new footwear sponsor for an athletic team may not. All the aforementioned may be considered timely and important to the operation of a sport organization, but media often prefer not to cover sponsorship agreements because they view such announcements as free advertisement for the sponsor.

Merely holding a news conference may not be enough to garner media attention. An organization that calls unnecessary news conferences may get a reputation similar to that of the boy who cried wolf. If and when something deserving of a news conference occurs, the media may be reluctant to attend based on previous experience. Opinions differ about what kinds of statements deserve a news conference. Smith (2017) provided three justifications for holding a news conference:

1. To announce news or give a response of major importance
2. To serve the media's interests when a prominent spokesperson is available only for a short time
3. To avoid accusations of playing favorites among reporters

Baus and Lesly (1998) outlined two instances when an organization should hold a news conference:

1. If it will provide the media with something that they could not get in simpler ways such as a news release

2. In the case of a major news event, such as a violent disruption, major accident, sudden death of a top official, or some other emergency

The common element of these circumstances is that the event is significant. In sport, major events may include coach firings, player trades, free-agent signings, and facility construction, to name a few. Note that an organization should hold a news conference only to announce major news or to make it easier for the media to report about the organization. Examples of newsworthy events include:

- Player trades
- Personnel changes
- Free-agent signings
- Facility construction
- Interviews with athletics director, CEO, or owner
- Visits by prominent alumni or hall of famer
- Banquet speakers
- New product launches
- Postevent news conferences
- Media days

Each sport organization must also consider other factors when assessing the newsworthiness of any given event, such as personnel changes. Assessing the news value of the firing of a head college football coach is relatively easy, but how important is the hiring of a running backs coach for the same team? Both events are personnel changes, but are both newsworthy? Certainly the new running backs coach thinks his hiring is newsworthy—but will the organization's publics, especially members of the media, agree? In deciding whether to hold a news conference, organizational objectives should be considered. It may be the goal of the football team to be competitive and increase attendance. The new running backs coach may help accomplish the former, but it is safe to assume few consumers will be motivated to attend games merely because of a new running backs coach.

After the organization has determined that it has an announcement worthy of a news conference, it should carefully consider who will speak on behalf of the organization and where and when the news conference will take place.

Identifying Spokespersons

The *who* of a news conference is as important as the *what* of the news conference. But regardless of who speaks the words, the organization should speak with a single voice, meaning that the message should be consistent from one person to the next (Smith, 2017).

Senior executives, such as the owner, general manager, university athletics director, and university president, usually speak on behalf of the organization at a news conference. But an organization should not automatically assume that senior executives are the best spokespersons. Often they are not. The best spokesperson will likely vary depending on the subject. For example, a university that is announcing plans to build a new stadium may want to have on hand the architect and construction planner, in addition to the athletics director, to answer questions regarding design and project planning.

Smith (2017, p. 211) identified several reasons not to presume that the CEO or someone else from senior management is the best organizational spokesperson in every case. First, the organization should save the CEO for big announcements. Second, the CEO may not be as prepared to respond to all the details of a project. Third, the CEO may not have the personality or charisma necessary to make a positive impression in public.

Many organizations use their PR professional as their spokesperson, but much debate surrounds this practice. Helitzer (1996) argued that because PR persons are professional communicators and usually have the best relationship with the media, they are best suited to speak for the organization. On the other hand, PR persons are often viewed with less credibility because of the perception that they are simply mouthpieces of the organization. Whether functioning as the spokesperson or preparing the spokesperson, the job of the PR person is vital to successful news conferences.

Location

Given that an objective of a news conference may be to generate publicity, an organization should go out of its way to maximize attendance at news conferences by holding them in a location that is convenient for both the media and the organization. Sport organizations generally have two options for location: on site and off site.

On Site

The most likely place for an organization to hold a news conference is on site at one of the sport organization's facilities. Obviously, an organization must first estimate the size of the audience that is likely to attend the news conference and then determine whether an on-site facility could accommodate that crowd.

Because most organizations already have an area designated in their stadium or arena for postevent interviews, holding news conferences in that same space, commonly referred to as an interview room, is advantageous for a variety of reasons. First, the organization likely owns or leases the facility, ensuring flexibility in timing and setup. Sport organizations frequently call news conferences about breaking news such as a coach firing or a player trade. As discussed later in this chapter, the organization may be unable to notify media more than an hour or two before the news conference takes place. Locating a venue for a news conference on such short notice may be difficult unless the organization already has control of the facility.

Second, the facility is likely familiar to members of the media who often cover the organization's events. They know where to park, how to enter the facility, and where the room is located, making it convenient for them to cover the event.

Third, having the news conference in the organization's home facility minimizes time demands on participating organizational personnel by eliminating the need for travel to a different location. Of course, this advantage applies only if the news conference is held in a stadium or arena that also houses the organization's offices.

Finally, staging the news conference on the organization's home turf allows the organization to have greater control over the news conference's message and atmosphere, including such things as backdrops and organizational banners. PR professionals should consider having visual items such as diagrams, trophies, or awards to supplement the verbal information. These visuals may be used by television stations to break up a long sound bite from one of the participants or by still photographers to help frame the person who is talking. For example, it is hard to imagine a news conference to announce the Heisman Trophy winner without the trophy being present.

Off Site

Many sport organizations such as sporting goods manufacturers and governing bodies may not be able to arrange for a home turf advantage because they have no permanent facility where events take place. An organization that does not have a meeting or conference room large enough to host the event may have to hold its news conference off site.

The same considerations for news conferences on site apply to choosing an off-site venue. Specifically, the organization should consider size, parking, and convenience for the media. A hotel ballroom or conference room often makes a good news conference location (Baus & Lesly, 1998; Helitzer, 1996). Hotels often have the flexibility to change the size of a ballroom or conference room to accommodate varying crowd sizes. This feature is helpful for an organization that may have small media attendance for its news conference. A large room with few people may present the image that the news conference is not important enough to fill a room.

A hotel probably also has ample parking near the front door, an important and often overlooked consideration for a number of reasons (Condron, 2001). First, members of the media, especially television and still photographers, carry heavy equipment. Having abundant parking near the front entrance to the facility makes the media's job easier. Second, if the news conference is important enough that local television stations will want to carry it live, adequate space must be available for large uplink trucks to park.

An organization usually chooses a hotel that is centrally located in its region, perhaps downtown (Helitzer, 1996). The news conference is then as convenient as possible for the media to attend. Most newspaper offices are located in the downtown area of a city, whereas television stations are frequently spread throughout a city. Choosing someplace in the middle minimizes the travel time for everyone involved.

Another advantage to using a hotel is the ability to capitalize on many of the services that it can provide. The hotel will likely have a podium and sound system, along with multimedia tools that might be needed. In addition, most hotels offer some form of beverage service for purchase as well as other touches such as coat racks and signage.

Two primary disadvantages associated with using a hotel for a news conference are cost and not having a home turf advantage. Most hotels charge a fee that varies with the size of the room. That fee generally includes basic microphone, podium, sound system, and room setup. Other services such as beverages and projectors can be added at additional cost.

Not using a facility owned or leased by the organization increases the time commitment required of participants. The organization will have less flexibility in arranging the room, displaying atmospherics, and creating an environment favorable to the organization.

Making the Announcement

After the organization has determined where the news conference will take place, planning for the announcement begins in earnest. Two of the most critical planning elements are timing and notifying the media.

Timing

For some announcements, such as the firing of a professional basketball coach, the timing of the news conference is irrelevant; the media will show up because of the magnitude of the announcement. For other announcements, especially those involving a crisis, the timing of the news conference is irrelevant because the media representatives will be aggressively seeking organizational comment.

In today's competitive media environment, where rumors surface online long before an official announcement is made, an organization cannot sit on an announcement for a long time. Keeping the name of a coach secret has become extremely difficult. Most news conferences should be held as quickly as possible after a decision has been made, often after just a couple of hours, to prevent inaccurate information from being reported (Davis, 1998). But if timing is less critical, certain considerations will help maximize media attendance.

First, know the media's schedule. Early mornings are not generally the best time for a news conference because most sporting events take place at night and on weekends. Reporters are often up late filing stories after an event has ended. The earliest that an organization should consider holding a news conference is late morning to noon. To maximize publicity for the announcement, a news conference should conclude by early afternoon to midafternoon, providing enough time for television stations to edit stories for the early newscast, usually at 5 p.m., as well as for radio stations to ensure that the story receives coverage during the evening drive time.

Second, know the competition. If, for example, the Kansas City Royals want to hold a news conference in November to announce a free-agent signing during the off-season, they should probably not schedule the announcement for a Monday morning after a Kansas City Chiefs game when the team's head coach is holding his mandated news conference.

Last, know the news cycle, or which days are best to release information to the media. As Baus and Lesly (1998) suggested, "Tuesday, Wednesday and Thursday are generally the best days of the week, with Monday slightly behind" (p. 339). Because most television stations have scaled-back staffs on weekends made up of different anchors, reporters, and producers, weekends should be avoided, unless the organization has bad news to release. Friday afternoons are often used by organizations to "take out the trash"—in other words, to disclose bad information in the hope that media outlets do not devote their scaled-back resources to covering the story.

Notifying the Media

Organizations typically notify the media of a news conference by distributing a media advisory. A media advisory is similar to a news release, except that its goal is to give the media enough information to get their attention but not so much information that they don't need to attend the news conference. Unlike a news release, which is written in ready-to-use form, a media advisory simply presents the basic who, what, where, when, why, and how of the announcement.

When notifying the media of a news conference, an organization should avoid playing favorites and notify all media representatives who may have an interest in the organization or the announcement (Smith, 2017). Such representatives may include media members who do not normally cover the organization. For example, assume that a professional football team is announcing a partnership with the local United Way organization. This story may be more interesting to the local business media than it is to the team's beat writer. The PR person should know who the business media representatives are and ensure that they are invited.

For a breaking news conference, the general rule is to give the media as much notice as possible, perhaps a couple of hours or more. The key is to give the media representatives enough time to alter their plans so that they can attend the news conference, but not so much time they will be able to announce the story before the announcement. Occasionally it works in the best interest of the organization to release the information as much as a day in advance of the announcement. Doing so can help prolong the news cycle of the story.

Benefits and Downsides of News Conferences

Besides releasing messages to targeted publics, news conferences have other benefits, including eliminating perceived favoritism by the media, assisting the PR staff in executing its job, and complying with rules of the league or governing body.

An organization may occasionally want to leak news to a media outlet in the hope of generating favorable coverage in exchange for exclusivity. A news conference is the opposite of exclusive—it releases information to all media at one time in one place (Helitzer, 1996). The nature of a news conference is such that all persons in attendance hear the same comments at the same time and in the same context, thus eliminating the possibility of perceived favoritism among journalists.

Because a news conference is designed to disseminate information to audiences simultaneously, the staging of a news conference, despite all the planning it requires, may make the PR person's job easier. For example, most of the media at an event will want to interview an athlete who scores a winning touchdown or hits a game-winning home run. Having that athlete attend a postevent news conference will help the PR person by eliminating the need to arrange a series of one-on-one interviews with the media and the athlete. The athlete also benefits by not having to answer the same media questions repeatedly.

Finally, many organizations are mandated to hold a news conference by their league or governing body. In a case study of the National Basketball Association (NBA), Fortunato (2000) pointed out the league's philosophy that the head coach is an integral part of the game and is therefore required to meet with the media following every game. A postgame news conference is the perfect opportunity for that coach to meet with the media.

Whether they are required or not, news conferences in sport are so commonplace that members of the media expect one to be held following an event at nearly every level of athletic competition. At the very least, the PR person should arrange for one-on-one interviews between the media and athlete following the event.

Although news conferences offer numerous benefits, downsides are present as well. In reality, most journalists view news conferences as cold, impersonal places to gather information. The basic format of a news conference is awkward and uncomfortable (Smith, 2017; Wilstein, 2002). Interviewees usually sit on a raised dais, above the interviewers, with bright lights focused on them, making it difficult for them to see the person asking the question.

Wilstein (2002) wrote, "The interview room, despite its name, is probably the worst place in sports to interview anyone. It is a concept that thwarts spontaneity and usually produces the most vapid quotes" (p. 127).

One reason for this lack of spontaneity may be the competitive nature of today's media. Most mass media outlets, like most businesses, exist to make money. A news site such as Bleacher Report can maximize profits by having access to information that its competitors do not. The news conference format of disseminating information to a large audience at the same time negates competition. A newspaper has no opportunity to get exclusive information at a news conference when its competitors get the information at the same time (Smith, 2017).

Given the number of reporters covering any one event and the competitive media environment, it is not surprising that many reporters wait to ask specific questions of interviewees until they are in a one-on-one interview.

Event Planning

For a PR professional, a news conference is equivalent to an athlete's game day. It provides an opportunity for PR professionals to showcase their abilities and skills on behalf of the organization. Therefore, the PR professional must attend to every detail well in advance to ensure smooth operation of the event.

PR professionals must have several reliable people to assist them with the duties outlined in the following section. One person cannot be everywhere at the same time, so having trustworthy assistants can enhance the efficiency of the news conference.

Five critical areas determine the success of a news conference: atmospherics, or the visual elements that can enhance the value of the news conference; press kits that can provide additional information for the media; adherence to a strict format; room setup and equipment, such as microphones and tape recorders; and a quote service, which provides excerpts of what was said to members of the media.

Atmospherics

Atmospherics—an element that Irwin, Sutton, and McCarthy (2008) addressed as a key marketing consideration—also apply to news conferences. The atmosphere at a news conference can be a positive promotional tool for the sport organization. Prominent placement of the organization's logo on the podium, a backdrop, and even clothing can help maximize media exposure. The sum of these elements affects the physical setting, resulting in additional promotional value for the organization.

One common atmospheric element at news conferences is some sort of backdrop. This backdrop is frequently a pattern of the organization's logo and perhaps a corporate sponsor. Given the intense media coverage of news conferences on cable television, organizations may be able to generate significant revenue by selling sponsorship of the backdrop to a corporation.

Attention should be paid to the color of the backdrop so that it presents the right image on television. A backdrop that is predominantly white will wash out on camera. Also, the backdrop should be portable enough that it can be erected in any location, even if the organization is playing a road game. The PR person must ensure that the backdrop is set up in time for postevent news conferences.

If a backdrop is unavailable, the news conference should be held against a solid wall if indoors, or if outdoors the participants should be positioned at such an angle so as not to cast shadows on their faces. Another alternative is to use some standard exposition-grade pipe and drape, preferably 8 feet (2.5 m) high. Most hotels and convention centers have a supply of these materials on site.

Other items that may enhance the setting of a news conference include anything that is visual and may make for a good picture, adding to the value of the news conference. Championship team trophies such as the Stanley Cup of the National Hockey League (NHL) or individual trophies such as the Heisman Trophy offer a reminder of past accomplishments. Banners or framed jerseys and photos hung on the walls may provide additional exposure for the organization's logo. As Hall and colleagues (2007) noted, the PR person's job is get the organization into the public eye: "One of the simplest and most effective ways to do so is to display the institution's name and logo in such a manner that

Sport organizations frequently use backdrops that feature both their logo and a key sponsor's logo.

Catherine Ivill - FIFA/FIFA via Getty Images

they appear prominently in photographs or video clips from the news conference" (p. 108).

Press Kits

Press kits contain a variety of publicity information about an organization and are usually assembled to support an event such as a news conference or media day. They typically contain a news release corresponding with the event and a schedule of events.

The schedule of events should include a detailed listing of what time the news conference will start and when certain spokespersons will speak. The schedule assists photographers and television camera crews with their preparation, because they need to have cameras trained at a certain spot at a certain time. Biographies should include correct titles for all spokespersons as well as past accomplishments, which helps ensure proper spelling of individuals' names.

Press kits, minus information critical to the announcement, may be distributed ahead of time along with the media advisory. More commonly, they are given to the media on site at the news conference. PR persons should ensure that all interested media representatives receive a press kit via e-mail or other electronic delivery.

Format

News conferences should be well organized and stick to the schedule of events distributed to the media in press kits. A moderator is often present at a news conference. This master of ceremonies, frequently the PR person, should be familiar with all participants as well as the media.

Moderators should welcome the media to the news conference and thank them for attending. They should introduce the primary spokesperson and clearly state the person's title. After the initial statements are concluded, it is appropriate for the media to ask questions. The moderator may facilitate this process by calling on individuals to voice their questions.

Some spokespersons may ask the moderator to repeat the question for the benefit of everyone in attendance. Doing so accomplishes two things. First, it allows everyone in the room to hear the question; second, it allows the spokesperson time to formulate an answer before speaking. The length of the question-and-answer session will vary depending on the nature of the news conference, but it should not exceed 30 minutes. The length of time allowed should be specified in advance.

As the time for questions winds down, the moderator can signal the end of the news conference by calling for the last question. Media members expect some time afterward for one-on-one interviews, which should be budgeted into the overall schedule.

These one-on-one interviews are important to electronic and print media alike. For electronic media, such interviews allow them to use their own microphones with station flags for the interview. This visual cue enhances the television station's credibility because it proves to viewers that the station was in attendance. In addition, the flag adds to the station's own promotional efforts. For print media, one-on-one interviews allow reporters to ask detailed questions that they do not want their competitors to hear. The business of mass media is to make money, and one way to accomplish that is through exclusive stories. Don't expect the media to ask all their questions in a news conference setting when competitors are present.

The PR person has the job of escorting the spokesperson from one interview to the next, as well as monitoring the interviews to know what is being asked and to ensure that no media outlet gets a longer interview than another.

Room Setup and Equipment

An often-overlooked element in the basic room setup for a news conference is some sort of check-in procedure. Check-in should take place outside the room in which the news conference will be held to minimize distractions caused by late arrivals. Organizations should request contact information such as name, affiliation, e-mail address, and phone number of all media representatives in attendance to enhance the organization's media list (Irwin, Sutton, & McCarthy, 2002). The check-in area is a good place to distribute press kits, and it should always be staffed by someone in the organization's PR office who is familiar with the schedule of events.

The basic setup of a news conference requires a podium where participants will stand or a head table where participants can sit in addition to ample chairs arranged in even rows where media representatives can sit and ask questions. A microphone and sound system must be in place for participants to speak into. In addition, chairs should be placed in a manner that creates adequate circulation space on either side and an aisle down the middle to allow smooth traffic flow (Condron, 2001). This setup also allows space for photographers and camera operators to move closer to the interview participants. PR staff members should develop protocols for movement of journalists during a formal news conference. Too much commotion in the middle of the room may distract the participants; therefore, the PR professional may consider restricting movement to the sides only.

If a head table is employed, it should be on a raised platform, called a dais. The dais should be about 18 inches (45 cm) off the ground and carpeted and draped to reduce noise (Condron, 2001). In addition, the table should be skirted in a color complementary to the backdrop and dais draping. A sufficient number of microphones, two at a minimum, should be located on the head table for the participants. One microphone should be reserved for the moderator, if there is one, and the other microphone can be shared. If the news conference involves more than two participants, an additional microphone should be added for every two persons.

The sound system into which the microphone is tied should include a multibox in the back of the room near where television cameras will be positioned. A multibox is a multiple outlet output device that allows media to patch directly into the audio from the sound system (Condron, 2001). Multiboxes are beneficial for both the media and the organization. From the media's standpoint, a multibox produces clear audio without the worry that the speaker will not talk directly into the media representative's microphone. From the organization's perspective, a multibox eliminates the need for multiple microphones with different media flags on the head table or podium. This setup presents a much cleaner visual image and may permit additional promotional exposure if the organization uses its logo on the main microphone.

The multibox may be placed on a camera platform, if one is available. If the news conference room has a dais for the head table, a similar dais that is the same height may be provided for cameras in the back. This second dais permits television crews to set up their tripods where people will not bump into them and where the cameras will not block the view of the head table.

Although it may add significantly to expenses, the organization should use its own lighting system. Optimal broadcast lighting is measured in terms of temperature, usually in degrees Kelvin. Standard indoor lighting for TV news shooting is 3,200 degrees Kelvin. Daylight and sunlight, considered natural light, measure up to 13,000 degrees Kelvin. Artificial light provided by overhead lighting and lamps is considerably darker than natural light, around 2,000 degrees Kelvin. Therefore, an organization must often provide supplemental lighting

for news conferences to enhance the artificial light already present in the room. Most electronic news-gathering (ENG) crews carry their own battery-powered light kits, which provide an additional 600 to 1,000 watts of artificial light at exactly 3,200 degrees Kelvin. Although those kits are sufficient for one ENG crew, if the news conference has multiple crews with multiple lights, participants in the news conference may find it difficult to see. Therefore, the organization should invest in key and fill lights. As the main light, the key light should be well above the cameras, about 7 feet (2 m) off the ground, and aimed at the subject. The fill lights fill in shadows caused by the key light and should be about 30 degrees to the either side of the cameras (Cremer, Keirstead, & Yoakam, 1996).

Teleconferences

A sport organization may consider adding a teleconference service to its news conference. A **teleconference** is a news conference using telecommunications to connect the interviewee with interviewers who are not physically present at the news conference. By dialing a predetermined phone number with a password or code, members of the media who cannot be present for a news conference may still listen to, and perhaps even participate in, the news conference.

Using a teleconference offers many benefits. From the organization's perspective, it allows maximum media exposure without the repetition of doing several individual interviews. From the media's perspective, it allows a reporter to dial into the news conference from anywhere (Miller & Zang, 2001). For example, if an international sporting goods organization on the West Coast is holding a news conference to release an earnings statement, the organization may arrange a teleconference with writers on the East Coast, where most business and magazine writers are located. If the CEO is delivering the statement, certainly business writers will be interested, especially if the company is publicly traded.

Perhaps during the teleconference, the CEO also announces plans for a new line of golf shoes to be unveiled in the next few months, along with a new endorsement agreement with a top golfer. This announcement is now certainly of interest to media that specialize in golf coverage, but it may also be of interest to media that cover sport business and marketing. A teleconference will make it easy for these diverse media groups to get information that they need for their stories. At the same time, the

CEO, whose time is extremely valuable, is spared from having to schedule multiple interviews about the same topic.

A critical factor that cannot be overlooked regarding teleconferences is geography. In the case of the sporting goods company, the CEO may want to hold the news conference at 9 a.m. on the West Coast, where the company is located; but this time falls during the middle of the business day on the East Coast. Thus, a teleconference such as this one may be better timed earlier in the day to make it easier for the media to participate.

Checklist

Many PR professionals find it helpful to use a checklist when planning a news conference because many details are involved (see figure 7.1). The PR person must monitor location, timing, notification, and equipment, and may choose to assign each task to a staff member or volunteer to ensure timely completion.

Media Days

Many sport organizations, particularly professional teams and NCAA Division I universities and conferences, hold media days before the beginning of the competitive season to maximize the team's or league's exposure and minimize demands on the organization. Media days are accomplished by inviting all members of the media interested in the organization to attend one session and by blocking out that day on the team's calendar to facilitate many interviews rather than initiating several interviews each day. In the case of major NCAA conferences, media days may be spread out over several days.

The Southeastern Conference held its 2019 football media days from July 15 through 18. Each of the 14 member schools was required to make its head coach and three players available to the media for nearly three hours. More than 1,000 media credentials were issued for the SEC media days in 2018, including national media as well as local university media and Internet-based media (Dennis, 2018).

Media days have been defined as "an elaborate news conference with a more social atmosphere" (Hall, Nichols, Moynahan, Taylor, 2007, p. 116). The basic goal of a media day is to provide media representatives with access to members of the organization, such as players and coaches, in a casual atmosphere. Media days at the beginning of a season should be upbeat. After all, each team begins the season without a loss and with lots of optimism. The organization has the opportunity to showcase its product, possibly producing favorable publicity and perhaps even additional revenue through tickets sales or sponsorships.

The distribution of materials at a media day will generally mirror that at a news conference. A press kit containing a schedule of events, biographies, and perhaps a media guide is expected.

A typical media day may begin with a lunch for members of the media and select organizational personnel, followed by a news conference with the team's coach and general manager or athletic director. The media then usually have access to players for interviews. Those interviews may be followed by a light scrimmage or practice that the media are able to watch. Figure 7.2 shows how a university might wish to schedule a media day for its women's basketball team.

The organization's PR staff may wish to consider several tactics to enhance media coverage. First, PR staff should anticipate that most media members will want to interview the same two or three players and prepare those players in advance. More players should be made available, however—particularly seniors who may be graduating. PR staff members should be sure to brief all players in advance regarding possible questions.

The PR staff should also encourage the athletes to wear uniforms with numbers to aid members of the media in identifying players whom they may wish to interview. In addition, because the uniform likely carries the organization's name and logo, the team receives additional publicity.

During the practice, the PR person should encourage the coach to run plays that are visually exciting, such as long passes or two-on-one basketball drills. Broadcast media will shoot the practice and use the video in their stories. Having positive images of players making baskets or catching passes may lead to positive publicity.

One final consideration relates to photographers who wish to make a creative image of media day. A photographer may stage a photo of a group of players, perhaps sitting on the basketball court around the team logo.

News Conference Checklist

Date: September 21, 2020
Time: 1:00 p.m.
Subject: Athletic Director Hiring News Conference
Location: Champions Club in Basketball Arena

Item	Person responsible	Complete by
Meet with sports information staff and students Assign specific responsibilities		Morning of September 16
Write and send media advisory Include parking instructions Include fax and e-mail info		Afternoon of September 16
Assemble media kit Write news release Write biography of athletic director (AD) Write biography of university president Include athletics schedules		Morning of September 17
Make name cards for AD and university president (if using a table)		Morning of September 18
Phone-call reminders to media		Afternoon of September 18
Set up room Set up backdrop Test sound system Arrange chairs Skirt table Set up podium or skirted table for speakers Set up additional lighting		12:00 p.m., September 21
Create media sign-in table Create sign-in sheet Include media kits Include miscellaneous athletics posters, schedules		12:30 p.m., September 21
Place bottled water on table for speakers and in back for media		12:45 p.m., September 21
Postevent activities Distribute quote sheets Deliver media kits to news outlets not in attendance Write story for organization website Post photos on organization website		As soon as possible after news conference

Figure 7.1 Sample checklist for planning a news conference.

Schedule for Media Day

Time	
12:00 p.m.	Welcome to media conducted by university sports information director
12:05 p.m.	Sit-down lunch for media
12:35 p.m.	Presentation by team's head coach, including introduction of assistant coaches
12:50 p.m.	Formal question-and-answer period
1:00 p.m.	One-on-one interviews with coaches and media
1:30 p.m.	Sports information director escorts media to practice gym
1:45 p.m.	One-on-one interviews with team players and media
2:15 p.m.	Practice open to media
3:00 p.m.	Media depart

Figure 7.2 Sample media day schedule for a university's women's basketball team.

SUMMARY

Because a sport PR professional functions as a conduit between the organization and the broader public, including mass media, the distribution of organizational information becomes one of the profession's key aspects. Understanding the methods accepted in the industry for identifying newsworthy information and distributing it can increase the likelihood that the organization will receive favorable coverage. Many tactics are employed to deliver information to the media. Interviews allow sport organizations the opportunity to communicate positive messages to targeted publics. The PR person for the organization should endeavor to make it as easy as possible for those messages to be communicated. Responding to media inquiries in a professional manner, preparing interviewees, and selecting appropriate spokespersons are essential to influencing the delivery of messages. Sport organizations may use controlled events such as news conferences and media days to assist media members in covering the organization. News conferences should be carefully planned by devoting attention to the timing, location, and setup of the conference.

LEARNING ACTIVITIES

1. Research a current professional athlete and write a news release as if she or he is retiring.

2. Visit several athlete social media sites and determine whether they are using front-stage or back-stage messages in their self-presentation. Which type of message is most effective and why?

3. As the sports information director for a Football Bowl Subdivision (FBS) university, you are approached by your athletic director about scheduling a news conference later that day to announce the firing of the head football coach. Detail a plan to notify the media and prepare a location for the news conference.

4. Write a media advisory for the scenario in activity 3. What information would you want to include? How would you distribute it?

5. Ask your university's sports information office for a credential to a home athletic event. Attend the postevent news conference and critique the behavior of the interviewees. Pay attention to their responses to questions and their mannerisms during the interview.

Communicating in Times of Crisis

After reading this chapter, students should be able to

- define crisis and crisis communications,
- recognize the importance of crisis readiness,
- identify the key elements of a crisis communications plan,
- distinguish between various crisis response strategies,
- articulate the critical role of social media in crisis communications, and
- understand how crisis responses may be assessed.

These are the key terms discussed in this chapter:

- call tree
- crisis
- crisis communications

- crisis communications plans
- crisis response strategy
- one-move chess

One of the most prominent crises in U.S. sport history involved a sport medicine physician who was found to have a long history of criminal sexual conduct while working with multiple organizations. After pleading guilty to multiple charges, Dr. Larry Nassar was sentenced to prison in 2018. During the sentencing hearing, more than 150 women and girls came forward with statements about his sexual abuse (Who is Larry Nassar?, n.d.). As the story unfolded, the organizations where Nassar served over his career of 30-plus years—Michigan State University, USA Gymnastics, and Gedderts' Twistars Gymnastics Club USA—were engulfed in the crisis as they were the subjects of lawsuits and related media coverage accusing them of failing to take action. At Michigan State, the sustained crisis resulted in the resignations of the university president and athletic director, campus protests, and subsequent controversy regarding the university's new leadership and its path forward. In reflecting on the university's response, a Michigan State trustee, who also happened to be a public relations executive, said, "It's a textbook example of how not to deal with a crisis" (Dianne Byrum, quoted in Mack, 2018).

This is one of the textbooks to which the trustee was alluding. And while there is much to be learned from the mistakes at Michigan State and USA Gymnastics, the reality is that many sports figures and organizations have endured prominent crises. Several prominent examples over the years include the following:

- Nike has endured a lengthy crisis that began in the 1990s about its labor practices. Critics have charged that Nike's overseas subcontractors paid their employees less than minimum wages, placed employees in unsafe working conditions, and allowed employees to be physically abused.

- The National Association for Stock Car Auto Racing (NASCAR) suffered tragedy in 2001 when star driver Dale Earnhardt was killed in an accident during the final lap of NASCAR's marquee event, the Daytona 500.

- Numerous athletes were implicated in the scandal that began in 2002 involving performance-enhancing drugs supplied by the Bay Area Laboratory Co-operative (BALCO). One of the most prominent was track star Marion Jones, who was ultimately sent to prison for lying to federal investigators about her steroid use.

- The National Football League (NFL) has faced a sustained crisis pertaining to long-term health effects of football on players, particularly the cognitive impact of brain trauma.

- The International Olympic Committee suspended and fined Russia's Olympic committee for state-sponsored doping and banned it from representation at the PyeongChang 2018 Winter Olympics.

All sport organizations are susceptible to crises, because even the most comprehensive risk management plans cannot protect against all potential problems. After a crisis occurs, the manner in which the sport organization's staff responds often has enormous public relations implications. All sport public relations professionals need to recognize the importance of preparing for crises and making sound decisions during crises.

Neal Gulkis, director of communications at Homestead–Miami Speedway, observed that this facet of professional preparation is easy to overlook as practitioners focus on developing core public relations skills (e.g., writing, research) that more frequently contribute to their organizations' growth and their own professional advancement. However, Gulkis (2016) warns, "How you approach and handle crisis situations can ultimately define you more than anything else you ever do as a PR professional—whether it is sports or any other field."

This chapter, designed to prepare students for crisis preparation and management, features four main sections on **crisis communications**. The first section discusses the nature of crises and their prevalence within sport. The second section describes how sport public relations professionals may prepare themselves for crisis episodes. It includes

- ways to anticipate the crises an organization is likely to face,
- the nature of crisis communications plans and the process of developing them, and
- key elements within a crisis communications plan.

The third section addresses considerations for sport public relations practitioners during crises, including strategies that may be employed to protect or repair the organization's reputation. An important aspect of this discussion relates to the importance of social media in crisis management. The fourth section considers how professionals can assess the effectiveness of a crisis response and offers a number of examples of both successful and unsuccessful crisis strategies.

Nature of Crises and the Need to Plan for Them

Not all negative incidents qualify as crises. Some are just that—incidents. Others may be severe enough to qualify as emergencies, but even emergencies are not necessarily crises. For instance, if a spectator who suffers a medical emergency receives prompt attention, the matter likely will not escalate into a crisis because it will have been resolved and probably not deemed newsworthy. Furthermore, not all crises are incident driven; some result from long-standing problems that have never been adequately resolved. For example, it does not take a lawsuit to plunge a sport organization that neglects gender equity into a crisis. Either a media report or social media posting could serve as the impetus for a hailstorm of public criticism.

Crises are sometimes serious threats to an organization's financial well-being, but their impact extends well beyond monetary considerations. Crises directly affect brands and reputations. Sometimes the crisis itself causes the impact, but more often it results from the organization managers' response or lack thereof to the crisis. For example, much of the criticism directed at Michigan State during the Nassar scandal focused on the university's attempts to minimize the issue and evade responsibility (Mack, 2018). Coverage by the mass and social media of poor organizational responses to crises can damage brands and related reputations in ways that outweigh any public goodwill established before the crisis (Grunig, Grunig, & Dozier, 2002).

A **crisis** is defined as "a situation or occurrence possessing the potential to significantly damage a sport organization's financial stability and/or credibility with constituents" (Stoldt, Miller, Ayres, & Comfort, 2000, pp. 253–254). This definition takes into account both the diverse nature of crises as well as their potential to affect brand, reputation, and financial well-being.

Purpose of Crisis Plans

Given the potential of crises to significantly damage an organization, some sport organizations have developed plans to guide them when crises occur. Sport managers sometimes confuse crisis plans with emergency plans. Although the two are clearly related, they are not identical. Emergency plans guide responses as an emergency occurs. They delineate responses to situations such as a patron having a heart attack, a packed facility being placed under a tornado warning, or a fire occurring at a manufacturing facility. Effectively employed, emergency plans can protect customers and employees and sometimes save lives, thus averting a crisis.

A **crisis communications plan** offers direction on how to proceed after a crisis has occurred. Because processing and sharing information are critical to managing crises, communications—both internal and external—are usually the focus of the plan. The plan specifies what roles people in the organization will play in responding to the crisis; sources of information that will support timely actions; and key steps to take in engaging with external publics such as the mass media, donors, and customers. Gulkis (2016) characterizes a crisis communications plan as "a must no matter what company you are with."

Need for Crisis Plans

Crisis planning is necessary for most sport organizations. Even organizations that do not usually face the glare of the media spotlight may find themselves under public scrutiny as a crisis evolves. For example, one state interscholastic athletics association found itself receiving national media attention when it was named in a federal lawsuit centering on the participation of transgender athletes. The lawsuit alleged that conference's application of state policy to allow sport participation based on gender identity discriminated against female athletes (Putterman & Riley, 2019).

Although saying precisely how many sport organizations are faced with crises is impossible, past studies (e.g., Hessert, 1998a; Stoldt, Miller, & Comfort, 2001) have indicated that the number is probably high. For instance, corruption is just one source of crises within the industry, yet corruption is, perhaps surprisingly, common. Using a model that recognized three types of corruption—doping, match-fixing, and insider information—Masters (2015) identified more than 300 instances of corruption over a 10-year period in just five sectors of the industry (Major League Baseball, the National Basketball Association, the NFL, the National Hockey League, and global football/soccer).

Despite the critical importance of crisis planning, many prominent sport organizations have been either slow to engage in such work or remain hesitant to do so. In a study focusing on communications professionals working with English Premier League football clubs, Manoli (2016) found that all 25 indicated that a proactive approach (i.e., planning) was not feasible. Further, planning for worst-case scenarios was only occasional, with "only a few details" being identified as to how to respond in such situations.

One can only wonder about the extent of crisis readiness among other sport organizations. If some organizations at the highest levels of sport—such as the major professional leagues and teams—are ill equipped for crises, the situation is likely even worse in minor league and smaller collegiate sport organizations in which staff members commonly assume multiple jobs. And that speculation does not even begin to take into account crisis readiness within other sectors of the industry.

Dealing with crises has become exponentially more challenging over the past decade for at least two reasons. First, the proliferation of media properties devoting themselves to 24-hour sport news coverage and possessing the digital technology capabilities to share information instantaneously has resulted in sport organizations finding themselves under greater media scrutiny. Second, the growth of social media and the tendency of social media to advance and escalate crises at breathtaking speed are having a profound effect on the sport industry. Sport public relations professionals must stand ready to respond to crises in a matter of minutes.

As noted earlier, the potential damage to sport organizations from not responding appropriately to a crisis is significant. Brands and reputations that have been carefully built through years of strong public relations and effective marketing can be irreparably harmed because of a single crisis. Crisis communications plans empower sport organizations to limit the damage and, in some cases, make positive impressions.

Preparing for a Crisis

Coombs (2019) contended that crisis management occurs in three stages: precrisis, crisis response, and postcrisis. Using that framework, figure 8.1 presents a recommended approach to **crisis communications**. The cyclical model starts with preparing for crises by forecasting crisis situations, then developing and maintaining a crisis communications plan. As noted earlier, the plan prescribes procedures for managing internal and external communications during a time of crisis. The onset of a crisis leads to the second stage in the model: managing the crisis. This phase includes both the activation of the crisis communications plan and

additional strategic considerations as the crisis management team defines strategies to protect or repair the organization's reputation. The conclusion of the crisis episode marks the transition to the third stage of the model: assessment of the effectiveness of the plan. Postcrisis evaluation may help organizational management prepare for and manage future crises. The following sections address each stage of the model in detail.

Forecasting Crises

The first step that sport public relations professionals should take in moving toward crisis readiness is to anticipate the types of crises that their organizations may face. This job is not pleasant, but it does offer two benefits. First, by identifying potential problems, sport public relations professionals enable their organizations to take preemptive measures and prevent crises from occurring. The second benefit is that the crisis forecast can provide a practical foundation for the development of the crisis communications plan.

As with any important public relations initiative, crisis forecasting should not be left to only the communications team. Forecasting should include managers from throughout the sport organization, including those specializing in human resources, finance, law, and security. A review of the organization's crisis-related history as well as an audit of the professional information regarding crisis-related trends across the field may serve as excellent starting points for planning team discussions. For example, if a minor league franchise has received a number of complaints about drunken fans, then it should consider fan misbehavior in its forecasting process. Similarly, if the public relations staff for a fitness center notices that several similar businesses around the country have endured crises because of being unprepared for medical emergencies, that concern should be included in the fitness center's forecast.

Some sport organizations have found it beneficial to hire external consultants to help forecast and plan for crises. Such companies offer services ranging from forecasting to developing plans to staging crisis simulations. Dan Beebe, who transitioned to a consultant role after serving as commissioner of the Big 12 conference, cited the advantage of involving experts outside the organization in the planning process (Elfman, 2017). Besides possessing expertise in crisis communications, these external consultants frequently bring fresh perspectives to the table and may enable an organization's

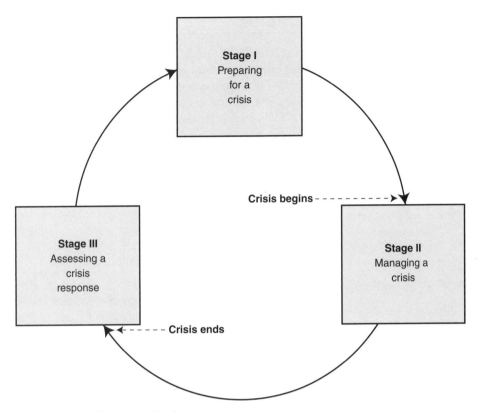

Figure 8.1 An approach to crisis communications.

sport managers to identify issues that would have been missed had all planning been conducted internally. Although the cost of hiring external consultants can sometime extend to six figures, the investment may prove to be money well spent given the potential for financial damage because of mismanaged crises.

The list of potential crises that a sport organization can face often seems limitless. Coombs and Holladay (1996) developed a framework distinguishing crises along two dimensions: whether they were internal or external and whether they were intentional or unintentional. While this framework has relevance across the sport industry, a nuanced application may need to include other factors such as gender, culture, geographic setting, and more. A similar crisis type may be perceived differently depending on whether it occurred in men's or women's sport or within a particular cultural context (Wilson, Stavros, & Westberg, 2009).

Favorito (2007) developed a typology that accounted for the following crises:

- Security threats, natural disasters, and construction problems that may imperil fans and impact facilities

- In-event incidents such as a competitor's death, fan injuries, and on-field or in-stand violence
- Off-field incidents in which organizational personnel commit legal infractions or become involved in celebrity scandals
- Organizational personnel decisions such as trading or releasing star players or coaches
- Organizational management issues, including financial crises, layoffs, compliance issues, and politically controversial decisions

Table 8.1 applies this framework and offers an example of a related crisis that has occurred in recent years.

As noted in the table, many sport organizations have been forced to consider terrorism as a relevant concern. Terrorism, however, is not a new reality in sport. The sidebar Terrorist Threats to Sport addresses this important issue.

Because a crisis communications plan cannot address every conceivable crisis that an organization may face, public relations experts have recommended prioritizing potential crises based on two dimensions: likelihood and impact (Coombs, 2019; Fearn-Banks,

Table 8.1   Sport Crisis Examples

Crisis type	Example
Threats to consumers, facilities	Terrorist bombing occurs outside Stade de France, a soccer stadium where the French president was in attendance as France played Germany. The attacks are part of a coordinated series of ISIS attacks in Paris that killed 130 people (2015).
In-event incidents	Several members of Australia's cricket team are discovered to be cheating by ball tampering while playing a third test match against South Africa. Cricket Australia issues bans to three players in response (2018).
Off-field incidents	Swimming star Ryan Lochte is suspended 10 months by the U.S. Olympic Committee and USA Swimming for his off-site behavior at the 2016 Summer Olympics in Rio de Janeiro. Lochte was found to have fabricated a story about being robbed (2016).
Organizational issue management	In the wake of California's passage of the Fair Pay to Play Act and other political pressure, the NCAA drafts new rules on whether college athletes can receive compensation for use of their name, image, and likeness (2019).
Organizational personnel decisions	Ohio State University endures fan backlash when it suspends football coach Urban Meyer for failing to take action after learning of domestic abuse allegations by one of his assistant coaches. Meyer subsequently resigns (2018).

Based on Favorito (2007).

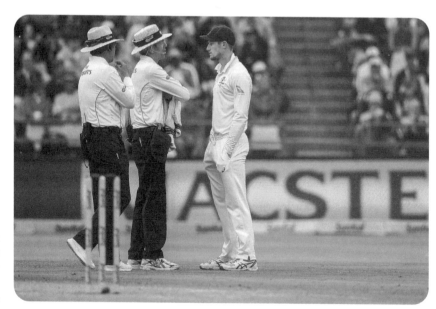

Cricket Australia faced a crisis when three of its players were found to have engaged in cheating by ball tampering.

GIANLUIGI GUERCIA/AFP via Getty Images

2017; Hessert & Gillette, 2002; Sports Media Challenge, 1997). If a particular type of crisis seems highly likely to occur, the organization should plan for it. Similarly, if a crisis possesses the potential to devastate the organization, such a crisis should also be addressed, even if it is deemed less probable to occur than others. For instance, many crisis plans address scenarios pertaining to both the arrest of a prominent player or coach and a transportation accident resulting in deaths or serious injuries. The first crisis is one that

Terrorist Threats to Sport

The visibility of many sport events and the density of the crowds attending such events make sport venues a possible target for terrorist attacks. That assessment has important implications for sport public relations professionals. The world of sport has endured multiple high-profile terrorist attacks. Four of the most prominent examples include the following:

- 1972 Olympic Summer Games in Munich, Germany: Eight terrorists slipped into the Olympic village, killed two members of the Israeli team, and took nine others hostage with the aim of forcing a prisoner exchange for Palestinian detainees. A day later, all the hostages and five terrorists were killed in a firefight at the Munich airport.
- 1996 Olympic Summer Games in Atlanta, Georgia: A bomb was detonated in the Centennial Olympic Park. One person was killed and more than 100 others were injured.
- 2013 Boston Marathon: Two bombs exploded near the finish line, killing 3 people and injuring more than 250 others.
- 2015 France–Germany International Friendly: Terrorists targeted an international soccer match as part of a coordinated attack on Paris. Only one person besides the suicide bombers was killed in the bombings outside Stade de France; however, at least one of the terrorists had a ticket to the match and tried to enter the stadium.

On other occasions, terrorist attacks in nonsport settings have affected the sport industry. In the wake of the September 11, 2001, attacks in New York City; Washington, D.C.; and Pennsylvania, numerous sport organizations, including the NFL, Major League Baseball, and many college athletics programs, postponed scheduled contests and reevaluated their readiness for future attacks (Brady, 2002; Muret, 2006).

Although recommendations aimed at preventing terrorist attacks were once resisted by sport executives, they were embraced in the climate following the September 11 attacks (Hessert & Gillette, 2002). Major sport properties adopted a series of best practices, including the placement of physical barriers to prevent explosive-laden vehicles from penetrating facilities and the screening of spectators to prevent people from carrying weapons into venues.

Some sport managers and government officials have made specific plans for responding to possible terrorist attacks. A number of communities and sport organizations have staged terrorism drills. One such drill was conducted at Tokyo Stadium ahead of the 2019 Rugby World Cup (Anti-terror drill . . . , 2019), the 2020 Summer Olympics Games, and the 2020 Paralympic Games.

most professional and college sport organizations are likely to encounter, even in programs that make every effort to recruit upstanding players and coaches. The latter crisis is one that programs are less likely to face, but the effects of such an event are devastating. For example, 16 people were killed when the bus carrying a Canadian junior hockey team was hit by a tractor trailer in April 2018. Fifteen of those killed were players or staff members of the Humboldt Broncos organization.

Finally, sport managers engaged in crisis forecasting should be aware that two types of crises occur (Carter & Rovell, 2003). The first happens suddenly and with no warning. Examples include an airplane crash or an explosion at a sport facility. The second type of crisis is one for which there is warning. Michigan State had received reports of Nassar's sexual abuse prior to the full onset of crisis. Lawsuits against the university alleged student–athletes began reporting Nassar's behavior as far back as 1998, and the university in 2014 cleared him after another reported assault (Who is Larry Nassar?, n.d.). At minimum, use of a well-developed crisis communications plan would have prevented some of the disastrous responses from university leaders as the crisis unfolded.

Developing a Crisis Communications Plan

Crises are by nature disruptive and difficult to manage, but by developing a crisis communications plan, sport managers can take a proactive approach.

A **crisis communications plan** provides a framework for responding to crisis situations. It empowers sport managers by specifying responsibilities in a crisis, the way information is to be shared internally during a crisis, and the way information is to be shared with other publics in a timely manner. By defining such considerations in advance of a crisis, the sport organization may be better positioned to respond in a manner that best protects its reputation and financial interests.

Crisis communications plans are not designed to prescribe responses for every conceivable crisis, nor are they detailed enough to specify every action that must be taken throughout a crisis episode. They are designed to provide general guidelines for the management team, particularly early on. Mark Fabiani, a public relations consultant for the National Hockey League (NHL), the Big East Conference, and the NFL team that at the time was the San Diego Chargers, has stated that the goal is to "get ahead of the story" (Mullen, 2004, p. 24). Getting ahead now means making an initial response within an hour of the onset of the crisis.

To prepare for crises in such a manner, sport managers must follow a number of steps in the process:

1. Ensure that stakeholders support the development of the plan

2. Involve key personnel on the planning committee

3. Communicate to the team the plan and the importance of using the plan

4. Test the plan and make improvements if necessary

5. Remain committed to using the crisis plan when needed

The first step in developing a crisis communications plan is to ensure that senior management supports the development of the plan. Without such support, people who should be involved in the planning process will not view it as a priority, and any plan that is developed will not likely be used when a crisis occurs.

A second step is to maintain the involvement of key personnel on the planning committee. The same staff members who were critical in the crisis forecasting process will likely have important insights in planning for crisis communications. Clearly, public relations staff members are integral to this process, but they are not alone.

One of the most important contributors to the plan is the sport organization's legal counsel.

Many crises lead to legal action against the sport organization. Therefore, the sport organization's attorneys need to offer insight about which actions may be legally defensible and which actions may not be. Unfortunately, some attorneys may advise sport organizations to say and do little when crises occur. After all, a statement never made cannot be held against the organization. Such advice is shortsighted, however, and fails to recognize the importance of the organization's reputation among key publics besides potential litigants.

A third critical step in preparing a crisis communications plan is to ensure that all employees recognize the existence of the plan and the importance of using it when a crisis occurs. Although not all employees need to have a copy of the complete plan, all members of the organization must understand that they have at least two important responsibilities. First, they must contact an appropriate crisis team member if they recognize a crisis developing. This means that all staff members should keep contact information for the crisis communications team at hand at all times (e.g., contacts directory on mobile devices). Second, they must refer crisis-related inquires to the appropriate crisis communications official. This means that the crisis communications plan must specify the appropriate people to contact immediately after the onset of the crisis.

Hessert (1998b) recognized that commitment from coaches may be particularly important in crisis communications plans. Coaches who wish to define their own course of action in a crisis may make statements or take actions that are damaging in the court of public opinion and maybe even in a court of law. A coach who takes a position contrary to that of the coach's organization may be setting the stage for an inevitable parting of ways.

A fourth step is to test the plan. These tests can range from complete mock drills to more limited forms such as callback exercises, in which members of the crisis communications team go through the sequence of mandated contacts to see how quickly important connections may be made.

The fifth and final step may seem obvious: Sport managers must remain committed to their plan and use it when a crisis occurs. The authors have spoken with a handful of public relations professionals who privately express frustration regarding this step. A crisis communications plan is sometimes developed but then left on the shelf because senior managers think that they can better manage the crisis by "winging it." If senior managers do not intend to use a plan, there is no reason to develop one.

Crisis communications plans can vary in structure. Because they are designed to prescribe general communication procedures at the onset of a crisis, however, most contain a number of common elements, as discussed in the following sections. The appendix also provides a sample crisis communications plan.

Crisis Scenario Tracks

Although some crisis communications plans are generic enough that they do not specify crisis scenarios, others are organized around particular crisis types. The rationale for such a recommendation is that responses vary based on the nature of the crisis. For example, the crisis communications plan for one National Collegiate Athletic Association (NCAA) Football Bowl Subdivision program specifies responses to the following crises:

- Death or catastrophic injury to a student–athlete
- Major brawl or riot
- Violence directed at an official
- Incidents involving law enforcement outside of competition
- Incidents involving NCAA rules violations
- Death of a staff member
- Death or catastrophic injury of a spectator
- Terrorist activity
- Transportation accidents

The makeup of the crisis management team and the types of initial responses vary within the plan based on the specific scenario.

Plan Initiation

When a crisis occurs, someone with the sport organization, usually the senior manager, is responsible for initiating the plan and activating the management team. Complete contact information (e.g., office, home, and cell phone numbers) for each member of the crisis team should be included in the plan. Further, team members should have easy access to others' contact information, whether they have the full plan in hand or not. Given the importance of this information in activating the crisis team, someone—likely the sport organization's top public relations person—should be charged with ensuring that all contact information remains current.

Knowing when and when not to declare a crisis and activate crisis communications procedures is critical. Manoli (2016) found that the majority of the

communications professionals in the English Premier League tended to wait until a potential crisis gained media momentum. Their rationale was that bad news is sometimes lost quickly in the media news cycle. By waiting, they could see whether the story would dissipate without an organizational response.

Although such an approach may sometimes work, there are numerous examples of sport organizations waiting too long to respond and suffering the consequences as a result. Again, Michigan State and USA Gymnastics (Kwiatkowski, Alesia, & Evans, 2018; Moffat, 2018) are examples. Regarding Michigan State's response, one crisis communications consultant observed, "It's understandable the university wishes this would all go away, but the fact is the snowball turns into an avalanche when you've got questions that aren't being answered" (Jeff Caponigro, quoted in Mack, 2018).

Research focusing on senior sports communicators in Northern Ireland indicated such professionals carefully monitor for tipping points at which issues escalate to full crises (Kitchin & Purcell, 2017). Interview respondents indicated that both the failure to recognize the advent of a crisis and the premature declaration of a crisis can be damaging to the organization.

Response Teams

Defining response teams is one of the most important elements of a crisis communications plan. Although some managers, such as those from public relations, legal, finance, and human resources, will be involved in responding to most crises, other team members may vary depending on the situation.

Delineating the general responsibilities of each team member on the crisis team may also be advisable. Table 8.2 displays the responsibilities of select members of the crisis management team for a college athletics department.

Internal Communications

In the heat of a crisis episode, it is easy to overlook one of the sport organization's most important publics: its own employees. Internal communications during a crisis event involves at least two distinct tasks. The first is informing important internal publics of what has happened and what they should be doing because of the crisis. Many organizations employ a **call tree**, in which the responsibilities for notifying employees of the situation are delegated to multiple parties, each of whom has specific contacts to make. Figure 8.2 displays the call tree used

Table 8.2 Responsibilities of Select Members of a Crisis Management Team

Title	Description
Director of Athletics	The Director of Athletics will lead the Emergency and Crisis Response Team and act as the final decision maker in any emergency situation. The Director of Athletics will be responsible for contacting the University President, General Counsel, Vice President for Student Life, the Vice President for University Advancement, and the Vice President for Administration and Finance. The Athletic Director will also be the designated spokesperson for the athletic department. All Athletics staff, as directed by the Director of Athletics, will work cooperatively with the appropriate law enforcement and medical officials as the situation warrants. The Director of Athletics will be responsible for coordinating with the Universities Emergency and Crisis Response Plan and will oversee communication with student–athletes, their families, the American Athletic Conference, the NCAA, the media, and the general public.
Senior Associate Athletic Director/ Senior Woman Administrator	The first priority of the Senior Associate Athletic Director/Senior Woman Administrator in the event of an emergency is to inform and brief the Interim Director of Athletics on the situation. Once the situation is defined the Senior Associate Athletic Director/ Senior Woman Administrator will be responsible for coordinating all communication with student–athletes, their families, and the University if the emergency directly or indirectly affects student–athletes. In the event the Director of Athletics is not available, the Senior Associate Athletic Director/ Senior Woman Administrator will assume leadership of the Emergency Response Team.
Associate Athletic Director-Strategic Communications	The Associate Athletic Director-Strategic Communications will be the designated media contact for Wichita State Athletics regarding any emergency situation. This individual will coordinate the release of information to the public with the Director of Athletics and the Emergency and Crisis Response Team. He or she will also be responsible for writing any press releases concerning the emergency situation. This individual will also be responsible for the handling of all media requests, from interview requests to requests for information.
Associate Athletic Director-Facilities and Operations Director	The Associate Athletic Director-Facilities and Operations will be responsible for the coordination of law enforcement and Emergency Medical Service needs, if any, at an event. This individual will be responsible for overseeing and providing for the safety of all spectators. This includes, but is not limited to, providing direction and assistance for spectators in the event of weather emergencies. If an emergency involves one of the facilities, this position will work with the University Physical Plant to determine the safety of the facility before any resumption in play. In the event of extensive damage, this individual will oversee any necessary repairs. This individual will also be responsible for the assembly of the Emergency Response and Crisis team as directed by the Director of Athletics. The Emergency Response Team will always meet in the conference room in the Athletic Director's Suite in Charles Koch Arena. Should an incident prevent that location from being available, the Team will meet in the Coastal Room at Eck Stadium.

Adapted by permission from ICAA Wichita State University.

Communicating in Times of Crisis

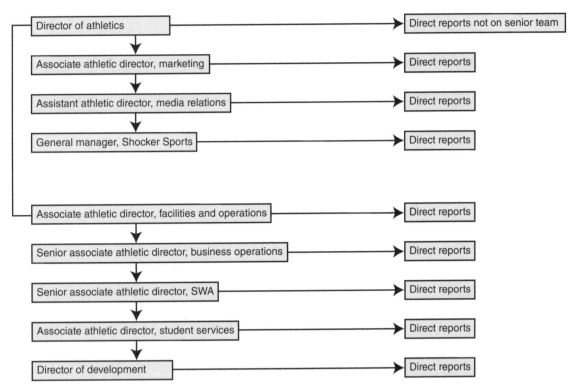

Figure 8.2 If conditions warrant it, a calling tree may be activated. The decision to activate the calling tree will be made by the Director of Athletics. Below is the progression of the tree, each department head or supervisor will be responsible for contacting their direct reports. If you are unable to contact your person on the flow chart, skip to the next person and then contact the immediate supervisor of the person you could not reach so they can make contact with direct reports.

Reprinted by permission from ICAA Wichita State University.

by the crisis management team for Wichita State University athletics (WSU ICAA, 2019).

The second task involves internal communications designed to secure additional information relevant to managing the crisis. Such information may include contact information in personnel records, documentation of existing organizational policies, and records regarding how past incidents were been handled.

External Communications

Crisis communications plans should be structured to enable external communication with a range of publics (e.g., family members, the media, fans). Figure 8.3 illustrates this concept. As indicated, the sport organization may use diverse forms of communication—direct communication, news releases and other media tactics, social media, and the organizational website and other forms of organizational communication. The media will also communicate with those other external publics, including some who will not receive information from any other source. To the degree that sport managers can successfully manage

communications with media representatives, they can also successfully share critical information with those other publics.

The dissemination of information via the various communication platforms will be discussed in greater detail later in the chapter. For now, one additional comment regarding the flow of information seems important. In figure 8.3, the flow of communication with publics such as affected family members, governing bodies, and the media is indicated by arrows in each direction. This indicates that two-way communication with those groups, to the extent possible, should be normative in crisis responses. Dialogue with audience members on social media is also two-way but tends to be limited in crisis situations. Communication via the organizational website is more one-way in nature.

Crisis communications experts recommend that organizations plan to make themselves the best source of information regarding the crisis for the media (Carter & Rovell, 2003; Broom, 2013; Poole, 1999). If the sport organization can successfully position itself in this manner, it may be able to reduce

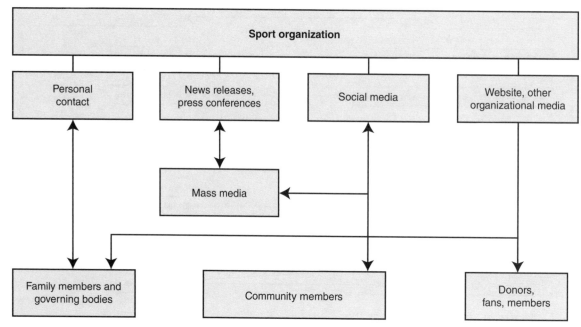

Figure 8.3 Flow of information to external publics.

the degree to which members of the media look to other sources, some of them possibly adversarial, for information. If a sport organization learns about a negative story brewing in the media, it may be in the organization's best interest to announce the negative news itself. As stated by communications consultant Kathleen Hessert (2006, p. 40), "Go for the quick hemorrhage, not the slow bleed." Manoli's (2016) research on how communicators working in the English Premier League managed crisis communications found that at least some practitioners supported such an approach. These professionals contended that when a crisis was likely to generate significant media attention, rapid communications from the organization could portray the club in a positive light and reduce media and public speculation.

In an insightful article on the subject of "stealing thunder," Moffat (2018) cites cyclist Lance Armstrong, USA Gymnastics, and the NFL as examples of sport entities failing to respond in an appropriate and timely fashion. The USA Gymnastics crisis was described earlier in this chapter; the controversy about Lance Armstrong is described later in the chapter. And while the NFL has endured multiple crises in recent years, Moffat's article specifically referenced the league's mishandling of discipline and public communication when one of its players, Ray Rice, assaulted his fiancée. Moffat argued that

> failing to self-disclose a crisis which is
> subsequently revealed by third parties

can be devastating. High levels of negative media coverage and widespread public indignation on social media will severely damage their reputation leading to loss of trust and confidence from sports fans and the general public, reduction in investment by sponsors, lawsuits and criminal proceedings, resignation of C-suite executives and the instigation of government inquiries and reports.

Crisis plans should delineate procedures for communicating with the media as quickly as possible. Two key considerations are the preparation of initial statements for the media and the identification of the organization's spokesperson.

Initial Statements

One tactic commonly employed is to prepare generic templates that can be customized for the circumstances of the crisis and quickly released to the media. Typically, such statements acknowledge the crisis and indicate that the organization is gathering more information. In some instances, these statements may specify there is no additional comment at the moment. In others, the organization states that it will commit to sharing additional information when it is available.

When appropriate, the initial statement will also express sympathy for those involved. For example, when Kendrick Norton, a player on the NFL's Miami

The sexual abuse scandal that engulfed USA Gymnastics included allegations by hundreds of gymnasts.
Sarah Silbiger/CQ Roll Call

Dolphins, was involved in a car accident that resulted in the amputation of one of his arms, the team issued the following statement via Twitter: "We were made aware this morning of a serious car accident involving Kendrick Norton. Our thoughts and prayers are with Kendrick and his family during this time" (Miami Dolphins, 2019).

Spokesperson Identification

One of the most important elements of the crisis communications plan is the identification of the sport organization's primary spokesperson during the crisis. Public relations professionals, although they are involved in preparing spokespersons for their tasks, often do not play the spokesperson role themselves. Instead, spokespersons are frequently the most prominent individuals within the organization.

The designated spokesperson may vary depending on the crisis scenario. The most serious crises demand a senior-level spokesperson such as a CEO, general manager, or director of athletics. Less serious episodes such as a player running afoul of the law may be effectively addressed by a head coach. Whatever the situation, the spokesperson must possess excellent public speaking and media relations skills. A prudent measure is to identify backup spokespersons in the event that the primary spokesperson is unavailable because of the crisis. The role descriptions listed in table 8.2 specify that if the director of athletics is not available to serve as spokesperson, the senior associate athletic director will assume that responsibility.

Managing a Crisis

When a crisis occurs, a well-prepared sport organization implements its crisis communications plan according to the specified procedures. As a result, the crisis communications team is activated, preliminary information regarding the situation is shared internally, and an initial statement is made available to members of the media or on social media. These actions position the crisis team to respond in a timely and appropriate fashion, but they represent only the initial steps in successfully managing the situation. When the crisis team gathers, it assembles as much information as possible, begins to formulate a strategy that will protect the organization's brand, and delineates subsequent communication tactics. The nature of the crisis determines not only the strategies and tactics employed in managing the episode but also the length and frequency of the crisis team meetings. Some crises, such as the trading of a star player, are fairly short-lived; others, such as a protracted labor dispute, are more enduring. Either way, the crisis communications team must determine when the crisis has ended, and sometimes the team must publicly state that the crisis is over.

Selecting a Strategy

Perhaps the single most important decision that the crisis communications team will make is what the organization's posture toward the crisis will be. Will the organization accept responsibility for the crisis? Will the organization counterattack those making accusations? Will it take steps to improve the situation? What else might be involved in the organization's response?

Coombs (2019) noted that the selection of an appropriate **crisis response strategy** is based on an accurate appraisal of two issues, the second of which has two parts. First, the type of crisis fundamentally affects how key publics are likely to perceive the organization. When a crisis is caused by something beyond the control of the organization, such as when a tornado struck the Georgia Dome in 2008 during the Southeastern Conference basketball tournament, key publics generally do not hold the organization responsible. When a crisis results from an accident, like the one that occurred in 2019 at a Pennsylvania speedway when an on-track crash sent a car over the fence killing a spectator, key publics tend to hold the organization only minimally responsible. But when human misdeeds or negligence result in a crisis, key publics hold the sport organization highly responsible. Major League Baseball came under fire in 2019 when a number of fans—including a two-year-old girl in Houston—were injured by foul balls. The league was criticized for failing to mandate expanded protective netting to keep fans safer. A second consideration in selecting the appropriate crisis strategy is evaluating the organizational context in which the crisis is occurring. There are two dimensions to this step. The first focuses on the sport organization's crisis history. Organizations that frequently suffer crises, such as college athletics programs that have repeatedly incurred major NCAA sanctions, face greater challenges in dealing with crises than those with cleaner records. The second contextual consideration is the reputation of the sport organization. Key publics tend to assign lower thresholds of responsibility to organizations with poor reputations.

Having assessed the situation and the organization's standing in regard to the crisis, the crisis communications team is well positioned to select a response that will either protect the organization's reputation or begin to repair it. A number of scholars have identified and described image repair strategies (see, e.g., Allen & Caillouet, 1994; Benoit 1995). Coombs (2019) compiled a number of these strategies, condensed them, and then categorized them into four general postures.

Denial Posture

Denial strategies are recommended when the organization is facing false rumors or unwarranted challenges (Coombs, 2019). Three specific strategies fall within this general posture. The first, attacking the accuser, involves challenging those making claims against the organization. This strategy occasionally involves the threat of a lawsuit against the accuser. A second strategy is straightforward denial, in which the organization denies that a crisis exists and offers explanations about why there is no crisis. A third strategy is scapegoating. When scapegoating, the organization blames people or groups outside the organization for the crisis.

Diminishment Posture

Diminishment strategies are recommended when a crisis is an accident or is caused by something beyond the control of the organization (e.g., workplace violence), especially when an organization has an unfavorable crisis history or poor reputation (Coombs, 2019). Two specific strategies fall under this category. The excusing strategy is employed when the organization wants to emphasize that it had minimal, if any, responsibility for the crisis. The justification strategy attempts to minimize the amount of perceived damage resulting from the crisis. Justification can be accomplished when the crisis produces minimal injuries or damage, or when victims bear significant responsibility for their injuries because of their own actions.

Rebuilding Posture

Rebuilding strategies are recommended whenever a preventable crisis occurs or when an organization with a weak crisis history and a poor reputation suffers an accident (Coombs, 2019). The two rebuilding strategies are apology and compensation. Apology includes both accepting full responsibility for the crisis and apologizing to victims. A study of sports fans' attitudes regarding professional athlete scandals found that athletes' sincere apologies were influential in regaining fan loyalty (Hwang, 2017). Compensation involves offering money or other gifts to those harmed in an effort to offset their suffering.

Bolstering Posture

Bolstering strategies are recommended as complements to the other postures (Coombs, 2019). They are not designed to stand alone. Coombs (2019) identified three bolstering strategies. The first is reminding, in which the organization reminds key publics of the many positive things that it has done in the past. The second is ingratiation, in which the organization heaps praise on its stakeholders for their support. The third is victimage, in which the organization emphasizes how it too has suffered because of the crisis.

Two other crisis response strategies not specifically included in Coombs' (2019) typology have emerged in sport-specific case studies. In their analysis of a salary cap scandal in Australasian men's rugby, Bruce and Tini (2008) observed a strategy that they described as diversion, in which the sport organization redirects attention away from itself to players and fans who suffer because of the crisis. The rugby club that they studied successfully garnered public sympathy by emphasizing how their own players had been harmed by the misdeeds of management. Diversion may sometimes be a successful strategy for sport organizations because of the emotional attachment between players and fans, but it should be employed only when the players or fans bear no responsibility for the consequences that they suffer (Bruce & Tini, 2008).

Another image repair strategy characterized as rallying emerged in Frederick and Pegoraro's (2018) study of how the University of Louisville responded to a college men's basketball scandal in 2017. The crisis resulted from a Federal Bureau of Investigation report about bribes paid to recruits or their representatives, and the resultant university response included the firing of prominent coach Rick Pitino. In crisis-related postings on its Facebook page, the university employed a number of strategies, including bolstering. However, the university also employed rallying, described as "university officials' calling on the community to unify and support the university and the athletics department in an effort to effectively 'move beyond' the scandal" (Frederick & Pegoraro, 2018, p. 424).

Communicating Effectively

As crisis management teams select protection and repair strategies, they also have to consider how to communicate the organization's position and share additional information with relevant publics. Accordingly, they must determine key messages and employ appropriate channels of communication to share those messages. Dietrich's (2014) PESO model, introduced in chapter 1, is again relevant here. While all four elements of the model may be employed in crisis communications, two in particular—shared (i.e., social) media and earned media (i.e., mass media coverage) warrant additional explanation in the sections that follow.

Determining Key Messages

One of the key responsibilities of public relations professionals serving on crisis management teams is to facilitate the crafting of key messages to be emphasized in communications. Key messages are often brief statements that are easily replayed in sound bites and may appear as succinct quotes in text. Of course, these messages are delivered to multiple publics, not just the media, and the organization must be consistent in emphasizing its selected key messages. Common key messages include expressions of concern for those negatively affected by the crisis and statements of commitment to improving the situation, even if the sport organization does not accept responsibility for the crisis.

Choosing Communication Channels

Sport managers frequently use multiple channels during crisis episodes, but the channels should be carefully selected. Some channels are more influential than others. Face-to-face interaction is arguably still the most persuasive, so personal contact with those most affected is highly recommended. In addition, having the designated spokesperson personally interact with members of the media through news conferences and interviews is highly advisable. Live interviews may be particularly effective ways to share key messages, because they are not subject to editing (Q&A: The interview, 2001).

The Internet can also play a key role. Information posted on a sport organization's website is not subject to filtering through the mass media, so sport organizations should use their websites to distribute crisis-related information. Usually, this information will be shared on the sport organization's regular website, but on some occasions special sites may be set up to deal with the crisis. The sidebar Be Your Own Media, on the NFL's "Play Smart. Play Safe" campaign, describes one such example. Beyond organizational websites, sport organizations may also use e-mail distribution lists and other forms of organizational communication to share information with members of key publics.

Dealing With Media

Despite the power of social media, especially in crisis episodes, working with representatives of mass media outlets continues to be highly important in the midst of crises. Sports communications professionals in Northern Ireland indicated that traditional media outlets were more important than

Be Your Own Media

As part of its response to the sustained crisis over player safety, the NFL in 2016 launched a "Play Smart. Play Safe" initiative with a dedicated website. The site serves as a hub for league communications around the issue, provides information that supports health and safety at other levels of football, and offers a league pledge to financially support independent research on player safety. The site also contains information ranging from a statement by Commissioner Roger Goodell to annual reports to information regarding relevant research and technological advances. Do you think the site is a persuasive platform for sharing the league's commitment to player health? Why or why not?

social media when addressing crises (Kitchin & Purcell, 2017). Crises are by definition newsworthy, and members of the media will attempt to generate as much information as possible about such stories. Accordingly, sport public relations professionals must take pains to establish themselves and their organizations as credible sources of information.

Frequent updates to the media are necessary to maintain the organization's position as the leading source of information. In some cases, the organization may need to provide an information center from which media representatives may work. Media centers are best set up in sites that are located some distance from the actual scene of the crisis (Davis & Gilman, 2002) and that may facilitate the delivery of media services such as news conferences, interviews, media advisories, and news releases.

Of course, several other principles should guide effective communication with members of the

Social Media Crisis Response

As with almost any aspect of public relations, a key role in crisis communications is played by social media. Senior sports communicators in Northern Ireland indicated support for incorporating social media as part of their crisis responses (Kitchin & Purcell, 2017). Similarly, communications professionals in the English Premier League stated that they used social media as part of their crisis responses (Manoli, 2016).

Research focusing on social media communication relating to the Lance Armstrong crisis underscored the value of the platform in a couple of respects (Coombs & Holladay, 2014). As readers may recall, Armstrong, a seven-time Tour de France champion, cancer survivor, and inspirational figure, became one of the most prominent athletes ever to fall as a result of a doping scandal. The researchers analyzed social communications posted on the blog of Livestrong (Armstrong's foundation) and an online news site, and ascertained that the messages served to effectively demonstrate public responses to the crisis. However, in order to truly get a sense of public reactions, monitoring of both organizational and nonaffiliated channels was critical, because the responses on the organizational platforms tended to be more positive. The researchers also found that people using social media can themselves serve as crisis communicators, amplifying and supporting the organization's key messages.

Brown and Billings (2013) chronicled the same phenomenon in their study of University of Miami fans who posted to Twitter about a crisis involving that school's athletics program. However, subsequent research focusing on crisis-related social media communications by fans revealed a significant danger associated with such engagement (Brown, Brown, & Billings, 2015). This study focused on fans of Pennsylvania State University's football program as they reacted to the sex abuse scandal in 2011 and 2012 that ultimately resulted in the conviction of a former assistant football coach, Jerry Sandusky, for sexual assault. As the university responded to criticism regarding what key personnel may have known and how they responded, both the university's president and its legendary football coach, Joe Paterno, were fired. "[Paterno's] firing altered not only the storyline for these fans but it altered their allegiance. Paterno's firing seemingly forced fans to choose a side between Paterno and Penn State, with most siding with their longtime coach" (Brown, Brown, & Billings, 2015). The study underscored that fans will likely engage on social media during a crisis but will not always be supportive of the organization and its crisis strategies.

When Penn State University fired football coach Joe Paterno, a riot ensued on campus.

Jeff Swensen/Getty Images

media during a crisis. The following list contains 10 recommendations that can guide sport public relations professionals as they interact with the media and as they prepare other individuals to serve as spokespersons:

1. Organizational spokespersons must be truthful and prompt in their responses. Attempts to mislead or stonewall members of the media are almost always discovered, and the resultant damage is even greater than what would have occurred had the truth been told in the beginning.

2. Public relations officials should anticipate difficult questions that the organizational spokesperson may face when talking with the media. This approach allows the public relations staff to assist the spokesperson in formulating responses that include key messages.

3. Organizational spokespersons should avoid the phrase "no comment." Even if they are not willing to answer a question, they must find more polite and informative responses.

4. Organizational spokespersons should not speculate when talking with the media. Speculation only fuels additional what-if questions and may limit response options at a later date.

5. Organizational spokespersons should avoid making statements off the record.

6. Organizational spokespersons should not attempt to promote their organization's products or services during a crisis. By attempting to use the crisis as a sales platform, they will likely be perceived as mercenary and unethical.

7. Sport public relations professionals should not ask media members to withhold damaging information. They can reasonably ask that the organization's side of the story be included in the news coverage.

8. Both the public relations staff and the organizational spokesperson should remain calm and professional, even in emotionally charged settings. Maintaining composure can be extremely challenging given the stress caused by crisis situations.

9. The public relations staff should anticipate that at least some of the media members assigned to cover a crisis will be different from those who may otherwise cover the sport organization (Helitzer, 2000). Some media organizations may replace their regular beat writers with other reporters who are perceived as more accustomed to dealing with hard news coverage. Additionally, a crisis will likely attract attention from media outlets that do not normally cover the sport organization.

10. Public relations officials should track media coverage during a crisis. As with social media, such monitoring can gauge how their organization is faring in the court of public opinion and whether they are being effective in disseminating key messages.

One other aspect of media relations in the midst of crises bears mentioning. The informal relationships sport public relations professionals have with members of the media can be highly advantageous in crisis situations (Manoli, 2016). On some occasions, media members may alert sports communicators about a forthcoming story and, in doing so, give the organization a head start in planning a response. Communications professionals working in the English Premier League reported that in some cases, they have negotiated story exchanges with media members, in which the organization offers attractive news content to media members in exchange for their agreement to not report on the crisis (Manoli, 2016). As indicated by the list of recommendations just set out, such exchanges may not fall within normative public relations practices, but practitioners do indicate some degree of success with the tactic.

Declaring the End of a Crisis

Sometimes, determining when a crisis is over is easy. For example, the NCAA issues a final report regarding its investigation. Charges are dropped. A problem coach is terminated.

In other situations, assessing when a crisis ends is more difficult. If people are killed in an accident, when does the crisis end? When does a sport organization put to rest a reputation-related crisis? The effects of such episodes can linger for years.

Publicly declaring that a crisis has ended may bring closure to the event. Practically speaking, such a public declaration may also signal to the media that the special services the sport organization has provided during the course of the crisis are coming to an end.

The difficulty with such pronouncements is that they must be based on an accurate assessment of the crisis event and its news life cycle. Just as the sport organization cannot control whether a crisis unfolds, it cannot mandate its ending. Attempts to declare an end to a crisis prematurely usually backfire and reignite simmering controversy. Athletes, coaches, and organizations who commit misdeeds, offer nonapologetic apologies, and then declare that the problem is all behind them fail to recognize that issues are not fully set aside until members of key publics are willing to consider that the issues are settled. By attempting to exert a level of control organizations do not possess, they exacerbate an already negative situation, usually resulting in additional publicity and public criticism.

Assessing a Crisis Response

Regardless of whether a crisis is short-term or sustained, when the management team decides to shift from crisis mode back to normal operations, the team must assess the effectiveness of its crisis communications plan. The best way to do this is by convening the same group of managers to review available data, such as media coverage of the event, consumer comments, sales records, and other indicators of the performance of the plan. These individuals should also debrief managers who served on the crisis communications committee but who were not included in formulating crisis communications plans to get their insights into the effectiveness of the plan.

Key questions that the crisis communications team should address include, but are not limited to, the following:

- Was the plan activated in a timely and efficient manner?
- Were initial communication procedures executed as assigned?
- Were initial communication procedures adequate given the situation?
- How quickly was the crisis communications team able to assess the situation and select a crisis response strategy?
- In retrospect, was the crisis response strategy appropriate?
- Were all important publics identified and served effectively?
- How effective were the key messages specified by the crisis communications team?
- How effective were the channels of communication used to carry those key messages?
- How effective was the organization's spokesperson in dealing with those key publics, particularly the media?
- How well did the public relations staff prepare the organization's spokesperson for interaction with members of the media or other key publics?
- Was the organization able to position itself as the best source of information regarding the crisis?
- How effective was the organization in using social media?

- How did social media audiences respond to organizational communication?
- Were all important services needed by members of the media or other key publics provided?
- How well did the plan perform in protecting the organization's brand and reputation?
- Most important, how can the plan be improved before the next crisis that the organization may face?

By addressing such questions, the crisis management team may better position their organization to navigate future crises successfully.

Crisis Response Case Studies

Although a sport organization will rarely endure a crisis unscathed, analyses of several high-profile crisis cases in sport indicate that some effectively managed the crises that they faced and, as a result, recovered rather quickly. One example focuses on tennis star Maria Sharapova, the other on the NFL.

Just as successful responses may serve as educational tools regarding how to communicate effectively during a crisis, case studies of unsuccessful responses also yield insights—especially about mistakes to avoid. The examples of how Michigan State University and USA Gymnastics mismanaged crises related to the Nassar crimes have already been referenced. Two additional examples are NCAA Division I institution Duke University and the Fédération Internationale de Football Association (FIFA).

Consider these questions as you read the case studies:

1. How do you think the crisis appraisal criteria (Coombs, 2019) described earlier in the chapter informed the crisis response?
2. Why do you think so many other sports figures and organizations are hesitant to adopt the "stealing thunder" approach?
3. How might reputations have been affected if different crisis response strategies had been selected?
4. How would you assess these brands today?

Maria Sharapova: Doping

Women's tennis star Maria Sharapova faced perhaps the most significant crisis of her career in 2016 when she failed a drug test and received a two-year suspension (later reduced to 15 months) by the International Tennis Federation. Sharapova was the winner of five Grand Slam events, and she had leveraged her tennis success through endorsement deals and other business ventures to become the world's top-earning female athlete for years. At the 2016 Australian Open, she tested positive for meldonium, a drug that had been added to the banned list months earlier.

Sharapova preemptively announced the failed drug test at a March 2016 news conference that was promoted via her social media and livestreamed over her website. At that news conference, she admitted her guilt but explained the context of the failed test, indicating that the substance was found in a prescription drug she had been taking for over a decade. Sharapova indicated difficulty in accessing the most current list of banned substances and stated the drug was not taken for performance enhancement. She subsequently posted additional explanation on her Facebook page to counter what she said was some incorrect media coverage of the story's details.

Sharapova utilized a "stealing thunder" approach to the crisis (Bell & Hartman, 2018). By personally breaking the news, taking ownership of the situation, and using her own social and digital platforms to elevate her story, she was able to communicate directly with her fan base and influence related media coverage. As stated by Bell and Hartman (2018, p. 381), "Media framing of Sharapova's approach ranged from mild to glowing as an exemplar that runs counter to any athlete strategy previously employed regarding drug use or suspensions." One public relations executive observed that Sharapova's response was refreshingly innovative: "Her tack was one of honesty, directness, and accountability. She did not use spokespeople or press releases or even Oprah to come clean. In doing so, she has saved herself countless hours of brand-damaging news reports" (Piedra, 2016).

As of 2019, Sharapova had not returned to tennis's elite, but her brand weathered the crisis in good fashion. Sharapova retained most of her sponsors and maintained her ranking among the top 10 highest-earning female athletes (Badenhausen, 2019). The earnings total is likely an indicator that Sharapova's marketability is not necessarily contingent on her tennis performance. However, her sustained popularity is likely also in part the result of a successful crisis response.

National Football League: Traumatic Brain Injury Link

As noted in the chapter's introduction, the NFL has dealt with a sustained crisis about the long-term health effects of the game on players, particularly brain trauma. Public discussion of the topic dates back more than 60 years (Paolini, 2019). The issue gained prominence in 2005 when an article in a medical journal reported that a prominent former player, who had died at age 50, suffered from chronic traumatic encephalopathy (CTE) as a result of multiple concussions. Subsequent studies supported the finding, with one influential researcher describing evidence of the linkage between repeated brain trauma and CTE as "overwhelming" (Hanna & Kain, 2010). Another article published in *JAMA: The Journal of the American Medical Association* reported that the brain tissue of 110 of 111 deceased former NFL players was diagnosed as having CTE (Mez et al., 2017). The authors explicitly stated the risk of CTE associated with playing American football.

The CTE crisis presents a threat to the NFL on multiple fronts. The league has already faced litigation with the resultant settlement costing hundreds of millions dollars. Broader public relations concerns include the impact on the league's brand and how the crisis might affect fan support and related revenue (e.g., value of broadcast rights, ticket sales). Another consideration is the effect on youth football participation rates and how a reduction could affect the talent pipeline and future fandom levels.

As the title of a prominent book (Fainaru-Wade & Fainaru, 2013) and related PBS *Frontline* documentary indicated, the NFL initially was a "League of Denial." It rejected the notion of a CTE linkage and established its own committee to publish research countering the argument. However, in the face of mounting information and public criticism, the league changed its position in 2016, acknowledging the connection between playing football and CTE. The NFL settled a class-action lawsuit with thousands of former players in 2015, although legal wrangling about terms of eligibility followed. The league also adopted rule changes designed to make the game safer. The aforementioned "Play Smart, Play Safe" initiative is an example of this shift in strategy. Another example was the league's measured response to the *JAMA* report. Rather than attack the study, which admittedly relied on a convenience sample of donated organs, the league affirmed the work being done to study CTE while cautioning about the many remaining unanswered questions (Coombs, 2017).

Crisis communications scholar Timothy Coombs (2017) observed, "The NFL may have found its method of dealing with the chronic issues of CTE—acknowledge the problem and consider CTE part of the price for American football." And legal scholar Mikayla Paolini (2019) likened the league's revised position as taken from the "Big Tobacco Playbook." While the issue will likely continue to be the basis for challenges to the league, the NFL continues to be the most popular sport in the United States, particularly as evidenced by television ratings.

Duke University: Rape Accusations

Duke University suffered one of the most prominent crises in the history of college athletics when three members of its men's lacrosse team were accused of rape and other crimes in 2006. The charge was made by an exotic dancer hired by members of the team to perform at an off-campus party. In the course of a controversial investigation, the district attorney indicated that as many as 46 members of the team were under suspicion of having violated the law (Associated Press, 2007).

Twelve days after the party, Duke officials forfeited two upcoming men's lacrosse games in response to team members' hiring exotic dancers and engaging in underage drinking at the party. Three days later, university officials suspended the program while awaiting "clearer resolution of the legal situation" (Associated Press, 2007). Less than 10 days later, Duke's men's lacrosse coach resigned, and the school president canceled the remainder of the team's season. The move followed the revelation of a vulgar e-mail from a lacrosse player about killing strippers. Two months after suspending the program, the university president reinstated the program with stricter monitoring (Associated Press, 2007). Months later, charges against all three players were dropped, and ultimately the district attorney resigned after a state bar panel concluded that he acted improperly during the course of the investigation (Wilson & Holusha, 2007).

Analysis of how Duke administrators managed the lacrosse incident revealed four key mistakes (Yaeger & Henry, 2009). First, Duke erred in that it did not use an established internal communications plan, as evidenced by the fact that the school president learned of the incident by reading the school newspaper (ABC News, 2007; Yaeger & Henry, 2009; Yaeger & Pressler, 2007). Second, Duke administrators failed to maintain consistent communication with the media throughout the crisis, thereby increasing the need for reporters to find other sources for their stories. Third, Duke administrators unsuccessfully attempted to reduce the news value of the story when they canceled the season. Fourth and most important, Duke administrators failed to wait on all relevant facts before acting. Yaeger and Henry (2009) likened the approach to **one-move chess**—that is, "making decisions with no respect for strategy."

FIFA: Corruption Charges

The international governing body for soccer (football), FIFA had long experienced reputational problems even before a corruption scandal in 2015 (Barrett, 2015). However, the 2015 crisis seriously escalated FIFA's credibility issues. The organization was already taking international criticism over human rights violations suffered by workers constructing facilities in Qatar where the 2022 World Cup is to be played. Then on May 27, 2015, the U.S. attorney general announced the indictments of nine FIFA officials on corruption charges. Swiss officials made related arrests in the case and announced their own investigation into FIFA corruption. A FIFA spokesperson denied the organization was in crisis, indicated the arrests were actually a positive development, and characterized the organization as "the damaged party" (Walter De Gregorio, quoted in Suleman, 2015).

Sepp Blatter, FIFA's president, was not among those arrested, but he was widely criticized as the leader of a corrupt organization. However, Blatter did not admit to a major problem, saying on May 28 that the scandal was limited to "the actions of a few" (quoted in Washkuch, 2015). Then remarkably, Blatter was elected to a fifth term as FIFA president on May 29. Days later, on June 2, he resigned, citing lack of support throughout FIFA's constituencies.

FIFA's employment of denial and victimage strategies proved ineffective, and Blatter's refusal to accept responsibility and recognize the need for organizational change further exacerbated the growing crisis. Again, crisis communications scholar Coombs (2015) offers insightful commentary:

> In a scandal, managers are recommended to take corrective action and apologize for the inappropriate actions in an effort to repair the damage inflicted by the crisis. When a scandal indicates the problem is a part of the organizational structure, the corrective action includes removing top management and creating new policies and procedures designed to prevent a repeat of the problem—the system needs change.

FIFA enacted reforms in 2016, but the investigations, bans, and arrests of FIFA officials and their business associates have continued. Much scrutinized World Cup site selections did not change, with the 2018 event being played in Russia and the 2022 event still scheduled for Qatar, as originally awarded. FIFA retained its major sponsors, so absent substantive consequences from its most critical stakeholders, the organization has avoided having to make more dramatic changes. Little wonder that a 2017 global survey of soccer fans indicated more than half had no confidence in FIFA, and only a third thought the organization was actively working against corruption (Transparency International, 2017). As Steve Barrett, editorial director for *PR Week*, stated, "From a business and communications point of view, [the FIFA crisis is] a stark reminder that the glamour and excitement of major sports and entertainment events can never be allowed to cloud the authenticity, ethics, and transparency that should always underpin brand and corporate reputation" (2015).

SUMMARY

Crises are events or controversies that may damage a sport organization's financial standing and credibility. Despite the widespread occurrence of crises within sport, many sport organizations are unprepared for them. Crisis communications plans specify the public relations responsibilities of various staff members during a crisis, and most focus on how information is shared both internally and externally. Effective crisis communications plans may address crises that are deemed likely to occur or are of significant potential impact.

Such plans include details about how the plans are to be activated, who should be involved in the crisis management process, who should be contacted regarding the crisis, and what should be said, at least initially. Perhaps the most important decision that a crisis response team will make is which strategy to employ in responding to the crisis. Such decisions are usually based on the type of crisis and the organization's history and reputation. By adhering to a number of crisis communications principles, sport public relations professionals and organizational spokespersons can effectively address the two most difficult aspects of a crisis: communicating with the media and engaging the broader public on social media. After a crisis ends, public relations staff and other managers should thoroughly review the performance of the crisis plan and make revisions to improve it.

LEARNING ACTIVITIES

1. Scan sports news sources on the Internet to gain a sense of the major sports stories of the day. Which sport organizations are dealing with crisis episodes? What types of crises are they facing? What strategies are they employing in response to the crisis?

2. Continuing with your examination of the same organization you identified in activity 1, review that organization's social media channels. To what extent is the organization using social media to communicate its crisis response? Is the organization interacting with followers or commenters, or is it simply sharing information in one-way fashion?

3. Conduct an interview with a sport public relations professional. Ask the public relations official about what her or his organization has done to prepare for crises. Does the organization have a written plan? If so, what things are specified in that plan? Has the organization ever used the plan? How well did it work? If the organization does not have a written plan, what would it do in the event of a crisis?

4. Develop a case study regarding a sport organization that has faced a crisis. Be sure to specify how the crisis unfolded, how quickly and in what ways the sport organization responded to the crisis, and what crisis response strategies appear to have been employed. Given the gift of hindsight, what would you have advised the organization to do differently, and what might have been the effects of your recommendations?

Cultivating Positive Relationships in the Community

Lisa A. Kihl, PhD

Director, Global Institute for Responsible Sport Organizations
Associate Professor, University of Minnesota

After reading this chapter, students should be able to

- understand the nature of social responsibility in sport organizations,
- describe the various dimensions of social responsibility,
- discuss the role of philanthropy in sport,
- characterize the different approaches to strategic social responsibility planning, and
- explain how to utilize the four principles of social impact planning.

These are the key terms discussed in this chapter:

- corporate social responsibility (CSR)
- philanthropy
- social impact
- strategic social responsibility
- unmediated communication

Sport **corporate social responsibility (CSR)** has grown considerably over the past 20 years and is now a global phenomenon across the sport industry. Most professional sport entities believe they have an ethical obligation to "do good" in society. National and international professional sport leagues (e.g., National Football League, English Premier League), corporations (e.g., Canucks Sports & Entertainment, Nike), teams (e.g., Memphis Grizzlies, Minnesota Timberwolves & Lynx), players (e.g., Lebron James, Serena Williams, Cristiano Ronaldo, J.J. Watt), and players' associations (e.g., National Basketball Players Association, Australian Football Players Association) understand that they possess a public face that affords them great influence over communities about making social change. Intercollegiate sport teams and athletes, and some community sport organizations, have also embraced an ethical obligation to act as role models and serve their communities. As CSR is exemplified in different "forms of community improvements, volunteerism, philanthropy, environmental initiatives, or educational and health programs, most sport organizations and many athletes identify the need to support some form of social involvement" (Walker & Parent, 2010, p. 200).

The connection between social responsibility and public relations is a close one, as most CSR activities are considered newsworthy and may result in considerable publicity. Further, since the messages that are delivered about CSR tend be controlled by the sport organization, most of the resultant publicity is likely to be favorable. This is an important feature for two reasons. First, many sport entertainment organizations (e.g., professional teams and Division I college athletics programs) have difficulty generating positive publicity because of poor team performance, frequent roster changes, and inappropriate behavior by players or coaches. In such cases, publicity from community relations ventures may be the only way to generate positive publicity for the team (Irwin, Sutton, & McCarthy, 2008). Second, sport organizations such as fitness providers and equipment manufacturers may find it challenging to obtain news coverage. Speeches, demonstrations, and open houses offer specific and positive story ideas that public relations professionals can pitch to members of the mass media.

Philanthropy encompasses sport entities' actions as good citizens in donating money and other resources (e.g., time, services, products, expertise) to social causes that benefit society or improve quality of life (Carroll, 1991; Porter, 2003). Society expects sport entities to give back to the community without

expecting anything in return because of the perception that charitable giving is the right thing to do. Philanthropy in sport is generally understood as donations to causes or nonprofit organizations, in-kind donations of products and services (e.g., free tickets, sponsorship of community events), and active volunteering by members of the organization (Sheth & Babiak, 2010). Monetary donations vary depending on the sport entity and context of the sport organization. For example, some professional organization will donate large amounts to certain causes or nonprofit groups. For example, over a two-year period (2017–19), the Philadelphia Eagles Charitable Foundation raised more than $7 million for autism research (Eagles Charitable Foundation, 2019), and various professional athletes, owners, teams, and leagues have donated or raised money to support different hurricane disaster relief initiatives. Specifically, in 2017 the National Football League (NFL), National Basketball Association (NBA), and Major League Baseball (MLB) donated a combined $3 million to nonprofit organizations such as the Hurricane Harvey Relief Fund, the American Red Cross, and United Way (Rafferty, 2017).

Most sport organizations are actively involved in community initiatives (Extejt, 2004; Sheth & Babiak, 2010), with their activities ranging from athletes visiting schools and hospitalized children; teams operating programs that promote healthy lifestyles and physical activity; and leagues, players, and player associations promoting athlete mental health awareness. In some instances, individuals are required to volunteer in the community. For example, some collegiate athletics departments require athletes to perform up to 10 hours per semester of service; various professional sport collective bargaining agreements mandate a certain number of team or individual appearances at community events. Communities expect sport entities to donate money, the use of facilities, and volunteer time to different causes, though it is not deemed unethical if the entities do not fully meet these expectations. Sport philanthropy is therefore discretionary or voluntary giving, despite society's expectation that sport entities should give back.

The main motivations for sport philanthropy are to enhance image and reputation, improve community relations, and counteract ethical issues experienced by the organization. Sport organizations using philanthropy to improve their images or guard against "ethical blowback" (negative public reaction to a sport entity's unethical behavior) run the risk of a negative public perception of their

Case Study

SUCCESSFUL FUNDRAISING

In the summer of 2017, a devastating hurricane hit Houston, Texas. Through his foundation, J.J. Watt, a member of the Houston Texans, launched a social media campaign to raise donations to support families displaced by Hurricane Harvey. Watt began the fundraiser by posting a social media video from his hotel room in Dallas, where the Texans had been rerouted following a preseason game. Within two hours, the JJ Watt Foundation had raised $200,000, the amount of his initial goal. Watt raised the goal to $500,000, and donations continue to pour in. Three weeks later, donations had surpassed $37 million. When all was completed, the campaign raised $41.6 million dollars, a record amount for a crowd-sourced fundraising endeavor. Monies were distributed to eight area nonprofit organizations (Barshop, 2018).

Two years after the hurricane, the foundation provided an update on how the monies were spent, suggesting that nearly 1,200 homes had been rebuilt with the donations. In addition, close to 1,000 childcare centers were rebuilt, benefiting 108,000 kids. Finally, more than 239 million meals were distributed to hurricane victims (Caron, 2019). Watt's efforts earned him the 2017 Walter Payton NFL Man of the Year Award, honoring a player's volunteer and charity work.

Discussion Questions

1. What made this philanthropic effort so successful?
2. What role do you believe social media played in generating engagement for this effort?
3. Would the effort have attracted as many donations if another Houston Texans player had started it?
4. Visit the JJ Watt Foundation website and find the 2019 report on how funds were disbursed. Why was it important for the foundation to publish this type of report?

---

philanthropic initiatives as public relations stunts rather than actions taken out of a sincere desire to do good in communities.

The purpose of this chapter is to discuss the evolution of social responsibility in the sport industry. The chapter is organized into three sections. The first section speaks to the uniqueness of CSR in sport. The second section discusses the evolution of CSR in sport from traditional philanthropy to strategic sport CSR, including considerations about decision making and social impact. The last section outlines a framework for communicating CSR.

Uniqueness of Sport Corporate Social Responsibility

In the sport industry, most sport entities believe that CSR is an important aspect of their organizational functions. Sport practitioners and scholars have not come to a consensus about what CSR means or should look like. Much variation in the use of this term exists, as well as the role of CSR in sport organizations, what stakeholders expect, and how CSR

should be delivered in the community. Despite the lack of a universally accepted definition of CSR, Carroll's (1991) four-part conceptualization—referred to as "the pyramid of CSR"—proves to be helpful. In this conceptualization, CSR consists of the following responsibilities:

1. Economic—the responsibility to maintain profitability and competitive strength
2. Legal—the duty to obey the law
3. Ethical—the obligation to do what is right, just, and fair
4. Philanthropic—the duty to be a good corporate citizen and meet societal expectations

Based on Carroll's pyramid, CSR goes beyond philanthropy and involves a business perspective that recognizes that being "socially responsible" is an obligation to fulfill economic, legal, ethical, and philanthropic duties that benefit both the social and economic interests of the organization.

Social responsibility (SR), however, can refer to both corporate and noncorporate entities, including community sport organizations; interscholastic, intercollegiate, and international sport federations; and national and international athlete advocacy

Corporate social responsibility for a sport organization may be linked to physical activity, such as support for the creation of a playground.

© Human Kinetics

organizations. Babiak and Wolfe (2009) summarized social responsibility as "an ethical ideology or theory that an entity, be it organization or individual, has the obligation to act in a manner that contributes to and benefits society at large" (p. 17). Sport entities might find it helpful to understand sport SR as a "custom-made process" reflecting the organization's mission that guides its determination of the organization's obligations to society and approach to policies and practices. Organizational entities can customize their SR programs by selecting the "concept and definition that best matches the sport organization's aims, intentions, resources, stakeholders, and where appropriate aligns with the organization's business strategy" (van Marrewijk, 2003, p. 96).

Compared with CSR in other industries, the practice of CSR in the sport context is unique. Babiak and Wolfe (2009) argued that passion, economics, transparency, and stakeholder management are four features that separate CSR in sport from CSR in other business sectors. Passion, emotion, and devotion to the sport product—athletes, teams, and the game—is the central characteristic that differentiates sport from other industries. The strong devotion toward teams and athletes generates a public image that differs in comparison with business leaders or their employees. Athletes and teams have greater influence in promoting socially responsible initiatives, such as environmental sustainability or active living, than the leaders of a business corporation like Target Corporation or 3M do.

Economically, the sport industry has unique elements (e.g., public subsidies for stadium construction and events, nonprofit status, antitrust exemptions) that place different expectations and perceptions of the social role of professional and nonprofessional sport teams and their leagues in the community. In addition, many aspects of the sport industry are transparent and reported in the media. Information about management decisions (e.g., collective bargaining agreements, sponsorship), team leadership (e.g., hiring and firings, salaries, injuries, trades), game-day activities, game outcomes (e.g., wins and losses), employee off-field behaviors (e.g., criminal arrests, positive drug test), and community initiatives is available to the public and heavily reported by the media. In comparison, other types of businesses do not receive such public scrutiny or coverage of their business practices.

Finally, the sport industry requires working with a diverse set of stakeholders (e.g., player agents, community, fans, government, media, medical staff, and players). Successful CSR initiatives require working collaboratively with different stakeholders. Often, CSR initiatives interact with public relations through publicity generated from the activities. The organization, because it is creating the publicity, can also control the message. Practitioners working in sport CSR should be cognizant of these four unique features of the sport industry when developing CSR initiatives in order to benefit society.

How sport entities perceive their obligations to society, and what contributing and benefiting society means, naturally have been subject to different interpretations and have changed over time. The next section speaks to this evolution.

Evolution of Sport Social Responsibility

Worldwide, how sport organizations have perceived their role in society has evolved. Over the past 15 to 20 years, sport organizations' understanding of their obligations to society has progressed from a philanthropic philosophy, to strategic philanthropy, to philanthropy that makes a social impact. Sport SR has moved from traditional sport philanthropic activities (see figure 9.1), to more strategic philanthropy that integrates the sport entities' core business objectives and core competencies to provide benefits to both the organization and society, to focusing on initiatives that address community priorities and make a social impact that may or may not financially benefit the organization. Traditional sport philanthropy reflects charitable giving such as donating money, volunteering in community activities, fundraising and awareness activities, and building new community sport fields or courts or rebuilding existing ones. Sport philanthropy is often delivered through community relations departments, foundations, intercollegiate athlete development units, and community sport organizations. Traditional sport philanthropy tends to be nonstrategic, with sport organizations often supporting a combination of charitable activities disconnected from these organizations' core business aims (i.e., sport, physical activity, and health). For example, Kihl and Inoue (2018) found that intercollegiate athletics departments in the state of Minnesota on average engaged in philanthropy addressed to five community needs, with the majority of causes supported outside of the departments' core competencies—for example, crime prevention, alleviation of poverty, cancer awareness, disability awareness, prevention of bullying, disaster relief, environmental awareness, and support for non-cancer diseases.

Decisions regarding issues to support and organizations to sponsor have been influenced by the preferences of team owners, players, and their spouses, as well as senior management and board directors. To make their philanthropic efforts visible in the local community, for many teams the philosophy is to give back by donating to as many causes and nonprofits as possible with the aim of satisfying as many individuals and community groups as possible. The check amounts are generally unsubstantial and have minimal benefit. Porter (2003) maintains that this approach to "charitable giving becomes fragmented, piecemeal, and arbitrary" (p. 4). Companies do not impose discipline on their giving. When sport philanthropy as such does not follow a coherent SR framework, charitable giving tends to be nonstrategic and unfocused. A "giving back" approach is not an effective philanthropic approach; therefore, **strategic social responsibility**, as explained in the following section, is perceived as a more effective means to benefit society.

Many professional sport entities have moved away from this traditional philanthropic approach and adopted strategic CSR. Leagues and teams are restructuring and rebranding their community relations departments to promote CSR. Strategic CSR integrates business practices (e.g., marketing,

Traditional philanthropy	Strategic philanthropy	Social impact
"Giving back"	Influences competitive context; social and economic benefits	Manage and respond to societal priorities; social change
Babiak and Wolfe (2009)	Kotler and Lee (2005) McAlister and Ferrell (2002)	Crampton and Patten (2008)

Figure 9.1 Shifting understandings of social responsibility.

sponsorship, sales, and human relations) and entrepreneurial and innovation decision making into the organization's overall business strategy. Sport organizations that have adopted CSR are recruiting experts to lead socially responsible units and develop strategic social programs that benefit both society and the organization. However, some professional sport leagues (e.g., English Premier League), teams (e.g., Minnesota Vikings Foundation), and players (e.g., LeBron James Family foundation) have adopted the philosophy that sport entities should address community priorities and create programs that make a social impact. These professional sport entities have changed their mission, rebranded their social responsibility units, and focused CSR programming on making a social impact. These types of CSR initiatives seek to address community priorities, which leads to social change.

Strategic Sport Corporate Social Responsibility

Given that professional sport entities are perceived to possess large amounts of resources, they are expected to support a wide range of initiatives. As discussed earlier, sport executives believe this expectation is unrealistic; consequently, they are shifting away from traditional philanthropy or an altruistic focus to a convergence of philanthropy and business strategy (Hamil & Morrow, 2011). Sport organizations are not only seeking to benefit the community, but also aiming to enhance the strategic position of the organization and ultimately the bottom line. **Strategic CSR** is defined as a "business strategy that integrates core organizational objectives and competencies of a firm" to "create business value and positive social change that is embedded in the day-to-day business culture and operations" (McElhaney, 2009, p. 35). It is a voluntary commitment to improve community well-being (i.e., human conditions and environmental issues) and organizational economic objectives by using core competencies and resources (Kotler & Lee, 2008).

Professional sport organizations are starting to realize the benefit of CSR as a means of advancing their business goals. Organizations are strategically restructuring their SR programming and utilizing their core competencies and abilities as a source of opportunity, innovation, and competitive advantage (Porter & Kramer, 2006). Sport entities adopting strategic CSR realize that certain social

issues (e.g., education, diversity, safety, workforce training) are also economic issues that can directly impact a sport organization's ability to be competitive within its business environment. Rather than giving donations in small amounts to a range of community initiatives, sport entities have become more focused, supporting initiatives that benefit both the organization and the community and that create a competitive advantage. For example, MLB recognized that the numbers of youth and, in particular, youth of color participating in baseball were declining. To help address this concern, the Reviving Baseball in Inner Cities (RBI) initiative was created to promote both baseball and softball to underserved youth. The program is an important means for MLB teams to develop the game at the grassroots level, while also enhancing and developing the number of minority youth playing baseball and softball. MLB's RBI program allows the organization to focus on its core business (e.g., baseball and softball), enhance the effectiveness and efficiency of its social responsibility initiatives (e.g., increase the numbers of youth and youth of color playing the sport), and position itself to create value for both the organization (e.g., cultivate fans and community relationships) and program recipients (e.g., develop baseball and softball skills).

The CSR strategy of the Union of European Football Associations (UEFA) is another good example of integrating the SR mission throughout an organization's various units to enhance its core business while fostering sustainable development, through several intentional SR programs (UEFA, 2019). In particular, to ensure national member associations and their stakeholders have access to talented and well-trained individuals, UEFA has developed customized education and knowledge-sharing initiatives. UEFA partners with European higher education institutions to allow program participants access to cutting-edge research and knowledge on managing football organizations. The program gives UEFA the opportunity to gain a competitive advantage through education innovation, which impacts society and economically benefits the organization.

Professional sport entities are confronted with different challenges, forcing them to make strategic decisions about the purpose of SR programs, the types of programs offered, and who will benefit from CSR initiatives. Babiak and Wolfe (2009) reported that in professional sport, both internal determinants (i.e., value, rareness, and inimitability) and external determinants (i.e., context, constituents, content, control, and cause) drive strategic SR decisions. (This framework might also be applicable to SR decisions in intercollegiate athletics, because this context also involves stakeholder influences and resource factors in adopting CSR.) Internal resources of professional sport organizations are uniquely valuable because of the way teams and athletes are admired, with public personas that afford them much social status and influence. Such resources are rare, distinct, and inimitable, giving sport organizations an advantage in addressing social issues. External forces take stakeholder concerns and societal needs as the guiding factors that drive SR decisions. The interconnectedness among professional sport organizations (e.g., teams, state and local governments, media, sponsors), consistency with organizational mission, key constituents (e.g., owners, players and their spouses, employees), legal and league regulatory mandates, and ethical obligations all serve as external drivers of SR initiatives. The type of SR program sport organizations adopt largely depends on the extent that they are stakeholder-centric (i.e., addressing societal needs) or corporate-centric (i.e., aiming at synergies between core business activities and social responsibility).

Examples of CSR programs that fall within the stakeholder-centric external perspective include the NBA's mind health program, which promotes healthy minds and bodies and raises awareness about emotional well-being and how to seek help, and the breast health awareness program of the Women's National Basketball Association (WNBA), which aims to increase women's understanding of their risk for breast cancer and how to reduce that risk. The program encourages women to complete the "Bright Pink Assess Your Risk" survey to evaluate their risk for breast and ovarian cancers. Mental health and breast cancer are important social issues, and the association with NBA and WNBA players and the brand is an important resource to encourage health and well-being; however, the core competencies of the league and the respective teams are not related to these two health initiatives.

Corporate-centric CSR programs include a sport and physical activity initiative of the United Kingdom's Aston Villa Foundation, involving a range of football (soccer) programs for girls and boys from 6 to 16 years of age that aims to develop football skills and pathways for development. USA Swimming Foundation's mission endeavors to build the sport across the country through "saving lives and building champions" initiatives that involve learn-to-swim programs and financial support for national representatives. Both organizations benefit from their respective CSR programs because they are developing grassroots participation in their

sports and future generation of fans by generating interest in soccer and swimming. In addition, the sport of swimming benefits through elite athletes' success at international competitions.

Sport organizations that have both an external and an internal CSR orientation are considered strategic, as they align social needs with core competencies. Strategic SR organizations use their unique abilities to benefit communities as well as return benefits to the organization. Netball Australia's Confident Girls Foundation is a strategic CSR initiative because its mission aligns with Netball Australia. The program partners with various community groups to provide opportunities for girls to participate in inclusive netball programs throughout Australia. The program aims to "break down gender bias, removing financial barriers and creating leadership opportunities for girls" (Netball Australia, 2019). The program uses resources such as coaches, umpires, volunteers, nonprofit partners, sponsors, and players to address local community needs that empower young girls to be successful both in the sport of netball and in life. These program goals coincide with Netball Australia's core competencies and resources.

The harmonizing of stakeholder-centric and corporate-centric CSR approaches makes this framework applicable to the intercollegiate athletics context. Intercollegiate athletics programs have various internal stakeholders (e.g., coaches, staff, administrators, faculty, students, and student–athletes) and external stakeholders (e.g., donors, fans, community members, sponsors, media). However, local communities make requests to athletics departments and teams for charitable giving to specific issues. Given that the mission of most higher education institutions involves public engagement and improving the lives of local communities (in addition to their research and teaching mission), and given the core competencies of athletics departments (e.g., sport and physical activity), athletics departments are well positioned to adopt a strategic CSR approach that addresses community social issues (stakeholder-centric) and develops programming that aligns with the departments' core competencies (corporate-centric). In turn, strategic CSR initiatives possess the potential to enhance the competitive advantage of athletics departments as well as benefiting or impacting society. To date, intercollegiate athletics departments have yet to recognize and take advantage of the business benefits of strategic SR programming. Most athletics departments and the National Collegiate Athletic Association (NCAA) adopt a traditional philanthropic approach by carrying out fundraising, promoting awareness campaigns, and making charitable donations (both financial and in kind). Adopting strategic CSR, intercollegiate departments could explore innovative ways to use their core competencies to benefit society while enhancing their revenues and return on investment through alignment of their social engagement with their own mission and vision and those of their institution.

Value of Strategic CSR

CSR creates both tangible and intangible benefits to a sport organization. Research has shown that the palpable advantages of adopting strategic CSR initiatives include

- improved competitive context,
- decreased operational costs, and
- enhanced brand image and reputation.

CSR efforts can improve organizations' competitive context, defined as "the quality of the business environment in the location or locations where they oper-

ate" (Porter & Kramer, 2002, p. 58). Several professional sport leagues and teams are making the most of their contexts by investing resources toward an initiative that aligns with their social and economic goals and therefore improves the long-term attractiveness of organizations. The CSR initiative of the Professional Golfers Association of America (PGA), for example, is tightly linked to its strategic mission to "serve the Member and grow the game" (PGA, 2018, para. 2). In addition to investing resources, the PGA leverages its capabilities and relationships to support five priority areas (Fostering Diversity & Inclusion, Engaging the Next Generation, Educating the Workforce of Tomorrow, Enhancing Lives Through Golf, and Growing the Game Around the Globe) that benefit both society (through, e.g., job creation and diversification of the workforce) and the long-term sustainability of the golf industry (through, e.g., diversification of participants and global expansion).

The potential for sport organizations to gain tangible benefits from their competitive contexts is an area of unrealized potential for enhancing their

In advance of the 2019 FIFA Women's World Cup, grants were awarded by the U.S. Soccer Foundation to organizations that focused on providing soccer participation opportunities to underrepresented girls.

© iStockphoto/Lilyana Vinogradova

bottom line. Sport organizational entities that seek to use the competitive context must rethink both where they focus their strategic SR efforts and how they go about giving (Porter & Kramer, 2002, p. 59).

Another strategic benefit is operational cost savings. Adopting sustainability practices dramatically decreases costs of operations and maintenance while also benefiting the environment. Many sport leagues and teams have partnered with the Sports Green Alliance, a global, environmentally focused trade organization that educates and consults sport entities on how to promote healthy, sustainable communities (Sports Green Alliance, n.d., para. 1). Organizations such as the Tokyo 2020 Olympic Organizing Committee demonstrate this practice through innovative programs such as creating athlete bed frames made completely out of recycled cardboard. Teams often adopt one or more of their programs (e.g., zero waste programs, renewable energy source practices, energy efficiency initiatives, energy conservation, water conservation, and environmental and human health programs) to be good corporate citizens as well as to reduce costs. Adopting these kinds of CSR programs motivates sport managers to reconsider their business practices and to seek more efficient ways of operating.

Strategic CSR also leads to enhanced organizational brand image and reputation. Fans and consumers are attracted to and value sport leagues, teams, and athletes with good reputations built on CSR-related programs. Furthermore, fans are more likely to purchase products (e.g., team merchandise, tickets) and speak favorably of the organization. Sport organizations that engage in strategic CSR activities are demonstrating their commitment to the community, which creates a positive perception of the organization. CSR initiatives can therefore help enhance the overall brand reputation of an organization beyond wins and losses. Brand image and reputation can be leveraged for low-identified fans during years when the organization is not performing well or when the organization is experiencing a rare negative event (e.g., a positive drug test, arrest for drinking while driving, or domestic violence on the part of a player).

Strategic Corporate Social Responsibility Planning

Strategic CSR allows a sport entity to achieve its organizational philanthropy goals. To realize their goals, organizational leaders must make a substantial, long-term commitment to strategic CSR, which entails "sound planning and careful implementation" (Bruch & Walter, 2005, p. 54). Furthermore, planning involves leaders working collaboratively with stakeholders to ensure that programs are clearly aligned with CSR goals, to identify potential partners for program implementation, and to mobilize resources to support strategy implementation. McElhaney (2009) recommended the following three steps in crafting a SR strategic plan.

Step 1

Senior organizational leadership or management (e.g., owners, president, commissioner, CEO), including the board, should make a genuine, strong, and public commitment to CSR and actively participate in initiatives. Successful CSR strategies are led and valued by senior management leaders who ensure that the vision of CSR is embedded in the organization and reflects its core values, mission, and vision. SR is treated as a central component of organizational operations, just as ticketing, sales, sponsorship, organizational operations, and human resources are. CSR directors therefore are high-level executives who report directly to the organization's CEO or president. For example, the Minnesota Timberwolves and Lynx vice president of social responsibility is a member of the senior management team and reports directly to the team president. Major League Baseball's vice president of social responsibility reports directly to the commissioner. In principle, the higher the executive role to which the SR reports in the organization, the greater value CSR has to the organization as a business strategy.

Step 2

Determine the three most important organizational objectives and priorities and develop an CSR strategy that will help realize the achievement of those organizational objectives. Deciding on specific CSR goals, determining the most effective strategies for achieving the goals given the organization's mission and vision, and planning how best to implement CSR strategies are essential steps for leaders. Management will need to determine how CSR is related to organizational priorities, team success, expected growth in revenue, and expected growth in new markets; how CSR can be used to increase innovation; how fan experience and engagement can be enhanced; and how CSR can be used as a recruiting strategy for seeking highly talented employees. For example, Nike Inc. declared that the Nike brand is a brand of innovation, growth, and purpose. Nike's "mission is to bring inspiration and innovation to every athlete in the world" (Nike, 2018). Nike's mission is accomplished through a focused strategy that incorporates its CSR into the fabric of the organization by "building creative and diverse global teams, making a positive impact in the communities where we live and work and by making products responsibly and more sustainably" (p. 2). Nike's CSR commitments and long-term goals are clearly stated to meet both stakeholder expectations and align with Nike's business priorities and resources. For example, under the priority issue of minimizing environmental impact, the company has the following product goal:

> Target—Deliver products for maximum performance with minimum impact, with a 10% reduction in the average environmental footprint. The goal is measured by assessing the extent that "greater than 80% of all NIKE, Inc. product will be scored on sustainability performance" (Nike, 2018, p. 3).

Nike is one of the few sport organizations whose strategic CSR plan coincides with its overall organizational mission and business priorities. In addition, Nike is a leader in clearly stating its priorities, goals, and assessments and reporting its findings. Sheth and Babiak (2010) examined professional teams' CSR priorities and found that executives identified CSR as a strategic priority. However, a range of factors influenced the CSR initiatives they sponsored, including philanthropy, ethical concerns, and the importance of partnerships and stakeholders, including the local community.

Generally, CSR initiatives are delivered internally through in-house programming or collaboratively through different social partnerships (Husted, 2003). Internal delivery typically involves program implementation by a unit within the organization that has sufficient financial and other resources. For example, Crystal Palace Football Club's foundation delivers a football program for women and girls that offers sessions for women and girls to enjoy football. The foundation has a set budget and provides the necessary resources to deliver the program—that is, trained coaches, facilities, curriculum, and so forth. Implementation of SR strategies has become quite challenging because of the complex nature of the various social issues sport entities are seeking to address. When sport organizations do not have the infrastructure or expertise to deliver programs, they seek out

social partnerships with nonprofits. Typically, the sport organization provides financial resources to the partner to implement the CSR program. For example, the NFL partners with the National Dairy Council and the United States Department of Agriculture (USDA) to create "Fuel Up to Play 60," a health and wellness program delivered by local schools. The NFL and National Dairy Council and the USDA transfer resources (e.g., curriculum, nutrition, awards) to local schools for them to effectively implement the program.

The CSR strategy should align with the organization's core competencies, which represent skills, technologies, and knowledge-based capabilities that are competitively unique and redeployable. For example, intercollegiate athletics departments' daily operations generally involve the promotion of sports as well as the athletic and academic development of student–athletes. Athletics departments should seek causes and social and environmental strategies for which they are well positioned to be part of the solution, such as community initiatives in the areas of youth sports engagement, youth education, and healthy lifestyles, which have a close connection with the departments' core competencies and resources. Initiatives focused on an organization's core competencies and organizational objectives tend to be more impactful in comparison with unplanned initiatives that are not integrated with an organization's expertise, knowledge, and capabilities.

Meeting strategic CSR goals requires fully integrating SR into the organization's culture, governance, and strategy development and into existing management and performance systems. Persuading organizational stakeholders and the organization itself to embrace and implement quality initiatives requires building SR functions into recognition and performance appraisals. Employees should be measured on both their functional job performance and their CSR performance. In addition, organizational performance indicators should also incorporate CSR achievements, including quality delivery and program outcomes. The National Hockey League (NHL) tracks and measures the league's impact on the environment (e.g., energy consumption of rinks, water usage, waste, etc.). The NHL uses the data to encourage local hockey clubs to implement changes to improve sustainability. For example, the "Montreal Canadians installed a closed-loop system that feeds melted ice shavings back into the ice resurfacer after being purified, saving around 208,000 litres of drinking water from being wasted every year" (Badloe, 2019, para. 9).

Step 3

To determine the impact and effectiveness of CSR strategies requires that organizations develop clear performance metrics or indicators and evaluate their strategies accordingly. Performance metrics are critical for defining CSR strategies' effectiveness and should include both internal metrics—such as increased sponsorship and ticket sales, reputation improvement, employee satisfaction, and decreased expenditures—and external metrics, including social and environmental impacts. Internal and external metrics can then be used to evaluate the quality of program delivery and outcomes. In addition, evaluation findings can assist organizations in identifying effective strategies and areas that require improvement, and can help organizations reassess overall strategies to ensure that resources (time, money, people, etc.) are used efficiently to benefit both the organization and society.

Social Impact Planning

Sport leaders are starting to recognize that sport organizations possess unique attributes that can be harnessed to make a **social impact** by responding to societal priorities. Social impact is different from

Be Your Own Media

The Aston Villa Foundation works in five thematic areas: disability, education and learning, health and well-being, sport and physical activity, and young people. Focusing first on Step 2 regarding organizational goals and objectives, identify the ways in which these themes are appropriate for Aston Villa Football Club. Explore the themes on the foundation's website and determine how Aston Villa has used its own organizational media to communicate aspects of these themes.

Now consider Step 3, determining the impact and effectiveness of CSR strategies through performance metrics. How would you measure the effectiveness of this CSR effort? Were these the correct tactics, given the focus on the foundation's themes? What additional tactics would you suggest to help Aston Villa meet its objectives? Should the foundation consider nonorganizational media tactics to help achieve objectives and measure effectiveness?

benefit. The Merriam-Webster dictionary defines a benefit as "something that produces good or helpful results or effects or that promotes well-being" ("Benefit," n.d., para. 1). A benefit might help people to feel good, but it does not necessarily lead to social change. In contrast, social impact seeks to make a change in behavior or attitude. CSR's social impact can be broadly understood as positive consequences to human populations based on specific initiatives or programs designed to address a pressing social challenge. Sport CSR initiatives that seek to have a social impact set specific goals around addressing a particular societal concern so as to effect a positive social change (e.g., decreased obesity rates, increased graduation rates, decreased crime rates). For example, in the United Kingdom, knife crime increased considerably in 2014–15, and metropolitan areas saw the greatest increases (Shaw, 2019). The English Premier League's Tottenham Hotspur Foundation is one of several team foundations that have developed initiatives through partnerships—such as with the English Premier League and the local Mayor's Office for Policing and Crime—to address the increased knife crimes carried out by youth 12 to 18 years old. Tottenham Hotspur's program uses a youth mentoring program based in football (soccer) to steer young people identified as at-risk to avoid becoming involved in crime. The program has had a social impact in addressing the community priority of knife crime in that over 60 of the 350 participants have reportedly found employment or enrolled in education and training programs.

It is possible that some CSR social impact initiatives delivered by sporting entities can be strategic (i.e., they benefit both the entity and the community), but some programs do not aim to financially benefit the organization. For example, Michael Jordan, former NBA player and part owner of the Charlotte Hornets, has partnered with Novant Health and donated $7 million to open two medical centers in Charlotte, North Carolina. The opening of the medical centers is focused on making a social impact by providing underprivileged residents without medical insurance with access to dental, behavioral, and physical health services. While there might be intangible benefits for the Jordan Foundation brand, Jordan's main objective is "to make an impact to a community that . . . in the future is going to make an impact back to the city of Charlotte" (Hudson, 2019, para. 4) because of access to quality health care.

Sport organizations seeking to make a social impact and address community priorities can use the following four principles, suggested by the

National Co-ordinating Centre for Public Engagement (2019) (see figure 9.2). The four principles serve as a guide for organizational decision making to create social initiatives that have social impact and make social change in local communities.

Principle 1: Purpose

Program decision makers and organizational leaders need to clearly state the purpose or clearly understand the reason for creating and delivering the CSR initiative. This decision will be based on how the specific sport entity defines community and determines which social priorities the entity will address. Organizational leaders work with local government, community nonprofits, and in some cases law enforcement to determine the community's priorities and collect relevant statistical data to understand the nature of a social challenge. They then create criteria for evaluating which community priorities the organization will choose to address. The criteria may or may not be based on the organization's mission and vision, what priorities are expected to make a return on the organization's investment, or the importance of the community issue.

Principle 2: People

It is important that organizational decision makers determine who will be the intended recipients of or the target population for the proposed initiative as well as assess recipients' priorities and determine how their priorities and interests will be taken into consideration in the development of the initiative. For example, decision makers consult with program partners, community nonprofits, and community members to learn about what is important to the recipients and what they expect from the program. Finally, decision makers should assemble a skilled delivery team to ensure quality programming. When sport is not used to address the community priority (e.g., food insecurity programs, STEM programs), organizational leaders must identify quality community nonprofits or educational institutions to ensure that knowledgeable and reputable individuals are implementing the programs.

Principle 3: Process

Organizational decision makers should ensure that the process for implementing the CSR program is the most suitable for achieving the aim of the social impact initiative. They must allocate sufficient resources to support program implementation and ensure that the staff responsible for delivering the program possess the right skills and knowledge to deliver the program effectively. Sport CSR social impact program implementation typically occurs through one or more of three main delivery modes: in-house, through a foundation, and through partnerships. Decision makers should select the appropriate implementation mode that will ensure quality

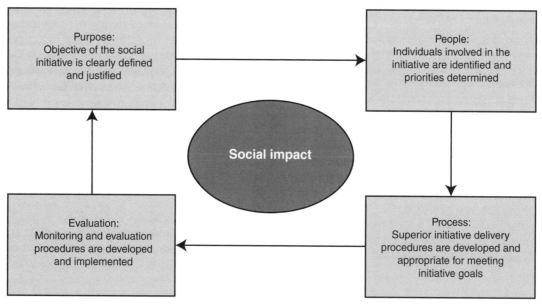

Figure 9.2 Four principles of social impact planning.

Adapted from the National Co-ordinating Centre for Public Engagement (2019).

delivery and meet social impact goals. In addition, it is critical to allocate sufficient resources and appoint knowledgeable and skilled staff to effectively deliver a quality program that meets social change outcomes. For example, the "I Promise" initiative of the LeBron James Family Foundation (LJFF) aims to address the high rate of students' dropping out of high school in Akron, Ohio. To increase high school graduation rates, the foundation recognized that it did not have the infrastructure itself to deliver a program. As a result, the foundation developed a partnership with Akron schools and designed an "I Promise" school that has a tailor-made curriculum and support program for children and youth (5 to 18 years of age) who are identified as being at high risk for dropping out. The program was created by trained educational experts and trained educational staff (e.g., educational scholars, teachers, educational administrators, mentors), all of whom have similar goals and sufficient educational and support resources (e.g., encouragement, mentorship, ways to meet day-to-day needs) to deliver a program that is making a social impact in the community by increasing high school graduation rates of Akron youth.

Principle 4: Evaluation

Evaluating the social impact of a CSR initiative is essential for two main reasons. First, the quality of delivery influences the extent to which program outcomes are realized. Second, the quality of delivery determines the social consequences of a SR initiative. Program decision makers therefore need to develop a process for evaluating the quality of the delivery and social impact outcomes. Kihl, Babiak, and Tainsky (2014) emphasized the importance of establishing "clear metrics" with respect to program implementation processes and the social impact outcomes expected. The nature of the delivery (e.g., in-house or via social partnerships) and the social impact goals will influence how each aspect is measured. For example, program theory (Chen, 2005) can assist with establishing metrics for partnership implementation programs where "evaluators can identify the steps required to implement a program/partnership and the quality of these steps in implementation" (Kihl et al., 2014, p. 326). While social impacts are often difficult to measure and quantify, a program's social impact goals can assist in operationalizing and then measuring social consequences. For example, the LJFF's "I Promise" school uses student math and reading scores as indicators of students' graduation potential and uses gradu-

ation rates to evaluate decreases in dropout rates. Once the evaluation data is collected, program decision makers should determine how they will use the data to inform future decisions and practices.

Communication of Corporate Social Responsibility

Communication of CSR has become a common practice for sport organizations; this communication benefits the organization by enhancing customer loyalty, patronage intentions, return on investment, employee commitment, and stakeholder engagement (e.g., Kolyperas & Sparks, 2011; Walker, Kent, & Vincent, 2010). Although many sport entities have adopted CSR initiatives and perceive benefits from these initiatives, sport entities may fail to effectively communicate their support for various social programs to their organizational stakeholders and the general public. This failure can undermine the benefits of engaging in strategic CSR programs. Creating stakeholder awareness and managing attribution toward the organization's CSR programs are critical to gaining strategic benefits; doing so requires designing an effective communication strategy (Du, Bhattacharya, & Sen, 2010). Tench, Sun, and Jones (2014) offer a helpful framework to guide CSR communications planning that addresses purpose, audience, message content, and message channels.

The main objective of strategic CSR communication is to convey a positive message that is sincere, reliable, and transparent about the organization's CSR initiatives. Communication involves a two-way exchange between the sender (i.e., the sport entity) and the recipient (i.e., stakeholders including the public), with a focus on a mutual understanding of the meaning of CSR and the shared benefits of initiatives (Tench et al., 2014). For example, it is vital that sport team stakeholders communicate their CSR expectations of the team and that the team in turn communicates how it has accurately understood and carried out stakeholders' expectations.

Sport organizations frequently use unmediated communication tactics to communicate SR initiatives to stakeholders. **Unmediated communication** has been defined as "two-way contact that does not pass through a channel or medium" (Fawkes, 2008, p. 19). Unmediated communication tactics such as public speeches, personal appearances, promotional tours, and clinics offer three distinct advantages as public relations tools.

The first is that the interaction is face to face and sometimes even person to person. When a sport organization's representatives make public speeches, they stand before their audiences. When they make personal appearances in other settings, representatives frequently talk one on one with those in attendance. When they host a special event, they are looking to make personal contact with their constituents. These are far more personal forms of contact than other public relations tactics such as news releases or even social media updates. These forms of contact also allow the representatives to respond to specific questions asked by their constituents.

The second major advantage of unmediated communication events staged by sport organizations is that audience members who attend are usually predisposed to be interested in and favorable toward the representatives and their organizations. Since most people are inclined to embrace messages that support existing interests, attitudes, and opinions, the potential is great for the sport organizations' representatives to successfully communicate intended messages. For instance, a room full of athletics boosters will likely respond favorably to coaches talking about their programs' exciting futures.

The third distinct advantage is that the sport organization can exert a high degree of control over the messages that are communicated in these settings (Helitzer, 2000). Person-to-person interaction is dynamic and occasionally unpredictable. However, the people representing the sport organization in unmediated communication activities are almost always employees or advocates. As a result, the sport organization has greater control over messaging than it does when it attempts to communicate with the public via the mass media. Ideally, public relations staff members will coach the organization's representatives regarding what messages are most important to emphasize and how to respond if faced with difficult questions.

Message Audience

The senders and receivers of CSR communications are generally the sport entity and organizational stakeholders (including the public). Remember that organizations have unique stakeholder groups who, in turn, have different expectations about CSR. A sport organization's fans and consumers may have different CSR expectations from the team owners or city officials. Targeting appropriate CSR messages toward addressing particular stakeholder expectations is an important consideration in this planning stage.

Message Content

The content of SR communication messages should address four main areas:

1. Convey the organization's SR philosophy—the meaning of SR and the organization's mission, culture, values, and beliefs regarding SR.

2. Inform stakeholders about the organization's involvement in specific CSR issues. Messages should clearly communicate the organization's commitment to a social issue by stating the amount, type, and consistency of support; explaining the organization's motivations for engaging with selected social issues; and being honest, emphasizing the convergence of social and business interests and frankly acknowledging that its CSR efforts benefit both the organization and society (Porter & Kramer, 2006).

3. Convey the implementation of CSR initiatives or programs, how they are delivered, and the impacts or outcomes measured and reported.

4. Provide ongoing communication to stakeholders about how respective CSR programs address stakeholders' identified social concerns.

For example, the NBA Charlotte Hornets' (n.d.) 2017–18 corporate social responsibility report's communication message explains its CSR philosophy, informs stakeholders about the four social pillars issues the team targets (i.e., education, wellness, hunger, and military care), speaks of the respective programs and their delivery through various partnerships, and communicates measured outcomes of the program (e.g., number of appearances, sponsorship dollars awarded to nonprofits, grant dollar amounts).

Message Channels

Sport organizations can use a variety of communication channels to convey their CSR activities and outcomes. Sport organizations can communicate their CSR activities through formal documents such as community or foundation annual reports and newsletters. To communicate the types of programs the organization supports and the mutual benefits to the organization and society, organizations may

The Minnesota Twins Community Foundation uses the slogan "Getting More Kids in the Game" in their outfield signage to highlight their community involvement.

Rob Leiter/MLB via Getty Images

use internal or controlled-content communication channels such as organizational social media (e.g., websites, Twitter, Facebook), traditional team or league media (e.g., television segments, commercials, public service announcements), or stadium or arena billboards, or some combination of these. For example, the Minnesota Twins Community Foundation promotes the mutual benefits of its youth baseball initiatives at Target Field by advertising that the team is encouraging more youth to play baseball in the community, which in turn benefits the team. Externally, the organization communicates CSR messages through TV commercials, local TV and radio reporting, and magazines. Using internal communication mechanisms allows the organization to control the message; in external communication mechanisms, an outside entity has the power to direct the message the organization wishes to convey to the public.

Sport entities can also communicate directly to stakeholder groups such as fans and consumers who serve as informal communication channels.

To date, this type of communication channel is a largely untapped resource that can benefit both sport entities and communities. The Minnesota Vikings Foundation uses management technology from Blackbaud to communicate with fans and donors and develop and strengthen fan relationships (Blackbaud, 2018). Blackbaud's communication technology allows the foundation to learn about fans and what they want to achieve through philanthropy, which the foundation uses to communicate different opportunities for fans to participate in different local community social programs. Teams and leagues should be proactive in using social media to engage stakeholders in SR dialogue with their CSR advocates.

Thoughtful planning about how sport organizations will use different channels to convey CSR initiatives used by different stakeholders is an important process for effective SR communication. Drawing on different channels can broaden stakeholder reach in communicating SR initiatives.

SUMMARY

Sport CSR is a common global practice for sport organizations, from nonprofit community sport organizations, to intercollegiate athletics, to the professional level. Social responsibility suggests that a sport entity believes it has an ethical obligation to contribute to society in a positive manner. Determining a sport entity's ethical obligation to society is a custom-made process in which organizations integrate their mission with social practices and policies that benefit society.

Sport organizations' perceptions of their obligation to society and how they contribute positively to society have evolved over the past two decades. Understandings of sport entities' obligations to society have emerged from traditional philanthropy, in which organizations give financial or in-kind donations to different causes. This charitable practice is a dominant way many sport organizations carry out their sense of obligation to society. An ancillary benefit to engaging in these practices is the resulting positive publicity the organization may receive.

However, many professional sport organizations have shifted to strategic CSR and understand the economic benefit of using their core competencies to address social issues. Organizations employing strategic CSR align their mission and core strengths and seek innovative ways to enhance their business environments in order to gain a competitive advantage. Sport entities are also seeking to engage in CSR decision making when they are addressing key community priorities to make a social impact. The evolution of CSR in sport demonstrates that sport entities do feel obligated to give back and that they are thinking about how they can make the most impact. However, the communication of CSR initiatives is an area that warrants more attention and thought by sport organizations. For CSR to effectively return economic benefits to the organization, it is important that the organization use a communication framework. In particular, the organization can use more innovative communication channels with different stakeholder groups to create stakeholder dialogue and enhance public awareness of the good the organization is doing in the community.

LEARNING ACTIVITIES

1. Contact a public relations official with a local sport franchise and ask several questions regarding the organization's CSR efforts. What does the organization do in this regard? What benefits does the official believe the organization receives as a result of its CSR? Based on what you learn, how would you characterize the organization's approach to CSR?

2. Contact a representative of a charitable organization and ask several questions. Does the representative's organization receive support from sport figures or organizations? If so, what kind? Does the representative know of a particularly effective partnership between a sport organization and a nonprofit organization? If so, how was it executed? How did each party benefit?

3. Visit the website of the major professional sport franchise of your choice. You will likely find a link to a page detailing the team's philanthropic initiatives. Has the organization established a charitable foundation? What causes does the team support? What type of support is provided? Does the team involve others (e.g., fans, corporate partners) in its philanthropic efforts?

4. Identify a sport social responsibility initiative and, using the four principles of social impact planning, break down how you categorize the strategy of the initiative.

Advancing Relationships With External and Internal Publics

After reading this chapter, students should be able to

- describe the role public relations plays in building and maintaining relationships with various external and internal stakeholders,
- describe the role public relations plays in the customer/member experience,
- identify how public relations efforts can enhance sponsor relationships,
- explain how donor relationships are nurtured through ongoing PR activity,
- discuss the need for effective influencing strategies when dealing with government regulation,
- outline the benefits of directing PR actions internally toward employees, and
- recognize the PR challenges that sport organizations encounter in balancing interests of investors with other stakeholders.

These are the key terms discussed in this chapter:

- 80-20 rule
- annual reports
- consumer-generated media (CGM)
- customer equity
- customer experience (CX)
- customer journey mapping
- customer lifetime value (CLV)
- customer relationship management (CRM)
- grapevine
- investor relations (IR)

- lobbying
- membership relationship management (MRM)
- Net Promoter Score (NPS)
- organizational culture
- public affairs
- recency, frequency, and monetary (RFM) analysis
- sponsorship activation
- touchpoints

Previous chapters have discussed the role of public relations with the media and the community at large. While these groups are significant, the success of sport organizations of all types depends on forming and maintaining relationships with external constituencies such as consumers, sponsors, members, and donors, and internal publics such as employees and investors. The goal of this chapter is to shed light on the benefits of PR efforts targeted to these publics that extend beyond traditional marketing activities.

As sport organizations have become increasingly attentive to long-term customer loyalty, they have increased their focus on building lasting relationships. This trend is occurring in all progressive sport organizations regardless of the sport industry segment. Developing a loyal consumer base makes good business sense, and PR efforts can help sustain loyalty. Similarly, other exchange-based connections, such as those with members, sponsors, and donors, benefit from building relationships that can be perpetuated over extended periods. Public relations efforts directed at these publics focus on building consistent and committed relationships. Associations with other external publics, such as government agencies and other regulatory and political groups, can be important in the sport world as well. A different type of PR approach is taken with these publics because the goal may be less oriented toward revenue generation and more toward gaining influence, support, and advocacy. Finally, PR efforts must also be directed internally, toward employees and investors. The value of having dialogue with these stakeholders creates a critical feedback loop and fosters a sense of engagement necessary in sustaining these important relationships.

The first portion of the chapter deals with the PR strategies used to build relationships with an organization's customers, members, sponsors, and donors. The chapter then looks at associations with government and other political or governing agencies and finally considers important aspects of relationships with internal publics such as employees and investors.

Customer and Member Relationships

Customers are referred to in many different ways. Timm (2001) noted that organizations may use terms such as *clients*, *members*, *patrons*, *associates*, *guests*, *buyers*, *viewers*, and *subscribers* to describe those with whom the organizations engage in transactions. A single sport organization may often use several of these terms to refer to specific target groups. In recent years, many spectator sport operations have adopted the Disney concept of customer service, considering visitors to be guests (see the 2011 book *Be Our Guest: Perfecting the Art of Customer Service* by Theodore B. Kinni). It is now routine for professional sport organizations to refer to their season ticket holders as members (a quick review noted that at least 22 of the 30 National Basketball Association teams used this designation). Such terms may be an effort to create a more contractual relationship with consumers rather than the noncontractual (come-and-go) relationship that many retailers tend to have with their customers. Regardless of terminology, the success of any revenue-driven sport organization is determined by how well it attends to the phases of the customer experience.

The primary focus for this section is looking at how PR can complement traditional marketing efforts tied to manipulation of the 4 *P*s of marketing—product, price, place, and promotion. These direct marketing efforts, tied to meeting the needs of consumers and resulting in an exchange, are very familiar. Price, as a very visible measure of value, is often manipulated to create an additional sense of value. Planet Fitness promotes its 20 cents down, $10 per month membership. While the core product for spectator sport (the game itself) is not manipulated as readily as price, leagues do look for ways to modify the games to make them more appealing. Baseball continues to look for ways to make the game move along faster. Manipulation of tangible products may be more controllable by marketers who, for example, may offer athletic shoes in multiple colors and styles. Sport retailers manipulate place by creating floor plans designed to encourage browsing (there is a reason that athletic shoes are usually located in the back of the store). For other operations like fitness clubs, place manipulation may be tied to aesthetics and appearance. Finally, the promotional mix of advertising, publicity, personal selling, and sales promotion presents numerous opportunities for manipulation. Advertising and personal selling can be tailored to particular consumer segments. Sales promotion can involve tactics like giveaways and coupons or virtually any activity that might elicit a product trial. Many of these marketing efforts occur during the prepurchase and purchase phases of the customer experience but may not do much to foster lasting relationships.

Customer Experience

PR can play an important role in building and sustaining relationships, but this first requires a thorough understanding of the customer or member experience. Figure 10.1 describes many of the possible areas of interaction between a consumer and an organization and can provide insight into some of the factors that likely contribute to satisfaction and dissatisfaction. Tincher (2014) reports that organizations must consider differences in the **customer experience (CX)** based on the person, the stage of the journey, and the unique perspective the customer brings to the experience. Tincher also suggests that the customer journey includes two critical moments: friction points and moments of truth. Friction points are steps in the journey that cause frustration or dissatisfaction. Moments of truth are those instants where the consumer decides to persist or abandon the journey. Attempts to map the customer journey often begin with identifying the physical and digital **touchpoints** (individual points of interaction) during various stages of the consumer experience, from awareness to consideration to acquisition to service. Tincher and Newton (2019) report that the three most important elements to successful **customer journey mapping** are

- broad cross-functional involvement (involving more than just the marketing department),
- involvement of customers in the process (seeing the journey through the eyes of the customer), and

- selecting the right journey map (recognizing the significance of various components of the journey, e.g., investigative phase).

More sophisticated journey maps will include efforts to identify questions consumers may have and emotions they may be experiencing during different stages of the journey (e.g., is a customer pleased with the available seating options, or frustrated with the inability to use a particular credit card?).

Creating a journey map may help identify some overlooked points of interaction. Connections can occur in a variety of ways, from advertising exposure to billing inquiries, and involve both direct and indirect contact. Some contacts may even involve interactions over which the organization has no control, such as review sites (unmanaged touchpoints). All these interactions contribute to the customer's perceptions about the organization. For example, the consumer may interact with a minor league baseball organization on the phone, at the ticket window, at the concession stand, through various facility services and amenities, and on the team website. The organization must then determine whether particular attributes of the CX are more crucial to each interaction. For instance, the concession interaction may be judged on criteria such as price, quality of food, breadth of menu, speed of service, and courtesy of service. Establishing the priority of these attributes for a consumer will provide insight into what is most influential to the customer's satisfaction. If consumers are simply asked to evaluate their satisfaction with the concession experience, the results may not

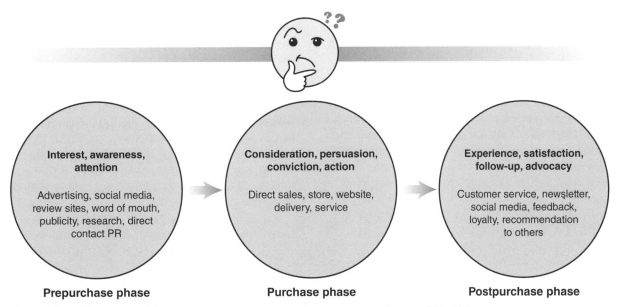

Figure 10.1 The phases of the customer experience contain many opportunities for PR activity.

reveal which attributes have the most influence on concession-buying behavior. Dissatisfaction with price may not alter buying behavior (since options are limited), whereas serving a hot dog that tastes like an old army boot may change consumption patterns a great deal. Rawson, Duncan, and Jones (2013) suggest that more touchpoints create additional complexity in managing the customer experience. Often customers will be dissatisfied with the cumulative experience rather than one particular component of the experience. Journey mapping that attempts to incorporate customer feelings and emotions will help clarify the nature of the customer experience with greater context.

Identifying where PR best fits into impacting the customer journey starts with looking at those phases of the customer experience where PR can contribute most to the building or sustaining of relationships. Direct contact PR activities can be a mechanism for both attracting consumers and nurturing relationships after purchase. Activities such as professional baseball teams' use of winter caravans to keep in touch with fans are primarily designed to build relationships rather than sell tickets. As an example, the Minnesota Twins' winter caravan is one of the most extensive in professional sports. The 2019 caravan traveled to 40 communities up to 500 miles (800 km) from Minneapolis–St. Paul to visit people who are hardly major ticket purchasers. Teams of current and former players visit schools, hospitals, businesses, and service groups with a traditional "hot-stove" program each evening (mlb.com/twins/community/winter-caravan). In many cases these efforts are directed toward smaller markets composed primarily of media consumers, and the marketing value may be tied to potentially higher media rights fees or additional value to sponsorship deals. Open houses, draft parties, preseason "fanfests," and grand openings can all be used to nurture relationships with consumers. While some direct marketing activity may occur during these events, it is often secondary to the chance to simply connect with clientele. Such occasions provide a chance to listen and engage in dialogue, an activity that is frequently overlooked when only transactional relationships exist. In addition, important information can be collected and prospects can be identified that can lead to more traditional marketing activity.

Another prepurchase PR role involves the efforts to craft image and tell compelling stories that resonate with the consumer. While advertising typically involves short targeted messages, storytelling deals with broader impressions about the organization and can be delivered through a variety of media. Helping consumers relate to people (e.g., athletes) or organizational contributions to the community (e.g., service activities) can create favorable and memorable feelings and may be received more readily than advertising.

The postpurchase phase also provides ample opportunity for PR to contribute to sustaining customer relationships. Complaint handling, follow-up communication, and satisfaction assessment (discussed later) are all PR-oriented activities that can be critical in fostering lasting customer relationships.

Customer Lifetime Value

While most discussion about consumer relationships is found in marketing literature, PR activity plays an increasingly important role in the development of relationships with consumers and members as sport organizations become more attentive to the value of long-term loyalty. Many of the strategies designed to build enduring relationships with customers are based on the idea that the customer is a financial asset. Blattberg, Getz, and Thomas (2001) used the concept of **customer equity** to address the value of a customer relationship over its life cycle, from prospect to early buyer to core customer to defector. Customer equity involves measuring both the costs of and revenue produced by the activities used to acquire and retain customers as well as efforts to add value to the relationship.

From a strategic standpoint, the value equity in spectator sport scale (VESSS) developed by Sweeney (2008) is an exceptionally thorough effort to address the factors that drive customer equity. Using a framework of value equity, brand equity, and relationship equity as the foundation (Rust, Zeithaml, & Lemon, 2000), Sweeney isolated a variety of elements within each of these categories as key factors contributing to customer equity (see figure 10.2). While the value equity and brand equity elements are primarily oriented toward marketing, the relationship equity factors are influenced by both strategic and tactical PR activities to some degree. Organizations attempt not only to provide products and services that customers value but also to create strong brand identity and retention strategies that increase customer equity.

Fader (2012) uses the concept of customer centricity—the alignment of product development and delivery with the current and future needs of the highest-value customers—as a way of focusing organizational attention and resources most efficiently. Fader and Toms (2018) define **customer lifetime value (CLV)** as a predictive measure that

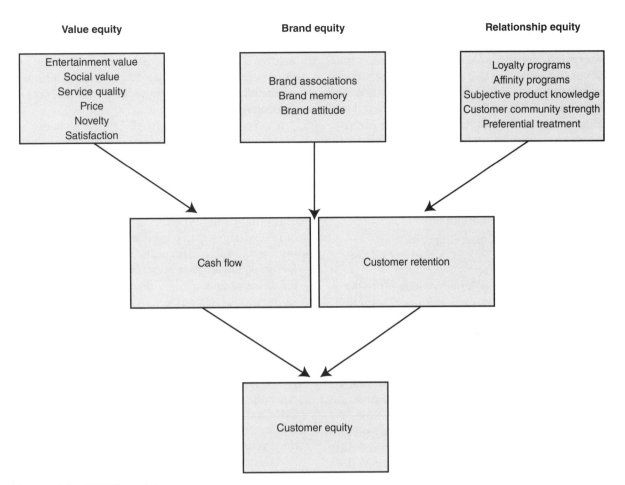

Value equity

Entertainment value
Social value
Service quality
Price
Novelty
Satisfaction

Brand equity

Brand associations
Brand memory
Brand attitude

Relationship equity

Loyalty programs
Affinity programs
Subjective product knowledge
Customer community strength
Preferential treatment

Cash flow

Customer retention

Customer equity

Figure 10.2 VESSS model.

Based on Sweeney (2008).

looks at the length of the customer relationship, the number of transactions, the value of those transactions, and other activities the customer may engage in (e.g., visiting the website, posting ratings, referring other customers). Fader and Toms suggest that CLV should be the driving force behind the development and delivery of products and services to the highest-value customers.

As relationships are established with customers and members, the goal is to expand and solidify those relationships by moving them into the core customer category. Core customers are characterized by larger and more repetitive purchase behaviors (e.g., season-ticket holders for multiple years). Consumers who shop with a retailer frequently or regularly make sizable purchases should receive treatment that matches their patronage. The value of loyal season-ticket holders to an organization clearly warrants a different level of attention than that offered to the occasional consumer who attends only sporadically.

A town hall meeting with season-ticket holders is an example of a PR activity designed to communicate directly with a team's most valuable customers. Organizations must be aware of CLV and allocate resources accordingly. The **80-20 rule** (also known as the Pareto Principle) is a reasonable rule of thumb. This principle suggests that 80% of revenue will be produced by 20% of customers. Customer equity management allows organizations to make reasoned decisions about where resources should be allocated in prospecting for new clientele, serving existing customers at various levels of consumption, retaining core customers, and reacting to defectors.

Customer Relationship Management Tools

One of the best ways to engender loyalty and increase retention is to know your customers and members well. In recent years sport organizations have become much more cognizant of the value of persistent and personalized relationships and **customer relationship management (CRM)** tools have been used to enhance that effort. There are broader perspectives of CRM such as that of Swift (2001), who defined CRM as the effort to understand and influence customer behavior in order to improve customer acquisition, retention, loyalty, and profitability. This effort includes

1. finding customers,
2. getting to know them,
3. communicating with them,
4. ensuring their satisfaction, and
5. retaining them.

Narrower descriptions often focus on CRM as the software used to track consumer transactions and other customer information to strengthen an operation's ability to serve its customers. "True CRM brings together information from all data sources within an organization (and where appropriate, from outside the organization) to give one, holistic view of each customer in real time" (Destination CRM.com, n.d.). What is CRM . . . (n.d.) outlines the specific benefits of CRM software, including greater efficiency and collaboration; greater accountability; increased customer engagement; and more data availability through a variety of features such as function automation, tracking, analytics and report generation, information access, and communication. Gaille (2015) cites the need for building a centralized consumer data bank that can be readily accessed by everyone in the organization who may have a need for it. Such information is valuable for a variety of marketing and communication purposes and for building consumer relationships while also providing data mining opportunities that can help organizations determine which marketing and PR strategies are working well and which might need to be changed. The features list for one brand of CRM software for sport organizations and clubs (SportsCRM, n.d.) could be categorized into four general areas:

- Organizational elements: registration, scheduling, tournament management
- Transactional elements: fee payments, account management, online store
- Informational elements: statistics, standings, awards
- Communication elements: announcements, targeted e-mail, newsletters

Each element provides potential insights about the clientele. Scott (2018) reports that sport teams are using CRM to build customer profiles, tailor and target communications and sales efforts, enhance sponsor integration with the fan base, and increase fan engagement.

Data collected through CRM results in better use of analytics tools to understand both individual consumers and identify or clarify various consumer segments. Sport organizations can now go well beyond collecting routine demographic information about their clientele. Computerized exercise equipment logs types of activity and frequency of use. Membership cards and access cards can be scanned to record times and days that patrons use facilities. Loyalty cards can be used to monitor the behavior of fans as they purchase tickets, concessions, and merchandise. Customer experience with websites can be assessed using click patterns. Ruth (2017) suggests that personalized marketing strategies enhance retention but require good data. She encourages incorporating social media profiles, web analytics, referral information, survey results, and experiential marketing information into the CRM database.

Customer relationship management tools have blurred traditional marketing and PR roles. Although much of the information collected in a well-designed CRM program will be used in direct marketing efforts (e.g., tailoring product offerings and modifications, targeting advertising, and adjusting pricing strategies), it can also be the basis for PR communications that can play a role in both the acquisition and retention of customers. Fitness clubs, tennis facilities, YMCAs, and country clubs are a few of the sport-related organizations that use membership as a primary source of revenue. These contractual relationships often result in transactions that are very intermittent in nature. Many of these operations function in a very competitive environment, and member retention is essential. The cost of acquiring a new member is typically five times greater than that of retaining a current member. CRM tools can help produce communication with members that occurs regularly rather than sporadically and provides the opportunity to solicit feedback about problems and difficulties. A consistent, systematic communication process conditions members to more regular interaction in the continual effort to meet member expectations (Gulko, 2003).

One important PR issue of concern when collecting and using client information is data security. Client trust and confidence can be quickly undermined by data breaches, as many organizations have discovered. For example, wearable fitness technology collects enormous amounts of information that might be problematic if shared or leaked. A Tufts University study (Greenwald, 2017) suggests that a variety of security precautions be taken to increase security awareness. Routine security audits, employee security education, and strong encryption and authentication protocols are among the best ways to make sure data is secure.

Membership Relationship Management Software

A variety of communication channels, from traditional communication forms to websites and various social media options, can be tailored to various membership segments and preferences. **Membership relationship management (MRM)** software (a specialized version of CRM software) is available to help maintain a member database; serve as a membership information portal; and manage dues, events and renewals. Many clubs have multigenerational memberships that require thoughtful decisions about appropriate communication channels. Using an ineffective medium while notifying members of an upcoming event may produce disappointing results.

Recency, Frequency, and Monetary Analysis

Several mechanisms are used to measure customer value. **Recency, frequency, and monetary (RFM) analysis** is one such tool. Information is collected about the frequency and recency of customer transactions as well as the amount spent on the transactions in an effort to identify the most valuable customers. The data can then be used to segment customers and more effectively target them based on their consumption patterns. CRM systems can assist in data collection and the categorization of customers based on purchase frequency, number of units purchased, and price paid, which can then serve to provide supporting rationale for marketing and PR decisions (Blattberg, Getz, & Thomas, 2001; Weinstein, 2002; Fader & Toms, 2018).

Net Promoter Score

Reichheld's **Net Promoter Score (NPS)** is one approach to assessing the customer experience. NPS is generated by asking customers a single question: "On a scale of 0 to 10, how likely would you be to recommend this company or product to a friend or a colleague and why?" Customers are then classified into one of three groups—promoters, passives, and detractors—based on how they respond (Markey, Reichheld, & Dullweber, 2009). Such a measure is an effort to provide information about both satisfaction and loyalty while providing valuable insights into customer likes and dislikes.

Consumer Satisfaction Survey

One of the best ways to assess customer satisfaction is to ask customers. Surveys are commonly used to help organizations generate feedback from customers about various aspects of the customer experience and can be tailored to specific elements of the customer journey. Nicholls, Gilbert, and Roslow (1998) developed a consumer satisfaction survey that is still a good starting point for the assessment of customer satisfaction; many of the items have a strong public relations orientation. The survey includes components of both personal service satisfaction and satisfaction with the service setting, each of which may be relevant for a variety of sport organizations. Carter (2017) created a list of satisfaction factors, recognizing that many consumers at least initiate the consumption process online. The following list provides a compilation of factors that are likely to impact customer satisfaction:

Basic Customer Satisfaction Factors

- Product quality
- Product choice
- Deliver on promises
- Courtesy
- Guarantees
- Timeliness and speed
- Responsiveness to problems
- Competence of assistance
- Access to products and services
- Website navigation ease
- Organizational memory of the customer
- Understandable language and communications ease
- Decisional and transactional convenience
- Sense of community
- Promptness
- Cleanliness
- Security and safety

Concern for the setting is especially relevant for many sport organizations because the setting is often an important component of the customer's overall experience. As an example, feeling safe in the parking lot of a stadium or aggravated by long lines to the restrooms may be important aspects of the customer experience. A clean and well-maintained workout area is an expectation for fitness club patrons.

For spectator sport, fan satisfaction is likely a function of several different elements of the experience. Yoshida and James (2010) attempted to distinguish between the influence of game satisfaction and service satisfaction on subsequent fan behavior. One interesting finding in this study was that game satisfaction was reported to have an influence on behavioral intentions in both the United States and Japan but that the relationship between service quality satisfaction and behavioral intentions was significant only in Japan.

Measuring customer satisfaction can produce important benefits for any sport organization, but measurements should be tailored to specific organizational circumstances and different consumers. Using customer journey mapping will help to identify critical aspects of the customer experience and serve as the basis for a well-designed assessment effort. Sources of information to achieve assessment objectives can be current and former customers, competitors' customers, and noncustomers, as well as employees. Beyond the obvious benefits of collecting information about the likes and dislikes of the consumer, periodic purposeful assessment provides a mechanism for regular two-way communication between the organization and its patrons. These efforts can serve as the foundation for product and service improvement and for nurturing, maintaining, and even repairing relationships with customers. Such information becomes even more valuable as it is shared among the different parts of the organization rather than kept in the customer service or marketing silo.

Customer Loyalty

It is common knowledge that keeping existing customers is less expensive and more profitable than finding new ones. Customer satisfaction fosters customer loyalty, which is reflected in higher retention rates (also referred to as lower "churn" rates). Kotler (2000) and Reichheld (n.d.) noted that satisfied customers stay loyal longer, talk more favorably about the organization, pay less attention to the competition, are less sensitive to price, and cost less to serve than new customers. As Severson (2017) points out, however, satisfaction and loyalty are not the same. Satisfaction looks backward at past experience rather than at future intent. Loyalty focuses on the customer's willingness to purchase again and recommend the product or service to others.

Satisfaction is the precursor to retention and loyalty. Effective customer retention helps control customer acquisition costs. Resources wisely spent retaining high-value customers may be more profitable than spending heavily trying to recruit new customers. Tracking retention rates is easier for some sport organizations that have contractual (renewable) relationships with their consumers. For example, teams that sell season tickets should have both industry benchmarks and organizational history to use as retention guidelines. Health and fitness clubs see average retention rates of around 72% (Archibald, 2016). New contractual subscription relationships with sport-related organizations such as Peloton Digital or Fitbit Premium can also readily track defection rates. Even small improvements in preventing defection can have a profound effect on profitability. Loyal customers tend to increase spending over time and often require less service. They also share their satisfaction with others and become less sensitive to price. Efforts directed at getting an existing ticket holder to renew or expand a ticket package adds value to a customer who has already exhibited an appealing level of commitment. A few fortunate sport franchises have even been able to capitalize on excess demand by creating waiting lists that contain many attractive prospective customers and keeping them more closely connected to the organization through regular contact.

Loyalty comes in several forms, some of which have little to do with consumer commitment or devotion. Monopoly loyalty, convenience loyalty, habitual loyalty, and incentivized loyalty often will not be tied to true allegiance. Committed loyalty, however, reflects consumers' belief that they are buying the best product or service (SaferPak, 2004). Most consumers will exhibit a certain level of loyalty tied to limited options (no other choices), convenience (closest or easiest option), or habit (what they have always done). Many sport operations use incentivized loyalty by encouraging repeat consumption through some form of reward. Loyalty cards that record consumption are commonly used by sporting goods stores (e.g., Dick's Sporting Goods ScoreCard

Facilitating the social component to sport consumption contributes to greater fan satisfaction and loyalty.

© J. Alan Paul Photography

Rewards Program) and professional teams (e.g., Red Sox Rewards).

As sport organizations try to foster greater commitment, loyalty programs can drive season-ticket holder engagement and satisfaction with the added benefit of providing data on fans that can be leveraged in efforts to improve sponsor engagement and activation. The IEG Sponsorship Report (2017) does recommend that these programs should not be overly complicated and should use fresh redemption items, perhaps tied to intangible experiences, since loyal fans already have much of the typical team-related merchandise. Research on loyalty programs in Japan revealed that the sense of community and special treatment received were of greater importance than price benefits provided by the program (Yoshida, Gordon, & Hedlund, 2018). Fader & Toms (2018) suggest that loyalty programs can be an important customer retention and development tool but are probably more effective when targeting low- and mid-value customers, while offering premium services may be more useful for high-value customers. Rosenbaum, Ostrom, and Kuntze (2005) suggested that communal loyalty programs—organizationally sponsored loyalty programs that provide members a sense of community and belonging—may be effective for certain organizations (an example is the Harley Owners Group—the HOG). Such communal groups need to provide a sense of belonging, offer a feeling of influence, meet some need (e.g., status), and create an emotional bond.

Because much sport consumption involves a social component with a strong emotional connection, sport organizations would be well served to nurture this aspect of consumption. A familiar sport example is tailgating—an experience that for some is as important as the game itself. Many sport operations might benefit from creating or facilitating these types of social experiences and connections and tap into the consumer's "fear of missing out," or FOMO. Digital communities can be enabled by sport organizations through their own websites using a range of social media sites like Facebook, Twitter, or Instagram. Communal connections can also be supported when communities are constructed outside the organization's direct control. Some examples include MyFitnessPal.com and GolfLink.com, which foster a sense of community for fitness buffs and golfers while providing a variety of information and resources about those respective activities.

The goal of committed loyalty, which reflects consumers' devotion tied to their belief in the product or service, resembles what Fullerton (2003) described as affective commitment, which can be closely associated with friendship, rapport, and trust. This type of emotional connection contrasts with continuance commitment, which is predicated on dependence, lack of choice, and the cost or inconvenience of switching. Consumer loyalty may be influenced by both types of commitment, but affective commitment tends to be more effective at producing the kind of dedication that manifests itself in consumers who may accept higher prices, travel farther, resist switching, and more readily recommend the product or service to others.

Organizations should constantly question what they are doing to merit consumer loyalty. Developing and keeping loyal customers is an increasingly challenging pursuit. The ability to maintain loyalty is eroding in the face of product innovation and technological advances that have expanded consumer options and information. The assortment of footwear choices is apparent in the inventory displayed in a large sporting goods store, and e-commerce now allows people to "shop the world" digitally with extraordinary convenience. Free shipping, free returns, price comparisons, service ratings, and product reviews are a few clicks away. This array of choices extends to sports spectators as well. Whereas a fan might once have loyally attended games of a small-college football team, the same fan might find it difficult to pass up the opportunity to watch multiple top-notch games in the comfort of the living room or with the convenience of a digital device.

Cable, satellite, and subscription services as well as the Internet provide access to so many games that loyalty in the form of live attendance is being challenged. Major League Baseball attendance dropped below 70 million in 2019 for the first time since 2003, experiencing its sixth decline in seven years (Fisher, 2019). While National Football League (NFL) attendance was still at 96%-of capacity in 2018, average game attendance was at its lowest since 2010 (McClung, 2019). Many college football and basketball programs are also experiencing rather significant attendance problems, particularly among the student population. There are a variety of explanations for these attendance problems, from pace of play and length of games, to expensive tickets, to the convenience of watching games on TV at home or digitally while doing other things. While fans may still have the loyalty to root for a particular team, such loyalty has less practical effect if it is no longer attached to attendance-related consumption.

A key to high retention rates is the ability to identify what makes customers happy and what irritates them along the journey. Timm (2001) identified six areas of opportunity for addressing consumer expectations and, by extension, six opportunities to build customer relationships. These six areas are value, information, speed, personality, add-ons, and convenience (VISPAC). Meeting or exceeding what the consumer expects in any or all of these areas increases the likelihood of retaining customers. While some of these areas are largely within the scope of direct marketing, others are oriented more toward PR. The ways these areas are addressed will have a powerful influence on the consumer's perception of the organization.

Value and Add-ons

Value and add-ons are largely connected to product or service quality. Timm (2001) defined value as the quality of a product or service relative to its price. Although value is, in the final analysis, a personal determination, it may be measured in more specific terms depending on the nature of the product. As an example, sports equipment may be purchased with relatively objective expectations about durability, reliability, or performance features. The purchaser of a ticket to an event may assess value based on a subjective set of expectations related to various aspects of the customer experience, such as entertainment quality, stadium aesthetics, or amenities like parking convenience or concession quality. A fitness club member may base the quality of his or her experience on criteria that could include anything from the cleanliness of the facility, to the variety of available equipment, to the quality of aerobics instruction or the convenience of the club's hours of operation. Regardless of what is being consumed, the organization must have some idea of criteria consumers use to assess value. As mentioned earlier in the chapter, understanding the CX through the customer's eyes is essential to establishing the parameters for satisfaction.

Add-ons can enhance the customer's sense of value. Supplementing the purchase of a set of golf clubs with a golf bag, or a new fitness club membership with a free fitness assessment, can make consumers feel as if their purchase has added value. Satisfaction or quality guarantees are also common add-ons that give the consumer some purchase security and instill confidence that the organization stands behind its product. In many cases, these additional benefits are directly associated with PR efforts to enhance customer relationships. Selling season tickets has become increasingly difficult in many sports because of a robust secondary market for tickets. Many consumers would prefer to pay a premium on the secondary market on a game-by-game basis rather than make the financial and time commitment required for the purchase of a season ticket. Add-ons may be a way to encourage season-ticket purchases. For example, the Chicago Bulls' description of season-ticket benefits specifically mentions "exclusive discounts, priority access, VIP access and experiences, convenience, gifts, and special add ons" (https://www.nba.com/bulls /tickets/seasons#).

Convenience and Speed

Convenience and speed are associated with quality of service. Meeting consumer expectations in these areas is particularly important in a culture that expects immediacy. In some cases these attributes are part of the product or service. For example, personal trainers who come to the client, and home exercise equipment with interactive displays, are examples of convenience built directly into the product or service. Professional teams have made it much more convenient to purchase and exchange tickets, while technology gives online ticket buyers a virtual view from various locations in the stadium as an added convenience. Morgan (2017) suggests that companies enhance their reputation when they make the consumer's life easier. Making customers do more work "when they assume customers know things that they don't, when they make customers go through extra steps to get the help they need, or when they aren't available at convenient times" often makes it easier on employees at the expense of the customers.

Speed of service, delivery, and response to complaints all influence consumer satisfaction. Anyone who has spent half an hour on the phone trying to reach the right person or any live person at all can identify with the frustration produced by slow or impersonal service. Long lines at the checkout counter or concession stand will result in annoyed customers. Failure to meet promised delivery dates for tournament T-shirts or deadlines for game programs will cost a supplier future business and damage its reputation. In the world of e-commerce, companies are becoming much more attentive to making the process as seamless as possible with free shipping and expeditious return systems and policies.

Information and Personality

Perhaps the two areas most directly associated with PR are information and personality. Sport organizations use information in a variety of ways to engage the consumer and add value to their product. Information may be part of a service such as personal instruction on how to use all the computer features on a new exercise bike. Information may take the form of a follow-up phone call to see how well the consumer is adjusting to a new set of fitted golf clubs. In some cases, information can be delivered in less personal ways, through e-mail or signage. Even the scoreboard can be used as a PR tool by providing information that shows an appreciation for the fans, such as greetings for groups, birthday and anniversary wishes, candid shots of spectators, and so on.

Personality is also an opportunity to create satisfied customers, and it provides a clear example of PR as the responsibility of everyone in the organization. Treating the consumer with courtesy and

Friendly and courteous frontline employees are critically important pieces in the PR landscape.

© Getty Images/andresr

consideration can make a powerful impression. Many people serve as the "face" of the organization, notably those who make the first direct contact with patrons. Employees such as greeters, ushers, ticket takers, salespeople, front-desk personnel, administrative assistants, and cashiers are on the PR front line. These are touchpoints that should not be ignored, and their influence on consumers should not be undervalued. Being polite, friendly, and sincere conveys the image that most organizations want to transmit to their clientele.

Customer Service and Support

Customer service and support are important antecedents to satisfaction, with poor customer service often resulting in defection. Dixon, Ponomareff, Turner, and DeLisi (2017) suggest that as organizations facilitate more customer self-service, front-line service representatives get increasingly difficult problems that the customers have not been able to solve on their own. Their research indicates that the most effective customer service representatives have the skills and tools to deliver quick and clear guidance that simplifies the customer experience. Toister (2017) contends that a customer-focused culture must be supported by hiring the right employees and training and empowering them to support the customer focus. In many cases, the "quality of service" aspect of the customer relationship focuses on customer problems and complaints. Timm (2001) put problems into three categories: value turnoffs, system turnoffs, and people turnoffs. Value turnoffs involve products or services that fail to meet the consumer's quality expectations. Without product improvements or price manipulation, value turnoffs may be difficult to resolve.

Responses to system turnoffs and people turnoffs have a much clearer connection to PR. Systems such as facilities, record keeping, sales and return policies, and communications are frequent sources of customer dissatisfaction. The extent to which these turnoffs can be addressed varies a great deal. Baer (2016) contends that there is a huge disconnect between how well businesses believe they are serving customers and how well customers believe they are being served. He mentions four benefits to answering complaints:

- Conversion of unhappy customers to happy or neutral customers
- Creation of customer advocacy
- Delivery of valuable information about problems
- Differentiation from competitors who are less responsive to complaints

Cook (2012) views customer dissatisfaction as an opportunity to reinforce the consumer relationship by encouraging customers to voice complaints. Quick and empathetic response to criticisms and problems can win over customers and may enhance the likelihood of a continued affiliation. Soliciting negative feedback can also ward off additional future complaints. And just as dissatisfied customers will spread the word of their discontent at a rapid rate, patrons whose problems were solved will become advocates for the competence and responsiveness of the organization. Word-of-mouth support is powerful because it has a credibility that organization-initiated messages do not. One challenge to handling many consumer complaints is they are often not made directly. In a world of **consumer-generated media (CGM)**, customers' ability to voice dissatisfaction to large numbers of people quickly has changed how organizations must approach customer service and monitor customer satisfaction. Problems and incidents that are chronicled on Facebook, described in a Yelp review, or documented on YouTube can create PR troubles that can persist and spread rapidly. Addressing these complaints may require the use of social listening services (Google Alerts and Hootsuite are two examples). These services can help find indirect complaints and allow a more rapid response. These efforts allow sport operations to be more proactive and control adverse situations more effectively (MacDonald, 2020).

Sponsor Relationships

One of the most important exchange relationships for many sport organizations is the relationship with sponsors. Mullin, Hardy, and Sutton (2014) define sponsorship as the "acquisition of rights to affiliate or directly associate with a product, person, organization, team, league or event for the purpose of deriving benefits related to that affiliation" (p. 315). These associations provide sport organizations and events with important financial resources and often other goods and services. Professional teams, college and high school athletics programs, sport governing bodies such as the National Collegiate Athletic Association (NCAA), and local youth sport leagues, as well as sport events of all types such as golf and tennis tournaments, bowl games, races,

Table 10.1 Sponsorship Examples

Sponsor	Partner	Contract value (begins in)
Uniqlo	Roger Federer	$300M/10 years (2018)
Mercedes-Benz	Atlanta Falcons Stadium	$324M/27 years (2015)
Chevrolet	Manchester United	$559M/7 years (2014)
Under Armour	University of California, Los Angeles	$280M/15 years (2016)
Outback Steakhouse	Outback Bowl	$48.5M/7 years (2019)
PGA title sponsors	PGA Tour event	$8M–$13M/year
Dreamstyle Remodeling	University of New Mexico	$9M/10 years (2017)
Nextier Bank	Seneca Valley (Pennsylvania) High School	$100K/10 years (2016)

and sport camps, use sponsors as a vital revenue source. About 70% ($17 billion) of North American sponsorship spending is directed toward sport (IEG Sponsorship, 2018). Multimillion-dollar sponsorship deals for stadium naming rights (Broughton, 2018) and the Olympic Partners (TOP) programme are just the tip of the sport sponsorship "iceberg." (See table 10.1 for sponsorship examples.)

Although an element of philanthropy may motivate a few sponsors, most substantive sponsorship arrangements are business deals with sponsors expecting a return on investment (ROI). The mindset has become one of developing corporate partnerships, and many partnership options exist as companies look to maximize their ROI.

Sponsor relationships have many of the same characteristics as customer relationships. The topics of customer equity, satisfaction, service, and retention that have been discussed in the previous sections can be applied to sponsor relationships as well. The development of ongoing relationships addresses many of the same concerns through the different phases, from prospecting and acquisition through service and support, to achieve high retention rates and minimize defection. Teams, sport organizations, and events must have the same understanding of the companies they target as sponsors as these entities have of the customers they target when marketing products and services. Sport organizations must customize their efforts in building and maintaining their affiliations with sponsors. Collecting data about sponsors is essential to building constructive, lasting relationships. Knowing about a company's sponsorship history, its decision makers, its sponsorship budget, its desired sponsorship benefits, and its decisional time frame will be invaluable in tailoring a sponsorship proposal and communicating it to the right

people in the right way. Just as efforts are made to encourage consumers to feel that they are part of the organization, sponsor relations now emphasize the "partnership" quality of the association. Four important elements in building and sustaining successful sponsor relationships include sponsor equity, service and support, sponsor satisfaction, and sponsor loyalty and retention.

Sponsor Commitment Levels

Most sport organizations have a tiered system of sponsorship opportunities so that the organizations can offer a variety of levels of sponsorship commitment. Few firms can afford the financial commitment required to be a title sponsor for a major event or to purchase the naming rights to a major sport facility. Tiered sponsorship broadens the prospect base and provides opportunities for a much wider range of corporate involvement. The financial commitment required for sponsors for major professional sport teams may range from a few thousand dollars to several million dollars. Although every sponsor is important, it is only logical that certain sponsors will receive extra attention based on the commitment that they have made. Replacing a small-scale sponsor may be inconvenient, but replacing a multimillion-dollar sponsor can take years. Attending to sponsor equity involves prioritizing relationship efforts based on the size and length of sponsorship commitment and is a way of recognizing the differential value of an organization's sponsors. Such attention may even require dedicating personnel to provide direct support for the most valuable sponsors.

Case Study

ALCOHOL SPONSORSHIP AND COLLEGE ATHLETICS

As the marketing director of a Football Championship Subdivision (FCS) athletics department at a university of 15,000 students, you are responsible for generating revenue through the sale of promotional and sponsorship opportunities. The university does not currently sell alcohol at athletic events although it is served in VIP areas (donor areas at football, basketball, and hockey games). The football stadium seats about 18,000 and the new basketball arena being built will hold about 4,000. Attendance rarely reaches half of capacity for basketball, and football attendance averages about 7,500 with students comprising about 20% of those attending.

Although the NCAA has discouraged alcohol advertising and sales in the past, numerous schools have developed more liberal alcohol sales policies in recent years, claiming alcohol sales will improve the fan experience. You have crafted a proposal for a wide-ranging promotional package that you would like to present to a large beer company. The proposal requests $150,000 in exchange for a variety of advertising and promotional benefits. The proposal *does not* include the sale of alcohol at events but does include a clause that could double the value of the sponsorship package if alcohol sales commence. The proposal would produce more far revenue than any sponsorship deal the program has ever had. The issue of alcohol and campus life is a particularly sensitive one at the university, which has a reputation as a party school; recurring incidents of binge drinking have resulted in a substantial amount of negative publicity. Additionally, there is growing evidence of the link between alcohol and sexual assault, particularly on college campuses. Most of the Title IX incidents reported on campus in the past three to four years have involved some degree of irresponsible alcohol use. From a financial perspective, the department is continually being asked to look for additional revenue to supplement its budget. Currently, the program generates only about $7 million (28%) of the $25 million athletics budget. The institution subsidizes the rest with student fees and money from the general fund (tuition).

Discussion Questions

1. What is the appeal of this sponsorship deal for the beer company?
2. Who are the decision makers at the school that you will need to persuade for approval of this deal? What kinds of information would you need to support your arguments?
3. Are there constituents who will likely oppose this proposal? How might you counter their arguments?
4. What response would you have for the contention that this is a money grab that ignores important social concerns?

Sponsor Service and Support

Servicing and supporting sponsorship partners will affect the organization's ability to satisfy and retain them. In many respects, basic customer service principles apply to sponsors just as they do to traditional customer relationships. Perhaps the most important mechanism for sponsor support is an effective communications system. Clear communications can minimize many of the problems that can hinder the organization's relationship with sponsors. Berg (2015) suggests nine ways to keep sponsors happy:

1. Cater to sponsors' unique needs
2. Get to know the sponsors on a personal level
3. Integrate sponsors into the event
4. Find digital space opportunities
5. Provide sponsors with on-site perks (e.g., exclusive "meet and greets")
6. Facilitate networking
7. Manage sponsor expectations
8. Provide post-event support and data
9. Send personalized thank-you notes

Helping sponsors achieve their sponsorship objectives and solve their problems will lead to the sponsors wanting to maintain the relationship.

"**Sponsorship activation** includes all the means one company/brand can use to maximize the exposure of the sponsorship program; promotions,

Many sponsors derive enormous PR benefits from their affiliation with charitable causes.
Andy Lyons/Getty Images

in-store activities, hospitalities, special events, licensing, show cases, PR activities and so on" (Tafa, 2017; emphasis added). This is certainly one area where sport organizations can be of tremendous assistance in providing service and support for their sponsors. While many activation activities are tied directly to marketing, many others are more PR-oriented. Many aspects of digital activation are driven by communication. Content, and storytelling that engages target audiences, taps into the strengths of PR to create and extend relationships (How to activate . . . , n.d.). Using social media platforms to create additional exposure leverages low-cost controlled media to add value to sponsorships. These activities are particularly important to sponsors of events that are tied to charitable causes and to sponsors of nonprofit organizations and events. The value of the goodwill generated by FedEx's long affiliation with the PGA tournament benefiting St. Jude Children's Research Hospital is hard to measure. Many local charitable events (e.g., road races, golf tournaments) have presenting sponsors along with an array of other sponsors seeking the benefits of being connected with worthy community causes.

Sponsor Satisfaction

Sponsor satisfaction is predicated on how well sponsor needs and expectations are met. Organizations that solicit sponsors need to know what benefits are being sought and how the sport organization might best accommodate sponsor interests. Sport organizations can accomplish this by matching the list of sponsor needs with a list of organizational deliverables. A list of sponsor needs should be developed based on thorough research of prospective sponsors so that sponsorship proposals can be constructed specifically for particular clients. Today, that list of needs almost certainly will include digital and social media opportunities (Jessop, 2014). IEG (IEG Sponsorship, 2018) reports that after exclusivity, presence on digital, social, and mobile media is most desired by sponsors. Tate (n.d.) addresses the importance of sponsorship to NASCAR and suggests that a social channel presence should be just the beginning of a digital strategy. Soliciting sponsor input and feedback will help cultivate the sponsor relationship, and integrating sponsors' insights will help ensure their goals are being met. Expanding social channel reach by creating engaging content throughout the NASCAR season adds value to the social component of the sponsorship.

Developing a list of deliverables involves conducting a complete assessment of organizational assets that might be of interest to sponsors. The following lists illustrate what sponsors might be looking for and what sport organizations might have to offer.

Sponsor Needs and Wants

- Exposure, visibility
- Increased sales
- Product distribution and trials
- Increased store traffic
- Goodwill
- Community involvement
- Media attention
- Image enhancement
- Corporate entertainment and hospitality
- Corporate networking (B2B)
- Employee recognition
- Competitive advantage
- Targeted market reach
- Cross-promotion opportunities
- Link to charity partner
- Audience information and data

Sport Organization Assets

- Tickets
- Signage space
- Media coverage
- Naming rights
- Logo usage
- Suites and luxury boxes
- Sponsor exclusivity
- Appealing market segments
- Advertising opportunities
- Special events
- Mailing lists
- Other sponsor partners
- Organizational prestige
- Charity affiliations
- Website exposure
- Customer data

- Social media presence
- Sports personalities

A sponsorship relationship is more likely to be formed and sustained when substantial congruity is found between sponsor needs and organizational assets. Satisfaction can be reinforced with post-event or postseason reports that demonstrate how sponsor expectations have been met and added value has been provided. Sport organizations can provide information about higher-than-expected attendance, media ratings, or participation that enhances the value of the sponsorship. The annual IEG Sponsorship Survey (IEG Sponsorship, 2018) reports that the most valuable service properties can provide to their partners is help in evaluating whether the sponsorship is meeting its goals. Properties who want to help their sponsors with measurement should note that the amount of positive social media activity was the second most valuable consideration behind brand awareness. Perhaps this desire for help with measuring sponsorship effectiveness stems from that fact that nearly 8 in 10 sponsors spend less than 1% of their sponsorship budget on measurement.

Sponsor Loyalty and Retention

One measure of the quality of the relationship with sponsors is their willingness to continue the relationship. For many sport organizations, sponsorship retention is the final stage of a perpetual process depicted in figure 10.3. Quality service and support produce satisfied, loyal sponsors that are easier to retain and move to higher levels of commitment. This approach is much more cost-effective than continually prospecting for new sponsors to replace those who are dissatisfied.

Donor Relationships

Donors are another public that requires special relationship attention. The donor public has become an increasingly important asset to many sport organizations in recent years, and the role of PR as a part of the fundraising process has evolved as well. Whereas fundraising (also known as development or advancement) was once largely used for special projects often known as capital campaigns (e.g., new facilities), many sport organizations now count on donors to provide funds for operational

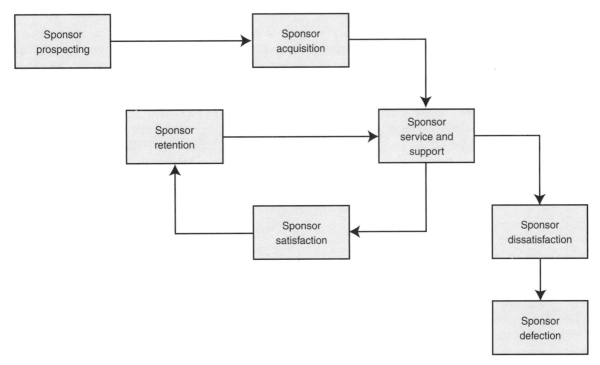

Figure 10.3 Overview of the sponsor relations process.

expenses. College athletics programs raise over $1 billion a year in donations, much of which is used for daily operations (Wolverton & Kambhampati, 2016). For many schools even at the highest levels of the NCAA (autonomy group of Division I), donor revenue is often as important as ticket revenue. As an example, between 2005 and 2018, contributions at both the University of Georgia and Auburn University of the Southeast Conference exceeded ticket revenue every year (NCAA Finances, n.d.). As you move to other tiers of NCAA athletics programs, donations as a proportion of total revenue generated by athletics are often five to six times as much as ticket revenue. In 2016, the typical Division I athletics department relied on contributions for about 23% of its generated revenue (revenue produced directly by the athletics department, including ticket sales, radio and television receipts, alumni contributions, guarantees, royalties, and NCAA distributions). The median amount for contributions at FBS schools was nearly $9.2 million (Fulks, 2017).

Hoffman (2019) states that reduced school funding is among the most serious challenges for high school athletics programs, and nearly 16% of schools report that fundraising provides at least 50% of the athletics budget. Nonprofit recreational organizations such as the YMCA rely on donors to supplement program-driven revenue and membership dues. A quick review on Charity Navigator (www.charitynavigator.org) reveals wide variation in reliance on contributions based on the size and nature of the particular Y. Donations as a percentage of total revenue may range anywhere from 10% to 60% or more. Even for-profit operations such as professional sport teams have developed nonprofit branches (e.g., Pirates Charities, Minnesota Wild Foundation, Manchester United Foundation) that raise significant amounts of money to benefit various community causes. Such efforts enhance public image and take advantage of the ardent support of the fan base.

Special project fundraising has a much clearer focus, and the goal and outcome are more easily communicated to donors. Whether the goal is renovating a weight room or building a new stadium, the costs and desired results are relatively clear. For these major capital projects, much of the early work involves PR elements aimed at cultivating relationships with donors who are being targeted for major contributions. Large gifts may take years to arrange. These donors may be individuals, corporations, or foundations that contribute to a variety of causes. When requesting large amounts of money, additional complications (e.g., tax consequences, terms of the gift, form of payment) likely require an extended period of discussion. Although soliciting large gifts is part of many fundraising efforts, it is especially important for special projects, because a few large gifts often encourage others to donate. Organizations typically announce a fund drive only after a substantial portion of the money has already been raised or at least pledged. Planned giving or legacy giving has also received more emphasis in recent years as organizations encourage donors to consider donating through estate planning. Relationship building is obviously critical to this type of fundraising.

For annual campaign fundraising, the sport organization has a more continuous relationship with donors, but how funds generated from annual campaigns are to be used is often more ambiguous. Annual campaign fundraising would likely benefit from clarifying specific purposes for such funds as a way of helping prospective donors attach tangibility to their gifts. In many respects, building this ongoing type of relationship with donors is similar to building relationships with customers. Many of the marketing strategies used to appeal to consumers can be used in attracting donors, and many CRM principles are useful in developing and retaining a donor base. Gathering demographic and contribution information (frequency of gifts, size of gifts, solicitation preference) and tailoring communication and fundraising approaches to the characteristics and motivations of each donor are basic to donor development. Such information may clarify the effectiveness of certain development tactics, supply data regarding retention and defection rates, and provide insight into the productivity of donors.

Fundraising

Effective fundraising of any type relies on knowing what motivates, satisfies, and inhibits donors. The process of identifying prospects and converting them into advocates requires patience and a combination of effective marketing and relationship-building strategies. Burnett (2002) uses the phrase *relationship fundraising* to describe the process of developing the special relationship between a cause and its supporters rather than focusing simply on raising money. Athletics programs often enjoy a special relationship with their donors. Alumni and other fans often exhibit a loyalty and passion that can be extremely beneficial in development efforts. Burchette's (2013) extensive study of athletics donor behavior repeatedly referred to the importance of relationship building. The study found that the "ability to build relationships is key to a successful athletic development," and discussed "building relationships between athletic donors and university

through regular communications and social events." Burchette wrote that the "development process is about building and maintaining relations," and "a significant relationship was found between former student-athletes that contributed to athletics . . . and their relationship with former teammates, former coaches, a current coach, an athletic fundraiser, and the athletic director." For nonprofit organizations such as the Y, supporters' attachment may be tied to membership in the organization or to the belief that the Y makes a worthy social contribution.

Wester's fundraising model in *The Four Pillars of Donor Relations* (2015) does an excellent job of identifying the elements (acknowledgment, stewardship, recognition, and engagement) crucial to building relationships with donors. She connects the gift to the science of fundraising and the donor to the art of fundraising.

The "science" of fundraising attends to the mechanics of the process, with data analytics and modeling often used to profile potential donors. The "art" of fundraising, on the other hand, focuses to a large extent on nurturing and maintaining relationships. This aspect of fundraising is "donor-centric" and focuses on the creative, storytelling aspects of the process, with the donor being cast as the hero of the story (Seven things you need . . . , 2018). Streiff (2017) outlines the mechanics of the process to include identification (prospecting), cultivation, solicitation, and stewardship. Public relations can play a role in all these phases, assisting in maintenance of donor relationships while preventing defection and improving donor productivity. Once the stewardship stage is reached, PR becomes central to extending the relationship. Weinger (2018) ties recognition and stewardship together, suggesting that the need to acknowledge donors both privately and publicly should be complemented by clear communication that donations are being used productively.

In ongoing fundraising efforts, the aim is to retain donors and move them to increased levels of contribution. But just as with consumers and sponsors, some donors are more valuable than others. Donorsearch.net (n.d.) notes that studies have shown that 88% of funds raised come from 12% of donors. This suggests that "donor lifetime value," or the monetary value a donor brings to the organization over the life of the relationship, needs to be a consideration in the different facets of the fundraising process; time, energy, and stewardship effort need to be allocated in ways appropriate to the level of donation. PR events such as luncheons, information sessions, meetings with leadership, and facility tours may be used to cultivate donors. Creating experiences and opportunities to acknowledge donors' contributions appropriately are critical to stewardship of donors. Several kinds of events may be employed both for cultivating donors and for stewardship of donors. These events often do not involve direct solicitations and are designed to develop and preserve the association with contributors. Alumni reunions during homecoming, "meet the team" parties, Hall of Fame induction dinners, and so on may involve no direct fundraising solicitation at all; they are simply opportunities to help donors feel more appreciated and connected to the program.

Because of the intermittent nature of direct interaction between fundraisers and donors, one of the most important PR roles in nurturing donor relationships is developing consistent lines of communication. Duff (2016) maintains that authentic relationships are built through the use of conversation that both asks questions and tells stories. Questions personalize donors and provide insight into their values, motivations, and priorities. The crafting and relating of stories shows donors how they are making a difference and reinforces their enthusiasm and advocacy. A variety of tactics are available to keep donors informed about organizational activities. PR skills are well suited for this informational role, using tools such as newsletters, mailings, personal contacts, thank-you notes, and acknowledgments to maintain communication continuity (Weir & Hibbert, 2000). Many college athletics departments employ newsletters and magazines to keep donors informed of activities and events, and these publications may include material that makes the recipients feel as if they are getting inside information. Social media platforms have created additional options for maintaining communication with donors, connecting them to one another, and enhancing the ability to tell the stories that will engage supporters.

Donor Motivation and Satisfaction

Understanding donor motivation is just as important to successful fundraising as understanding consumer needs is to successful marketing. Attention must be given to what prompts donors to give and to maintain and increase their support as well as what might inhibit donor involvement or produce defection. One key difference between the donor relationship and the consumer relationship is that although donors provide money, goods, or services, what they get in return is often less tangible. While some donors may contribute for the benefits they receive (e.g., preferential seating or parking), others may donate for more philanthropic reasons. Verner, Hecht, and Fansler (1998), and more recently Ko and colleagues (2013), studied the motivation of donors to athletics programs and isolated several key influencers of donor behavior. Table 10.2 lists some key motives and offers examples of ways athletics departments might accommodate these motives.

Attention to these factors is important to accommodating the needs of donors, and PR can be an important part of the overall fundraising effort. Popp, Barrett, and Weight (2016) summarized research on athletics giving by characterizing the motives as transactional and altruistic. This is an important distinction when considering donor motivation across all elements of the sport industry. While donors to college athletics organizations may be more transaction oriented (focused on what they get for the donation), someone donating to a high school

Table 10.2 Donor Motivations

Motivational factor	Fulfilled through
Recognition	Naming rights, plaques, print acknowledgment
Vicarious involvement	Inside information, connections to successful teams
Tangible benefits	Priority seating, designated parking
Power	Access to leadership, influence on decisions
Commitment	Volunteer opportunity, helping meet needs
Socialization/affiliation	Booster clubs, social events, giving societies
Impact	Contributions to new facilities, team-specific gifts
Philanthropy	Endowed scholarships, communicating gift benefits

athletics program or a Y may have more altruistic motives (focused on how the gift helps others). The motivational complexity driving donor behavior provides additional evidence of the importance of getting to know donors on a more personal level. Donor satisfaction is vital to sustaining relationships. In some cases, donors will have very explicit expectations for their contributions, while for others (particularly those whose motives are primarily altruistic), satisfaction criteria may be somewhat more ambiguous. Organizations must make donors feel they have made important contributions to organizational progress, and PR plays a vital role in telling the stories that demonstrate donor impact.

Donor Retention

Determining the barriers to donor retention is crucial to reducing donor defection rates. Sargeant (2001) reported that only one in five donors defects because of a change in financial circumstances. Donors discontinue their support for many other reasons, such as the following:

- Competition from other more deserving causes
- Support provided in other ways
- Not reminded to give again
- Failure to acknowledge previous support
- Asking for inappropriate amounts
- Failure to accommodate wishes
- Failure to inform how money was used
- Perception that support is no longer needed
- Poor quality of service or communication

PR solutions exist for many of these retention barriers. Several causes of defection have roots in poor communication. Not acknowledging gifts, not providing information on how the gifts were used, and poor service quality can be remedied by better PR efforts. Public relations can also play an important part in altering perceptions about the worthiness of the cause or the need for continued support. Just because the local YMCA has reached its fundraising goal for a new expansion does not mean that it has no other needs. Improvements in telling the story of how donations are used and how impactful the gifts are can play a critical role in donors' willingness to continue support. Relationship fundraising concentrates on creating an ongoing connection rather than viewing the association with the donor as purely transactional. The fundraising environ-

ment is highly competitive, as donors have many opportunities for giving. A good cause is simply not sufficient to ensure sustained support.

Government Relationships

Managing an organization's interest in political issues and its relationships with government organizations comes under the umbrella of **public affairs** (Gruber & Hoewing, 1980). Sport organizations of all types, from major governing bodies to trade associations to local sport enterprises, can benefit from healthy relationships with any number of governmental, political, and regulatory entities. Sport operations are likely to profit from having a voice in the political process and the opportunity to wield influence in many instances. Sport organizations can be affected by anything from federal legislation such as Title IX, to minimum wage laws, to local government actions such as zoning laws and sales and amusement taxes. Political and regulatory activity such as California passing a law allowing athletes to profit from the use of their likeness can have a significant effect on the operating environment of nearly any sport organization, so it only stands to reason that developing relationships with influential governmental and regulatory units is prudent.

Power Centers

Much of the political relationship building done by organizations falls within the scope of PR and begins with strategic planning to identify the external power centers that make the rules and regulations affecting organizational operations. This process also involves determining key issues that confront the organization and identifying the political and regulatory settings in which the organization will most benefit from having influence and contacts. Organizations such as the major professional sport leagues may need to forge relationships with Congress and individual legislators or other state or federal agencies to address such issues as antitrust legislation, tax laws, concussion legislation, or broadcasting rules—any of which may affect league or team operations. Both the Sports and Fitness Industry Association (SFIA) and the National Sporting Goods Association (NSGA) are actively lobbying Congress for passage of the Personal Health Investment Today (PHIT) Act, which would allow people to pay for certain fitness activities using health savings accounts and flexible spending accounts. For a small local fitness club, it may be necessary to develop a relationship with the zoning board that controls whether the operation can expand to include child care. A group desiring to run an event such as a marathon on city streets will certainly benefit from a positive relationship with the city council and law enforcement. College and high school athletics programs must form relationships with regulatory bodies such as the NCAA or the state high school athletics association as the programs navigate the system of rules to which they must conform.

People charged with helping organizations comply with the rules are not routinely considered part of an organization's PR team, but these individuals have the task of maintaining good relations with regulatory groups by monitoring their organization's activity and engaging in regular dialogue that minimizes the likelihood of rules violations. For example, a college athletics department's compliance director must forge relationships with conference and NCAA personnel as the director guides the department's efforts to adhere to rules and, in some cases, reports rules violations.

An effective association with government and regulatory agencies involves establishing connections with people. Identifying who has power within these organizations allows PR resources to be deployed effectively. Distinguishing those who support organizational interests from those who are opposed is often important. For example, making a case before the city council for funding a new community recreation center requires knowing who can be counted on for support and who may be uncommitted or opposed to the proposal. Public relations efforts may be directed toward convincing those who are not supportive but may also be aimed

at encouraging influential supporters to sway the opinions of detractors or those who are undecided.

Influence Strategies

Public relations planning must include decisions on the strategies of influence. Determining where influence needs to be directed is useful only if the organization can establish relationships that create an environment conducive to influence and persuasion. Cialdini (1984) outlined six principles of persuasion that can serve as fundamental to the process of influence. He added a seventh in the book *Pre-suasion* in 2016. His website, Influence at Work (influenceatwork.com/principles-of-persuasion), provides an array of resources and insights on harnessing the powers of influence. His seven universal truths of influence are as follows:

1. Liking—"People like those who like them"

2. Reciprocity—"People repay in kind (return a favor)"

3. Social proof—"People follow the lead of similar others"

4. Authority—"People defer to experts"

5. Consistency—"People align with their commitments (are true to their word)"

6. Scarcity—"People want more of what they can have less of"

7. Unity—"Shared identity of being part of a group"

Most of these principles focus on actions tied to the ability to foster relationships with the targets of influence. Most success in collective bargaining occurs when reciprocity is part of the negotiations. When a sales tax increase was proposed to fund new stadiums for the Pittsburgh Pirates and Steelers, both proponents and opponents tried to sway the voters by using economic data, hoping that their experts were more persuasive. The Power Five conferences unified to get the NCAA membership to agree to allow them to operate under some different rules.

Holyoke (2003) noted that identifying the appropriate audience is only the first component of influencing effectively. Decisions must also be made about the timing and intensity of influencing efforts as well as the alliances that might be useful in applying additional pressure and support. As an example, persuading a political official to support funding for a community recreation center in an election year may be much easier if the issue has

Be Your Own Media

Trade organizations often serve as the lobbying or influencing agent for an entire industry. Visit the website of the Sports and Fitness Industry Association (sfia.org) or the National Sporting Goods Association (nsga.org). What is the stated mission statement of the organization? Look under the Public Affairs/Industry Affairs or Advocacy tabs on the sites and identify some of the issues that seem to be of interest to these groups. What organizations appear to be the targets of their influencing efforts?

substantial public backing. The politician may see support of the issue as an asset in the effort to retain or gain office. Conversely, if the issue is controversial, getting an official to make a public statement of support may be difficult unless doing so can deliver some political benefit.

Lobbying

Sport organizations from sporting goods manufacturers, to the major professional leagues, to outdoor recreation areas are all affected by legislative and regulatory agencies. Regulations such as product safety rules, guidelines for nonprofit status, antitrust laws, and environmental directives can significantly influence the operations of certain sport organizations. For large organizations with a national or international presence, the scope of desired influence may be expansive and include many audiences in high places. **Lobbying** is a common tool used by organizations as they seek to influence government and political activity. In some cases, lobbying efforts may be more informal and involve organizational personnel interacting with a government agency when a situation calls for efforts to influence the agency. For example, the owners of a professional team may seek an audience with city or state officials to discuss what types of support could be provided for the construction or renovation of an arena or stadium. In other cases, lobbying may be more systematic and involve a more consistent presence.

Organizations may staff an office, hire lobbyists, or use trade associations to lobby on the organization's behalf. As an example, the NCAA has had an office of government relations in Washington, D.C., since 1995 to provide the organization with up-to-date information on federal activities of interest and to advise management on policy decisions related to governmental interaction. This office works closely with other associations of higher education and serves as an information resource for members of Congress, education associations, and the media on issues relevant to the federal government and intercollegiate athletics (NCAA, 2004). The NFL has its own in-house lobbyist and formed a political action committee (PAC), and the NFL Players Association employs a lobbying firm to address the players' interests in Washington, D.C. (Frommer, 2010). In 2011 a congressional push to come up with safety standards for children's football helmets prompted Riddell, a major football helmet manufacturer, to sharply increase its lobbying activities. The company framed its more aggressive lobbying efforts by saying, "We believe it is only prudent to follow this legislation and to help members (of Congress), and their staffs, better understand the leadership role that Riddell has played in designing the best head protection we can manufacture for athletes who play football" (Associated Press, 2011).

Lobbyists can provide a variety of services that include collecting and interpreting information, serving as an advocate, and functioning as a liaison and communication link (Grunig & Hunt, 1984). The NCAA has ramped up lobbying efforts, spending $400,000 in 2018 with much attention paid to the issue of college athlete compensation and amateurism (Murphy & Lightman, 2019). The major professional leagues have spent more than $40 million since 1999 lobbying on issues such as tax law and antitrust law, concussion legislation, and broadcasting. The Washington Redskins have spent more than $500,000 since 2014, much of it related to legal battles over the Redskins name (Sinn et al., 2017). Perhaps the most prominent issue involving sport organization lobbying efforts of late has revolved around various efforts to expand sports wagering. Until recently, sport organizations had been quite successful in their lobbying efforts to restrict sports wagering. In 2018, the Supreme Court declared the Professional and Amateur Sports Protection Act (PASPA) of 1992 (the law restricting where sports wagering could occur) to be unconstitutional. The freedom states now have to enact their own gambling laws may result in sport organizations shifting their focus to lobbying at the state level as they try to influence the development of the sports gambling landscape (Perez, 2018). Any sport organization that is regularly subject to the actions of political entities should consider the benefits of lobbying as a potential means of shaping the organization's political environment.

Employee Relationships

Many sport organizations do not have units or departments with employee relations in the title. As in nonsport organizations, the function is commonly housed in human resources departments (Grunig, 1992). The employee relations function has been conceptualized as one of numerous human resource (HR) practices, including recruitment, performance management, and training and development (Taylor, Doherty, & McGraw, 2008). But positive employee relations and effective internal communications benefit workplace dynamics by

- increasing employee engagement and morale,
- building trust and rapport with senior management,
- decreasing rumor mills and uncertainty,
- establishing and reinforcing cultural values, and
- creating a clear understanding of expectations (Zottola, 2019).

The foundations of effective employee relations are the same as they are for other forms of public relations. These foundations include understanding the nature of key publics, carefully planning communication activities that will connect with people within those key publics, and assessing the effectiveness of those activities. Although employee relations activity largely involves channeling messages within the sport organization, it also relates to broader concerns such as employee morale, employee behaviors, and organizational culture (Mogel, 2002). Mireles (2015) states that today's employees are more important than ever, and maintaining ongoing dialogue can provide valuable feedback and foster employee engagement. Trends impacting PR as a whole are also impacting strategic internal communication and include greater use of storytelling, analytics, video and visuals, internal social networks, and mobile information platforms, among other things.

The employee relations function poses certain challenges because employees can be skeptical about management-initiated communications (Guiniven, 2000). Employees often question whether their organization's leadership is forthright and fully discloses information that employees believe they need to know. Such an environment may produce employee suspicion or hostility toward management and fuel a belief that management is unfair and manipulative. The "us versus them" mentality that many employees have concerning management is difficult to eliminate. Effective employee communications are not likely to eradicate that perception, but interaction that fosters a more trusting environment will promote a more collaborative work culture.

The State of the American Workplace study (Gallup, 2017) provides an extensive look at the modern workforce and the changes that are impacting the nature of employee relations and communications. Changes in attitudes about work, technology that affords the opportunity to work remotely and with more flexibility, fewer face-to-face interactions, more electronic communications, and changes to traditional work spaces are some of the circumstances facing organizations of all types

today. The study also reports that only about one-third of employees are engaged in their work, while 16% are actively disengaged and miserable at work, suggesting that current employee relations efforts are not particularly effective.

Employee relations, in concert with other human resource (HR) activities, affect organizational performance in general and desirable HR outcomes in particular (Taylor et al., 2008). Three specific outcomes merit mention. First, employees who are satisfied with their work environment are easier to retain than are dissatisfied employees. Because the cost of replacing employees is almost always high, sport organizations logically desire to keep productive employees. Second, happy, engaged employees are likely to be more productive in their jobs than their dissatisfied counterparts.

This point leads to the third reason why employee relations are critical. Every employee of a sport organization is a public relations representative. Employees' job titles may not include the term *public relations*, but nearly all of them interact with the sport organization's key stakeholder groups. Employees on the front line of customer service, such as ticket representatives, front-desk personnel, ushers, and security staff, likely log more hours in direct contact with consumers than members of the public relations staff. Employees also interact with people outside of the work environment. The messages that they communicate about their employers influence how others perceive the sport organization. Sport organizations must cultivate employees who will advocate for their organizations whether on the clock or off. In light of these considerations, it is not surprising that a survey regarding competencies for sport event managers found that both practitioners and academics rated "maintains effective communications with staff" as the most important competency that managers can possess (Peng, 2000). Sport organizations, therefore, should make sure that their public relations planning is oriented not just externally but internally as well.

Organizational Pride

Unlike media relations and community relations, the employee relations function in sport shares many elements with the same practice in nonsport settings. The goals, practices, and challenges are similar. Nevertheless, several unique features of employee relations in sport warrant discussion. One such feature is that because of the popularity of sport, employees of sport organizations often enjoy a sense of social prestige because of their organizational affiliation (Acosta Hernandez, 2002; Todd, 2003). For example, Xing and Chalip (2009) reported that lower-level employees with the Beijing Organizing Committee for the Olympic Games understood the high-profile nature of their organization and valued the opportunity to participate in a historic event. Similarly, researchers at ESPN may never see a second of camera time, and ticket sellers for a big-league sport franchise may not even see their team's home games, but these employees may enjoy a level of prestige because of their professional associations. For these reasons, sport organizations are uniquely positioned to build employee commitment by stressing organizational pride. Organizations may provide apparel with the organization's logo to employees, recognize employees in organizational publications, and allow lower-profile employees to work with higher-profile employees in public initiatives such as volunteer ventures.

Labor Unions

Another unique aspect of employee relations relates to professional sport in which **labor relations** with powerful players' unions are often contentious and have intense public interest. (Carter & Rovell, 2003). Antagonistic negotiations are not unique to sport, but the amount of scrutiny and fans' interest in the negotiations do seem to be. Since players' unions began gaining power in the 1970s, collective bargaining negotiations have often been very combative. There have been several instances of work stoppages, and the resulting business interruptions have been only part of the fallout. Fans have been alienated, and the reputations of owners, union leaders, and players have been tarnished. A battle between billionaire owners and millionaire players doesn't evoke much sympathy from fans. When owners are flying in to negotiations on private jets and players are arriving in stretch limousines, each side claiming they aren't getting their fair share, the result is often a need for PR damage control. The critical nature of player relations has meant that leagues have hired executives at senior-level positions to work primarily with their players' associations on an ongoing basis, not just when collective bargaining agreements need to be negotiated.

Communication Strategies

Communication flow within sport organizations may be conceptualized in several ways (Lussier & Kimball, 2014). Vertical communication is formal in nature and flows downward from senior management to other employees as well as upward from employees to senior management. Horizontal communication is also formal in nature but takes place among peers who are essentially at the same level within the organization. This communication often takes the form of memorandums and meetings. While line managers are responsible for most day-to-day communication both vertically and horizontally, senior leaders can help reinforce communication engagement through open and authentic interactions from the top down. These interactions are usually carried out in very formal ways, through speeches or memoranda ("From the desk of:"), but informal "walking around" interactions may seem more genuine in the eyes of employees (Boughey & Munro, 2014). Many sport organizations are small enough that this type of interaction is viable.

For larger organizations, such personal interactions are more of a challenge. Hall (2018) suggests that the best leaders are personable, approachable, visible, and open and describes a variety of ways senior leaders can improve the effectiveness of downward communication even in larger organizations. Using social media tools, even short message formats (e.g., Instagram, Twitter), can be beneficial as a way to share thoughts or information, and this approach both creates a sense of informality and matches the way many employees process information today. Organizational newsletters are particularly common—so common that many PR practitioners may not give them the attention they deserve. In some cases, this downward communication may also be used to generate upward communication. Vdovin (2017) suggests that newsletter content such as a regular contribution by the CEO, success stories, employee profiles, infographics, visuals, and surveys may help produce employee engagement. Downward communication often involves "big picture" messages about future direction, changes, or uncertainty. Senior managers who have established a credible communication strategy provide a sense of transparency that allows them to provide more believable reassurance to employees and reduce some of the speculative communication (e.g., Is the store closing? Are they going to fire the manager? I heard that Bob is going to work for a competitor!) often associated with the informal communication network discussed later.

Upward communication is at least as important as downward communication to organizational success. Upward communication often takes the form of questions, suggestions, or complaints. Productive organizational communications practices facilitate the two-way interaction that enables management to better utilize the knowledge and skills of front-line employees while also more quickly recognizing and responding to employee problems (Taylor et al., 2008). Upward communications can be stifled by employee fear that reporting problems or asking questions will make them look less competent. Creating a culture where such communication is encouraged fosters trust and confidence while stimulating a more collaborative environment.

Horizontal communication (peer-to-peer or lateral) is primarily used as a means for coordinating activity. Such communication is typically shorter and more impromptu in nature and facilitates work coordination and clarification. Horizontal communication also enhances operational efficiency because feedback tends to be more immediate. Efforts to control this form of communication may stem from managerial concerns about loss of control or an undermining of authority. Because of the informal nature of much horizontal communication, suppression is very difficult.

Another form of communication that occurs within the sport organization is the informal com-munication network often known as the **grapevine**. This type of communication often fills the gaps left by formal vertical and horizontal communications. While the general perception of the grapevine may be tied to gossip and rumor, the existence of the grapevine is inescapable and not necessarily negative. The American Management Association estimates that as much as 70% of all organizational communication emanates through the grapevine. For this reason, monitoring the grapevine merits attention both in addressing false or incomplete information being circulated as well as in taking advantage of the speed and message control that often comes with active engagement with this form of communication (Wroblewski, 2018).

Solar (2019) suggests managers should make every effort to promote meaningful and productive conversation within the organization. Fostering connections among employees and providing channels for sharing and for feedback will fuel a productive communication environment. This does pose challenges in a multigenerational workforce with different communication preferences that may result in the need to overcome resistance to some

Maintaining reliable and meaningful communications with staff is a sign of a skillful manager.

Klaus Vedfelt/DigitalVision/Getty Images

of the modern collaboration tools available. Most employees indicate that their preferred method of communication is direct interaction with their immediate supervisor (Bobo, 2000; Broom, 2009). Organizational managers who build strong relationships with their staffs greatly increase the likelihood that communication is characterized by honesty and openness.

Communication Tools

Facilitating and managing employee communication has a tremendous upside for organizational productivity, and technology has provided additional tools to supplement traditional forms of communication such as employee newsletters. While newsletters still have a role, particularly in downward communication, new social, intranet, and collaboration platforms address employee communications in all its forms. Terms such as *enterprise social networks*, *team communication platforms*, and *workplace communication platforms* (e.g., Slack) are used to describe what could be termed the modern intranet. Anders (2016) outlines the advantages of such platforms to include enhanced collaboration and connectivity, knowledge sharing across diverse sources, and social engagement and cohesion. These platforms can be used to enable communication and collaboration, manage documents, manage workflow, arrange schedules, create social profiles, store forms and data, create reports, and support analytics (What is an intranet . . . , 2017). These centralized communication platforms provide many potential benefits and are likely to be embraced more enthusiastically as the workforce is increasingly composed of people for whom social networking is second nature. Cardon and Marshall (2015) and Anders (2016), among others, do caution, however, that using these tools must be balanced with more traditional communications, such as in-person meetings and phone calls. Fragmented messages and information overload often impede organizational productivity.

Organizational Culture

The subject of internal public relations cannot be adequately addressed without considering organizational culture. **Organizational culture** consists of the shared values, attitudes, and behaviors that characterize the way an organization operates and that provide guidelines and boundaries for the behavior of members of the organization. Meng and Berger (2019) report that a supportive organizational culture, in which decision making is shared, the value of public relations is appreciated, two-way communication is practiced, and diversity is embraced, will have a positive impact on PR professionals' work engagement, organizational trust, and job satisfaction.

Racial and gender diversity and inclusion are aspects of organizational culture that often prove to be problematic. The U.S. Bureau of Labor Statistics (2019) reports that the ethnic makeup of the public relations industry is nearly 88% white. Chitkara (2018) suggests that even if there are measures in place to create a more diverse workplace, retaining minority employees is often difficult if the culture is not welcoming and inclusive.

Issues of gender diversity in the PR industry are more related to lack of power rather than lack of representation. The public relations profession is one in which women are the majority. Arenstein (2019) states that women hold 75% of PR positions but only 20% of the senior leadership positions. Such disparity is also seen in sport. The 2017 report on diversity in college athletics indicated that women hold fewer than 15% of the sports information (media relations) director positions at NCAA institutions (Lapchick, 2017). Diversity extends beyond the mere presence of women and members of racial and ethnic minorities within sport organizations. Representation must be followed by leadership opportunity. As noted by Lapchick and colleagues (2009), "This element of diversity can provide a different perspective, and possibly a competitive advantage for a win in the boardroom as well as on the athletic fields of play" (p. 2).

Sport organizations have had their diversity and hiring practices scrutinized more closely in recent years. The Institute for Diversity and Ethics in Sport (TIDES-www.tidesport.org/) publishes annual reports that assess the hiring practices of many amateur, college, and professional sport organizations using a racial and gender report card (RGRC). These reports have directed more attention to diversity initiatives and attention to the barriers that women and minorities have faced in accessing jobs that have historically been dominated by white males. Women within the field have other resources at their disposal as well. The Association for Women in Sports Media (AWSM) "works to promote and increase diversity in sport media through career-enhancement networking and mentoring initiatives as well as the internship/scholarship program—which has placed more than 150 female college students in paid summer positions since 1990" (awsmonline.org/we-are-awsm).

Building Volunteer Relationships

Volunteers are essential to many sport organizations. Volunteers are critical to sport organizations in countries like Canada and Australia that have club-based sport systems (Cuskelly, Hoye, & Auld, 2006), and nonprofit sport organizations in the United States routinely rely on volunteer labor. Estimates are that 63 million Americans, 13 million Canadians, 20 million English, 6 million Australians, and 24 million Germans volunteer each year (Wilson, 2015). The Beijing Olympics had 70,000 volunteers and Brazil had 80,000 volunteers for the 2014 World Cup (Ringuet, 2012). The U.S. Bureau of Labor Statistics (2016) reports that nearly 4 million people volunteer for sport, cultural, and arts organizations, and the median number of hours volunteered is just over 50. Independent Sector estimates that the value of volunteer time is currently just over $25 per hour, with a cumulative value of more than $200 billion (2019).

Volunteers come in all shapes and sizes—women, men, teens, seniors. They perform all sorts of critical and routine tasks—handing out water at a fun run, coaching and refereeing youth soccer, welcoming people to the Y. There are clear parallels between volunteer relations and donor relations in that volunteers are donors of time and talent. Volunteer management involves cultivation and recruitment, assessment and training, engagement, and retention.

Recruiting volunteers starts with understanding the motivations for volunteerism. Wilson (2015) mentions several motivations, including altruism, social interaction, ego enhancement, developing new skills, and career development. Understanding motivation is vital to successful recruitment. Just as important is a clear understanding of the organization's volunteer needs. Knowing and communicating the types of work expected of volunteers will expedite the recruitment process and result in fewer situations in which volunteers are disillusioned by the experience.

One important factor in volunteer satisfaction is the sense of contribution and impact. Wyche (2012) advises that volunteers need to be properly trained and equipped to perform their assigned tasks. Regularly checking with volunteers to see how things are going gives volunteers a sense of support and often provides invaluable feedback on how things might be done more effectively.

Wilson (2015) identifies three overriding strategies for a successful volunteer program:

1. Focus on the individual—understand their motivations and match their talents to the most appropriate roles.

2. Communicate—pre-event communication should clarify expectations and address any apprehension. Communication during an event should address problem solving and provision of necessary support. Postevent communication should involve debriefing, feedback, and acknowledgment.

3. Encourage engagement—Promote a sense of teamwork and inspire commitment through recognition of volunteers' contributions and the value of their input.

A variety of volunteer management software tools, resembling CRM software, can help create volunteer profiles, communicate, and track volunteer time. VolunteerMatch is a website that can aid in recruiting volunteers for many types of nonprofit causes. Finding good volunteers and managing them well will greatly increase volunteer retention. Volunteers who have a seamless and rewarding experience assisting in a cause for which they have enthusiasm are not only more likely to return but may help recruit additional volunteers as well.

A diverse workforce can foster a sensitivity toward other cultures, opinions, and ideas as employees draw from different backgrounds and bring unique perspectives to the consumption process among key audiences. It is critical to promote diversity and nurture a culture of mutual respect to enhance workplace productivity and organizational success (Ramaswami, 2018).

Investor Relationships

Also referred to as financial relations, **investor relations (IR)** is a specialized public relations function that seeks to establish desirable relationships with individual investors, investment firms, and financial analysts. IR has been described as "a strategic management responsibility that integrates finance, communications, marketing, and securities law compliance to enable the most effective two-way communication between a company, the financial community, and other constituencies, which ultimately contributes to a company's securities achieving fair valuation" (NIRI, 2009). A number of large sport-related organizations are publicly owned. Such organizations must consider investor relations to be a critical public relations function. The following are examples of publicly owned sport-related organizations:

- Callaway Golf Company (ELY)
- Brunswick (BC)
- Lululemon Athletica (LULU)
- Under Armour (UA)
- Dick's Sporting Goods (DKS)
- Madison Square Garden (MSG)
- Fitbit (FIT)
- Foot Locker (FL)
- Nautilus Inc. (NLS)
- V.F. Corporation (VFC)
- International Speedway Corporation (ISCA)
- Nike (NKE)
- World Wrestling Entertainment Inc. (WWE)
- Manchester United Football Club (MANU)

A strategic communication model developed by Argenti, Howell, and Beck (2005) summarized investor relations practice as having two broad objectives (transparency and meeting financial expectations) and three constituencies (investors, analysts, and the media). Often nested within an organization's corporate communications department, investor relations practitioners must be accomplished in both public relations and finance (Broom, 2009). The main responsibilities for the head of IR position are as follows:

- Develop investor confidence and belief in the company's vision and strategy for delivering shareholder value
- Develop a robust investor relations strategy and framework
- Create and manage a strong reputation by demonstrating consistent and clear communication between internal and external parties
- Manage equity research and investor relationships
- Provide insights on market activity and present them to the leadership team

- Analyze and present financial trends, competitor behavior, shareholder issues, and anything else that could impact the business
- Oversee and manage quarterly earnings and conference calls
- Work with legal counsel to ensure compliance on regulatory matters
- Help prepare the company's annual report and Form 10-K filing (Corporate Finance Institute, n.d.)

Like other aspects of public relations, IR professionals may approach their work either reactively or proactively. Those practicing in a reactive mode limit their activities to complying with government laws, responding to inquiries, and managing traditional organizational activities (e.g., annual reports, stockholder meetings). People practicing in a proactive mode will not only meet those requirements but also structure a program and develop plans designed to promote the sport organization's financial position to investors.

In the wake of corporate scandals coupled with cynicism about corporate greed, investors are understandably wary of business leadership. Frequent and open communication may alleviate some of those suspicions. Investor confidence is often based on variables that are not necessarily addressed in corporate financial statements. These less objective elements include the company's leadership, the strategies it employs, the value of its brand, the state of its reputation, and the way that it is evolving technologically (Kalafut, 2003). Communicating with investors regarding those intangibles may mean overcoming managerial inclinations toward secrecy. But if investors are ultimately the group to which company leadership must answer, then such steps are necessary. Investors have many options to choose from. The IR professional is charged with helping to make the company an attractive investment choice.

Among the more important activities of IR practitioners are the development of annual reports, the planning and management of annual shareholder meetings, and the use of interactive technologies to communicate with various constituencies.

Annual Reports

Annual reports are among the most important aspects of the IR professional's job. In the United States, the Securities and Exchange Commission (SEC) mandates that certain financial information be disclosed by publicly traded companies so that investors can make informed decisions. An annual report is "a state-of-the-company report, including an opening letter from the Chief Executive Officer, financial data, results of operations, market segment information, new product plans, subsidiary activities, and research and development activities on future programs" (U.S. SEC, 2014). The SEC requires an annual report to be filed using Form 10-K, which may be used in place of or in addition to a company-generated report.

In nonprofit settings, the Internal Revenue Service (IRS) also requires some financial reporting (typically a Form 990), and many organizations produce complete annual reports. Nonprofit annual reports are often less focused on detailed financial data (although these data are typically included) and more focused on the organization's stories. Zhang (2018) suggests that nonprofit annual reports use visuals such as pictures and infographics, personalize and humanize the messages, be specific in citing accomplishments, thank supporters, and serve as inspiration for future action.

Shareholder Meetings

Shareholder meetings are a regulatory requirement, which means most public and private companies must hold them. Annual shareholder meetings provide stockholders with the opportunity to hear from the corporation's leadership, learn more about the company, and vote on matters ranging from the election of board members to proposals submitted for shareholder consideration. A company's public relations staff is typically involved in planning and executing annual shareholder meetings in the following ways (Richman & Hermsen, 2018):

- Meeting logistics
- Q&A preparation
- Meeting rules
- Shareholder proposal information
- Social media content
- Security
- Media coverage
- Voting results

Most annual meetings tend to be rather routine proceedings, but there are occasions where controversy or consideration of some high-profile issue may result in a more exciting event.

Interactive Communications

A third set of activities that is increasingly important to IR involves the use of interactive communication channels. Conference calls and webcasts are well-established tools in providing access to events such as annual meetings (Marshall & Heffes, 2004). Investors and analysts who tune into the meetings indicate that they are better able to determine how open management is regarding the company's finances. Websites are also critical platforms for investor communications. For instance, the investor relations tab on the Dick's Sporting Goods website (investors.dicks.com) provides information on the company, financial and stock data, governance, investor services, corporate social responsibility, and SEC filings. Social media such as Facebook, Twitter, blogs, and message boards are also becoming increasingly influential communication channels for IR professionals. Although a 2016 survey indicated that 72% of investment relations professionals said they do not use social media for IR functions, studies indicate that fewer investors are using traditional media and paying more attention to social media. This shift will inevitably result in the need for greater awareness of social media both as a platform that must be monitored as well as an asset to be used to advance investor relations (Social media monitoring is . . . , 2017).

Balancing Stakeholder Interests

Managers of publicly owned sport companies are clearly concerned with providing returns to their investors and enhancing the value of the organization's stock. The sacrifices managers are willing to make in their relationships with other stakeholder groups may depend on the extent to which these individuals are solely concerned with providing value to investors (shareholders). Smith (2003) contrasted two basic approaches to this issue. The first is the shareholder approach, in which the primary responsibility is to investors. The second is the stakeholder approach, in which managers attempt to balance the interests of investors with other constituents such as employees, customers, and the community. "The fundamental distinction is that the stakeholder theory demands that interests of *all* stakeholders be considered *even if it reduces company profitability*" (p. 86). The reality is that most organizations are not purely in either camp; their philosophies are somewhat mixed in that they serve the interests of both shareholders and other stakeholders. Therefore, it is most helpful to view the shareholder–stakeholder dichotomy as a continuum, with few organizations stationed on either extreme. Nasdaq (2019) reports that institutional investors and other stakeholders are pressing companies on their environmental, social, and governance (ESG) initiatives and expecting boards of directors to look beyond shareholder returns as the only metric of success. An example of the stockholder–stakeholder balance is Dick's Sporting Goods' attempt to balance the profit from gun sales with social concerns about gun violence. Corporations should expect public scrutiny in dealing with such issues, which will likely continue to pose PR challenges and opportunities for investment relations professionals.

SUMMARY

The public relations function plays a key role in developing and maintaining relationships. Sport organizations must make a concerted effort to nurture their relationships with a variety of external publics including customers, members, sponsors, donors, and government and regulatory agencies as well as addressing internal publics, specifically employees and investors. The quality of the relationship between an organization and its customers and members is critical to success. Public relations can take interaction with consumers beyond a transactional relationship and increase the possibility that customers are satisfied, loyal, and committed. A better understanding of the customer journey will help in developing strategies for delivering quality service and in crafting direct marketing and PR tactics that will reduce defection and lower the barriers to loyalty. Sponsors and donors are also vitally important to many sport organizations. Both sponsors and donors provide significant revenue to a variety of sport operations; building strong relationships is particularly important given the numerous options that exist for sponsors and donors to direct their resources.

Public relations professionals play an important role in political relationships as well. Sport organizations should identify the regulatory agencies that are likely to influence their operating environment and then determine the appropriate methods for influencing political actions and promoting organizational interests. The employee relations function relates to managers' efforts to foster desirable relationships with employees. Sport organizations are likely to benefit from strong employee relationships through greater employee satisfaction and productivity. Frequent, open communication between employees and direct supervisors is essential, and a variety of communication platforms are available to accommodate that goal. Some of the unique attributes that are a part of employee relations in sport (e.g., volunteers, high-profile labor unions) present interesting employee relations challenges. As in other sectors, however, public relations professionals must be attentive to the notion of organizational culture, because it significantly influences overall public diverse effectiveness.

Finally, investor relations programs are needed to offer transparency and support positive financial outcomes. The practice of investor relations is diverse, IR professionals are usually involved in the production of annual reports, the staging of annual shareholder meetings, and the use of web-based technologies to facilitate management–investor communications. Senior managers must also deal with the PR challenges that come with balancing the interests of investors with the interests of other stakeholders.

LEARNING ACTIVITIES

1. Go to the website of a sport-related CRM software service (e.g., ssbinfo.com). Describe what types of services the CRM platform offers, the kinds of information it collects, and the benefits the company says come with using CRM software.

2. Find and critique a sport organization's newsletter for its content, presentation, and reader engagement (e.g., nassm.com/NASSM/Newsletter, Sports Geek News, Sport-Techie Daily News, Hashtag Sports Daily, fortwaynesportclub.com, brickyardgolf.com /newsletter/).

3. Visit a sporting goods retailer's website and assume that you are interested in making a purchase. Using the list of basic customer satisfaction factors listed earlier in the chapter as a guideline, which of the factors on the list are likely to be most important to your satisfaction with the buying experience? How well does the website accommodate some of your major concerns?

4. Find a template for a customer journey map and apply it to a sport-related purchase. Identify the key touchpoints and pinpoint aspects during the journey that might be critical to the level of satisfaction or to completing the purchase (friction points and moments of truth).

5. Go to the corporate sponsorship web page for a professional sport franchise (e.g., mlb .com/pirates/sponsorship). Describe the ways in which the franchise promotes the value of professional team sponsorship. What assets does the team promote to potential sponsors? Are digital assets mentioned in conjunction with possible sponsorship opportunities?

6. For many college athletics programs, fundraising is essential. Go to the donor page for an athletics department (e.g., nittanylionclub.com/) and outline the giving options and benefits described there. Discuss how well the donor page engages and excites prospective donors.

7. Assuming that your class has guest speakers from time to time, ask one or more of them to describe their sport organization's culture. Does it seem to be more authoritarian than participative? Have measures been taken to support women and minorities within the organization? If so, are those steps relatively basic (e.g., discrimination policies) or more advanced (e.g., mentoring programs)?

8. Visit the website of a publicly owned sport organization and identify what information is provided to investors. What elements go beyond the mandated financial disclosure data? Describe the key messages conveyed that are designed to promote investor confidence.

Sample Crisis Communication Plan

A crisis communications plan provides a framework for responding to crisis situations. It empowers sport managers by specifying the responsibilities in a crisis, the way information is to be shared internally during a crisis, and the way information is to be shared with other publics in a timely manner. By defining such considerations in advance of a crisis, the sport organization may be better positioned to respond in a manner that best protects its reputation and financial interests.

Crisis communications plans are not designed to prescribe responses for every conceivable crisis, nor are they detailed enough to specify every action that must be taken throughout a crisis episode. These plans are designed to provide general guidelines for the management team, particularly early on. To prepare a crisis communication plan, sport managers must follow a number of steps to develop a plan containing certain key elements.

In addition to creating various crisis plans, a crisis assessment committee (CAC) should create the following four contact lists:

1. CAC contact list, with names; positions; and all office, mobile, and home phone numbers of members
2. Names, positions, and phone numbers of individuals who may be added to a specific crisis communication committee or team

3. Names, positions, and phone numbers of key individuals who may need to be contacted regarding crisis situations
4. Media outlets and specific contacts that cover university athletics on a frequent basis

The first list should be widely distributed because it covers the four-member team that will be responsible for the initiation of the crisis response plan.

The second list should cover the internal staff on the front line of crisis management, such as all lead sport coaches, the athletics director (AD), the senior associate AD/senior woman administrator, the associate AD for strategic communications, the vice president and general counsel, the associate AD for development, the faculty athletic representative, the assistant AD for marketing and promotions, the assistant AD for facilities and events, the assistant AD for compliance and student services, the chief of campus security, the dean of students, the vice president (VP) for student affairs, the university director of news and media relations, and the director of environmental control.

The third list should cover key university positions, such as the university president, VP and general counsel, VP for academic affairs, associate AD for development, faculty athletic representative, assistant AD for marketing and promotions, assistant AD for facilities and events, assistant AD for compliance and student services, chief of campus security, dean of students, VP for student affairs, director of multicultural affairs, environmental health and safety director, and physical plant manager.

The fourth list should cover local and national news outlets that routinely cover your university. Each outlet should be included when releasing information regarding a crisis situation. Media members inquiring about the crisis situation will likely need to be added to this list as the crisis unfolds. Detailed records regarding those inquiries and relevant contact information should be maintained throughout the episode.

University Athletic Department Crisis Communications Plan

A crisis is defined as a situation or occurrence possessing the potential to significantly damage the university's and athletic department's reputation. This document describes the steps that are to be taken to (1) identify emerging crises and (2) respond appropriately to such crises.

All athletic department staff members should be familiar with their responsibilities when a crisis occurs. This will enable the department to respond in an appropriate and coordinated manner. It is critical that all potential crises be addressed only within the framework of this plan. While not comprehensive, the following is a brief list of some crises that may be encountered:

1. Accusations of criminal activity against a staff member or student–athlete
2. Accidents involving student–athletes and staff members resulting in serious injury or death
3. Accusations of NCAA rules violations
4. Fan-related incidents involving serious injuries or criminal activity at an athletic event

Athletics department staff members encountering these or other potentially damaging incidents should quickly gather as much information as possible and then immediately contact a member of the crisis assessment committee (CAC). The CAC consists of four members—the senior associate AD/senior woman administrator, associate AD for business affairs, associate AD for strategic communications, and assistant AD for operations.

Upon being notified of the situation, the CAC, in consultation with appropriate parties (i.e., director of athletics, university counsel, university president), will determine whether to fully implement the crisis communication plan. If the situation involves student–athletes or staff members specific to a program, that program's head coach will also be contacted.

The following sections summarize initial CAC response plans. They address the four crisis scenarios previously listed and also provide a generic response plan that may be used for crises that do not fall in the first four categories.

Scenario 1: Accusation of Criminal Activity against a Staff Member or Student–Athlete

Objectives

1. Ensure that all parties involved—the accused, the accuser, and others—are treated fairly and in accordance with existing legislation and university policy.
2. Communicate to key publics that the athletics department holds its members to high standards of behavior and upholds its obligation to treat its members with fairness.
3. Take action as quickly as circumstances will permit, given objectives 1 and 2.

Procedures

1. The CAC chair will contact other personnel who serve as members of the crisis communications committee (CCC) for the duration of the crisis episode. They include the following:

   - Athletics director (AD)
   - Senior associate AD
   - Associate AD for strategic communications
   - Assistant AD for compliance and student services
   - University general counsel
   - Head coach (if student–athlete is accused)
   - Campus security chief (if incident took place on campus)
   - University director of news and media relations

2. AD informs university president of the situation.

3. If a student-athlete is involved, head coach contacts the student–athlete's parent or legal guardian.

4. Associate AD for strategic communications, in conjunction with the athletics director and general counsel, prepares a media statement. Previously drafted templates may be used to expedite this step.

5. Associate AD for strategic communications makes initial statement available to media officials who are making inquiries. Associate AD for strategic communications informs media members that subsequent inquiries should be directed to, and additional information will be released from, the athletics department's communications office. The associate AD for strategic communications will also maintain a record of all media inquiries, responses, and follow-up actions.

6. Depending on the situation, the initial statement may be shared on the department's social media channels.

7. AD's office apprises other university key officials. Depending on the situation, these may include human resources (HR), the dean of students, or the Title IX officer, or some combination of these.

8. Associate AD for strategic communications informs appropriate staff members (e.g., athletics department communications officers assigned to the program involved).

9. Senior associate AD gathers as much information as possible regarding who is involved in the incident, what happened, when and where it happened, and how it unfolded.

10. CCC meets to plan subsequent actions. Key issues to address include the following:

   • Who will serve as primary spokesperson?

   • What will be the department's response regarding the accused (e.g., no action until trial, suspension, dismissal)?

   • How may the department best communicate that information to the mass media?

   • How quickly can the department make additional public comment regarding the situation?

11. As quickly as possible, take those actions deemed important in the crisis committee meeting.

12. As quickly as possible, release additional information regarding the department's response to members of the mass media.

The previous 12 steps provide a framework for how to proceed. Additional CCC meetings may be necessary given the circumstances.

Scenario 2: Accident Involving Student– Athletes and Staff Members Resulting in Serious Injury or Death

Objectives

1. Ensure that the privacy of those directly and indirectly involved is protected.

2. Release information to key publics as quickly as possible in accordance with objective 1.

3. Communicate the athletic department's

   • sincere concern and sadness regarding the accident,

   • commitment to fully investigate what happened, and

   • commitment to minimize the possibility of such an event occurring again.

4. Minimize exposure to possible legal action.

Procedures

1. The CAC chair will contact other personnel who will serve as members of the CCC for the duration of the crisis episode. They include the following:

   • Athletics director

   • Senior associate AD

   • Associate AD for strategic communications

   • Assistant AD for compliance and student services

   • University general counsel

   • Head coach (if student–athletes or staff members of specific programs are involved)

- Campus security chief (if accident took place on campus)
- University director of news and media relations
- Student–athlete counselor

2. AD informs university president of the situation.

3. AD and senior associate AD make preliminary contact with family of parties involved in the accident. Contact information is available in student–athlete personnel records.

4. Associate AD for strategic communications, in conjunction with the athletics director and general counsel, prepares a media statement. Previously drafted templates may be used to expedite this step.

5. Associate AD for strategic communications makes the initial statement available to media officials who are making inquiries. Associate AD for strategic communications informs media members that subsequent inquiries should be directed to the athletics department's communications office. All additional information will be released from the communications office as well. Associate AD for strategic communications will maintain a record of all inquiries, responses, and follow-up actions as needed.

6. Depending on the situation, the initial statement may be shared on the department's social media channels.

7. AD's office apprises other university key officials. Depending on the situation, these may include HR, the dean of students, or the director of counseling services, or some combination of these.

8. Senior associate AD gathers as much information as possible regarding the accident including who was injured and to what extent, who else was involved, when and where the accident occurred, and what may have caused the accident.

9. The communication crisis team meets to make the following decisions:

- Who will serve as primary spokesperson?
- How will the department communicate the information?

- How quickly can the department release additional information?
- What other university personnel need to be contacted and who is going to do this?
- How will senior staff liaisons be assigned to each affected family?

10. AD and senior associate AD contact family units of those involved to update them regarding the situation and to introduce the senior staff liaison assigned to each family, who will arrange for their transportation to the city if warranted.

11. As quickly as possible, take other actions deemed important in the CCC meeting.

12. The athletics department holds a news conference. Update the media, providing as much information as possible while keeping regard for the families and parties involved. Work with law enforcement to ensure only facts are released and not speculative information. Share key points from the news conference via social media channels.

13. Release additional information to the mass media as quickly as possible regarding the department's response. Make updates to mass and social media as appropriate. All additional information will be given to families before it is released to media.

The previous 13 steps provide a framework for how to proceed. Additional CCC meetings may be necessary given the circumstances.

Scenario 3: Accusation of NCAA Rules Violations

Objectives

1. Ensure that all parties involved—the accused, the accuser, and others—are treated fairly and in accordance with existing legislation and university policy.

2. Communicate to key publics that the athletic department holds its members to high standards of behavior and upholds its obligation to treat its members with fairness.

3. Take actions as quickly as circumstances will permit given objectives 1 and 2.

Procedures

1. The CAC chair will contact other personnel who will serve as members of the CCC committee for the duration of the crisis episode. They include the following:

   - Athletics director

   - Senior associate AD

   - Associate AD for strategic communications

   - Assistant AD for compliance and student services

   - University general counsel

   - Head coach (if student–athlete is accused)

   - University director of news and media relations

2. AD informs university president of the situation.

3. AD's office apprises the faculty athletics representative.

4. Assistant AD for compliance gathers as much information as possible regarding who is involved, what has happened, and how it happened.

5. If appropriate at this stage, assistant AD for compliance contacts the NCAA.

6. Associate AD for strategic communications, in conjunction with the athletics director and general counsel, prepares a media statement. Previously drafted templates may be used to expedite this step.

7. Associate AD for strategic communications makes the initial statement available to media officials who are making inquiries. Associate AD for strategic communications informs media members that subsequent inquiries should be directed to the athletics department's communications office. All additional information will be released from the communications office as well. Associate AD for strategic communications will maintain a record of all inquiries, responses, and follow-up actions as needed.

8. Depending on the situation, the initial statement may be shared on the department's social media channels.

9. CCC meets to plan subsequent actions. Key issues to address include the following:

   - Who will serve as primary spokesperson?

   - What will be the department's response to the accusations?

   - How may the department best communicate that information to the mass media?

   - How quickly can the department make additional public comment regarding the situation?

   - Who else needs to be contacted regarding the situation, and who should make those contacts?

   - What additional steps need to be taken to facilitate the internal investigation of what has been reported?

10. As quickly as possible, take all actions specified in the CCC meeting.

11. As quickly as possible, release additional information regarding the department's response to members of the mass media.

The previous 11 steps provide a framework for how to initially proceed. Additional CCC meetings may be necessary given the circumstances.

Scenario 4: Fan-Related Incident Involving Serious Injuries or Criminal Activity at an Athletic Event

Objectives

1. Ensure that the privacy of those directly and indirectly involved is protected.

2. Release information to key publics as quickly as possible in accordance with objective 1.

3. Communicate the athletic department's

   - sincere concern and sadness regarding the accident,

   - commitment to fully investigate what happened, and

   - commitment to minimize the possibility of such an event occurring again.

4. Minimize exposure to possible legal action.

Procedures

1. The CAC chair will contact other personnel who will serve as members of the CCC for the duration of the crisis episode. They include the following:

   - Athletics director
   - Senior associate AD
   - Associate AD for strategic communications
   - Assistant AD for compliance and student services
   - University general counsel
   - Head coach (if student–athletes or staff members are involved)
   - Campus security chief (if incident took place on campus)
   - University director of news and media relations
   - Director for environmental control (determined by incident)
   - City law enforcement liaison (determined by incident)

2. AD informs the university president of the situation.

3. AD and senior associate AD make preliminary contact with appropriate officials, the injured parties, and organizational members who may have relevant information to gather as much information as possible.

4. If a student is involved, the AD will work in conjunction with the dean of students to contact the parent or legal guardian. If a student–athlete is involved, the head coach will contact the parent or legal guardian.

5. Associate AD for strategic communications, in conjunction with the athletics director and general counsel, prepares a media statement. Previously drafted templates may be used to expedite this step.

6. Associate AD for strategic communications makes the initial statement available to media officials who are making inquiries. Associate AD for strategic communications informs media members that subsequent inquiries should be directed to the athletic communications office. All additional information will be released from the athletic communications office as well. Associate AD for strategic communications will maintain a record of all inquiries, responses, and follow-up actions as needed.

7. Depending on the situation, the initial statement may be shared on the department's social media channels.

8. Associate AD for strategic communications informs all athletics department communications personnel of the situation. If necessary, all these personnel report to the athletics department to assist with media services.

9. Senior associate AD gathers as much information as possible regarding the incident. Sustained contact with campus security and community law enforcement is critical.

10. CCC meets to discuss subsequent action for the following issues:

    - Do any immediate public safety issues at athletic facilities need to be addressed?
    - Who will serve as the primary contact for the individuals who were involved and their families?
    - Who will serve as the primary spokesperson for media inquiries?
    - How will the process be coordinated so that public comment never precedes the sharing of information with the individuals who were involved and their families?
    - How will information be shared with the media?
    - What will be the department's position regarding the accused?
    - What messages will the department attempt to communicate to fans regarding their safety at athletic events?
    - Who else needs to be contacted regarding the situation and who should make those contacts?

11. Promptly take actions deemed important in the CCC meeting.

12. Release additional information to the media as it becomes available, ensuring the privacy of the patrons and families involved. All additional information will be given to families before it is released to media. Share information via organizational communication channels, including social media.

The previous 12 steps provide a framework for how to initially proceed. Additional CCC meetings may be necessary given the circumstances.

Scenario 5: Other Crises

Objectives

1. Fulfill the athletic department's obligations to its various constituents while protecting its reputation.
2. Adhere to existing department and university policies that may be relevant to the situation.
3. Communicate effectively with the mass media and other key publics regarding the crisis.

Procedures

1. The CAC chair contacts the director of athletics. Together, they identify other department and university personnel who may need to be temporarily added to the CCC.
2. AD informs university president of the situation.
3. If a student–athlete is involved, head coach contacts the student–athlete's parent or legal guardian.
4. Associate AD for strategic communications, in conjunction with the athletics director and general counsel, prepares a media statement. Previously drafted templates may be used to expedite this step.
5. Associate AD for strategic communications makes the initial statement available to media officials who are making inquiries. Associate AD for strategic communications informs media members that subsequent inquiries should be directed to the athletic communications office. All additional information will be released from the athletics department's communications office as well. Associate AD for strategic communications will maintain a record of all inquiries, responses, and follow-up actions as needed.
6. Depending on the situation, the initial statement may be shared on the department's social media channels.
7. Associate AD for strategic communications informs appropriate staff members (e.g., athletics department communications officers assigned to any programs involved).
8. Senior associate AD gathers as much information as possible regarding what has happened.
9. CCC meets to assess the situation and determine responses. Key issues to address include the following:

   - Who will serve as primary spokesperson?
   - How quickly can the department make additional public comment regarding the situation?
   - How may the department best communicate with the mass media?
   - What messages should be communicated?
   - Who else needs to be contacted regarding the situation, and who should make those contacts?

10. As quickly as possible, take actions as specified in CCC meeting.
11. As quickly as possible, release additional information regarding the department's response to members of the mass media.

The previous 11 steps provide a framework for how to proceed. Additional CCC meetings may be necessary given the circumstances.

glossary

80-20 rule—The axiom that 80% of sales come from 20% of clients.

acquisition metrics—A type of social media measurement focused on building relationships on social networking sites. Sport public relations professionals use these types of measures to prove value of social media efforts. Referrals are an example of this type of metric.

active public—A group of people who recognize that they have some common interest or link to the organization, and as a result, take action to affect the relationship.

annual reports—A "state-of-the-company" summary that reports financial data, results of operations, market segment information, new product plans, subsidiary activities, and research and development activities on future plans.

average engagement rate—Calculated by the number of engagement actions on a social network post, divided by the number of total followers of the organization on the network.

aware public—Group of people who recognize that they have some common interest or link to the organization.

blogging—The process of producing a journaled website containing the experiences, opinions, and observations of a writer or writers.

bounce rate—The ratio of website visitors who navigate away from the site after viewing only the exact page of the site they landed upon.

brand—All the representations, including names, marks, intangible attributes, of an entity (e.g., product, organization, individual) that distinguish the entity from other entities in the minds of consumers.

brand equity—The relative value a brand holds in the minds of its consumers as compared with a generic competitor.

B-roll—A taped series of unedited video shots and sound bites related to a news story.

call tree—Internal communications sequence in which the responsibilities for notifying employees of a crisis are delegated to multiple parties, each of whom has specific contacts to make.

campaigns—Limited duration public relations initiatives within an organization to attain a specific public relations result with a defined public or publics.

community relations—A public relations function focused on building strong relationships with members of the community.

consumer-generated media (CGM)—Various social media platforms used by customers to share opinions with large numbers of people quickly.

conversion metrics—A type of social media measurement focused more on the marketing functions of sales and revenue that are generated from social media efforts. The number of fans who used a coupon in store that was distributed using social media is an example of this type of metric.

conversion rate—The ratio of website visitors who eventually complete a call to action, such as a purchase or sign-up.

corporate communications—A public relations structure often found in professional-level organizations that assumes functional responsibility for media relations for corporate partnerships, community relations, and other public relations programs.

corporate social responsibility (CSR)—The responsibility of organizations to consider and respond to broader social needs and expectations in addition to their own financial interests.

credential—A pass that allows the holder access to certain areas of an event venue to which the public does not have access. Often, these areas include media work spaces such as interview rooms, media seating, and media work rooms.

crisis—A situation or occurrence possessing the potential to significantly damage a sport organization's financial stability and credibility with constituents.

crisis communications—An aspect of public relations practice related to how organizations engage internal and external publics during situations that threaten the organizations' financial stability, credibility with key stakeholders, or both.

crisis communications plan—A framework that directs an organization's members on how to proceed after a crisis has occurred. Because processing and sharing information are critical to managing crises, communications—both internal and external—are usually the focus of the plan.

crisis response strategy—A sport organization's selected position in regard to a crisis and its chosen method of communicating that position.

customer equity—The total expected profitability to be generated from a customer base over time.

customer experience (CX)—The product of the interactions between an organization and a customer over the duration of their relationship.

customer journey mapping—The method of identifying the physical and digital touchpoints (individual points of interaction) during various stages of the consumer experience, from awareness to consideration to acquisition to service.

customer lifetime value (CLV)—The total amount of money a customer is expected to spend on an organization's products or services during the customer's lifetime.

customer relationship management (CRM)—The software used to bring together information from all data sources to give a holistic view of each customer in real time.

demographics—In social media, includes the age, gender, and location of a particular user.

domain name—An identification string that provides specific context and control of a web address.

e-commerce—The buying and selling of goods and services, or the transmitting of funds or data, over an electronic network, primarily the Internet.

game notes—A sport public relations organizational media tactic made up of numerous bite-sized notes designed to provide up-to-date information to media and information-seeking publics throughout the contest season both in print and online.

game programs—An organizational media tactic usually distributed by the organization and sold to consumers on the day of an event.

gatekeepers—Members of the media who choose to write about a specific topic and not others. The media are opening the gate, allowing the public access to certain pieces of information.

grapevine—An informal communication network that fills the gaps left by formal vertical and horizontal communications.

Grunig's four models of public relations—Models depicting the basic approaches to public relations practice as well as its evolution as a profession. Includes press agentry, public information, and two-way asymmetrical and two-way symmetrical models.

hashtags—The # symbol, which, followed by a key phrase, represents a searchable topical grouping on social networks.

intranet—An internally managed website or private network within an organization used to share private business-related information among employees.

integrated communication—A synergistic approach to communication that allows congruent brand-related messages to be delivered across multiple platforms (e.g., paid, shared) to attain consistency of message.

inverted pyramid—A journalistic writing style in which the most important information is placed at the beginning of a news story, followed by supportive and less-relevant information.

investor relations (IR)—a public relations function that seeks to establish desirable relationships with individual investors, investment firms, and financial analysts.

issues management—An organizational process of identifying and addressing interest-driven actions by a public that stand to affect the relationship between the organization and that public.

key performance indicators (KPI)—A varied set of metrics, closely aligned with a website's purpose and goals, that provide data on the effectiveness of the website in meeting those goals.

latent public—A group of people who have some common interest or link to the organization but fail to recognize it.

lead—The opening one to two paragraphs of a news story, which typically contain the factual elements of who, what, where, when, why, and how.

lobbying—A persuasion strategy used by organizations as they seek to influence government and political activity.

media content—The photos, video, or GIFs and other animations shared by a user on a social networking site.

media guides—An annual and highly detailed sport public relations organizational media tactic designed primarily for media and information-seeking publics distributed in print and online.

media relations—A public relations function focused on building strong relationships with members of the mass media.

media rooms—Spaces available to working members of the media and organizational public relations professionals. These rooms typically have work areas and access to technology, power, and media information, such as statistics.

media-sharing networks—Social networking sites that have the distinct purpose of sharing photos, videos, and graphical elements.

membership relationship management—Systematic approach to establishing, tracking, and advancing relationships with an organization's members. Typically involves securing relevant information (e.g., contact information, purchase history) and tailoring engagement based on the members' interests and preferences.

message development—The process of preparing organizational representatives to purposefully convey intended content.

mobile application—Commonly referred to as an app; software designed to specifically run on mobile devices such as a smartphone or tablet.

Net Promoter Score (NPS)—An approach to assessing the customer experience by categorizing customers into one of three groups: promoters, passives, and detractors.

news conference—A staged media event in which an organizational spokesperson makes an opening statement, followed by an exchange with reporters.

newsletters—An organizational media tactic distributed in print and by e-mail that communicates a variety of information to wide or very targeted publics.

news value—Helps journalists decide whether or not to cover a particular story. Attributes such as timeliness and proximity can impact a story's news value.

nonpublic—A group of people who have no common interest in or connection to an issue confronting an organization.

one-move chess—A crisis response in which a sport entity is observed to be "making decisions with no respect for strategy" (Yaeger & Henry, 2009).

organizational app—An application downloaded by a user to a mobile device that is an organizational media tactic made available to the general public.

organizational culture—The values, attitudes, and behaviors that characterize the way that an organization operates.

organizational media—Internally published public relations tactics that do not rely on the involvement of mass media to translate the organization's message.

PESO model—communications model from Dietrich (2014) comprising four communication categories: paid, earned (i.e., publicity), and the "two new kids in town" (p. 38), shared and owned media.

philanthropy—A term used to describe an act of trust by a donor when giving something of value, financial or otherwise, to an organization.

podcasting—The production of a series of digital audio or video files available to users for download to listen or watch.

proactive public relations—An approach to public relations practice in which the organization predominantly initiates actions to build stakeholder relationships and anticipates issues that need to be addressed before they become problems.

programs—Formalized and sustained public relations efforts within an organization to manage and build relationship with a defined public or publics.

promotion—Organizational messages regarding the brand, products, or services designed to motivate publics to behave in desired fashions.

psychographics—In social media, includes a variety of behaviors of users on social media (e.g., the time of day a user is online).

public affairs—Managing an organization's interest in political issues and its relationships with government organizations.

publics—Groups of people who relate to the sport organization in similar ways. May include members of the mass media, members of the sport organization's community, employees, customers, donors, and investors.

reach—Estimated measurement of the size of a potential audience for a post on a social network.

reactive public relations—Approach to public relations practice in which the organization predominantly responds to stakeholder actions only after problematic issues have arisen.

recency, frequency, and monetary (RFM) analysis—Data collected about the frequency and recency of customer transactions as well as the size of those transactions.

reputation—Publicly held perceptions of an organization or individual based on constituencies' experiences and resultant relationships with the organization or individual.

retention metrics—A type of social media measurement focused on evaluating the relationship with publics on social networking sites. Satisfaction rates, reviews, and testimonials are all examples of this type of metric.

rights fee—An amount of money paid by a media company to a sport team, conference, or governing body for the right to broadcast that organization's events.

schedule card—A pocket-sized printed organizational media tactic that features the organization's schedule and potentially advertisements as well.

score bug—Part of a livestreamed or televised event graphical interface that the viewer sees and that is updated by an operator or through digital connections to a scoreboard on site. The score bug is usually found in the lower or upper third of the screen and includes sport-specific information such as the score, identification of teams, time remaining, which quarter or half is being played, and other information such as time-outs remaining and a shot clock.

search engine optimization (SEO)—The building and maintaining of a website in such a manner as to make it easily accessed and read by search engine bots or search quality raters to improve the ranking when someone searches for a topic related to the website.

self-presentation—How individuals choose to disclose information textually or display themselves visually on social media.

shared media—An element of the PESO model that describes social media as communication-based curated content that creates engagement and community.

site structure—The arrangement or grouping of information and the ways website users navigate the content of those groupings.

social impact—Positive consequences to humans based on specific initiatives or programs designed to address a pressing social challenge.

social listening—The monitoring of a brand's social networks for customer feedback and direct mentions that indicate sentiment of the brand.

social media—"Interactive media technologies that allow consumers to create and disseminate their own content, connect with media outlets and other network users and voice their opinions on any number of topics" (Sheffer & Schultz, 2013, p. 210).

social media activity—The amount of social network content produced by a public relations professional.

social media content—Original text, photos, video, and links produced by the organization or shared on the platform from another entity—such as a highlight video from a traditional media outlet such as local news or ESPN or from a governing body such as a college athletics conference.

social media voice—Communication across all of an organization's social media platforms that is aligned to consistently express the personality of the brand.

social networking sites—Web-based services that allow individuals to construct a profile, articulate a list of others with whom they share a connection, and view and traverse their list of connections and those made by others within the system.

social networks—Broad methods to connect to people and brands for the purpose of sharing information and ideas.

spam—Systems produced to send unsolicited and repeated messages and advertisements while on the same website.

sponsorship activation—All the means one company or brand uses to maximize the exposure of a sponsorship program.

sport public relations—A brand-centric communication function designed to manage and advance relationships between a sport organization and its key publics.

Sports Broadcasting Act—Passed by Congress in 1961, the act allows professional sports leagues the ability to pool the rights of member teams and resell them for one rights fee, as opposed to having each member team negotiate individual media rights fees.

statistics—Detailed pieces of information generated throughout the course of a sporting event. The exact statistics vary by sport. Members of the media expect access to these statistics throughout an event.

stealing thunder—A crisis response approach in which a sport organization itself announces the bad news and shares its response before the news is reported elsewhere. The advantage of this approach is that it enables the sport organization to take a lead position in framing the public discussion around the crisis.

strategic management—Mission- and vision-driven process in which strategies are defined that organize, coordinate, and activate all the organization's assets to attain its goals and objectives

strategic social media management—The process of creating, scheduling, analyzing, and engaging with content posted on social media platforms.

strategic social responsibility—A voluntary business strategy that emphasizes improved community well-being (i.e., human conditions and environmental issues) and organizational economic objectives by using core competencies and resources.

teleconference—A news conference using telecommunications to connect the interviewee with interviewers who are not physically present at the news conference.

touchpoints—Individual points of interaction during various stages of the consumer experience, from awareness to consideration to acquisition to service.

unmediated communication—Direct communications between an organization and its publics without the use of a channel or medium.

viral marketing—The encouraged spread of a message through a variety of digital sources that can easily and quickly be spread from user to user.

virtual communication community—A group of people with shared interests who use electronic communication in the form of instant messaging, blogs, and forums as the primary form of communication between members of the group.

website accessibility—The ability for a website to be used by all people, regardless of disability type or impairment.

website service provider—A company that provides any variety of website creation and management services that can include domain hosting, construction of a website, maintenance of a website, and analytical evaluation of a website in a package based specifically on the user's needs.

references

Chapter 1

Aaker, J. (n.d.). *How to use stories to win over others* [Video]. Retrieved from https://leanin.org/education/harnessing-the-power-of-stories

Aaker, J., & Smith, A. (2010). *The dragonfly effect: Quick, effective and easy to use social media to drive social change.* San Francisco, CA: Wiley.

Abernathy, P.M. (2018). *The expanding news desert.* University of North Carolina, Hussman School of Journalism and Media, Center for Innovation and Sustainability in Local Media. Retrieved from www.usnewsdeserts.com/reports/expanding-news-desert/

Abeza, G. (2018). The past, present and future of social media in professional sports: Interview with Shannon Gross, director of content strategy, Dallas Cowboys. *International Journal of Sport Communication, 11,* 295–300.

ANA/USC Annenberg Center for Public Relations. (2017). *The evolution of public relations.* Retrieved from https://annenberg.usc.edu/sites/default/files/ii-evolution-public-relations.pdf

Andrew, D.P.S., Pedersen, P.M., & McEvoy, C.D. (2020). *Research methods and design in sport management* (2nd ed.). Champaign, IL: Human Kinetics.

Berkhouse, J., & Gabert, T. (1999, June). *Community relations within Major League Baseball, National Basketball Association, National Football League, and the National Hockey League.* Paper presented at the meeting of the North American Society for Sport Management, Vancouver, British Columbia, Canada.

Black, A. (2007, August 22). Football feature: Football's unsung heroes. *PR Week.* Retrieved from www.prweek.com/article/732718/football-feature-footballs-unsung-heroes

Broom, G. (2013). *Cutlip and Center's effective public relations* (11th ed.). Upper Saddle, NJ: Pearson.

Carter, D.M. (1996). *Keeping score: An inside look at sports marketing.* Green Pass, OR: Oasis Press.

Clark, M.S., & Mills, J. (1979). Interpersonal attraction in exchange and communal relationships. *Journal of Personality and Social Psychology, 37,* 12–24.

Clavio, G. (2013). Emerging social media and applications in sport. In P.M. Pedersen (Ed.), *Routledge Handbook of Sport* Communication (pp. 259–268). New York, NY: Routledge.

Dietrich, G. (2014). *Spin sucks: Communication and reputation management in the digital age.* Indianapolis, IN: Que Publishing.

Dozier, D.M., Grunig, L.A., & Grunig, J.E. (1995). *Manager's guide to excellence in public relations and communication management.* Hillsdale, NJ: Erlbaum.

Drew, N. (2016, August). Closing the gap between brand and reputation. *FleishmanHillard True.* Retrieved from https://fleishmanhillard.com/2015/10/true/closing-the-gap-between-brand-and-reputation/

Edwards, L. (2018, January 24). Phil Neville deletes Twitter account after controversial posts about women are unearthed. *The Telegraph.* Retrieved from www.telegraph.co.uk/football/2018/01/23/phil-neville-deletes-twitter-account-controversial-posts-women/

Fontaine, M. (2018, December 11). Twitter has become the modern-day Roman Colosseum. *Fortune.* Retrieved from http://fortune.com/2018/12/11/twitter-mob-mentality-ancient-rome/

Freitag, A. (2008). Staking claim: Public relations leaders need to shape CSR policy. *Public Relations Quarterly.* Retrieved June 24, 2009, from www.allbusiness.com/company-activities-management/business-ethics/10635842-1.html

Funk, D.C., & Pritchard, M.P. (2006). Sport publicity: Commitment's moderation of message effects. *Journal of Business Research, 59,* 613–621.

Germann, M. (2015, July 12). The rise and evolution of the chief communications officer. LinkedIn. Retrieved from www.linkedin.com/pulse/rise-evolution-chief-communications-officer-mitch-germann/

Gibbs, C., & Haynes, R. (2013). A phenomenological investigation into how Twitter has changed the nature of sport media relations. *International Journal of Sport Communication, 6,* 394–408.

Gray, G. (2017, July 21). Why public relations agencies are evolving. *Forbes.* Retrieved from www.forbes.com/sites/forbescommunicationscouncil/2017/07/21/why-public-relations-agencies-are-evolving/#23338ab017f4

Grieco, E. (2018, July 30). Newsroom employment dropped nearly a quarter in less than 10 years, with greatest decline at newspapers. *Pew Research Center.* Retrieved from www .pewresearch.org/fact-tank/2018/07/30/newsroom -employment-dropped-nearly-a-quarter-in-less-than-10 -years-with-greatest-decline-at-newspapers/

Grunig, J.E. (Ed.). (1992). *Excellence in public relations and communication management.* Hillsdale, NJ: Erlbaum.

Grunig, J.E., & Hunt, T. (1984). *Managing public relations.* New York, NY: Holt, Rinehart, and Winston.

Grunig, J.E., & Repper, F.C. (1992). Strategic management, publics, and issues. In J.E. Grunig (Ed.), *Excellence in public relations and communication management* (pp. 117–157). Hillsdale, NJ: Erlbaum.

Henniger, W. (2003, May 5–11). Preakness' wild 2-week ride a challenging piece of reactive PR. *Street & Smith's SportsBusiness Journal, 6,* 12.

Hopwood, M. (2010). Public relations and communication in sport. In M. Hopwood, P. Kitchin, & J. Skinner (Eds.), *Sport public relations and communication* (pp.13–32). Oxford, England: Elsevier.

Hoyt, J. (2019, May 25). From "a Texas treasure" to a town that "sold its soul": Art Briles' shocking hire sent tiny Mount Vernon into national news. *The Dallas Morning News.* Retrieved from https://sportsday.dallasnews.com /high-school/high-schools/2019/05/25/texas-treasure -town-sold-soul-art-briles-shocking-hiring-sent-tiny -mount-vernon-national-news

Humphreys, B., & Ruseski, J. (2008). *The size and scope of the sports industry in the United States* (IASE/NAASE Working Paper Series, No. 08–11). Working paper.

Irwin, R.L., Sutton, W.A., & McCarthy, L.M. (2008). *Sport promotion and sales management* (2nd ed.). Champaign, IL: Human Kinetics.

Jones, J.M. (2017, October 13). Pro football losing fans; other sports holding steady. Retrieved from https:// news.gallup.com/poll/220562/pro-football-losing-fans -sports-holding-steady.aspx?g_source=link_newsv9&g _campaign=item_224864&g_medium=copy

Lasswell, H.D. (1948). The structure and function of communication in society. In L. Bryson (Ed.), *The communication of ideas* (pp. 37–51). New York, NY: Harper.

Lawhon, D. (2019, March 20). Bradley coach Brian Wardle contrite after controversy over targeting reporter: "You've got to own it." *The Des Moines Register.* Retrieved from www.desmoinesregister.com/story/sports/college /2019/03/20/march-madness-bradley-brand-ncaa -tournament-brian-wardle-peoria-journal-star-reporter -michigan-state/3220736002/

Lee, M.K., Ryu, S., Clavio, C., Lovell, M.D., Lim, C.H., & Pedersen, P.M. (2014). The effect of Twitter on sports fans' information processing: An analysis of the controversial referee's decision in the 2012 London Olympic Games. *International Journal of Sport Management and Marketing, 15*(3/4), 102–119.

L'Etang, J. (2013). *Sports public relations.* London, England: Sage.

Londergan, J. (2018, April 9). How the Colorado Buffaloes embrace digital storytelling. *Front Office Sports.* Retrieved from https://frntofficesport.com/how-the -colorado-buffaloes-embrace-digital-storytelling/

Londergan, J. (2019, January 2). Three predictions for sports digital media in 2019. *Front Office Sports.* Retrieved from https://frntofficesport.com/digital-social-media -predictions-2019/

MacCambridge, M. (2018, April 11, 2018). "Who can explain the athletic heart?" The past and perilous future of Sports Illustrated. *The Ringer.* Retrieved from www.theringer .com/2018/4/11/17220176/sports-illustrated-future -meredith-sale-history

Maese, R. (2018, May 31). NBA Twitter: A sports bar that doesn't close, where the stars pull up a seat next to you. *The Washington Post.* Retrieved from www .washingtonpost.com/news/sports/wp/2018/05/31/nba -twitter-a-sports-bar-that-doesnt-close-where-the-stars -pull-up-a-seat-next-to-you/?utm_term=.004a6873a775

Mazique, B. (2017, March 14). LaVar Ball: Marketing genius, out of control dad, or both? *Forbes.* Retrieved from www .forbes.com/sites/brianmazique/2017/03/14/lavar -ball-marketing-genius-out-of-control-dad-or-both /#31a8906a9d50

McCarthy, E.J. (1960). *Basic marketing: A managerial approach.* Homewood, IL: Irwin.

Milne, G.R., & McDonald, M.A. (1999). *Sport marketing: Managing the exchange process.* Sudbury, MA: Jones and Bartlett.

MLSE (Maple Leaf Sports and Entertainment Inc.) Foundation. (n.d.). *Staff.* Retrieved from www.mlsefoundation .org/About/Staff.aspx

Mullin, B.J., Hardy, S., & Sutton, W.A. (2014). *Sport marketing* (4th ed.). Champaign, IL: Human Kinetics.

MVPindex. (2018, December 20). MVPindex presents the year's most valuable sports teams on social. Retrieved from https://mvpindex.com/mvpindex-presents-the -years-most-valuable-sports-teams-on-social/

New Balance. (2012). *Made to move.* Retrieved from www .newbalance.com/on/demandware.static/-/Sites -newbalance_us2-Library/default/dw36cfbc3e/inside -nb/inside-nb-overview/171206508.pdf

Nielsen Sports. (2018). *Commercial trends in sports 2018: Top 5 global sports industry trends.* Retrieved from https:// nielsensports.com/reports/commercial-trends-sports -2018/

Norman, J. (2018, January 4). *Football still Americans' favorite sport to watch.* Retrieved from https://news.gallup .com/poll/224864/football-americans-favorite-sport -watch.aspx

Pedersen, P.M., Laucella, P.C., Kian, E.M., & Guerin, A.N. (2021). *Strategic sport communication* (3rd ed.). Champaign, IL: Human Kinetics.

Perper, R. (2019, October 22). China and the NBA are coming to blows over a pro-Hong Kong tweet. Here's why. *Busi-*

ness Insider. Retrieved from www.businessinsider.com /nba-china-feud-timeline-daryl-morey-tweet-hong -kong-protests-2019-10

Pettinger, R. (1999). *Effective employee relations: A guide to policy and practice in the workplace*. London, England: Kogan Page.

Public Policy Forum. (2017, June 6). *The shattered mirror: FAQ*. Retrieved from https://ppforum.ca/articles/the -shattered-mirror-faq/

PwC. (2019). A new video world order. Retrieved from www.pwc.com/us/en/services/consulting/library /consumer-intelligence-series/video-consumer -motivations.html

Ries, A., & Ries, L. (2002). *The fall of advertising and the rise of PR*. New York, NY: HarperCollins.

Right to Play. (n.d.). *About us*. Retrieved from www .righttoplayusa.org/en/about-us/

Rush, B.C. (2014, August 28). Science of storytelling: Why and how to use it in your marketing. *The Guardian*. Retrieved from www.theguardian.com/media -network/media-network-blog/2014/aug/28/science -storytelling-digital-marketing

Sanderson, J., & Yandle, C. (2015). *Developing successful social media plans in sport organizations*. Morgantown, WV: FiT Publishing.

Shannon, C.E., & Weaver, W. (1949). *The mathematical theory of communication*. Urbana, IL: University of Illinois Press.

Sheffer, M.L., & Schultz, B. (2013). The new world of social media and broadcast sports reporting. In P.M. Pedersen (Ed.), *Routledge handbook of sport communication* (pp. 2510–218). New York, NY: Routledge.

Sports Biz Mom: Gina Lehe, College Football Playoff. (2019, May 1). Retrieved from https://sportsbizmom .com/2019/05/01/sports-biz-mom-gina-lehe-college -football-playoff/

Sriramesh, K., Grunig, J.E., & Buffington, J. (1992). Corporate culture and public relations. In J.E. Grunig (Ed.), *Excellence in public relations and communication management* (pp. 577–598). Hillsdale, NJ: Lawrence Erlbaum Associates.

Statista. (2019a). *Number of monthly active Twitter users worldwide from 1st quarter 2010 to 4th quarter 2018 (in millions)*. Retrieved from www.statista.com/statistics/282087 /number-of-monthly-active-twitter-users/

Statista. (2019b). *Number of social media users worldwide from 2010 to 2021 (in billions)*. Retrieved from www.statista .com/statistics/278414/number-of-worldwide-social -network-users/

Statista. (2019c). *Number of mobile phone users worldwide from 2015 to 2020 (in billions)*. Retrieved from www.statista .com/statistics/274774/forecast-of-mobile-phone-users -worldwide/

Stoldt, G.C., Dittmore, S.W., & Branvold, S.E. (2003, May). *Teaching about sport public relations*. Paper presented at the meeting of the North American Society for Sport Management, Ithaca, NY.

Strunk, W., Jr., & White, E.B. (2008). *The elements of style* (50th anniversary ed.). New York, NY: Longman.

The influence 100. (2015). *PRovoke*. Retrieved from www .provokemedia.com/research/article/link-between -corporate-reputation-market-value-strengthens -study\

Top podcast genres in U.S. households. (2018, July 27). *Marketing charts*. Retrieved from www.marketingcharts .com/charts/popular-podcast-genres-us-households /attachment/nielsen-top-podcast-genres-in-us -households-aug2018

Turney, M. (2011). Parallels between interpersonal relations and public relations can enhance your understanding of both. *On-line Readings in Public Relations by Michael Turney*. Retrieved from www.nku.edu/~turney/prclass /readings/interpersonal.html

Value Based Management.net. (n.d.). *Corporate reputation quotient*. Retrieved June 26, 2009, from www .valuebasedmanagement.net/methods_corporate _reputation_quotient.html

Waters, R.D. (2013). Applying public relations theory to increase the understanding of sport communication. In P.M. Pedersen (Ed.), *Routledge handbook of sport communication* (pp. 66–74). New York, NY: Routledge.

Wilder, C. (2019, January 29). How the Super Bowl's Opening Night has evolved into the spectacle it is today. *Sports Illustrated*. Retrieved from www.si.com/nfl/2019 /01/29/super-bowl-opening-night-patriots-rams-media -day

Young, R. (2019, May 3). Kanter draws support of union after drawing jeers. *ESPN*. Retrieved from www.espn .com/nba/story/_/id/26657954/kanter-draws-support -union-drawing-jeers

Zheng, J. (2018). Interview with Rong (DanDan) Hua, digital media manager of the National Football League's China office. *International Journal of Sport Communication, 11*, 301–307.

Chapter 2

Adams, W.M. (2006). *The future of sustainability: Re-thinking environment and development in the twenty-first century*. Report of the IUCN Renowned Thinkers Meeting, January 29–31, 2006. Retrieved August 29, 2010, from cmsdata .iucn.org/downloads/iucn_future_of_sustanability.pdf

AdNews Australia. (2013, May 28). Nike "She Runs" case study—MFA Awards 2012 (Best Integrated Media Campaign) [Video]. Retrieved from www.youtube.com /watch?v=RqGIemVf4cY

Ahles, C.B. (2003). Campaign excellence: A survey of Silver Anvil award winners compares current PR practice with planning, campaign theory. *Public Relations Strategist, 9*(3), 46–53.

Allen, S. (2011, August 12). 7-pound dumbbells and 14 more gimmicky Heisman campaigns. *Mental Floss*. Retrieved from http://mentalfloss.com/article/28496 /7-pound-purple-dumbbells-and-14-more-gimmicky -heisman-campaigns

AMEC (International Association for Measurement and Evaluation of Communications). (2011, June 7). *Valid metrics for PR measurement: Putting the principles into action*. Retrieved from http://apps.prsa.org/Intelligence /BusinessCase/Documents/AMEC/20110607ValidMe tricsforPRMeasurement.pdf

Amway Center. (n.d.). *About the city of Orlando*. Retrieved from www.amwaycenter.com/venue-information/about -the-city-of-orlando

Austin, E.W., & Pinkleton, B.E. (2015). *Strategic public relations management: Planning and managing effective communication campaigns* (3rd ed.). New York, NY: Routledge.

Balfour, F., & Jana, R. (2008, August 4). Sponsors walking away from the Olympics. *Business Week*.

Barnett, M., Jermier, J., & Lafferty, B. (2006). Corporate reputation: The definitional landscape. *Corporate Reputation Review, 9*(1), 26–38.

Block, J. (2016, April 19). Why ads on NBA jerseys aren't the end of the world. *HuffPost*. Retrieved from www .huffingtonpost.com/entry/why-ads-on-nba-jerseys -arent-the-end-of-the-world-according-to-a-soccer-fan _us_57112ae7e4b0060ccda32e05

Broom, G. (2013). *Cutlip and Center's effective public relations* (11th ed.). Upper Saddle, NJ: Pearson.

Chia. (2018, May 9). How an athletic brand preferred by men drove a 9% Q4 revenue increase with a killer marketing campaign for women. *Brand24*. Retrieved from https://brand24.com/blog/nike-drove-q4-revenue -increase-with-killer-marketing-campaign/

Connors, K. (2014). Public relations. In B. Mullin, S. Hardy, & W. Sutton (Eds.), *Sport marketing* (4th ed., pp. 311–341). Champaign, IL: Human Kinetics.

Coombs, T. (2017). How the NFL has handled the recent CTE crisis risk from the JAMA article. *Institute for Public Relations*. Retrieved from https://instituteforpr.org/nfl -handled-recent-cte-crisis-risk-jama-article/

Corporate reputation quotient. (n.d.). Retrieved October 20, 2004, from www.valuebasedmanagement.net/methods _corporate_reputaton_quotient.html

Dale, M. (2002). Issue-driven strategy formation. *Strategic Change, 11*, 131–142.

Dietrich, G. (2014). *Spin sucks: Communication and reputation management in the digital age*. Indianapolis, IN: Que Publishing.

DiMeglio, S. (2010, February 16). "Down year" has an upside as LPGA season begins. *USA Today*.

Dougall, E. (2008, December 12). Issues management. *Institute for Public Relations*. Retrieved from https:// instituteforpr.org/issues-management/

Dozier, D., & Ehling, W. (1992). Evaluation of public relations: What the literature tells us about their effects. In J. Grunig (Ed.), *Excellence in public relations and communications management* (pp. 159–184). Hillsdale, NJ: Erlbaum.

Dozier, D.M., Grunig, L.A., & Grunig, J.E. (1995). *Manager's guide to excellence in public relations and communication management*. Hillsdale, NJ: Erlbaum.

Drew, N. (2016, August). Closing the gap between brand and reputation. *FleishmanHillard True*. Retrieved from https://fleishmanhillard.com/2015/10/true/closing-the -gap-between-brand-and-reputation/

Edelman, R. (2010). *2010 trust barometer executive summary*. Retrieved from www.scribd.com/doc/26268655/2010 -Trust-Barometer-Executive-Summary

Ettenson, R., & Knowles, J. (2008, Winter). Don't confuse reputation and brand. *MIT Sloan Management Review*, 19–21.

Festinger, L. (1957). *A theory of cognitive dissonance*. Evanston, IL: Row, Peterson.

Fombrun, C. (1996). *Reputation: Realizing value from the corporate image*. Boston, MA: Harvard Business School Press.

Fombrun, C., Gardberg, N., & Sever, J. (1999). The reputation quotient: A multi-stakeholder measure of corporate reputation. *Journal of Brand Management, 7*(4), 241–255.

Forbes. (2017). The Forbes Fab 40 2017: The world's most valuable sports brands. Retrieved from www.forbes .com/pictures/59e62ee431358e542c03d5be/10-nesn /#6a2a8dd62f65

Freberg, K. (2016, December 11). *Social media and sports lessons from the Heisman Trophy campaigns*. Retrieved from https://karenfreberg.com/blog/social-media-and -sports-lessons-from-the-heisman-trophy-campaigns/

Frederick, D. (2017, June 2). Qualtrics teams up with Utah Jazz to fund cancer research. *PR Week*. Retrieved from www.prweek.com/article/1435464/qualtrics-teams -utah-jazz-fund-cancer-research

Fryer, J. (2010, July 27). NASCAR fights its perception problem. *Detroit News*.

Funk, D.C., & James, J.D. (2004). The Fan Attitude Network (FAN) model: Exploring attitude formation and change among sport consumers. *Sport Management Review, 7*, 1–26.

Gaio, M. (2013, December). Technology and social media alter the future of Heisman trophy campaigns. *Athletic Business*. Retrieved from www.athleticbusiness.com /marketing/technology-and-social-media-alter-the -future-of-heisman-trophy-campaigns.html

Gibson, H., Fairley, S., & Kennelly, M. (2019). Sport tourism. In P. Pedersen & L. Thibault (Eds.), *Contemporary sport management* (6th ed., pp. 226–245). Champaign, IL: Human Kinetics.

Grunig, J. (1993). Image and substance: From symbolic to behavioral relationships. *Public Relations Review, 19*, 121–139.

Grunig, J. (2006). *After 50 years: The value and values of public relations*. Institute for Public Relations: 45th Annual Distinguished Lecture, The Yale Club, New York, November 9, 2006.

Grunig, J.E., & Grunig, L.A. (2001). *Guidelines for formative and evaluative research in public affairs*. Retrieved from https://www.instituteforpr.org/wp-content/uploads/Guidelines-for-Formative-and-Evaluative-Research-in-Public-Affairs.pdf

Grunig, L., Grunig, J., & Dozier, D.M. (2002). *Excellent public relations and effective organizations*. Mahwah, NJ: Lawrence Erlbaum.

Grunig, J., & Hunt, T. (1984). *Managing public relations*. New York, NY: CBS College.

Heath, R. (1997). *Strategic issues management: Organizations and public policy changes*. Thousand Oaks, CA: Sage.

Hendrix, J. (1998). *Public relations case* (4th ed.). Belmont, CA: Wadsworth.

Henninger, W. (2002, March 4–10). Upper Deck regroups behind gizmo after a PR launch that wasn't. *Street & Smith's SportsBusiness Journal, 4*, 10.

Hon, L. (1998). Demonstrating effectiveness in public relations: Goals, objectives, and evaluation. *Journal of Public Relations Research, 10*(2), 103–105.

Hon, L., & Grunig, J. (1999). *Guidelines for measuring relationships in public relations*. Gainesville, FL: Institute for Public Relations, Commission on Public Relations Measurement and Evaluation.

Hopwood, M.K. (2007). Sport public relations. In J. Beech, S. Chadwick (Eds.), *The marketing of sport* (pp. 292–317). Harlow, England: Prentice Hall.

Hopwood, M.K. (2010a). Public relations and communication in sport. In M. Hopwood, P. Kitchin, & J. Skinner (Eds.), *Sport public relations and communication* (pp. 13–32). Oxford, England: Elsevier.

Hopwood, M.K. (2010b). Sport marketing public relations. In M. Hopwood, P. Kitchin, & J. Skinner (Eds.), *Sport public relations and communication* (pp. 55–68). Oxford, England: Elsevier.

Hoye, R., Smith, A.C.T., Nicholson, M., & Stewart, B. (2018). *Sport management: Principles and applications* (5th ed.). London: Routledge.

Humphreys, B., & Ruseski, J. (2008). *The size and scope of the sports industry in the United States* (IASE/NAASE Working Paper Series, No. 08–11). Working paper.

Hunsberger, D. (2009, July 18). Can the LPGA tour be fixed? *Daily Commercial*.

Hyman, H.H., & Sheatsley, P.B. (1947). Some reasons why information campaigns fail. *Public Opinion Quarterly, 11*, 412–423.

Irwin, R.L., Sutton, W.A., & McCarthy, L.M. (2008). *Sport promotion and sales management* (2nd ed.). Champaign, IL: Human Kinetics.

Jackowski, M. (1999, November 8). In pure dollars, what's your reputation worth? *Street & Smith's SportsBusiness Journal*. Retrieved from www.sportsbusinessdaily.com/Journal/Issues/1999/11/08/No-Topic-Name/In-Pure-Dollars-Whats-Your-Reputation-Worth.aspx

Jackson, P. (2000). PRoSpeak: Strategy is everything. In F.R. Matera & R.J. Artigue (Eds.), *PR campaigns and techniques: Building bridges into the 21st century* (pp. 104–105). Boston, MA: Allyn and Bacon.

Jang, W., Ko, Y.J., & Chan-Olmsted, S.M. (2015). Spectator-based sports team reputation: Scale development and validation. *International Journal of Sports Marketing and Sponsorship, 16*(3), 52–72.

Keller, K. (1993). Conceptualizing, measuring, and managing customer-based brand equity. *Journal of Marketing, 57*(1), 1–22.

Kelly, K. (2001). Stewardship: The fifth step in the public relations process. In R. Heath (Ed.), *Handbook of public relations* (pp. 279–289). Thousand Oaks, CA: Sage.

Kendall, R. (1996). *Public relations campaign strategies* (2nd ed.). New York, NY: HarperCollins.

Kitchin, P.J., & Purcell, P.A. (2017). Examining sport communications practitioners' approaches to issues management and crisis response in Northern Ireland. *Public Relations Review, 43*, 661–670.

Kotler, P., & Keller, K.L. (2016). *Marketing management* (15th ed.). Boston, MA: Pearson.

Kristiansen, E., & Williams, A.S. (2015). Communicating the athlete as a brand: An examination of LPGA star Suzann Pettersen. *International Journal of Sport Communication. 8*, 371–388.

Kutz, S. (2017, November 13). 19 NBA teams have now sold ad space on their jerseys. *MarketWatch*. Retrieved from www.marketwatch.com/story/this-company-will-pay-the-golden-state-warriors-20-million-a-year-for-an-ad-on-its-jerseys-2017-09-12

Ledingham, J.A., & Bruning, S.D. (2010). *Public relations as relationship management: A relational approach to the study and practice of public relations*. Mahwah, NJ: Lawrence Erlbaum.

Lesly, P. (1998). *Lesly's handbook of public relations and communications*. Chicago: NTC Business Books.

L'Etang, J. (2013). *Sports public relations*. London, England: Sage.

LPGA (Ladies Professional Golf Association). (n.d.). *Suzanne Pettersen*. Retrieved from http://www.lpga.com/players/suzann-pettersen/81622/bio

Macnamara, J. (2006). *Reputation measurement and management* (Research paper). Retrieved from http://195.130.87.21:8080/dspace/bitstream/123456789/232/1/Macnamara-reputation%20measurement%20and%20management.pdf.

Marker, R.K. (1977). The Armstrong/PR data measurement system. *Public Relations Review, 3*(4), 51–59.

Matera, F.R., & Artigue, R.J. (2000). *PR campaigns and techniques: Building bridges into the 21st century.* Boston, MA: Allyn and Bacon.

Mez, J., Daneshvar, D.H., Kiernan, P.T., Abdolmohammadi, B., Alvarez, V.E., Huber, B.R., . . . McKee, A.C. (2017). Clinicopathological evaluation of chronic traumatic encephalopathy in players of American football. *JAMA, 318*(4), 360–370.

Millman, C. (2009, July 24). Sports leagues sue to stop betting. *ESPN the Magazine.*

Mitrook, M. A., Parish, N. B., & Seltzer, T. (2008). From advocacy to accommodation: A case study of the Orlando Magic's public relations efforts to secure a new arena. *Public Relations Review, 34,* 161–168.

Mogel, L. (2002). *Making it in public relations* (2nd ed.). Mahwah, NJ: Erlbaum.

National Collegiate Athletic Association (NCAA). (2010a). *2010–11 Revenue distribution plan.* Indianapolis, IN: NCAA.

National Collegiate Athletic Association (NCAA). (2010b). *2010–11 NCAA Division I manual.* Indianapolis, IN: NCAA.

Ozanian, M. (2017, October 24). The Forbes Fab 40: The world's most valuable sports brands 2017. *Forbes.* Retrieved from www.forbes.com/sites/mikeozanian/2017/10/24/the-forbes-fab-40-the-worlds-most-valuable-sports-brands-2017/#58e4773b84b1

Pedersen, P.M., & Thibault, L. (2018). *Contemporary sport management* (6th ed.). Champaign, IL: Human Kinetics.

Pinkham, D. (2004). *Issues management.* Public Affairs Council. Retrieved October 19, 2004, from www.pac.org/public/issues_management.shtml

Poole, M. (2004, March 15). Companies that use PR effectively multiply value of their sponsorships. *Street and Smith's SportsBusiness Journal, 6,* 13.

PRSA (Public Relations Society of America). (n.d.a). *About PRSA.* Retrieved from www.prsa.org/about/about-prsa/

PRSA (Public Relations Society of America). (n.d.b). *APR frequently asked questions.* Retrieved from http://www.praccreditation.org/apply/apr/APR_FAQ

Rawlins, B. (2006). *Prioritizing stakeholders for public relations.* Gainesville, FL: Institute for Public Relations: Commission on Public Relations Measurement and Evaluation.

Ries, A., & Ries, L. (2002). *The fall of advertising and the rise of PR.* New York, NY: HarperCollins.

Sammer, P. (2016). Don't let storytelling become a fantasy. *The Ketchum Blog.* Retrieved from www.ketchum.com/dont-let-storytelling-become-a-fantasy/

Schultz, B., Caskey, P.H., & Esherick, C. (2013). *Media relations in sport* (4th ed.). Morgantown, WV: FiT Publishing.

She runs the night—strategy, execution, results of Nike's groundbreaking campaign. (2013, May 6). *Marketing.* Retrieved from www.marketingmag.com.au/hubs-c/she-runs-the-night-strategy-execution-results-of-nikes-groundbreaking-campaign/

Shilbury, D., & Rowe, K. (2010). Sport relationship management. In M. Hopwood, P. Kitchin, & J. Skinner (Eds.), *Sport public relations and communication* (pp. 33–54). Oxford, England: Elsevier.

Siang, S. (2016, March 3). 3 lessons from sports for effective storytelling. *Forbes.* Retrieved from www.forbes.com/sites/sanyinsiang/2016/03/03/3-lessons-from-sports-for-effective-storytelling/#6dd35cfc785f

Sims, M.P. (2018, March 8). Link between corporate reputation & market value strengthens: Study. *PRovoke.* Retrieved from www.provokemedia.com/research/article/link-between-corporate-reputation-market-value-strengthens-study

Smith, R.D. (2017). *Strategic planning for public relations* (5th ed.). New York, NY: Routledge.

Stareva, I. (2014). How to become a break through storyteller. *Iliyana's Blog.* Retrieved from www.iliyanastareva.com/blog/how-to-become-a-break-through-storyteller-infographic

Stoldt, G.C., Ratzlaff, SE. & Ramolet, A. (2009). The "Vote Yea" campaign: A case study in two-way asymmetrical communication. *International Journal of Sport Management, 10,* 410–428.

Tomiyama, K. (2012, September 18–21). *Understanding the sports organizational reputation.* Paper presented at the annual meeting of European Association for Sport Management, Aalborg, Denmark. Retrieved from www.easm.net/download/2012/d4613da15cf5e7410b9ff17e28009347.pdf

Zillgitt, J. (2018, July 30). LeBron James opens new public school in Akron: "One of the greatest moments" of his life. *USA Today.* Retrieved from www.usatoday.com/story/sports/nba/2018/07/30/lebron-james-promise-school-akron-ohio/862159002/

Chapter 3

Amaresan, S. (2018, August 20). What is social listening & why is it important? *Hubspot.* Retrieved from https://blog.hubspot.com/service/social-listening

Boyd, D.M., & Ellison, N.B. (2007). Social network sites: Definition, history, and scholarship. *Journal of Computer-Mediated Communication, 13*(1), 210–230.

Carr, C.T., & Hayes, R.A. (2015). Social media: Defining, developing, and divining. *Atlantic Journal of Communication, 23*(1), 46–65.

Cawley, C. (2018, July 23). What is social media management? Retrieved from https://tech.co/digital-marketing/social-media-management-guide

Chang, J., Kapetaneas, J., & Valiente, A. (2015, May 15). How the stars behind Dude Perfect made YouTube their day job. *ABC News.* Retrieved from https://abcnews.go

.com/Entertainment/stars-dude-perfect-made-youtube-day-job/story?id=31075377

Chi, C. (2019, February 12). 51 YouTube stats every video marketer should know in 2019. *Hubspot*. Retrieved from https://blog.hubspot.com/marketing/youtube-stats

Chugh, R., & Ruhi, U. (2018). Social media in higher education: A literature review of Facebook. *Education and Information Technologies, 23*(2), 605–616.

Clarke, T. (2019, March 12). 22 Instagram statistics that matter to marketers in 2019. *Hootsuite*. Retrieved from https://blog.hootsuite.com/instagram-statistics/

Facebook. (July 24, 2019). Number of monthly active Facebook users worldwide as of 2nd quarter 2019 (in millions) [Graph]. *Statista*. Retrieved from www.statista.com/statistics/264810/number-of-monthly-active-facebook-users-worldwide/

Foreman, C. (2017, June 20). 10 types of social media and how each can benefit your business. *Hootsuite*. Retrieved from https://blog.hootsuite.com/types-of-social-media/

Forsey, C. (n.d.). What is Twitter and how does it work? *Hubspot*. Retrieved from https://blog.hubspot.com/marketing/what-is-twitter

Freberg, K. (2016). Social media. In C. Carroll (Ed.), *Encyclopedia for corporate reputation* (pp. 773–776). Thousand Oaks, CA: SAGE.

Jahns, M. (2019, March 26). Top 10: These are the most popular athletes on Instagram. *Ispo*. Retrieved from www.ispo.com/en/people/top-10-these-are-most-popular-athletes-instagram

Kapoor, K. K., Tamilmani, K., Rana, N. P., Patil, P., Dwivedi, Y. K., & Nerur, S. (2018). Advances in social media research: past, present and future. *Information Systems Frontiers, 20*(3), 531–558.

Larson, L. (2019, September 9). The most subscribed YouTube channels in 2019. *Digital Trends*. Retrieved from www.digitaltrends.com/web/biggest-youtube-channels/

Muniz, A. M., Jr., & Schau, H. J. (2007, Fall). Vigilante marketing and consumer-created communications. *Journal of Advertising, 36*(3), 35–50.

MVPindex. (2019, April 1). MVPindex presents the year's most valuable sports teams on social. Retrieved from https://mvpindex.com/mvpindex-presents-the-years-most-valuable-sports-teams-on-social/

Newberry, C. (2019, December 2). 37 Instagram statistics that matter to marketers in 2020. Retrieved from https://blog.hootsuite.com/instagram-statistics/

Search Sports Jobs. (n.d.). *TeamWork Online*. Retrieved from www.teamworkonline.com/

Seiter, C. (2018, November 30). 61 social media metrics, defined. *Buffer Marketing Library*. Retrieved from https://buffer.com/library/social-media-metrics

Sheffer, M.L., & Schultz, B. (2013). The new world of social media and broadcast sports reporting. In P.M. Pedersen (Ed.), *Routledge handbook of sport communication* (pp. 210–218). New York, NY: Routledge.

Shleyner, E. (2019, November 8). 19 social media metrics that really matter—and how to track them. *Hootsuite*. Retrieved from https://blog.hootsuite.com/social-media-metrics/

Social media. (2013, September 27). Retrieved from https://excellencetheory.wordpress.com/tag/social-media/.

Statista. (2019a). *Number of monthly active Twitter users worldwide from 1st quarter 2010 to 4th quarter 2018 (in millions)*. Retrieved from www.statista.com/statistics/282087/number-of-monthly-active-twitter-users/

Statista. (2019b). *Number of social media users worldwide from 2010 to 2021 (in billions)*. Retrieved from www.statista.com/statistics/278414/number-of-worldwide-social-network-users/

Twitter. (April 23, 2019). Number of monthly active Twitter users worldwide from 1st quarter 2010 to 1st quarter 2019 (in millions) [Graph]. *Statista*. Retrieved from www.statista.com/statistics/282087/number-of-monthly-active-twitter-users/

Chapter 4

Adams, R. (2004, November 8–14). Keying on growth, nfl.com rolls out new fantasy game. *Street & Smith's SportsBusiness Journal, 7*, 5.

An, D. (2018, February). Find out how you stack up to new industry benchmarks for mobile page speed. *Think with Google*. Retrieved from www.thinkwithgoogle.com/marketing-resources/data-measurement/mobile-page-speed-new-industry-benchmarks/

Baehr, C. (2007). *Web development: A visual-spatial approach*. Upper Saddle River, NJ: Pearson Prentice Hall.

Barnett, B. (2017). Girls gone web: Self-depictions of female athletes on personal websites. *Journal of Communication Inquiry, 41*(2), 97–123.

Brown, A., & Green, T. (2008). Video podcasting in perspective: The history, technology, aesthetics, and instructional uses of a new medium. *Journal of Educational Technology Systems, 36*(1), 3–17.

Bruno, R., & Whitlock, K. (2000). Nothin' but net. In M. Helitzer (Ed.), *The dream job: $port$ publicity, promotion and marketing* (3rd ed., pp. 429–441). Athens, OH: University Sports Press.

Chiu, W., & Won, D. (2016). Relationship between sport website quality and consumption intentions: Application of a bifactor model. *Psychological Reports, 118*(1), 90–106.

Coombs, W. (2002). Assessing online issue threats: Issue contagions and their effect on issue prioritisation. *Journal of Public Affairs, 2*(4), 215–229.

Cooper, C. (2008). NCAA website coverage. *Journal of Intercollegiate Sport*, 1(2), 227–241.

Dellarocas, C. (2010, Spring). Online reputation systems: How to design one that does what you need. *Sloan Management Review*, 33–38.

Delpy, L., & Bosetti, H. (1998). Sport management and marketing via the World Wide Web. *Sport Marketing Quarterly*, 7(1), 21–27.

Domain.com. (2019, September 12). How much does a domain name cost? Retrieved from www.domain.com /blog/2018/09/13/how-much-does-a-domain-name -cost/

Farkas, D.K., & Farkas, J.B. (2002). *Principles of web design*. New York, NY: Longman.

Funk, T. (2009). *Web 2.0 and beyond*. Westport, CT: Praeger.

Garrett, D. (1996). *Intranets unleashed*. Indianapolis, IN: Sams.net.

Harmonson, T. (2004, February 4). Fans and schools in a tangled web, as sites may violate rules. *Orange County Register*.

Hart, T. R. (2002). ePhilanthropy: Using the Internet to build support. *International Journal of Nonprofit and Voluntary Sector Marketing*, 7(4), 353–360.

Hatch, C. (2019, May 16). Be in the know: 2018 ecommerce statistics you should know. *Disruptive Advertising*. Retrieved from www.disruptiveadvertising.com/ppc /ecommerce/2018-ecommerce-statistics/

Hess, E., & Kean, J. (2000, June 27). *Basics of keeping Web pages current*. Paper presented at the College Sports Information Directors of America Conference, St. Louis, MO.

Hur, Y., Ko, Y. J., & Claussen, C. L. (2012). Determinants of using sports web portals: An empirical examination of the sport website acceptance model. *International Journal of Sports Marketing and Sponsorship*, 13(3), 6–25.

Hur, Y., Ko, Y. J., & Valacich, J. (2011). A structural model of the relationships between sport website quality, e-satisfaction, and e-loyalty. *Journal of Sport Management*, 25(5), 458–473.

IAB. (2019a). Q1 2019 reaches $28.4 B in U.S. digital ad revenues, according to IAB. Retrieved from www.iab .com/news/iab-advertising-revenue-q1-2019/

IAB. (2019b). U.S. podcast ad revenues hit historic $479 million in 2018, an increase of 53% over prior year, according to IAB & PWC Research. Retrieved from www.iab .com/news/u-s-podcast-ad-revenues-hit-historic-479 -million-in-2018/

ICANN. (2010, December 6). Beginner's guide to domain names. Retrieved from www.icann.org/resources/files /domain-names-beginners-guide-2010-12-06-en

King, D. (2005, January). A blog to remember. *Information Today*, 22(1), 27–29.

Krug, S. (2006). *Don't make me think: A common sense approach to web usability* (2nd ed.). Berkeley, CA: New Riders Publishing.

Layden, T. (2003, May 19). Caught in the net. *Sports Illustrated, 98*, 46–50.

Licata, A. (2019, August 2). 42 states have or are moving towards legalizing sports betting—here are the states where sports betting is legal. *Business Insider*. Retrieved from www.businessinsider.com/states-where-sports -betting-legal-usa-2019-7

Lowes, M., & Robillard, C. (2018). Social media and digital breakage on the sports beat. *International Journal of Sport Communication*, 11(3), 308–318.

Luong, R. (2019, October 2). LAFC scores brownie points with mobile ordering. *National Sports Forum*. Retrieved from https://sports-forum.com/lafc-selling-it/?inf _contact_key=8b2067aaeb7378d0a16cbc052fe6366f680f 8914173f9191b1c0223e68310bb1

Matuszewski, E. (2000, February). Tangled Web. *CoSIDA Digest, 50*, 7.

Murphy, M. (2019, April 29). You might not have heard of Fanatics yet—but it's taking over sports apparel one league at a time. *Quartz*. Retrieved from https://qz .com/1600107/fanatics-has-found-a-way-to-make-itself -effectively-amazon-proof/

O'Connell (2020, April 9). Sporting goods industry in the U.S. Retrieved from www.statista.com/topics/961 /sporting-goods/

Olsen, M., Keevers, M., Paul, J., & Covington, S. (2001). E-relationship development strategy for the nonprofit fundraising professional. *International Journal of Nonprofit and Voluntary Sector Marketing*, 6(4), 364–373.

Patel, S., Willens, M., Barber, K., Peterson, T., Southern, L., & Lucinda Southern. (2019, February 21). Barstool Sports has 25 podcasts and brought in $15 million from them last year. *Digiday*. Retrieved from https://digiday.com /media/barstool-sports-made-more-than-15-million -from-podcasts/

Perry, P.M. (2003, May). Server ace. *Athletic Business*, 27(5), 44–47.

RGB Colors. (n.d.). Retrieved from www.w3schools.com /colors/default.asp

Rouse, M. (n.d.). E-commerce (electronic commerce)? *WhatIs.com*. Retrieved from https://searchcio.techtarget .com/definition/e-commerce

Russ, H. (2019, February 12). Global esports revenues to top $1 billion in 2019: Report. *Reuters*. Retrieved from www.reuters.com/article/us-videogames-outlook /global-esports-revenues-to-top-1-billion-in-2019-report -idUSKCN1Q11XY

Ryan, D. (2016). *Understanding digital marketing: marketing strategies for engaging the digital generation*. London, England: Kogan Page.

SIDEARM Sports. (2019). Official athletic websites. Retrieved from www.sidearmsports.com/websites/

Smith, M. (June 27, 2016). Sidearm's pitch well-received as college website portfolio grows. *Street &*

Smith's Sports Business Journal. Retrieved from www .sportsbusinessdaily.com/Journal/Issues/2016/06/27 /Colleges/Sidearm.aspx

Stoldt, G.C., Seebohm, B., Booker, J., Kramer, J., & Laird, A.J. (2001). In-house management versus outsourcing: An examination of mid-level NCAA Division I web sites. *National Association of Collegiate Marketers of Athletics Ideas, 8,* 2, 6.

Summerfield, L. (n.d.). Lessons: HubSpot Academy. Retrieved from https://academy.hubspot.com/lessons /conducting-user-research

Tallos, C. (2016, January 21). Why all sports organizations should have a website in 2016. *League Lineup.* Retrieved from www.leaguelineup.com/blog/sports -organizations-website-2016/

The size of the World Wide Web (the Internet). (n.d.). Retrieved from www.worldwidewebsize.com/

Thomas, V. (2020, January 22). Successful web design—5 things all successful websites have in common. Retrieved from https://thomasdigital.com/successful -web-design/

US Census Bureau. (April 11, 2019). U.S. online shop and mail-order sales of sporting goods from 2003 to 2017 (in million U.S. dollars) [Graph]. *Statista.* Retrieved from www.statista.com/statistics/185459/us-online-shops -and-mail-order-houses-sales-figures-for-sporting -goods/

Waters, R.D. (2007). Nonprofit organizations' use of the internet: A content analysis of communication trends on the internet sites of the philanthropy 400. *Nonprofit Management and Leadership, 18*(1), 59–76.

Weaver, J. (2019, July 19). The Top 10 Things to Look for in a Modern Intranet. Retrieved from www.intranetpro .com/blog/the-top-10-things-to-look-for-in-a-modern -intranet

Wilson, R. (2000, February 1). The six simple principles of viral marketing. *Web Marketing Today,* 70.

Winn, R., Blair, A., Ross, & Schwan, J. (2019, June 27). How to start a podcast: A complete step-by-step tutorial. *Podcast Insights.* Retrieved from www.podcastinsights.com /start-a-podcast/

World Internet Users Statistics and 2020 World Population Stats. (n.d.). Retrieved from www.internetworldstats .com/stats.htm

Chapter 5

Abicht, A. (2004, June 28). *Basics of the profession.* Paper presented at the College Sports Information Directors of America Workshop, Calgary, Alberta, Canada.

Anderson, C. (1997, July 1). *Getting your publication to the printer.* Paper presented at the College Sports Information Directors of America Workshop, New Orleans, LA.

Bauer-Wolf, J. (2019, September 11). California passes bill allowing athletes to be paid for name, image and likeness. *Inside Higher Ed.* Retrieved from www.insidehighered .com/news/2019/09/11/california-passes-bill-allowing -athletes-be-paid-name-image-and-likeness

Brown, G.T. (2004). Out of print? Proposal threatens publication of popular media guides. The NCAA News. Retrieved November 11, 2019, from http://ncaanews archive.s3.amazonaws.com/2004/Division-I/out-of -print---2-16-04.html

Cherner, R., Kushlis, J., Rupp, A., O'Toole, T., & Bennett, C. (2005, July 26). NCAA reins in hefty college media guides. *USA Today.* Retrieved from www.usatoday.com /sports/college/2005-07-26-media-guides_x.htm

CoSIDA (College Sports Information Directors of America). (2018). *CoSIDA publications & digital design contest general information.* Retrieved from https://cosida .com/documents/2018/10/16//2018_19_Publications _Contests_General_Information.pdf?id=2687

CoSIDA (College Sports Information Directors of America). (2015) NCAA media guide legislation explained. Retrieved from https://cosida.com/news/2005/8/23 /GEN_867.aspx?path=general

Dallas Wings. (2019). 2019 media guide. Retrieved from https://ak-static.cms.nba.com/wp-content/uploads /sites/69/2019/07/2019-Dallas-Wings-Media-Guide.pdf

Davis, H.M. (1998). Media relations. In L.P. Masteralexis, C.A. Barr, & M.A. Hums (Eds.), *Principles and practice of sport management* (pp. 356–379). Gaithersburg, MD: Aspen.

DiLorenzo, M. (2010, September 17). Personal communication.

Hall, A., Nichols, W., Moynahan, P., & Taylor, J. (2007). *Media relations in sport* (2nd ed.). Morgantown, WV: FiT Publishing.

Harris, T.L. (1998). *Value-added public relations: The secret weapon of integrated marketing.* Lincolnwood, IL: NTC Business Books.

Helitzer, M. (2000). *The dream job: $port$ publicity, promotion and marketing* (3rd ed.). Athens, OH: University Sports Press.

Liberman, N. (2000, August 21–27). Oakland University dumps traditional media guides, uses Internet. *Street & Smith's SportsBusiness Journal, 2,* 16.

Los Angeles Dodgers. (n.d.). *Keep in touch with the Dodgers.* Retrieved from http://losangeles.dodgers.mlb.com/la /fan_forum/newsletters.jsp

Lourim, J. (2018, July 18). The story behind Louisville football's media guide cover with Justify. *Louisville Courier Journal.* Retrieved from www.courier-journal.com/story /sports/college/louisville/2018/07/18/louisville-football -media-guide-justify-horse-bobby-petrino/795856002/

Madej, B. (2009, September 8). *U-M, OSU agree to halt printing sports guides. University of Michigan Record Update.* Retrieved from www.ur.umich.edu/update/archives /090529/56

Miller, K. 2017. *Organizational communication: Approaches and processes* (7th ed.). Stamford, CT: Cengage Learning.

Mullin, B.J., Hardy, S., & Sutton, W.A. (2014). *Sport marketing* (4th ed.). Champaign, IL: Human Kinetics.

National Collegiate Athletic Association (2018, August). *2018–19 NCAA Division I Manual*. Indianapolis, IN: Author.

Poe, S., Emory, A., & McDowell, E. (2015, January 29). Print it? *Great American Media Services*. Retrieved from http://athleticmanagement.com/2009/10/19/print_it/index.php

Sadowski, M. (2018, January 5). Five reasons why video will be crucial for PR in 2018. *Forbes*. Retrieved from www.forbes.com/sites/forbescommunicationscouncil/2018/01/05/five-reasons-why-video-will-be-crucial-for-pr-in-2018/#d9635d93e9b5

San Francisco 49ers. (2019). San Francisco 49ers 2019 media guide. Retrieved from https://49ers.1rmg.com/

Smith, R.D. (2017). *Strategic planning for public relations* (4th ed.). Mahwah, NJ: Erlbaum.

Top 10: Media guide absurdities. (1998, November 2). *Sports Illustrated, 89*, 88.

University of Tulsa Athletics. (2018). Golden Hurricane basketball 2018–19 record and fact book. Retrieved from https://tulsahurricane.com/documents/2018/10/8//TU_MBB18_19_MediaGuide_web.pdf?id=21421

U.S. Environmental Protection Agency. (2009). *EPA communications stylebook*. Retrieved from www.epa.gov/stylebook

U.S. Soccer Communications Department. (2019). 2019 WNT media guide. Retrieved from www.flipsnack.com/ussoccer/2019-wnt-media-guide.html

USOPC (United States Olympic & Paralympic Committee). (n.d.). *Media information*. Retrieved from www.teamusa.org/media

Vance, D. (2018, November 16). CoSIDA membership recognition week featured by Rece Davis on College Gameday. Retrieved from https://cosida.com/news/2018/11/16/espns-college-gameday-salutes-cosida-membership-recognition-week-over-80-game-notes-submitted.aspx

Wilcox, D.L., Cameron, G.T., & Reber, B.H. (2016). *Public relations: Strategies and tactics*. Boston, MA: Pearson.

Chapter 6

Andrews, D.L. (2003). Sport and the transnationalizing media corporation. *Journal of Media Economics, 16*(4), 235–251.

Arledge, R. (2003). *Roone: A memoir*. New York, NY: Harper Collins.

Armour, N. (2014, May 7). NBC Universal pays $7.75 billion for Olympics through 2032. *USA Today*. Retrieved from www.usatoday.com/story/sports/olympics/2014/05/07/nbc-olympics-broadcast-rights-2032/8805989/

Ashwell, T. (1998). Sport broadcasting. In L.P. Masteralexis, C.A. Barr, & M.A. Hums (Eds.), *Principles and practice of sport management* (pp. 380–400). Gaithersburg, MD: Aspen.

Austin, W. (2015, April 7). Modern college football, information management, and the importance of spring games. *SBNation*. Retrieved from www.collegeandmagnolia.com/2015/4/7/8360675/modern-college-football-information-management-and-the-importance-of

Bernstein, A., & Blain, N. (Eds.). (2003). *Sport, media, culture: Global and local dimensions*. New York, NY: Routledge.

Betts, J.R. (1953). The technological revolution and the rise of sport, 1850–1900. *Mississippi Valley Historical Review, 40*, 230–256.

Black, J., & Bryant, J. (1995). *Introduction to media communication* (4th ed.). Dubuque, IA: Brown & Benchmark.

Clavio, G. (2011). Social media and the college football audience. *Journal of Issues in Intercollegiate Athletics, 4*, 309–325.

Condron, B. (2001). Media operations when hosting an event. In K. Neuendorf (Ed.), *Olympic public relations association handbook*. Colorado Springs, CO: Author.

Crupi, A. (2011, June 7). Update: NBC bids $4.38 billion for Olympic Gold. *Adweek*. Retrieved from www.adweek.com/tv-video/update-nbc-bids-438-billion-olympic-gold-132319/

Crupi, A. (2019, Jan. 3). Network TV can't survive without the NFL. *AdAge*. Retrieved from https://adage.com/article/media/top-50-u-s-broadcasts-2018/316102/

Dart, J. (2014). New media, professional sport and political economy. *Journal of Sport & Social Issues, 38*, 528–547.

Douglas, M. (2013, Dec. 13). Plan for "exclusive" paid-for Newcastle United access gathering pace. *ChronicleLive*. Retrieved from www.chroniclelive.co.uk/sport/football/football-news/plan-exclusive-paid-for-newcastle-united-6401153

Evens, T., Iosifidis, P. & Smith, P. (2013). *The political economy of television sports rights*. Basingstoke, England: Palgrave Macmillan.

Fielding, L.W., & Pitts, B.G. (2003). Historical sketches: The development of the sport business industry. In J.B. Parks & J. Quarterman (Eds.), *Contemporary sport management* (2nd ed., pp. 41–78). Champaign, IL: Human Kinetics.

Finale of M*A*S*H draws record number of viewers. (1983, March 3). *The New York Times*. Retrieved from www.nytimes.com/1983/03/03/arts/finale-of-m-a-s-h-draws-record-number-of-viewers.html

Garmire, C. (2000). The Super Bowl III problem: A review of the development of the property right in live professional sports broadcasts and a practical application of copyright law to an infringement action for the unauthorized reproduction and distribution of a taped broadcast of Super Bowl III. *Chicago-Kent Journal of Intellectual Property, 2*(1). Retrieved from http://jip.kentlaw.edu/jip_archives.asp?vol=2&iss=1

Gerrard, B. (2000). Media ownership of pro sports teams: Who are the winners and losers? *International Journal of Sports Marketing & Sponsorship, 2*, 199–218.

Goldfarb, C.B. (2011). How changes in the economics of broadcast television are affecting news and sports programming and the policy goals of localism, diversity of voices, and competition. *Journal of Current Issues in Media and Telecommunications, 3*(2), 111–144.

Gomery, D. (2000). The television industries. In B. Compaine & D. Gomery (Eds.), *Who owns the media? Competition and concentration in the mass media industry* (3rd ed., pp. 193–284). Mahwah, NJ: Erlbaum.

Goodwill Games ceases operations. (n.d.). Goodwill Games. Retrieved August 6, 2004, from www.goodwillgames.com

Hall, A., Nichols, W., Moynahan, P., & Taylor, J. (2007). *Media relations in sport* (2nd ed.). Morgantown, WV: Fitness Information Technology.

Harvey, J., Law, A., & Cantelon, M. (2001). North American professional team sport franchises ownership patterns and global entertainment conglomerates. *Sociology of Sport Journal, 18*, 435–457.

Helitzer, M. (1996). *The dream job: $port$ publicity, promotion and marketing* (2nd ed.). Athens, OH: University Sports Press.

Hums, M.A., & MacLean, J.C. (2004). *Governance and policy in sport organizations*. Scottsdale, AZ: Holcomb Hathaway.

Hutchins, B. (2011). The acceleration of media sport culture. *Information, Communication & Society, 14*, 237–257.

Hutchins, B. (2018, August 22). Mobile media sport: The case for building a mobile media and communications research agenda. *Communication & Sport*. https://journals.sagepub.com/doi/10.1177/2167479518788833

International News Service v. Associated Press, 248 U.S. 215 (1918).

Keeney, C.J. (2008). Kentucky Fried Blog: How the recent ejection of a blogger from the College World Series raises novel questions about the First Amendment, intellectual property, and the intersection of law and technology in the 21st century. *Journal of Technology Law & Policy, 13*, 85–113.

Koppett, L. (2003). *The rise and fall of the press box*. Toronto, Canada: Sport Classic.

Littleton, C. (2018, December 2). Tribune Media to be acquired by Nexstar Media Group. *Variety*. Retrieved from https://variety.com/2018/tv/news/tribune-media-acquired-nexstar-media-group-1203073621/

McChesney, R.W. (1989). Media made sport: A history of sports coverage in the United States. In L. A. Wenner (Ed.), *Media, sports, and society* (pp. 49–69). Newbury Park, CA: Sage.

McChesney, R.W. (2000). The political economy of communication and the future of the field. *Media, Culture, and Society, 22*, 109–116.

McChesney, R.W. (2004). *The problem of the media: U.S. communication politics in the 21st century*. New York, NY: Monthly Review Press.

McChesney, R.W. (2008). *The political economy of media: Enduring issues, emerging dilemmas*. New York, NY: Monthly Review Press.

McIntire, J. (2013, January 25). The PGA is threatening to pull credentials from journalists who tweet at the Farmer's Insurance Tournament in La Jolla. *The Big Lead*. Retrieved from https://thebiglead.com/2013/01/25/the-pga-is-threatening-to-pull-credentials-from-journalists-who-tweet-at-the-farmers-insurance-tournament-in-la-jolla/

Morales, A. (2015, October 19). Clarion-Ledger halts beat coverage of JSU sports. *Clarion Ledger*. Retrieved from www.clarionledger.com/story/sports/college/jackson-state/2015/10/19/clarion-ledger-halts-beat-coverage-jsu-sports/74232126/

National Basketball Association v. Motorola, Inc., 105 F.3d 841 (2d Cir. 1997).

National Exhibition Co. v. Fass, 143 N.Y.S.2d 767 (N.Y Sup. Ct. 1955).

Notre Dame football practice coverage restricted. (2017, August 5). *ND Insider*. Retrieved from www.ndinsider.com/football/notre-dame-football-practice-coverage-restricted/article_c61d4322-7a30-11e7-bd53-0341fd3f34fb.html

Ostrow, A. (2009, August 18). Common sense wins: Social media to be allowed at SEC games. *Mashable*. Retrieved from http://mashable.com/2009/08/18/sec-social-media-policy/#ioOe1fBDiZq0

Patel, S. (2018, December 14). "Every big tech company is a competitor": ESPN boss Jimmy Pitaro on the future of sports. *Digiday*. Retrieved from https://digiday.com/media/espn-jimmy-pitaro-qa/

Patten, D. (2015, February). Touchdown! NBC's Super Bowl scores record-smashing viewership—update. *Deadline*. Retrieved from https://deadline.com/2015/02/super-bowl-ratings-patriots-seahawks-2015-superbowl-xlix-1201364688/

Pedersen, P.M., Miloch, K.S., & Laucella, P.C. (2007). *Strategic sport communication*. Champaign, IL: Human Kinetics.

Peles, J.M. (2014). The most expensive seats in the house: How sports franchises and sports networks profit at fans' expense. *Virginia Sports and Entertainment Law Journal, 13*, 295–315.

Pitts, B.G., & Stotlar, D.K. (2007). *Fundamentals of sport marketing* (4th ed.). Morgantown, WV: Fitness Information Technology.

Pittsburgh Athletic Company v. KQV Broadcasting Co., 24 F. Supp. 490 (W.D. Pa. 1938).

Rader, B.G. (1984). *In its own image: How television has transformed sports*. New York, NY: The Free Press.

Rader, B.G. (1999). *American sports: From the age of folk games to the age of televised sports* (4th ed.). Upper Saddle River, NJ: Prentice Hall.

Read, D. (2015, August/September). Looking to connect. *Athletic Management, 27*(5), 32.

Reeve, S. (2000). *One day in September*. New York, NY: Arcade.

Rice, G. (1954). *The tumult and the shouting: My life in sport*. New York, NY: A.S. Barnes.

Roberts, R., & Olson, J.S. (1989). *Winning is the only thing: Sports in America since 1945*. Baltimore, MD: Johns Hopkins University Press.

Sage, G.H. (1998). *Power and ideology in American sport: A critical perspective* (2nd ed.). Champaign, IL: Human Kinetics.

Samaranch, J.A. (1996*).* Introduction. In *The Olympic movement and the mass media* (pp. 9–10). Lausanne, Switzerland: Author.

Semiao, R. (2004, June 21). *The creation of the X Games*. Retrieved July 12, 2004, from www.espneventmedia.com/pr.php?p=942&e=554

Senn, A.E. (1999). *Power, politics and the Olympic Games*. Champaign, IL: Human Kinetics.

Seymour, H. (1960/1989). *Baseball: The early years*. New York, NY: Oxford University Press.

Sheppard, J.R. (2010). The thrill of victory, and the agony of the tweet: Online social media, the non-copyrightability of events, and how to avoid a looming crisis by changing norms. *Journal of Intellectual Property Law, 17*, 445–477.

Sherman, E. (2015, December 3). The problem with the dwindling media access to college athletes. *Poynter*. Retrieved from www.poynter.org/reporting-editing/2015/the-problem-with-the-dwindling-media-access-to-college-athletes/

Smith, G. (2019, January 4). Comcast, Dish, AT&T to raise TV prices to counter cord-cutting. *Bloomberg*. Retrieved from www.bloomberg.com/news/articles/2019-01-04/comcast-at-t-raise-prices-to-counter-cord-cutting-higher-costs

Solomon, W.S. (1997). The newspaper business. In A. Wells & E.A. Hakanen (Eds.), *Mass media and society* (pp. 71–83). Greenwich, CT: Ablex.

Spence, J. (1988). *Up close and personal: The inside story of network television sports*. New York, NY: Antheneum.

Suggs, Jr., D.W. (2016). Tensions in the press box: Understanding relationships among sports media and source organizations. *Communication & Sport, 4*, 261–281.

Taaffe, W. (1986, July 21). Goodwill, but not a very good show. *Sports Illustrated, 65*(3), 55.

Umstead, R.T. (2018, November 15). DAZN steps to the plate with MLB digital rights deal. *Multichannel News*. Retrieved from www.multichannel.com/blog/dazn-steps-to-the-plate-with-mlb-digital-rights-deal

Weiler, P.C., & Roberts, G.R. (1998). *Sports and the law: Text, cases, problems* (2nd ed.). St. Paul, MN: West Group.

Wenner, L. (Ed.). (1989). *Media, sports, and society*. Newbury Park, CA: Sage.

Wenner, L.A. (1998). *MediaSport*. London, England: Routledge.

Wenner, L.A. (2006). Sports and media through the super glass mirror: Placing blame, breast-beating, and a gaze to the future. In A.A. Raney & J. Bryant (Eds.), *Handbook of sports media* (pp. 45–60). Hillsdale, NJ: Erlbaum.

What is StatCrew? (n.d.). *CBS Statcrew*. Retrieved from www.statcrew.com/index.html

Wong, G.M. (2002). *Essentials of Sports Law* (3rd ed.). Westport, CT: Greenwood Publishing Group.

Zimbalist, A. (1994). *Baseball and billions: A probing look inside the big business of our national pastime*. New York, NY: Basic.

Chapter 7

Baus, H.M., & Lesly, P. (1998). Preparations for communicating. In P. Lesly (Ed.), *Lesly's handbook of public relations and communications*. Chicago, IL: Contemporary.

Brinson, W. (2014, January 19). Richard Sherman calls Michael Crabtree "sorry receiver" in wild rant. *CBSsports.com*. Retrieved from www.cbssports.com/nfl/news/richard-sherman-calls-michael-crabtree-sorry-receiver-in-wild-rant/

Clemson Football. (2019, September 28). Retrieved from https://clemsontigers.com/wp-content/uploads/2019/09/2019-05-UNC.pdf

Condron, B. (2001). Media operations when hosting an event. In K. Neuendorf (Ed.), *Olympic public relations association handbook*. Colorado Springs, CO: Author.

Cremer, C.F., Keirstead, P.O., & Yoakam, R.D. (1996). *ENG television news*. New York, NY: McGraw-Hill.

Davis, H.M. (1998). Media relations. In L.P. Masteralexis, C.A. Barr, & M.A. Hums (Eds.), *Principles and practice of sport management* (pp. 356–379). Gaithersburg, MD: Aspen.

Dennis, R. (2018, July 16). SEC Media Days open in Atlanta with state of conference speech. *Athens Banner-Herald*. Retrieved from www.onlineathens.com/sports/20180716/sec-media-days-open-in-atlanta-with-state-of-conference-speech

Fortunato, J. (2000). Public relations strategies for creating mass media content: A case study of the National Basketball Association. *Public Relations Review, 26*(4), 481–497.

Gatorade® launches original docu-series "Cantera 5v5." (2019, September 5). *Cision: PR Newswire*. Retrieved from www.prnewswire.com/news-releases/gatorade-launches-original-docu-series-cantera-5v5-300912063.html

Geurin-Eagleman, A.N., & Burch, L.M. (2016). Communicating via photographs: A gendered analysis of Olympic athletes' visual self-presentation on Instagram. *Sport Management Review, 19*, 133–145.

Greene, H. (2003, July 23). Personal communication.

Grunig, J.E., & Hunt, T. (1984). *Managing public relations.* New York, NY: Holt, Rinehart and Winston.

Hall, A., Nichols, W., Moynahan, P., & Taylor, J. (2007). *Media relations in sport* (2nd ed.). Morgantown, WV: Fitness Information Technology.

Harris, T.L. (1998). *Value-added public relations: The secret weapon of integrated marketing.* Lincolnwood, IL: NTC Business Books.

Helitzer, M. (1996). *The dream job: $port$ publicity, promotion and marketing* (2nd ed.). Athens, OH: University Sports Press.

Hessert, K. (2000, June/July). Jousting with the press. *Athletic Management, 12*(4), 17.

Hessert. (2002, February/March). Framing the facts. *Athletic Management, 14*(2), 24.

Irwin, R., Sutton, W., & McCarthy, L. (2002). *Sport promotion and sales management.* Champaign, IL: Human Kinetics.

Irwin, R., Sutton, W., & McCarthy, L. (2008). *Sport promotion and sales management* (2nd ed.). Champaign, IL: Human Kinetics.

Lebel, K., & Danylchuk, K. (2012). How tweet it is: A gendered analysis of professional tennis players' self-presentation on Twitter. *International Journal of Sport Communication, 5*(4), 461–480.

Lebel, K., & Danylchuk, K. (2014). Facing off on Twitter: A generation Y interpretation of professional athlete profile pictures. *International Journal of Sport Communication, 7*(3), 317–336.

Lechner, T. (1996). Sports photography: A sight for more eyes. In M. Helitzer, *The dream job: $port$ publicity, promotion and marketing* (2nd ed., pp. 157–178). Athens, OH: University Sports Press.

Lorenz, A.L., & Vivian, J. (1996). *News reporting and writing.* Needham Heights, MA: Allyn and Bacon.

Mathews, W. (2004, May-June). What should I tell them? Why every organization should have an official policy for communicating. *Communication World,* 46–60.

Miller, C., & Zang, F. (2001). Teleconference calls: Maximizing interview time. In K. Neuendorf (Ed.), *Olympic public relations association handbook.* Colorado Springs, CO: United States Olympic Committee.

Newport, K. (2015, January 27). Marshawn Lynch at Super Bowl Media Day: "I'm here so I won't get fined." *Bleacherreport.com.* Retrieved from https://bleacherreport.com/articles/2344416-marshawn-lynch-at-super-bowl-media-day-im-here-so-i-wont-get-fined

Rowe, S., Alexander, N., Earl, R., & Esser, A. (2001, July). Media interview tips to make the most of your expertise. *Nutrition Today, 36*, 4.

Simon, R., & Zappala, J.M. (1996). *Public relations workbook: Writing & techniques.* Lincolnwood, IL: NTC Business Books.

Smith, R.D. (2017). *Strategic planning for public relations* (5th ed.). New York, NY: Routledge.

Thompson, W. (1996). *Targeting the message: A receiver-centered process for public relations writing.* White Plains, NY: Longman.

Treadwell, D., & Treadwell, J.B. (2000). *Public relations writing: Principles in practice.* Needham Heights, MA: Allyn and Bacon.

Troutner wins PLL Rookie of the Year (2019, September 20). *HighPointPanthers.com.* Retrieved from https://highpointpanthers.com/news/2019/9/20/mens-lacrosse-troutner-wins-pll-rookie-of-the-year.aspx

Weisman, L. (2002, December 2). Image follows suit. *USA Today,* 1C.

Wilstein, S. (2002). *Associated Press sports writing handbook.* New York, NY: McGraw-Hill.

Chapter 8

ABC News. (2007, January 5). *Lacrosse player sues Duke professor who failed him in wake of scandal.* Retrieved September 18, 2009, from http://abclocal.go.com/ktrk/story?section=news/national_world&id=4907958

Allen, M.W., & Caillouet, R.H. (1994). Legitimate endeavors: Impression management strategies used by an organization in crisis. *Communication Monographs, 61*, 44–62.

Anti-terror drill held at Tokyo stadium ahead of Rugby World Cup. (2019, July 4). *Tokyo Daily News.* Retrieved from https://tokyodailynews.com/anti-terror-drill-held-at-tokyo-stadium-ahead-of-rugby-world-cup/

Associated Press. (2007, April 13). *Timeline of Duke lacrosse investigation.* Retrieved August 28, 2009, from http://nbcsports.msnbc.com/id/18041327//

Badenhausen, K. (2019, August 6). The highest-paid female athletes 2019: Serena and Osaka dominate. *Forbes.* Retrieved from www.forbes.com/sites/kurtbadenhausen/2019/08/06/the-highest-paid-female-athletes-2019-serena-and-osaka-dominate/#739d45c12fcc

Barrett, S. (2015, May 29). Sponsors beware: FIFA's reputation has stunk for decades. *PR Week.* Retrieved from www.prweek.com/article/1349344/sponsors-beware-fifas-reputation-stunk-decades

Barshop, S. (2018, Aug. 27). J.J. Watt foundation says $41.6M in Hurricane Harvey relief is largest crowd-sourced fundraiser in history. *ESPN.com.* Retrieved from www.espn.com/nfl/story/_/id/24491493/jj-watt-foundation-says-416m-hurricane-harvey-relief-largest-crowd-sourced-fundraiser-history

Bell, T.R., & Hartman, K.L. (2018). Stealing thunder through social media: The framing of Maria Sharapova's drug suspension. *International Journal of Sport Communication, 11*, 369–388.

Benoit, W.L. (1995). *Accounts, excuses, and apologies: A theory of image restoration.* Albany, NY: State University of New York Press.

Brady, E. (2002, September 11). Continuity of sports helped ease the pain. *USA Today,* p. 1C.

Broom, G. (2013). *Cutlip and Center's effective public relations* (11th ed.). Upper Saddle, NJ: Pearson.

Brown, N.A., & Billings, A.C. (2013). Sports fans as crisis communicators on social media websites. *Public Relations Review, 39*(1), 74–81.

Brown, N.A., Brown, K.A., & Billings, A.C. (2015). "May no act of ours bring shame:" Fan-enacted crisis communication surrounding the Penn State sex abuse scandal. *Communication and Sport, 3*(3), 288–311.

Bruce, T., & Tini, T. (2008). Unique crisis response strategies in sports public relations: Rugby league and the case for diversion. *Public Relations Review, 34*, 108–115.

Caron, E. (2019, August 29). JJ Watt's Hurricane Harvey relief funds has built more than 1,100 homes. *Sports Illustrated.* Retrieved from www.si.com/nfl/2019/08/29/texans-jj-watt-hurricane-harvey-funds-homes-built-meals-houston

Carter, D., & Rovell, D. (2003). *On the ball.* Upper Saddle River, NJ: Prentice Hall.

Clavio, G., Eagleman, A.N., Miloch, K.S., & Pedersen, P.M. (2007). Communicating in crisis. In J. James (Ed.), *Sport marketing across the spectrum: Research from emerging, developing, and established scholars* (pp. 15–27). Morgantown, WV: FiT Publishing.

Coombs, T. (2015, June 3). Why FIFA was so slow to adopt an effective crisis response. *Institute for Public Relations.* Retrieved from https://instituteforpr.org/fifa-slow-adopt-effective-crisis-response/

Coombs, T. (2017, July 26). How the NFL has handled the recent CTE crisis risk from the *JAMA* article. *Institute for Public Relations.* Retrieved from https://instituteforpr.org/nfl-handled-recent-cte-crisis-risk-jama-article/

Coombs, W.T. (2019). *Ongoing crisis communication* (5th ed.). Los Angeles: Sage.

Coombs, W.T., & Holladay, S.J. (1996). Communication and attributions in a crisis: An experimental study in crisis communication. *Journal of Public Relations Research, 8*(4), 279–295.

Coombs, W.T., & Holladay, S.J. (2014). How publics react to crisis communication efforts. *Journal of Communication Management, 18*(1), 40–57.

Davis, S.C., & Gilman, A.D. (2002). Communications coordination. *Risk Management, 49*(8), 38–44.

Dietrich, G. (2014). *Spin sucks: Communication and reputation management in the digital age.* Indianapolis, IN: Que Publishing.

Dorn, M.S. (2004, August). Keys to survival: Crisis media relations. *College Planning & Management, 7*, 16.

Elfman, L. (2017, January 24). Experts: Game plan key to managing campus sports crisis. *Diverse Issues in Higher Education.* Retrieved from https://diverseeducation.com/article/91633/

Fainaru-Wade, M. & Fainaru, S. (2013). *League of denial: The NFL, concussions, and the battle for truth.* New York, NY: Three Rivers.

Favorito, J. (2007). *Sports publicity: A practical approach.* Burlington, MA: Elsevier.

Fearn-Banks, K. (2017). *Crisis communications: A casebook approach* (5th ed.). New York, NY: Routledge.

Frederick, E., & Pegoraro, A. (2018). Scandal in college basketball: A case study of image repair via Facebook. *International Journal of Sport Communication, 11*, 414–429.

Grunig, L.A., Grunig, J.E., & Dozier, D.M. (2002). *Excellent PR and effective organizations.* Mahwah, NJ: Erlbaum.

Gulkis, N. (2016). Team crisis communications. *PRsay.* Retrieved from http://prsay.prsa.org/2016/10/04/team-crisis-communications/

Hanna, J.M., & Kain, D. (2010). The NFL's shaky concussion policy exposes the league to potential liability headaches. *Entertainment, Arts and Sports Law Journal, 21*(3), 33–40.

Helitzer, M. (2000). *The dream job: $port$ publicity, promotion and marketing* (3rd ed.). Athens, OH: University Sports Press.

Hessert, K. (1998a). *The 1998 Hessert sports crisis survey.* Retrieved March 17, 1999, from www.sports.mediachallenge.com/crisis/0106.htm

Hessert, K. (1998b, October/November). The management before the crisis. *Athletic Business, 10*, 22–24.

Hessert, K. (2006). Working as a public relations consultant. In G.C. Stoldt, S.W. Dittmore, & S.E. Branvold (Eds.), *Sport public relations: Managing organizational communication* (2nd ed., pp. 39–40). Champaign, IL: Human Kinetics.

Hessert, K., & Gillette, C. (2002, October/November). Part of the game plan. *Athletic Business, 14*, 22–25.

Hwang, G. (2017). An examination of crisis response in professional athlete scandals: A sport fan's perspective. *International Journal of Crisis Communication, 1*(2), 64–71.

Kitchin, P.J., & Purcell, P.A. (2017). Examining sport communications practitioners' approaches to issues management and crisis response in Northern Ireland. *Public Relations Review, 43*(4), 661–670.

Kwiatkowski, M., Alesia, M., & Evans, T. (2018, January 31). A blind eye to sex abuse: How USA Gymnastics failed to report cases. *Indy Star.* Retrieved from www.indystar.com/story/news/investigations/2016/08/04/usa-gymnastics-sex-abuse-protected-coaches/85829732/

Mack, J. (2018, February 6). Michigan State a "textbook" case of how not to do crisis management. *MLive.*

Retrieved from www.mlive.com/news/2018/02/under_simon_msu_communications.html

Manoli, A.E. (2016). Crisis communications management in football clubs. *International Journal of Sport Communication, 9*(3), 340–363.

Masters, A. (2015). Corruption in sport: From the playing field to the field of policy. *Policy and Society, 34* (2), 111–123. https://doi.org/10.1016/j.polsoc.2015.04.002

Mez, J., Daneshvar, D.H., Kiernan, P.T., Abdolmohammadi, B., Alvarez, V.E., Huber, B.R. . . . McKee, A. (2017). Clinicopathological evaluation of chronic traumatic encephalopathy in players of American football. *JAMA, 318*(4), 360–370.

Miami Dolphins. (2019). We were made aware this morning of a serious car accident involving Kendrick Norton. Our thoughts and prayers are with Kendrick and his family during this time [Twitter post]. Retrieved from https://twitter.com/miamidolphins/status/1146775232927227904

Moffat, S. (2018, July). "Stealing thunder" in sport public relations. *PR Academy*. Retrieved from https://pracademy.co.uk/insights/stealing-thunder-in-sports-public-relations/

Mullen, L. (2004, January 12–18). Ex-Clinton aide brings political tactics to sports. *Street & Smith's SportsBusiness Journal, 6*, 24.

Muret, D. (2006, March 8–12). Staying on guard. *Street & Smith's SportsBusiness Journal, 8*, 19–25.

Paolini, M. (2019). NFL takes page from the big tobacco playbook: Assumption of risk in the CTE crisis. *Emory Law Journal, 68*(3), 607–642.

Piedra, M. (2016, March 9). Why the "Sharapova response" will go down as a crisis communications blueprint. *PR Week*. Retrieved from www.prweek.com/article/1386760/why-sharapova-response-will-go-down-crisis-communications-blueprint

Poole, M. (1999, September 20–26). Draft your emergency plan before bad news hits. *Street & Smith's SportsBusiness Journal, 2*, 11.

Putterman, A. & Riley, L. (2019, June 18). Connecticut high school athletes file complaint over transgender policy. *Hartford Courant*. Retrieved from www.courant.com/sports/high-schools/hc-sp-transgender-high-school-track-lawsuit-20190618-20190618-4mjx7gllrjarlpidhnjeecfosq-story.html

Q&A: The interview—Gail Brown. (2001, November/December). *SportsTravel, 5*, 22–23.

Sports Media Challenge. (1997). *Crisis barometer*. Retrieved March 17, 1999, from www.sports.media.challenge.com/crisis/0106.htm

Stoldt, G.C., Miller, L.K., Ayres, T.D., & Comfort, P.G. (2000). Crisis management planning: A necessity for sport managers. *International Journal of Sport Management, 1*, 253–266.

Stoldt, G.C., Miller, L.K., & Comfort, P.G. (2001). Through the eyes of athletic directors: Perceptions of sports information directors, and other PR issues. *Sport Marketing Quarterly, 10*(3), 164–172.

Suleman, K. (2015, May 27). FIFA comms director Walter De Gregorio denies there is a crisis. *PR Week*. Retrieved from www.prweek.com/article/1348826/fifa-comms-director-walter-de-gregorio-denies-crisis

Transparency International. (2017, March 2). FIFA must do more to win back trust of football fans. *Transparency International*. Retrieved from www.transparency.org/news/feature/fifa_must_do_more_to_win_back_trust_of_football_fans

Who is Larry Nassar? (n.d.). *USA Today*. Retrieved from www.usatoday.com/pages/interactives/larry-nassar-timeline/

Washkuch, F. (2015, May 27). Timeline: FIFA in crisis. *PR Week*. Retrieved from www.prweek.com/article/1348954/timeline-fifa-crisis

Wilson, B., Stavros, C., & Westberg, K. (2009). A sport crisis typology: Establishing a pathway for future research. *International Journal of Sport Management and Marketing, 7*(1–2), 21–32.

Wilson, D., & Holusha, J. (2007, June 15). Duke prosecutor says he will resign. *The New York Times*. Retrieved September 2, 2011, from www.nytimes.com/2007/06/15/us/15cnd-duke.html

Wilson, S., & Patterson, B. (1987, November). When the news hits the fan. *Business Marketing, 72*, 92–94.

WSU ICAA (Wichita State University Intercollege Athletic Association Inc.). (2019, July). *Emergency management plan*. Wichita, KS: Author.

Yaeger, D., & Henry, J. (2009, July 2). *Institutional reputation management*. Paper presented at the College Sports Information Directors of America Convention, Tampa, FL.

Yaeger, D., & Pressler, M. (2007). *It's not about the truth: The untold story of the Duke lacrosse case and the lives it shattered*. New York, NY: Threshold.

Chapter 9

Babiak, K., & Wolfe, R. (2009). Determinants of corporate social responsibility in professional sport: Internal and external factors. *Journal of Sport Management, 23*(6), 717–742.

Badloe, N. (2019, September 10). Protecting our planet: Governing bodies and leagues. *Sportanddev.org*. Retrieved from www.sportanddev.org/en/article/news/protecting-our-planet-governing-bodies-and-leagues

Barshop, S. (2018, Aug. 27). J.J. Watt foundation says $41.6M in Hurricane Harvey relief is largest crowd-sourced fundraiser in history. *ESPN.com*. Retrieved from www.espn.com/nfl/story/_/id/24491493/jj-watt-foundation-says

-416m-hurricane-harvey-relief-largest-crowd-sourced -fundraiser-history

Benefit. (n.d.) In *Merriam-Webster dictionary of the English language*. Retrieved from https://www.merriam-webster .com/dictionary/benefit?utm_campaign=sd&utm _medium=serp&utm_source=jsonld

Blackbaud. (2018, April). *Customer story: Minnesota Vikings Foundation*. Retrieved from https://s21acms01blkbsa02 .blob.core.windows.net/prod/docs/default-source /customer-showcase-pdfs/mn_vikings_foundation _customerstory_final_rev.pdf?sfvrsn=1f193f9b_3

Bruch, H., & Walter, F. (2005). The keys to rethinking corporate philanthropy. *MIT Sloan Management Review, 47*(1), 49.

Caron, E. (2019, August 29). JJ Watt's Hurricane Harvey relief funds has built more than 1,100 homes. *Sports Illustrated*. Retrieved from www.si.com/nfl/2019/08/29 /texans-jj-watt-hurricane-harvey-funds-homes-built -meals-houston

Carroll, A.B. (1991). The pyramid of corporate social responsibility: Toward the moral management of organizational stakeholders. *Business Horizons, 34*(4), 39–48.

Charlotte Hornets. (n.d.). *Charlotte Hornets: Swarm to serve: 2017–2018 corporate social responsibility report*. Retrieved from www.nba.com/resources/static/team/v2/hornets /PDFs/18_AnnualReport.pdf

Chen, H.T. (2005). *Practical program evaluation: Assessing and improving planning, implementation, and effectiveness*. Thousand Oaks, CA: Sage Publications.

Crampton, W., & Patten, D. (2008). Social responsiveness, profitability and catastrophic events: Evidence on the corporate philanthropic response to 9/11. *Journal of Business Ethics, 81*, 863–873.

Du, S., Bhattacharya, C.B., & Sen, S. (2010). Maximizing business returns to corporate social responsibility (CSR): The role of CSR communication. *International Journal of Management Reviews, 12*(1), 8–19.

Eagles Charitable Foundation. (2019). *Eagles Autism Foundation*. Retrieved from www.philadelphiaeagles.com /eaglesautismfoundation/

Extejt, M.M. (2004). Philanthropy and professional sport teams. *International Journal of Sport Management, 5*(3), 215–228.

Fawkes, J. (2008). Public relations and communications. In A. Theaker. *The public relations handbook* (3rd ed., pp. 18–32). New York, NY: Routledge.

Hamil, S., & Morrow, S. (2011). Corporate social responsibility in the Scottish Premier League: Context and motivation. *European Sport Management Quarterly, 11*(2), 143–170.

Helitzer, M. (2000). *The dream job: $port$ publicity, promotion and marketing* (3rd ed.). Athens, OH: University Sports Press.

Hudson, C. (2019, October 21). Michael Jordan, Novant Health partner to open clinic in west Charlotte. *Charlotte Business Journal*. Retrieved from www.bizjournals.com /charlotte/news/2019/10/17/michael-jordan-novant -health-partner-to-open.html

Husted, B.W. (2003). Governance choices for corporate social responsibility: To contribute, collaborate, or internalize? *Long Range Planning, 36*, 481–498.

Irwin, R.L., Sutton, W.A., & McCarthy, L.M. (2008). *Sport promotion and sales management* (2nd ed.). Champaign, IL: Human Kinetics.

Kihl, L., Babiak, K., & Tainsky, S. (2014). Evaluating the implementation of a professional sport team's corporate community involvement initiative. *Journal of Sport Management, 28*(3), 324–337.

Kihl, L.A., & Inoue, Y. (2018). *Minnesota intercollegiate athletics community service: An overview and recommendations for best practices*. Unpublished report. Minneapolis, MN: University of Minnesota.

Kolyperas, D., & Sparks, L. (2011). Corporate social responsibility (CSR) communications in the G-25 football clubs. *International Journal of Sport Management and Marketing, 10*(1–2), 83–103.

Kotler, P., & Lee, N. (2005). Best of breed: When it comes to gaining a market edge while supporting a social cause, "Corporate Social Marketing" leads the pack. *Social Marketing Quarterly, 11*(3–4), 91–103.

Kotler, P., & Lee, N. (2008). *Corporate social responsibility: Doing the most good for your company and your cause*. Hoboken, NJ: John Wiley & Sons.

McAlister, D. T., & Ferrell, L. (2002). The role of strategic philanthropy in marketing strategy. *European Journal of Marketing, 36*(5), 689–705.

McElhaney, K. (2009). A strategic approach to corporate social responsibility. *Leader to Leader, 52*(1), 30–36.

National Co-ordinating Centre for Public Engagement. (2019). Quality engagement: Discover the four principles behind high quality engagement and why they matter. Retrieved from www.publicengagement.ac.uk /do-engagement/quality-engagement

Netball Australia (2019). *Confident Girls Foundation*. Retrieved from https://netball.com.au/confident-girls -foundation

Nike, Inc. (2018). *Impact report: Purpose moves us*. Retrieved from https://purpose-cms-production01.s3.amazonaws .com/wp-content/uploads/2019/05/20194957/FY18 _Nike_Impact-Report_Final.pdf

Panepento, P. (May 4, 2008). Sports philanthropy gets more sophisticated. *The Chronicle of Philanthropy*. Retrieved from www.philanthropy.com/article/Sports -Philanthropy-Gets-More/190729

PGA. (2018, January 18). PGA of America releases first-ever social responsibility report. Retrieved from www .pga.com/news/pga/pga-of-america-releases-first-ever -social-responsibility-report

Porter, M.E. (2003). Corporate philanthropy: Taking the high ground. *Foundation Strategy Group, 13*, 1–12.

Porter, M.E., & Kramer, M.R. (2002). The competitive advantage of corporate philanthropy. *Harvard Business Review, 80*(12), 56–68.

Porter, M.E., & Kramer, M.R. (2006). The link between competitive advantage and corporate social responsibility. *Harvard Business Review, 84*(12), 78–92.

Rafferty, S. (August 30, 2017). Hurricane Harvey: How the sports world is helping disaster victims. *Rolling Stone.* Retrieved from www.rollingstone.com/culture/culture-sports/hurricane-harvey-how-the-sports-world-is-helping-disaster-victims-195173/

Sports Green Alliance. (n.d.). Who we are and what we do. Retrieved from https://greensportsalliance.org/about/

Shaw, D. (2019, July 18). Ten charts on the rise of knife crime in England and Wales. *BBC.* Retrieved from www.bbc.com/news/uk-42749089

Sheth, H., & Babiak, K.M. (2010). Beyond the game: Perceptions and practices of corporate social responsibility in the professional sport industry. *Journal of Business Ethics, 91*(3), 433–450.

Tench, R., Sun, W., & Jones, B. (2014). Introduction: CSR communication as an emerging field of study. In R. Tench, W. Sun, & B. Jones (Eds.). *Communicating corporate social responsibility: Perspectives and practice* (Critical Studies on Corporate Responsibility, Governance and Sustainability, Vol. 6) (pp. 3–21). Bingley, England: Emerald Group Publishing.

UEFA (Union of European Football Associations). (2019). *Respect: UEFA football and social responsibility report.* Retrieved from www.uefa.com/MultimediaFiles/Download/uefaorg/General/02/60/26/72/2602672_DOWNLOAD.pdf

van Marrewijk, M. (2003). Concepts and definitions of CSR and corporate sustainability: Between agency and communion. *Journal of Business Ethics, 44*(2–3), 95–105.

Walker, M., Kent, A., & Vincent, J. (2010). Communicating socially responsible initiatives: An analysis of US professional teams. *Sport Marketing Quarterly, 19*(4), 187–195.

Walker, M., & Parent, M.M. (2010). Toward an integrated framework of corporate social responsibility, responsiveness, and citizenship in sport. *Sport Management Review, 13*(3), 198–213.

Chapter 10

Acosta Hernandez, R. (2002). *Managing sport organizations.* Champaign, IL: Human Kinetics.

Anders, A. (2016). Team communication platforms and emergent social collaboration practices. *International Journal of Business Communication, 53*(2), 224–261.

Archibald, M. (2016). Calculating retention and understanding the impact on your health club's performance. *Club Industry.* Retrieved from www.clubindustry.com/trp/calculating-retention-and-understanding-impact-your-health-clubs-performance

Arenstein, S. (2019). PR news' top women in PR speak: Onus on us and industry to close leadership gap. *PR News.* Retrieved from www.prnewsonline.com/women-Top+Women+in+PR-leadership.

Argenti, P.A., Howell, R.A., & Beck, K.A. (2005). The strategic communication imperative. *MIT Sloan Management Review, 48*(3), 82–89.

Associated Press. (2011). Helmet bill stokes lobbying effort. *Boston Herald.* Retrieved May 16, 2011, from www.bostonherald.com

Association for Women in Sports Media (n.d.). *About AWSM.* Retrieved from http://awsmonline.org/we-are-awsm

Baer, J. (2016). *Hug your haters.* New York, NY: Portfolio/Penguin.

Berg, J. (2015). Checklist: 9 ways to keep sponsors happy before and after the event. *BizBash.* Retrieved from www.bizbash.com/production-strategy/experiential-activations-sponsorships/article/13232436/checklist-9-ways-to-keep-sponsors-happy-before-and-after-the-event.

Blattberg, R., Getz, G., & Thomas, J. (2001). *Customer equity.* Boston, MA: Harvard Business School Press.

Bobo, C. (2000). Gaining support for a strategic emphasis on employee communications. *Tactics, 7*(2), 18.

Boughey, T. & Munro, L. (2014). *The role of communication in creating engagement.* Insights Group. Retrieved at https://www.insights.com/media/1101/the-role-of-communication-in-employee-engagement.pdf

Broom, G. (2009). *Cutlip and Center's effective public relations* (10th ed.). Upper Saddle, NJ: Pearson.

Broughton, D. (2018, September 30). Top naming-rights deals. *Sports Business Journal.*

Burchette, B. (2013). *Factors that influence donor motivation among former student-athletes and NCAA DI classification* (Dissertation). Drexel University, Proquest Dissertations.

Burnett, K. (2002). *Relationship fundraising: A donor based approach to the business of raising money* (2nd ed.). San Francisco, CA: Jossey-Bass.

Cardon, P.W., & Marshall, B. (2015). The hype and reality of social media use for work collaboration and team communication. *International Journal of Business Communication, 52*(3), 273–293.

Carter, D., & Rovell, D. (2003). *On the ball.* Upper Saddle River, NJ: Prentice Hall.

Carter, R. (2017). The 15 key factors that influence customer satisfaction. *Zoovü.* Retrieved from https://zoovu.com/blog/customer-satisfaction-factors/

Chitkara, A. (2018, April 12). PR agencies need to be more diverse and inclusive: Here's how to start. *Harvard Business Review.*

Cialdini, R. (1984). *Influence: The psychology of persuasion.* New York, NY: William Morrow & Company.

Cialdini, R. (2016). *Pre-suasion: A Revolutionary Way to Influence and Persuade.* New York, NY: Simon & Schuster.

Cook, S. (2012). *Complaint management excellence: Creating customer loyalty to service recovery.* London, England: Kogan Page.

Corporate Finance Institute. (n.d.). *Role of investor relations.* Retrieved October 25, 2019, from https://corporatefinanceinstitute.com/resources/careers/jobs/role-of-investor-relations-ir/

Cuskelly, G., Hoye, R., & Auld, C. (2006). *Working with volunteers in sport.* London, England: Routledge.

Destination CRM.com. (n.d.). What is CRM? *Destination CRM.* Retrieved October 25, 2019, from www.destinationcrm.com/About/What_Is_CRM

Dixon, M., Ponomareff, L., Turner, S., & DeLisi, R. (2017, January-February). Kick-ass customer service. *Harvard Business Review,* 110–117.

Donorsearch.net. (n.d.). *Major gifts and major gift officers: The basics.* Retrieved October 25, 2019, from www.donorsearch.net/major-gifts-guide/

Duff, K. (2016). Donor conversations: What's often missing (and needn't be). *Academic Impressions.* Retrieved October 25, 2019, from www.academicimpressions.com/blog/donor-conversations-whats-often-missing-and-needn't-be/

Fader, P. (2012). *Customer centricity: Focus on the right customers for strategic advantage.* Philadelphia, PA: Wharton Digital Press.

Fader, P. & Toms, S. (2018). *The customer centricity playbook.* Philadelphia, PA: Wharton Digital Press.

Fisher, E. (2019). MLB ends '19 regular season at 16 year attendance low. *SportBusiness.* Retrieved from www.sportbusiness.com/news/mlb-ends-19-regular-season-at-16-year-attendance-low/

Frommer, F. (2010, February 3). The influence game: Fearing a lockout, NFL players ramp up lobbying effort. *ABC News/ESPN Sports.* Retrieved May 24, 2010, from abcnews.go.com/Sports/wireStory?id=9738278

Fulks, D. (2017). *2004–2016 revenues and expenses of Division I intercollegiate athletics program report.* Indianapolis, IN: National Collegiate Athletic Association.

Fullerton, G. (2003, May). When does commitment lead to loyalty? *Journal of Service Research, 5*(4), 333–344.

Gaille, B. (2015, October 30). 12 pros and cons of customer relationship management. *Brandon Gaille: Small Business & Marketing Advice.* Retrieved from https://brandongaille.com/12-pros-and-cons-of-customer-relationship-management/

Gallup. (2017). *State of the American workplace.* www.gallup.com/workplace/238085/state-american-workplace-report-2017.aspx

Greenwald, M. (2017). *Cybersecurity in sports.* Retrieved from www.cs.tufts.edu/comp/116/archive/fall2017/mgreenwald.pdf

Gruber, W., & Hoewing, R. (1980). The new management in corporate public affairs. *Public Affairs Review, 1,* 13–23.

Grunig, J., & Hunt, T. (1984). *Managing public relations.* New York, NY: CBS College.

Grunig, J.E. (1992). Symmetrical systems of internal communication. In J.E. Grunig (Ed.), *Excellence in public relations and communication management* (pp. 531–575). Hillsdale, NJ: Erlbaum.

Guiniven, J. (2000). Suggestion boxes and town hall meetings: Fix 'em or forget 'em. *Public Relations Tactics, 7*(2), 22.

Gulko, L. (2003, November). Managing member relationships. *Fitness Management,* 30–32.

Hall, B. (2018, August 28). Who's the boss? How to make senior leaders more visible to employees. *Interact Blog.* Retrieved from www.interact-intranet.com/blog/whos-the-boss-how-to-make-senior-leaders-more-visible-to-employees/

Hoffman, K. (2019, January). 2019 state of the industry. *Coach and Athletic Director, 88*(4), 22–26.

Holyoke, T. (2003, September). Choosing battlegrounds: Interest group lobbying across multiple venues. *Political Research Quarterly, 56*(3), 325–336.

How to activate . . . (n.d.). How to activate a sponsorship—12 top tips to greater success. *The Sponsorship Awards 2020.* Retrieved from www.sponsorship-awards.co.uk/how-activate-sponsorship-%E2%80%93-12-basic-ways

IEG Sponsorship. (2018). *What sponsors want & where the dollars will go in 2018.* Retrieved from www.sponsorship.com/IEG/files/f3/f3cfac41-2983-49be-8df6-3546345e27de.pdf

IEG Sponsorship Report. (2017, October 10). The ins and outs of team loyalty programs. *In Depth.* Retrieved from www.sponsorship.com/Report/2017/10/10/The-Ins-and-Outs-Of-Team-Loyalty-Programs.aspx

Independent Sector. (n.d.). *Value of volunteer time.* Retrieved from https://independentsector.org/value-of-volunteer-time-2018/

Jessop, A. (2014, October 28). In the new sports marketplace, teams and leagues must create digital and social media opportunities for sponsors. *Forbes.* Retrieved from www.forbes.com/sites/aliciajessop/2014/10/28/in-the-new-sports-sponsorship-marketplace-teams-and-leagues-must-create-digital-and-social-media-opportunities-for-sponsors/#7522c8a3cf03

Kalafut, P.C. (2003, July-August). Communicate value to boost investor confidence. *Financial Executive, 19,* 19–20.

Ko, Y., Rhee, Y., Walker, M., & Lee, J. (2013, March). What motivates donors to athletic programs: A new model of donor behavior. *Nonprofit and Voluntary Sector Quarterly,* 523–546.

Kotler, P. (2000). *Marketing management: Analysis planning, implementation, and control* (10th ed.). Englewood Cliffs, NJ: Prentice Hall.

Lapchick, R. (2017). *2017 college sports racial & gender report card*. Orlando, FL: University of Central Florida, Institute for Diversity and Ethics in Sports.

Lapchick, R., Little, E., Lerner, C., & Mathew, R. (2009). *2008 racial and gender report card: College sport*. Orlando, FL: University of Central Florida, Institute for Diversity and Ethics in Sports.

Lussier, R.N., & Kimball, D. (2014). *Applied sport management skills* (2nd ed., p. 314). Champaign, IL: Human Kinetics.

MacDonald, S. (2020, March 9). 7 ways to use social listening for customer service. *SuperOffice*. Retrieved from www.superoffice.com/blog/social-listening/

Markey, R., Reichheld, F., & Dullweber, A. (2009, December). Closing the customer feedback loop. *Harvard Business Review, 87*(12).

Marshall, J., & Heffes, E.M. (2004, May). Investor relations: Conference call, Web usage grows. *Financial Executive, 20*, 10.

McClung, B. (2019, January 2). NFL attendance lowest since '10 despite Chargers rebound. *Sports Business Daily*.

Meng, J. & Berger, B. (2019). The impact of organizational culture and leadership performance on PR professionals' job satisfaction: Testing the joint mediating effects of engagement and trust. *Public Relations Review, 45*(1), 64–75.

Mireles, A. (2015). PR and internal communications: Changing with the times? *Cision*. Retrieved from www.cision.com/us/blogs/2015/01/pr-and-internal-communications-changing-with-the-times/

Mogel, L. (2002). *Making it in public relations* (2nd ed.). Mahwah, NJ: Erlbaum.

Morgan, B. (2017, July 31). Reducing customer effort is your best investment. *Forbes*. Retrieved from www.forbes.com/sites/blakemorgan/2017/07/31/reducing-customer-effort-is-your-best-investment/#4d67fce67807

Mullin, B., Hardy, S. & Sutton, W. (2014). *Sport Marketing*. Champaign, IL: Human Kinetics.

Murphy, B., & Lightman, D. (2019, March 28). NCAA lobbies to keep congressional efforts on paying players at bay. *McClatchy Washington Bureau*. Retrieved from www.mcclatchydc.com/news/politics-government/congress/article228138694.html

Nasdaq. (2019, September 9). *How your company can build a robust ESG strategy with Nasdaq ESG advisory program*. Retrieved from www.nasdaq.com/articles/how-your-company-can-build-a-robust-esg-strategy-with-nasdaq-esg-advisory-program-2019-09

NCAA (National Collegiate Athletic Association). (2004). *Government relations*. Retrieved November 1, 2004, from www1.ncaa.org/eprise/main/Public/hr/about.html

NCAA Finances. (n.d.). NCAA finances: 2017–18 finances. *USA Today*. Retrieved November 7, 2019, from https://sports.usatoday.com/ncaa/finances/

Nicholls, J., Gilbert, G., & Roslow, S. (1998). Parsimonious measurement of customer satisfaction with personal service and the service setting. *Journal of Consumer Marketing, 15*(3), 239–253.

NIRI (National Investor Relations Institute). (2009). *About us*. Retrieved October 9, 2009, from www.niri.org/FunctionalMenu/About.aspx

Peng, H. (2000). *Competencies of sport event managers in the United States* (Doctoral dissertation). University of Northern Colorado.

Perez, A. (2018, May 14). What it means: Supreme court strikes down PASPA law that limited sports betting. *USA Today*.

Popp, N., Barrett, H., & Weight, E. (2016). Examining the relationship between age of fan identification and donor behavior at an NCAA division I athletics department. *Journal of Issues in Intercollegiate Athletics, 9*, 107–123.

Ramaswami, S. (2018, September 27). Diversity and inclusion in the PR industry: A case for change. *PR Week*.

Rawson, A., Duncan, E., & Jones, C. (2013, September). The truth about customer experience. *Harvard Business Review*.

Reichheld, F. (n.d.). Prescription for cutting costs. *Bain & Company*. Retrieved from www2.bain.com/Images/BB_Prescription_cutting_costs.pdf

Richman, L., & Hermsen, M. (2018, April 11). 10 tips for upcoming annual shareholders meetings. *Harvard Law School Forum on Corporate Governance*. Retrieved from https://corpgov.law.harvard.edu/2018/04/11/10-tips-for-upcoming-annual-shareholder-meetings/

Ringuet, C. (2012). Volunteers in sport: motivations and commitment to volunteer roles. *Aspetar Sports Medicine Journal, 1*(2), 154–161.

Rosenbaum, M., Ostrom, A., & Kuntze, R. (2005). Loyalty programs and a sense of community. *Journal of Services Marketing, 19*(4), 222–234.

Rust, R.T., Zeithaml, V.A., & Lemon, K.N. (2000). *Driving customer equity*. New York, NY: Free Press.

Ruth, A. (2017, November 30). 7 data sources you should absolutely be plugging into your CRM. *Entrepreneur*. www.entrepreneur.com/article/305309

SaferPak. (2004). *Customer loyalty: How to measure it, understand it and use it to drive business success. The leadership factor*. Retrieved October 23, 2004, from www.saferpak.com/csm_sat_loyal.htm

Sargeant, A. (2001, Winter). Relationship fundraising: How to keep donors loyal. *Nonprofit Management & Leadership, 12*(2), 177–192.

Scott, G. (2018, November 2). 5 ways sports teams use CRM systems. *BizTech Magazine*.

Season Ticket Benefits (n.d.). NBA.com. Retrieved October 17, 2019, from www.nba.com/bulls/tickets/seasons#benefits

Seven things you need . . . (2018, July 1). Seven things you need to know about the art and science of fundraising. *The Ringer: TrueSense Marketing.* Retrieved from www.truesense.com/ringer/7-things-you-need-to-know-about-the-art-and-science-of-fundraising

Severson, D. (2017). Customer satisfaction vs. customer loyalty (companies can lose millions by getting this wrong). *Inc.* Retrieved from www.inc.com/dana-severson/customer-satisfaction-vs-customer-loyalty-companies-can-lose-millions-getting-th.html

Sinn, D., Zielonka, A., Hoyt, C., & Brice-Saddler, M. (2017, December 18). Pro sports leagues, teams spend millions lobbying Washington. *Capital News Service.* Retrieved from https://cnsmaryland.org/2017/12/18/pro-sports-leagues-teams-spend-millions-lobbying-washington/

Smith, H.J. (2003). The shareholders vs. stakeholders debate. *MIT Sloan Management Review, 44*(4), 85–90.

Social media monitoring is . . . (2017). Social media monitoring is critical for investor relations. *Cision.* Retrieved from www.cision.com/content/dam/cision/Resources/white-papers/Social%20Media%20Monitoring.pdf

Solar, A. (2019). Best practices for your internal communications strategy. *Sprout Social.* Retrieved from https://getbambu.com/blog/internal-communications-guide/#bestpractices

Sports CRM. (n.d.). Features list. Retrieved October 8, 2019, from www.sportscrm.com/featureslist/

Streiff, E. (2017, April 14). The four steps of the fundraising process. *Medium.com.* Retrieved from https://medium.com/@ericstreiff/the-four-steps-of-the-fundraising-process-26a887964e98

Sweeney, D. (2008). *An integrated model of value equity in spectator sports: Conceptual framework and empirical results* (Doctoral dissertation). Florida State University.

Swift, R. (2001). *Accelerating customer relationships.* Upper Saddle River, NJ: Prentice Hall.

Tafa, R. (2017, October 3). What is sports sponsorship activation? *RTR Sports Marketing.* Retrieved from https://rtrsports.co.uk/blog/what-is-sports-sponsorship-activation/

Tate, C. (n.d.). What do sponsors want from team and driver websites. *Digital Momentum Blog.* Retrieved October 31, 2019, from www.digitalmomentum.com/blog/what-do-sponsors-want-from-team-and-driver-websites

Taylor, T., Doherty, A., & McGraw, P. (2008). *Managing people in sport organizations: A strategic human resource management perspective.* Burlington, MA: Butterworth-Heinemann.

Timm, P. (2001). *Customer service* (2nd ed.). Upper Saddle River, NJ: Prentice Hall.

Tincher, J. (2014, August). Using customer journey maps to improve health insurance customer loyalty. *FC Business Intelligence.* Retrieved from https://heartofthecustomer.com/wp-content/uploads/2016/04/White-Paper-Health-Insurance-Create-Loyalty-through-an-Improved-Customer-Journey-White-Paper.pdf

Tincher, J., & Newton, N. (2019). *How hard is it to be your customer? Using journey mapping to drive customer-focused change.* Rochester, NY: Paramount Market Publishing.

Todd, S. (2003, May). *Towards a framework for examining distinct job attitudes in the job industry.* Paper presented at the meeting of the North American Society for Sport Management, Ithaca, NY.

Toister, J. (2017). *The service culture handbook: A step-by-step guide to getting your employees obsessed with customer service.* San Diego, CA: Toister Performance Solutions.

Twins winter caravan (n.d.). MLB.com. Retrieved from www.mlb.com/twins/community/winter-caravan

U.S. Bureau of Labor Statistics. (2016, February 25). *Volunteering in the United States, 2015* (Economic news release). Retrieved at www.bls.gov/news.release/volun.nr0.htm

U.S. Bureau of Labor Statistics. (2019). *Labor force statistics from the current population survey.* Retrieved from www.bls.gov/cps/cpsaat11.htm

U.S. SEC (Securities and Exchange Commission). (2014, October 15). *Annual report.* Retrieved from www.sec.gov/fast-answers/answers-annrephtm.html

Vdovin, A. (2017, September 22). Nine internal newsletter content ideas to try in your company newsletter. *DeskAlerts.* Retrieved from www.alert-software.com/blog/nine-internal-newsletter-content-ideas-to-try-in-your-company-newsletter

Verner, M., Hecht, J., & Fansler, A. (1998). Validating an instrument to assess the motivation of athletics donors. *Journal of Sport Management, 12*(2), 123–137.

Weinger, A. (2018, November 19). 5 best practices to strengthen your fundraising cycle. *GuideStar Blog.* Retrieved from https://trust.guidestar.org/5-best-practices-to-strengthen-your-fundraising-cycle

Weinstein, A. (2002). Customer retention: A usage segmentation and customer valuation method. *Journal of Targeting, Measurement and Analysis for Marketing, 10*(3), 259–268.

Weir, L., & Hibbert, S. (2000, April). Building donor relationships: An investigation into the use of relationship and database marketing by charity fundraisers. *Service Industries Journal, 20*(2), 114–132.

Wester, L. (2015, September 21). Donor relations: what you "should" do and what you "must" do. Retrieved November 1, 2019, from www.academicimpressions.com/blog/donor-relations-what-you-should-do-and-what-you-must-do/

What is an intranet . . . (2017, August 21). What is an intranet and why do you need it? *Noodle.* Retrieved from https://vialect.com/blog/collaboration-and-communication-software/what-is-an-intranet

What is CRM . . . (n.d.). What is CRM process? *FinancesOnline: Reviews for Business*. Retrieved from https://financesonline.com/what-is-crm-process/

Wilson, L. (2015, November 5). Opportunities and challenges in working with volunteers in local parks. *The Nature of Cities*. Retrieved from www.thenatureofcities.com/2015/11/05/opportunities-and-challenges-in-working-with-volunteers-in-local-parks/

Wolverton, B., & Kambhampati, S. (2016, February 5). Colleges raised $1.2 billion in donations for sports in 2015. *Chronicle of Higher Education*, 62(21).

Wroblewski, M. (2018, November 6). The importance of the grapevine in internal business communications. Retrieved from https://smallbusiness.chron.com/importance-grapevine-internal-business-communications-429.html

Wyche, C. (2012). Building relationships with volunteers. *Sport public relations*. Human Kinetics: Champaign, IL.

Xing, X., & Chalip, L. (2009). Marching in the glory: Experiences and meaning when working in a sport mega-event. *Journal of Sport Management, 23,* 210–237.

Yoshida, M., Gordon, B. & Hedlund, D. (2018). Professional sport teams and fan loyalty programs: A perceived value perspective. *International Journal of Sport Management.* 19. 235–261.

Yoshida, M., & James, J. (2010). Customer satisfaction with game and service experiences: antecedents and consequences. *Journal of Sport Management, 24*(3), 338.

Zhang, C. (2018, August 12). 7 tips for creating an effective nonprofit annual report. *Donorbox Nonprofit Blog.* Retrieved from https://donorbox.org/nonprofit-blog/nonprofit-annual-report-tips/

Zottola, J. (2019, July 11). Your PR strategy is missing one thing: Internal communications. *Stern Strategy Group.* Retrieved from https://insights.sternstrategy.com/internal-communications-missing-pr-strategy/

Glossary

Dietrich, G. (2014). *Spin sucks: Communication and reputation management in the digital age.* Indianapolis, IN: Que Publishing.

Sheffer, M.L., & Schultz, B. (2013). The new world of social media and broadcast sports reporting. In P.M. Pedersen (Ed.), *Routledge Handbook of Sport Communication* (pp. 210–218). New York, NY: Routledge.

Yaeger, D., & Henry, J. (2009, July 2). *Institutional reputation management.* Paper presented at the College Sports Information Directors of America Convention, Tampa, FL.

index

about the authors

Photo courtesy of Wichita State University.

G. Clayton Stoldt, EdD, is associate dean, a professor of sport management, and the faculty athletics representative at Wichita State University in Kansas. He has taught and conducted research in sport public relations for more than 20 years, was a college sport information director for 10 years, and currently maintains involvement in sport public relations practice through media service roles for select events with ESPN, CBS Sports, and Fox Sports Midwest.

In addition to *Sport Public Relations,* Stoldt has published 11 book chapters and 51 articles in academic and professional publications, and he has made 30 presentations on the subject of sport public relations at various academic and professional conferences. His work as a sport information director has also been recognized in various state and national competitions, and in 2019 he received the Committed Service Award from the Commission on Sport Management Accreditation (COSMA) and was inducted into the COSMA Hall of Fame. Stoldt is a member of the North American Society for Sport Management (NASSM) and the College Sports Information Directors of America (CoSIDA).

Stoldt enjoys spending time with his family and friends, attending sporting events, and reading.

Courtesy of the University of Arkansas.

Stephen W. Dittmore, PhD, is the assistant dean for outreach and innovation as well as a professor of recreation and sport management at the University of Arkansas in Fayetteville. He worked in sport public relations in both the 1996 and 2002 Olympic Games as director for the Salt Lake Olympic Organizing Committee, coordinator for the Atlanta Committee for the Olympic Games, and public relations manager for USA Wrestling. In 2015, he served as the venue media manager for the Special Olympics World Games in Los Angeles. He is an assistant editor for the AthleticDirectorU site and is on the editorial board of *International Journal of Sport Communication.*

Dittmore is a member of the Society for American Baseball Research. He has been recognized with multiple awards from the University of Arkansas, including the Rising Star Award in 2011 and the Outstanding Advising and Mentoring Award in 2016.

Dittmore enjoys traveling with his family, supporting his son's athletics activities, reading, and writing.

Photo courtesy of Wichita State University.

Mike Ross, EdD, is an assistant professor of sport management at Wichita State University (WSU), with teaching specializations in sport public relations, technology in sport management, and sport marketing. Prior to joining the faculty in 2010, Ross was the assistant media relations director for WSU Athletics. He has sustained his involvement in sport communication practice in a number of ways, most recently serving as director of media operations for the 2018 NCAA men's basketball regional hosted in Wichita.

Ross is a member of the College Sports Information Directors of America (CoSIDA). He was the recipient of the Leadership in the Advancement of Teaching Award in 2016 and the College of Education Emory Lindquist Faculty Teaching Award in 2018, both from WSU.

Courtesy of Life Touch.

Scott E. Branvold, EdD, is a professor of sport management at Robert Morris University and a former faculty athletics representative at the university. He has over 30 years of teaching experience in the sport management field and practical experience in sport information and event management. In 2017 he was the recipient of the university's School of Business Service Award.

Branvold earned his doctorate in education from the University of Utah. He has contributed chapters to two publications dealing with ethics in sport management and marketing and public relations in college athletics. He has written articles for several sport marketing and management journals and has given several presentations on topics relating to sports.